Beyond Tomorrow

Studies in German Literature, Linguistics, and Culture

Beyond Tomorrow

German Science Fiction and Utopian Thought in the 20th and 21st Centuries

Ingo Cornils

Rochester, New York

Copyright © 2020 Ingo Cornils

All Rights Reserved. Except as permitted under current legislation,
no part of this work may be photocopied, stored in a retrieval system,
published, performed in public, adapted, broadcast, transmitted,
recorded, or reproduced in any form or by any means,
without the prior permission of the copyright owner.

First published 2020
by Camden House

Camden House is an imprint of Boydell & Brewer Inc.
668 Mt. Hope Avenue, Rochester, NY 14620, USA
www.camden-house.com
and of Boydell & Brewer Limited
PO Box 9, Woodbridge, Suffolk IP12 3DF, UK
www.boydellandbrewer.com

ISBN-13: 978-1-64014-035-6
ISBN-10: 1-64014-035-2

Library of Congress Cataloging-in-Publication Data

CIP data is available from the Library of Congress.

This publication is printed on acid-free paper.

Printed and bound in Great Britain by
TJ International Ltd, Padstow, Cornwall

Contents

Acknowledgments vii

Note on the Translations ix

Introduction 1

Part I. The Great Discourse on the Future

1: Utopians and Utopian Thought 17

2: Futurists and Futures Studies 33

3: Utopian/Dystopian Writers and Utopian/Dystopian Fiction 46

4: Science Fiction: The Nexus of Utopianism, Futurism, and Utopian Fiction 61

Part II. German Science Fiction in the Twentieth and Twenty-First Centuries

5: Some Preliminary Thoughts on German Science Fiction 77

6: First Contact: Martians, Sentient Plants, and Swarm Intelligences 84

7: The Shock of the New: Mega Cities, Machines, and Rockets 104

8: Utopian Experiments: Island Idylls, Glass Beads, and Eugenic Nightmares 110

9: To the Stars! Cosmic Supermen and Bauhaus in Space 122

10: Visions of the End: Catastrophism and Moral Entropy 133

11: Virtual Realities: Caught in the Matrix 149

12: Alternative Histories: Into the Heart of Darkness	157
13: Big Brother Is Watching Us: Who Is Watching Big Brother?	170
14: Artificial Intelligences: The Rise of the Thinking Machines	178
15: Eternal Life: At What Cost?	188
16: Social Satires: Of Empty Slogans and Empty Hearts	193
17: Critical Posthumanism: Twilight of the Species or a New Dawn?	207
18: High Concept: Time, the Universe, and Everything	215
Conclusion	229
Appendix 1: Chronological List of German SF Novels—A Selection	237
Appendix 2: Chronological List of German SF Films—A Selection	239
Notes	241
Bibliography	275
Index	315

Acknowledgments

I would like to thank

- The School of Languages, Cultures and Societies, the Leeds Arts and Humanities Research Institute, and the Faculty of Arts, Humanities and Cultures, at the University of Leeds, for their support.
- My academic teachers who encouraged my lifelong fascination with Science Fiction: Professor Johann N. Schmidt at the University of Hamburg, and Professor Mark Rose at the University of California, Santa Barbara.
- Professor Robert Weninger, for his wisdom and astute comments on the manuscript.
- Professor Tom Shippey, for challenging the naysayers.
- My colleagues at the University of Leeds, especially my collaborators, Dr. Sarah Dodd and Dr. Liz Stainforth, in our research project *The Transcultural Fantastic*.
- My students in the seminar *German Utopian Thought in Fiction and Film* who helped me understand the liberating power of speculative thought.
- My colleagues in the weekly "shut up and write" sessions.
- Mike Collins and Dr. Hilary Potter, for their help with my translations.
- Dr. Lars Schmeink and colleagues at the Gesellschaft für Fantastikforschung/Association for Research in the Fantastic.
- Professor Rebecca Braun and the participants of "The Future is Now" panel at the 2017 ACLA conference in Utrecht.
- Dr. Amanda Rees, and colleagues in the *Unsettling Scientific Stories* AHRC project.
- The two anonymous readers, for their constructive criticism.
- As ever, Jim Walker, the editorial director of Camden House, for support and encouragement beyond the call of duty.

Ingo Cornils, Leeds, February 2020

Note on the Translations

I HAVE MADE a conscious decision to include a broad selection of voices from German utopian discourse and science fiction so that readers without German can get a sense of the range of utopian ideas and a flavor of the debates built on them but can also appreciate the quality and variety of SF writing (and filmmaking) on offer. Much of this material has never been translated into English. Unless indicated otherwise, the translations are my own.

Introduction

CAN LITERATURE TELL US anything meaningful about the future? Can it shape our expectations of things to come and help us decide which of the many possible futures to choose? Science Fiction (SF) has a long tradition of engaging with social change as well as scientific and technological progress, and it is an ideal medium through which to address such questions. My book argues that this popular art form that grew out of the industrial revolution not only holds valuable messages that can help us come to terms with the digital revolution but can make us more resilient in the face of the unknown, and can provide us with a toolkit that allows us to make informed choices in an increasingly complex world. SF can also tell us much about cultural differences and give us fascinating insights into alternative ways of approaching problems. Such a "transcultural" approach can open our eyes to alternatives to the status quo.

German SF has a long tradition and a distinct cultural identity. Yet not enough is known about it in the anglophone world. Apart from the film *Metropolis* (1927), few works of German SF have crossed the language barrier—to the detriment of a richer, transcultural conversation about the kind of world we want to live in. The aim of this book, therefore, is twofold: to provide an anglophone reader with an overview of the history and trajectory of German SF and utopian thought, and to explore how its distinctive voice can contribute to the global discourse on the future.

In an arc that spans 125 years, German utopians have moved from the cultural fringes to the center of German public discourse while maintaining their critical edge. The writer Kurd Laßwitz challenged the authoritarian Wilhelmine order while film director Fritz Lang provided a searing commentary on Weimar society. Utopian thinkers like Ernst Bloch and Herbert Marcuse insisted on the possibility of hope, even in the face of totalitarianism. During the Cold War, German utopian/dystopian writing and filmmaking became increasingly important both as an "early warning system" and as a creative imagining of possible futures. While SF remained marginal in the eyes of academics and critics who dismissed it as escapist entertainment, more recently "mainstream" writers like Thomas Lehr, Christian Kracht, Juli Zeh, Karen Duwe, Dietmar Dath, and Thomas Steinaecker, as well as filmmakers such as Lars Kraume, Tim Fehlbaum, and Tom Tykwer, have adopted the mode of SF to produce increasingly dystopian imaginings of the future, thus giving it, by investing it with their cultural capital, greater urgency, and visibility.

In an extraordinary explosion of creative urgency over the last two decades, German SF has bridged the gap between C. P. Snow's "two cultures" and engaged with the latest scientific and technological research and developments, be that particle research, bioengineering, artificial intelligence, climate change, electronic voting, or nanotechnology. German SF extrapolates current trends and visualizes potential futures that are characterized by human mastery of technology as well as the consequences of human hubris and miscalculation. These fictions express our fear of the unknown future but, by giving it shape and plausibility, they can help us make far-reaching decisions that will directly affect our lives. On a higher level, they critically reflect on the pitfalls of the "utopian impulse" (Bloch): the frustrating experience when good intentions to perfect humanity create new strictures and totalitarian controls. Thus, Juli Zeh (*Corpus Delicti*, 2009) envisions a modern society in which the desire to maximize human health and well-being has led to an all-pervasive ideology that enforces compliance through ubiquitous surveillance and harsh sanctions, while Uwe Timm (*Ikarien*, 2017) explores the history of eugenics as a utopian endeavor that has become one of the most abhorrent aspects of an inhuman ideology.

German SF and German utopian thought tend to reflect specifically "German" concerns stemming from the country's dark history that in turn has given rise to specific fears and sensitivities about totalitarian control, the fragility of civil society, and the environment. Precisely because of the Holocaust, German writers' awareness of the dark side of our scientific and technological capabilities means they are particularly able to influence the moral and ethical debates about the direction and social distribution of scientific and technological progress. These ideas and concerns are also part of a global context of recent anticipatory writing about possible futures—for instance, Cixin Liu's *The Three-Body Problem*, Ahmed Khaled Towfik's *Utopia*, Don DeLillo's *Zero K*, Boualem Sansal's *2084: The End of the World*, Vladimir Sorokin's *Kremlin made of Sugar*, Michel Houellebecq's *The Possibility of an Island*, and Naomi Alderman's *The Power*. These works all illuminate the social consequences of advances in medicine, computing, bioengineering, and electronic communications but also more generally the rapid changes in modes of working, gender roles, political systems, and mobility that started with the industrial revolution.

This book combines a discussion of German utopian thought with a survey of the German utopian/dystopian literary and cinematic tradition, both set in the context of the respective anglophone debates. Through an analysis of the tradition of anticipatory writing and a close reading of selected examples of German SF from around 1900 to the present day that represent key milestones and major artistic achievements, it explores how German writers and filmmakers have responded to the question of how humanity can match its scientific and technological advances with a commensurate social, ethical, and moral progress. It examines their visionary responses to global challenges and plots the trajectory of this ongoing inquiry.

While scientific and technological progress has revolutionized our ability to alter ourselves and our physical world, literary and cinematic responses have become increasingly skeptical in their outlook. They reflect fears and misgivings about the consequences of globalization, artificial intelligence, and genetic engineering alongside ongoing challenges such as climate change, migration, and digitalization. I will show that German utopian imaginaries offer conceptual frameworks and potential solutions for dealing with these seismic shifts.

German Studies and Science Fiction

German Studies has a blind spot when it comes to speculative literature: SF and utopian/dystopian narratives rarely feature in academic discussions of German literature and film, whether in an established "Kanon" (canon) such as the one promoted by the late "Literaturpapst" (literature pope) Marcel Reich-Ranicki or in reading lists at universities that teach German. Nor can we find much SF in the academic discourse on German literary and cinematic production—whether post 1945 or postunification or in the literary criticism produced by Germanists around the world. A trawl through key literary histories and overviews of German literature and film from the last three decades confirms that SF simply does not exist in their frame of reference.[1] The mode of SF seems to sit outside the established boundaries of German literature, confirming my view that even following the transition from "German Language and Literature" to "German Studies" in the 1980s and 1990s, anticipatory literature and film continue to be regarded either with great suspicion or with complete disinterest. As a consequence, very little makes it onto the short lists of the German Book Prize,[2] the New Books in German recommendation list,[3] or into volumes on new or emerging writers.[4] And while there is a sizeable research literature on utopian thought and SF in German (discussed in part 1), it is rarely referred to by "serious" Germanists. Only in the last ten years, owing to the foundation of the Gesellschaft für Fantastikforschung (Association for Research into the Fantastic) with its annual conferences and journal (*Zeitschrift für Fantastikforschung*), have we seen a sustained effort to give research on SF and Fantasy greater visibility and respectability in the German-speaking world. In spite of such attempts to open the academic debate to include "popular genres," it still comes down to traditions of perception, distinctions between "high" and "mass" culture, snobbery and cultural hegemony.

There is another explanation for why German Studies ignores SF: for three quarters of a century, the discipline has focused on *Vergangenheits-*

bewältigung (coming to terms with the past). In light of the Holocaust and the two world wars with millions of dead and widespread devastation, and in light of the further consequences such as the Cold War, the division of Germany, and ideological confrontation, the process of working through Germany's traumatic past, with all its attached guilt and shame, has rightly taken precedence. Thus, the names of authors like Siegfried Lenz, Günter Grass, Heinrich Böll, Christa Wolf, and Peter Schneider, and of film directors like Alexander Kluge, Volker Schlöndorf, and Margarete von Trotta have come to stand for a cultural preoccupation with the past and not the future, with historical identifiers like "Gruppe 47," "1968/RAF," or "Wenderoman" reflecting their backward-looking gaze. Even after reunification, when Germany seemed to go through a process of "normalization" and had every reason to look forward, global events like 9/11 and the challenges of the 2008 financial crisis have served as reminders of past decisions and a confirmation of a skeptical mindset regarding any chances for a better future.[5]

It is entirely understandable that German studies have concentrated almost exclusively on how writers, filmmakers, and other opinion shapers deal with Germany's dark and complex past. However, there is a risk that such a singular focus on the past gives diminishing returns,[6] and that it bypasses the rapid developments in science and technology that require a thorough understanding of, and a critical engagement with, what Rosi Braidotti has called "the four horsemen of the posthuman apocalypse"— namely, nanotechnology, biotechnology, information technology, and cognitive science.[7] All these developments have a direct impact on the way we organize ourselves in terms of participation and equality, work and leisure, medicine and healthcare, trade and commerce, education and the public sphere.

While "old" Germany still struggles to come to terms with its past amid rapidly changing political, technological, social, and economic conditions, a more forward-looking Germany is emerging.[8] One example of this newly confident Germany is the recently built Futurium Berlin on the Alexanderufer, which is a joint initiative by the federal government of Germany and leading German research organizations, foundations, and business enterprises. The Futurium is intended as a platform for dialogue and networking between state, science, business, and society. Another, very public example of the high significance the future is accorded in Germany is the parliamentary study commission "Artificial Intelligence— Social Responsibility and Economic Potential," which the German Bundestag (parliament) constituted in September 2018. The results of this far-reaching inquiry that aims to assess the opportunities and risks of new technologies are fed into the government's digital strategy.

The cultural forms that reflect such efforts to anticipate, think through, and emotionally explore the impact of rapid technological change (and that have done so since Germany's belated industrialization in the late nineteenth century) are popular, but not normally the object of German studies. There is a lack of interest in and little background knowledge about science and technology among literary critics and academics. This blind spot becomes even bigger when we consider that in English departments around the world, utopian studies, futures studies, and SF are much more "mainstream" and considered key objects of inquiry spearheaded by eminent scholars like Fredric Jameson, Tom Moylan, Gregory Claeys, or Sherryl Vint.

SF continues to be viewed with suspicion by literary critics and academics in Germany. While the words "Schundliteratur" (trash literature) or "Trivialliteratur" (trivial literature) are no longer used, SF is still suspected of escapist, popular, and apolitical, if not reactionary, tendencies. In the 1970s it was fashionable to put the whole genre under "Ideologieverdacht" (suspicion of revanchist and violent tendencies) while the proliferation of the German equivalent of the "Pulps" in the shape of the *Perry Rhodan* series and its associated fandom was regarded with deep suspicion by those who preferred to write culture with a capital "C". We live in more enlightened times today, yet the programs of the Germanistentag 2019 in Saarbrücken (on the theme of "Time") and that of the Gesellschaft für Fantastikforschung in Berlin (on the theme of "Romantik") couldn't be more different.[9] There is little overlap between these tribes.

Very few of the major publications and critical works from recent years on German literature—or German film, for that matter—mention research on German SF. And, as we will see, when there has been research on German SF texts or films, it has tended to appear in single articles or in specialist journals, which means that it has never reached a broader audience.[10] Nor are there many reviews of German SF in the German press, unless they are written about works by "mainstream" writers who happen to "dabble" in SF but are still seen to conform to prevalent literary norms. The best example of this attitude is the scandalous silence among German literary critics on one of the most trenchant and disturbing German novels of recent times, Andreas Eschbach's *Nationales Sicherheitsamt* (National Security Office, 2018).

Does that mean that there are no contributions from German SF worthy of note, apart from, perhaps, Fritz Lang's 1927 film *Metropolis?* In this book, I set out to prove that this is emphatically not the case. I delineate the tradition of German utopian thought and discuss outstanding contributions from speculative literature and film that can easily match the quality of their Anglophone siblings, as well as that of "mainstream" German literature. I argue that these make important contributions to a *Zukunftsbewältigung* that enable audiences to engage with, imagine, and come to terms with the challenges of the future and the choices we will have to make in order for it to be worth living in.[11]

As to German SF in Anglo-American bookstores, things are improving, starting with Franz Rottensteiner's anthology of German SF stories and translations of recent novels by Juli Zeh, Andreas Eschbach, Frank Schätzing, and others.[12] Compared to the wealth of anglophone SF that is translated into German, though, these translations into English rarely make an impact. One reason for this lack of engagement that is given again and again by Anglo-American scholars is a (freely admitted) ignorance of foreign languages/cultures.[13]

In spite of efforts to bridge the gap between the humanities and science and technology studies (STS) by US scholars like Sherryl Vint (University of California Riverside) and Colin Milburn (University of California Davis), and the AHRC-funded research project Unsettling Scientific Stories in the United Kingdom, there is a continuing divide between the "two cultures," a sorry state of affairs given that literature should aim to reflect *all* human activities and passions.[14] While it is understandable that novelists may not feel competent to write about science and technology other than as background for human-interest stories, what happens in these fields is now touching every single life on the planet, and the political, social, economic, ecological, and cultural consequences of technological advances in manufacturing, global communication, biosciences, and computing are becoming increasingly obvious, so they ought to provide a focus for writers interested in the world around them.[15]

Just as our concern about the impact of science and technology dates back to Romantics, so does the division between the arts and the natural sciences.[16] While Achim von Arnim saw these as two different realms, both Novalis and Schlegel argued that they were two sides of the same coin. In her introduction to *The Third Culture*, Elinor Shaffer has suggested that a fusion of the arts and natural sciences is sorely needed today:

> Despite their apparent differences, Romanticism and Post-Modernism may have the similar function of providing a half-way house in which both art and sciences may be accommodated—and this accommodation is the major need of the intellect in our time.[17]

I argue that SF can act as such a "half-way house." Once writers (and readers) realize that it has much more to offer than spaceships and gadgetry, there is a lot to be gained and learned. As a rule of thumb, we can say that SF doesn't portray a perfect future or a better world or society, but one that is, as a consequence of scientific or technological progress (understood in the broadest possible sense), *different* from our present one. Thanks to its chameleon-like ability to adapt to (and borrow from) any literary form, SF as a "mode" can offer genuinely new and imaginative perspectives on the human condition and human psychology and at the same time engage with the "bigger picture" by taking its readers or viewers into alternative worlds, allowing them to experience, emotionally as well as cognitively, truly novel ideas. Accordingly, by arguing that German SF makes a vital contribution to *Zukunftsbewältigung*, our managing and coping with the future, this book goes beyond the objectives of a literary history, especially since it aims to be as inclusive as possible in terms of what can be subsumed under the heading "Science Fiction." To adequately describe, and take account of, this complex and interconnected phenomenon of anticipatory thought and cultural production, we need to consider some parameters.

The Context of German SF

The first point to make is that German SF is part of a *Gesamtzusammenhang* (a holistic context): it cannot be considered in isolation from the Anglo-American tradition with which it lives in parallel (e.g., Kurd Laßwitz's *Auf zwei Planeten* and H. G. Wells's *War of the Worlds*), in symbiosis (e.g., American SF in German translation), in artistic dialogue (Rainer Werner Fassbinder's adaptation of Daniel Galouye's novel *Simulacron 3* as the two-part television series *Welt am Draht* that in turn inspired the Wachowski siblings to write *The Matrix*), or in playful competition (Carl Amery's 1975 novel *Der Untergang der Stadt Passau* as a "local" version of Walter Miller's *A Canticle for Leibowitz*, 1959). But it is also part of a *Medienverbund* (an intermedial and multimodal agglomeration), in which books beget films and films beget books, or computer games, comic books, and art. This book will therefore make regular references to anglophone SF literature and film.

Beyond the Anglo-German relationship, we have a transcultural dimension that has brought a postcolonial perspective to the field of SF studies in recent years.[18] No doubt, and in order to ward off accusations of advocating outdated notions of national literatures or national cinemas, one could establish lines of influence on German SF from Russian or French SF, or construct a broader, "European SF identity." The European Science Fiction Society was founded back in 1972, precisely in order to "promote Science Fiction in Europe and European Science Fiction worldwide."[19] Similarly, there have been attempts to challenge the American dominance in SF films.[20] I do not argue for a German "Sonderweg" (special path); rather, this case study of German SF and utopian thought (defined by being published in the German language) is intended to identify its contribution and add its voice to the global conversation.

The second point is that the complexity of this *Gesamtzusammenhang* requires us to look beyond the strictly limited field of SF. The "genre" has grown out of, and continues to be intimately connected to, not only utopian *literature* (for Thomas More's *Utopia* wasn't intended to be read as literature in the sense of Geoffrey Chaucer's "sentence and solace"), but to utopian *thought*—both in terms of form and in content. Thus, especially when writing about German SF, we cannot cut it off from the vital tradition of German utopian (philosophical) thought that has developed chronologically in parallel to German SF. Similarly, the tradition of forecasting/predicting and evaluating likely future scenarios (under the terms "foresight," "futurology," or "futures studies") has directly influenced the form and content of SF, as has the tradition of utopian (and dystopian) fictional writing that sees itself, or is positioned, as separate from SF. It is therefore essential to understand these three interconnected discourses of the future before focusing in detail on the literary and filmic productions that emerge from this fertile ground.

Thirdly, a point about the selection of texts, films and case studies. I make no apologies for casting my net wide to include all the SF novels, films, and television series that I believe have something worthwhile to say not just in a German context, but also to a broader international audience. Obviously, more recent works will have been produced with an international audience in mind (e.g., Frank Schätzing's SF novels *Der Schwarm*, 2004 and *Die Tyrannei des Schmetterlings*, 2018), and it may be more challenging in such cases to identify a distinctly "German" flavor. But I believe that the sheer imaginative power and generally high artistic standards of my selection will give the reader a clear overview and enough background to make his or her own informed choices when venturing deeper into German SF.

My working definition of SF is that it is a body of imaginative works that looks at the world in a "science fictional" way—that is, a way of approaching our human condition as one that is defined by an ever advancing scientific and technological capability that has significant and lasting social, economic, and emotional impacts. The *emotional* aspect is often overlooked: SF responds to expressions of hope and despair; it is high-minded and aspirational or skeptical and worried (and occasionally both). It responds to change—whether that change is due to natural causes or is made by human beings. With sometimes playful, often serious, and, on occasion, desperate attempts, writers and filmmakers of SF engage their audiences with the challenges and opportunities of the future by thinking through, imagining, extrapolating, and concretizing possible realities in artistic and creative ways ranging from the prosaic to the transcendental, while always endeavoring to catch a memorable glimpse of a possible future.

How we feel about change *is* important: The annual Allensbach survey, begun in 1949, about how Germans view the future shows distinct peaks and troughs depending on the socioeconomic and political situation.[21] Cultural production—in literature, film, music, and art—follows suit: Witness the explosion of dystopian visions over the last two decades in the wake of the terror attacks on 9/11, climate change, civil wars, financial crashes, and the rise of nationalism. We all know the challenges facing us on a global scale, be they environmental (climate change, diminishing natural resources), biological (genetic engineering, tailored pathogens), technological (artificial intelligence, weapons of mass destruction), social (political control, migration, unemployment, inequality), or psychological (mental health, information overload). I will demonstrate that German SF has a significant role in helping its audiences to face up to these problems: not by solving them, but by creating awareness of, and helping its audiences to develop emotional resilience to, the changes that these challenges inevitably lead to.

My hypothesis is that German SF is an ongoing project of *Zukunftsbewältigung* to help us cope with the impact of scientific and technological advances that promise us Promethean capabilities but require us to make far-reaching ethical choices. The speed of change caused by scientific and technological progress has already led to fears and misgivings about increasingly porous boundaries (ownership of data, multiple realities, cultural identities), conceptual paradigm shifts (artificial intelligence, nanotechnology, genetic engineering), and a persistent sense of threat (climate change, pollution, and war/terrorism), all of which require a response from us. To test this hypothesis, I explore three discourses on the future that may appear to be concerned with very similar questions but tend to have separate traditions, networks, and conventions: utopian thought (how the world should be), futurology (how the world is likely to be) and utopian fiction (how the world could be). These three discourses are presented as key tributaries of an anticipatory thought that insists that the status quo is not enough and that a different life is possible.

The German discourse on the future is part of a global debate dominated by cultural historians like Fredric Jameson, futurists like Max Tegmark and Nick Bostrum, and theorists like Donna Haraway, whose visions of post- and transhuman futures are amplified by the cultural reach of Hollywood and the economic power of Silicon Valley. To be sure, German utopian thought once was essential to think "beyond tomorrow": thinkers like Karl Marx, Ernst Bloch, Hannah Arendt, and Herbert Marcuse fired the imagination of entire generations. They influenced the countercultural protest of the late 1960s, as well as the women's, the green, and the peace movements. Today, utopian discourse, and an interest in alternatives to the status quo, are on the rise again. While seriously compromised by the experience of the totalitarian nightmares of fascism and Stalinism, utopian thinking has resurfaced in a somewhat chastened but reenergized mood in recent years, from the Arab Spring to the Occupy movement, as well as from Silicon Valley visions of a global village to scientists promising a longer, healthier, and happier life for those who can afford it.

Of course, the concept of utopia itself is fraught with difficulties, ranging from confusion about terminology (do we mean "eutopian" [the good place] when we speak of "utopian" [the nowhere place]?) and attitudinal differences ("one person's vision of utopia is another person's vision of hell") to competition over the power of definition between scholars and learned societies, and political controversies about the legacy of "1968" or the European "project."[22]

Television programs and popular science books tend to offer us dazzling visions of the future in response to the accelerating social, environmental, and technoscientific change and the narrative of "progress," generally depicting a bright future in which we all live longer, healthier, and happier lives. Not all predictions are so rosy, though. Public intellectual Richard David Precht's bestselling book *Jäger, Hirten, Kritiker: Eine Utopie für die digitale Gesellschaft* (2018) reflects on the difficulties in navigating the inevitable consequences of *Digitalisierung* (digitalization): finding an appropriate response to the capital-driven demand for "progress" while acknowledging that past scientific and technological advances have not always improved our cultural well-being, let alone our happiness. To cope with these challenges of the future (and other unforeseen ones), we need to develop the ability to make informed choices. This is also the message of historian Yuval Noah Harari, who has been charting humanity's future history in his books *Homo Deus* (2016) and *21 Lessons for the 21st Century* (2018), which depict future scenarios familiar to readers of SF. He states:

> In the 21st century, AI will open up an even wider spectrum of possibilities. Deciding which of these to realise may well be the most important choice humankind will have to make in the coming decades.[23]

Harari has consistently argued that more of us need to be informed, and he warns that since this important choice is a matter of politics, abstaining from it is no longer an option: when science becomes politics, scientific ignorance becomes a recipe for political disaster. This may sound rather abstract and sensationalist, but if we consider that artificial intelligence will give scientists the computing power necessary to hack the human organism, then decisions have to be made not just by the scientists themselves or the markets but by an informed society.

With the need to make informed choices comes the need to deal with information overload, the ability to identify risks and prioritize actions, but, most importantly, the ability to cope with an ever-increasing speed of change. When asked whether he thought humans could withstand such rapid rates of change, Harari responded:

> We'll have to wait and see. My main fear is really psychological—whether we have the psychological resilience to sustain such a level of change. The rate of change has been accelerating for the past two centuries. My grandmother is 93 and she is OK. By and large we survive. Whether we can do it again, there is no guarantee. We must invest more resources in the psychological resilience of people.[24]

Large corporations, especially those that are currently focusing on developing the next generation of artificial intelligence, claim to look for guidance from "society." As Amazon's chief technology officer Werner Vogels explained in a recent interview with BBC North America's technology reporter Dave Lee, his company did not feel that it was its responsibility how its products—for example, its facial recognition software Rekognition—was being used:

> Mr Vogels doesn't feel it's Amazon's responsibility to make sure Rekognition is used accurately or ethically. "That's not my decision to make," he tells me. "This technology is being used for good in many places. It's in society's direction to actually decide which technology is applicable under which conditions. It's a societal discourse and decision—and policy-making—that needs to happen to decide where you can apply technologies." He likens ML [machine learning] and AI [artificial intelligence] to steel mills. Sometimes steel is used to make incubators for babies, he says, but sometimes steel is used to make guns.[25]

This leads me to the core of my argument: science works within a market and a regulatory framework defined by society. SF can help society (us) make better decisions as the imagination can run through a range of scenarios and allow us to emotionally feel, as well as rationally weigh, the consequences of a given choice. Moreover, by exercising our *Möglichkeitssinn* (sense of possibility), we become used to the consequences of new ideas, and we acquire a resilience to the actual experience of change.

This is what SF does in its best moments—not in the hackneyed form of spaceships and robots and voluptuous women in distress from the era of the "pulps" but in the shape of serious and imaginative engagement with issues that matter, exploring the conceptual and emotional consequences of making far-reaching choices in an aesthetic that allows audiences to participate and engage with scientific and technological issues while potentially even influencing scientific discourse itself.

Of course, all this presupposes that literature can have an influence on its audiences, that films leave a lasting impression on their viewers, and that both art forms have the potential to raise consciousness and critical awareness. My point of departure is that they produce popular narratives that allow readers to experience, in a safe and hypothetical way, possible futures. These may be descriptions of the impact of scientific and technological change on society; extrapolations of demographic developments; warnings about consequences of social control; or reflections on human nature in the face of imagined and real environmental threats. If this assumption is correct, then SF is not just responding to scientific and technological progress (understood in its broadest sense) but is itself part of the discourse, anticipating and influencing its future direction.

In the following chapters, I embark on a detailed investigation of the "grand discourse on the future" and an analysis of the key themes in German SF, pursuing three distinct but interconnected research questions. The first seeks to understand how German SF has responded to the scientific and technological revolutions over the last 125 years. How do writers and filmmakers negotiate the dual lure of techno-euphoric anticipation and dystopian apprehension? How do they envision science and technology's impact on society? The second question seeks to identify the distinctive features of German utopian/dystopian thought and anticipatory writing/filmmaking. Is there a "typically" German SF, and, if so, what makes it so? Are there specific themes, concerns or messages that stand out? The third question asks what strategies German SF can offer a global audience to imagine, understand, and respond to, the challenges of the future. Are its protagonists painted as role models or antiheroes? Do its narratives offer solutions to problems? Are desirable futures depicted as attainable, and are those depicted as dead ends avoidable?

The Organization of the Chapters

Part I

In order to understand the unique contribution that German SF makes to our ability to cope with the challenges of the future, we need to acknowledge that it operates in a larger context, a *Gesamtzusammenhang*. Since the end of the nineteenth century, global and national speculative discourses on the future have been fed by three tributaries: utopian thought (philosophizing about ideal futures), futurism (anticipating probable futures), and utopian fiction (imagining possible futures). Each of these fields is vast, interdisciplinary, and contains tightly knit networks. They sometimes burst their appointed channels and form new affinities. I therefore explore them separately in three chapters, both in their anglophone and in their German variety, before presenting a synopsis in the fourth chapter and linking them to SF in general and German SF in particular.

Part II

Following a brief discussion of the history, development, and distinctiveness of German SF (including German SF film). I discuss key works in thirteen chapters in roughly chronological order, singling out particularly representative texts or films for extended analysis. Thematic strands identified are the "First Contact" or "Alien Encounter," the "Shock of the New," "Utopian Experiments," the "Journey to the Stars," "Visions of the End," "Virtual Realities," "Alternative Histories," "Totalitarian Futures," "Artificial Intelligence," "Eternal Life," "Social Satires," "Critical Posthumanism," and "High Concept." The aim is to outline developments within each strand as well as to describe and critically reflect on the overall trajectory of German SF over the last 125 years.

Part I.

The Great Discourse on the Future

1: Utopians and Utopian Thought

U<small>TOPIAN THOUGHT HAS</small> a long tradition and has for centuries been both feted and condemned. While the literary manifestations of utopian thinking will be discussed as the third tributary, the visioning of ideal societies (political and social utopias) has escaped its merely literary confines and has provided blueprints for humanity's noblest aspirations (the United Nations, the European Union), as well as its vilest ideologies (fascism, National Socialism). "Being human means having a utopia" declared German theologian Paul Tillich, but we do not always wear this characteristic with pride. Politicians and the media use the term "utopian" to denigrate ideas and proposals for change; and in everyday parlance the term suggests impossible schemes, pipe dreams, and hare-brained projects. And yet, despite this, a certain type of person will vehemently defend the right to imagine the world differently, and work to radically change it accordingly. There are "utopians" who plan better, if not ideal, worlds at their desks, and there are those who actively fight for them in the public arena in the attempt to turn them into a lived reality. And there are those who are fascinated by the idea of utopianism, and who study its history and manifestations. The political and social utopias they advocate or study tend to share a holistic perspective, and they are ostensibly oriented toward "happiness." But what makes people happy depends on context and an individual's perspective. In the 1970s, Frank and Fritzie Manuel laid the groundwork for a systematic study of utopias and utopian thought, and they wrote about the "thinkers and dreamers" who envisaged an ideal social order.[1] As Dan Chodorkoff points out, the focus on the individuals who conceived of utopias was key for their generation of researchers:

> Philosophical and literary utopias are the work of individuals and as such tend to reflect their creators' likes and dislikes. These idiosyncratic approaches have given rise to the cliché that "One man's utopia is another man's hell."[2]

Sociologists often speak of a "utopian impulse" that drives individuals and groups to envision better worlds and push for their realization when reality becomes unbearable:

The utopian impulse is a response to existing social conditions and an attempt to transcend or transform those conditions to achieve an ideal. It always contains two interrelated elements: a critique of existing conditions and a vision or reconstructive program for a new society. Utopias usually arise during periods of social upheaval, when the old ways of a society are being questioned by new developments.[3]

The last two decades have seen a revival in interest in utopian thought, spearheaded in North America by the Society for Utopian Studies and its sister organization in Europe, the Utopian Studies Society.[4] Their most eminent members like Lyman Tower Sargent and Gregory Claeys have published extensively and over a sustained period, contributing to a discourse in the anglophone world that is both inter- and transdisciplinary. Their definitions of utopianism and of the utopian impulse have changed little over time, and build on Lewis Mumford's famous distinction between "utopias of escape" and "utopias of reconstruction."[5]

In 2005, in a seminal text on the state of utopian studies and the position of the utopian in a world that seemed to have lost faith in utopias, Fredric Jameson reasserted their political potential, albeit in an argument that required all the skills of a seasoned dialectician:

> The Utopians not only offer to conceive of . . . alternative systems; Utopian form is itself a representational meditation on radical difference, radical otherness, and on the systemic nature of the social totality, to the point where one cannot imagine any fundamental change in our social existence which has not first thrown off utopian visions like so many sparks from a comet.[6]

Jameson argued that, far from seeking out a happy place in an idealistic manner (which, to his mind, rather belonged to the idyll or the pastoral), utopias have a radical function: to critically challenge the status quo and the famous phrase used by politicians that "there is no alternative" (TINA): "The Utopian form itself is the answer to the universal ideological conviction that no alternative is possible, that there is no alternative to the system" (232).[7]

Attempts to define the utopian as a political factor always run the risk of vagueness and wishful thinking. When Lyman Tower Sargent talks about "definitional disagreements," especially those caused by confusion between definitions of utopianism as a general category and the utopia as a literary genre, he cannot help but be prescriptive:

> Utopianism refers to the dreams and nightmares that concern the ways in which groups of people arrange their lives and which usually envision a radically different society from the one in which the dreamers live. And utopianism, unlike much social theory, focuses

on everyday life as well as matters concerned with economic, political and social questions.[8]

Gregory Claeys sees aspirations for a better—or even perfect—society as an ongoing quest: "The concept of utopia in every age is some variation on an ideal present, an ideal past and an ideal future, and the relation between the three."[9] This quest, he argues, takes place in three different domains: that of utopian thought, that of utopian literature, and in practical attempts to found improved communities. But even this differentiation does not yield sufficient clarity, and in the face of the vast range of utopian texts, Claeys opts for a metaphor: "utopia explores the space between the possible and the impossible" (15).

As far as seeing the utopian impulse as a motor for social change, Ruth Levitas recently made the case for using the imagination of utopias as a distinctive method of sociology:

> A utopian method . . . provides a critical tool for exposing the limitations of current policy discourses about economic growth and ecological sustainability. It facilitates genuinely holistic thinking about possible futures, combined with reflexivity, provisionality and democratic engagement with the principles and practices of those futures. And it requires us to think about our conceptions of human needs and human flourishing in those possible futures. The core of utopia is the desire for being otherwise, individually and collectively, subjectively and objectively. . . . It is thus better understood as a method than a goal.[10]

As this brief overview has shown, and in spite of a "vast cultural despair" that manifested itself in the rise of negative utopias in the second half of the twentieth century, utopian thinking in the United States and the United Kingdom is alive and well at the beginning of the twenty-first century.[11] This revival may have to do with new generations forgetting or ignoring the failures of the past, with our human nature that, having achieved a given objective, is keen to move on to the next one, or simply with the belief that optimism trumps pessimism.[12]

Utopian visions have been promoted in recent years by Eric Olin Wright,[13] Mark Featherstone,[14] and, perhaps most vocally, by Rutger Bregman.[15] Like many of his left-leaning colleagues, this Dutch thinker no longer believes in an ideal world; but he certainly believes in a better world, in this case one defined by a fifteen-hour workweek, open borders, and the introduction of a universal basic income. He and his fellow utopians are united in their insistence that, whatever the practical obstacles may be, utopian thinking itself is sorely needed to reignite our ability to believe that a different life could be possible:

It's time to return to utopian thinking. We need a new lodestar, a new map of the world that once again includes a distant, uncharted continent—"Utopia." By this I don't mean the rigid blueprints that utopian fanatics try to shove down our throats with their theocracies or their five-year plans—they only subordinate real people to fervent dreams. . . . What we need are alternative horizons that spark the imagination.[16]

One of these "alternative horizons" is offered by Paul Mason, who argues that the time has come to replace capitalism and build a socialist society, one that avoids the pitfalls of strict doctrine, central control, and curtailment of individual freedom, instead offering the possibility of free, abundant goods and information in a new form of society:

Is this utopian? The utopian socialist communities of the mid-nineteenth century failed because the economy, technology and the levels of human capital were not sufficiently developed. With info-tech, large parts of the utopian socialist project become possible: from cooperatives, to communes, to outbreaks of liberated behaviour that redefine human freedom.[17]

Another highly visible manifesto for utopian thinking comes from George Monbiot, who argues in his latest book that humans are basically altruistic and cooperative, but that they need to "take back control" from undemocratic forces that have blighted our political and economic life through egoism and greed.[18] His "policy of belonging" is built on a set of values and principles that most of us would happily sign up for. They include the following examples:

1. We want to live in a place guided by empathy, respect, justice, generosity, courage, fun and love.
2. We want to live in a place governed by judgments that are honestly made, supported by the evidence, accountable and transparent.
3. We want to live in a place in which everyone's needs are met, without harming the living world or the prosperity of future generations.[19]

What is interesting in Monbiot's list is not only that he rephrases the aspirations of generations of utopians—from the authors of the United States' Declaration of Independence to the *Déclaration des droits de l'homme et du citoyen* (Declaration of the Rights of Man and of the Citizen)—or that he synthesizes basic ethical and moral norms from the United Nations' Declaration of Human Rights and the German Basic

Law to the principles of Mark Anholt's "Good Country" project,[20] but that he recognizes we require a coherent narrative to convince ourselves that a better life is possible.

Such a narrative is elusive, as Zygmunt Bauman acknowledged in *Retrotopia*, his final book.[21] There he described developments and trends in globalized societies that have lost their sense of security in the face of increasing violence and now seek reassurance in concepts such as nationalism that were long thought to have been overcome. Bauman argued that "liquid modernity" had created a vacuum: as the state retreats, responsibility is passed on to the individual to ensure its security and well-being, in a state of constant competition with others. He did not share the optimism of the social utopians cited above (apart from supporting the "utopia for realists"—a universal basic income for everyone, 145) but warned, in an ironic turn, that there was "no alternative" but to persevere with the utopian project (202).

One thinker who doesn't seem to be daunted by this task is Aaron Bastani, a rising British left-wing provocateur, who, in his aptly titled book *Fully Automated Luxury Communism*, expresses great optimism in humanity's long-term future.[22] He argues that, by combining a wise use of technology with an updated form of communism as the twenty-first-century society's organizing principle, the world can overcome the current environmental, economic, social, and demographic crises, not through self-restraint and regulation, but through a "third disruption" and by harnessing solar power and artificial intelligence. While some of his ideas sound more like the scenarios dreamed up by the futurists discussed in the next chapter (a reviewer described them as "Lenin-goes-to-Silicon-Valley rhetoric"),[23] Bastani's utopian vision is political, philosophical, energizing, as well as thought-provoking, and it is thus worthy of inclusion in this section.

The German Utopian Discourse

German utopian thought has played a vital role in shaping utopian discourse. Friedrich Gottlieb Klopstock provided a blueprint for an ideal society with his epic poem *Die Gelehrtenrepublik* (The Republic of the Learned, 1774). Immanuel Kant was instrumental in conceptualizing the idea of human progress,[24] and he applied his moral philosophy to politics, noting that states would eventually have to adhere to reason and maxims that follow the categorical imperative.[25] Johann Wolfgang Goethe made his contribution with his drama *Faust*, where he reflected on human nature and our inability to be content with the status quo.[26] Heinrich Heine enthusiastically announced that it was possible to build heaven right here on earth in his satirical poem *Deutschland, ein Wintermärchen* (Germany, a Winter Fairytale, 1844), and Karl Marx described his vision of the ideal communist society of the future in *Die deutsche Ideologie* (The German Ideology, 1846):

> While in communist society—where nobody has one exclusive sphere of activity but each can become accomplished in any branch he wishes—society regulates general production and thus makes it possible for me to do one thing today and another tomorrow, to hunt in the morning, fish in the afternoon, rear cattle in the evening, critique after dinner, as the fancy takes me, without ever becoming hunter, fisherman, shepherd or critic.[27]

August Bebel's *Die Frau im Sozialismus* (The Woman in Socialism), originally circulated in 1879 but expanded over five decades as the Social Democratic Party of Germany developed, offered an encouraging utopian vision for women.[28] In the chapter "Die Frau in der Zukunft" (The Woman in the Future), Bebel writes:

> In the new society a woman will be entirely independent, both socially and economically. She will not be subjected to even a trace of domination and exploitation, but will stand alongside man, free and equal, and mistress of her own destiny. Her education will be the same as a man's, with the exception of those deviations necessitated by the differences of the sexes. Living a natural life, she may fully develop and employ her physical and mental faculties. She chooses an occupation suited to her wishes, inclinations, and abilities, and works under the same conditions as man. Engaged in some field of industrial activity as a practical working woman in the first part of the day, she may, during the second part of the day, be educator, teacher, or nurse; during a third she may practice a science or an art; and during a fourth she may perform some administrative function. She studies, works, enjoys entertainment and recreation with other women or with men, as she may choose, and as the opportunity presents itself.

But it was the German philosopher Ernst Bloch (1885–1977) who established the principles of our utopian desire, initially in his metaphysical ravings against the madness of World War I where he sought to reconcile the individual's sense of loss and hopelessness with the collective's need to find meaning in the carnage.[29] Driven by sheer will to overcome the unsatisfactory reality, he imagined a new and better world emerging out of the ashes:

> Finally, however, after this *internal* vertical, may the expanse—the *world* of the soul, the *external, cosmic* function of utopia, which is set against misery, death, and the crustacean that is physical

nature—unfold. This light still burns in all of us, and the fantastic journey, the journey to interpret the waking dream, toward it, toward the utopic and fundamental concept, commences. To find this meaning, for which it behooves us to live, to be organized, to have time, for this we keep going, hewing the metaphysical constitutive paths, summoning up what not yet is, building into the blue sky. We build into the blue sky and search there for what is true, what is real, where the merely real disappears—*incipit vita nova*.[30]

Expanding on his vision after the even more horrific experiences of the World War II and the Holocaust, Bloch explained in *The Principle of Hope* (1959) that, while the past often suffocated the potentiality of the future, it was essential to learn to hope.[31] Seeing the potentiality of a better future, he stressed, required "illumination" and a form of individual engagement through art and literature.[32]

German philosophers who maintained the possibility of a better future after World War II included the theologians Martin Buber (1878–1965), who believed in the aspirational utopian ideal of community but denied that it had to come in the form of a Marxist straightjacket,[33] and Paul Tillich (1886–1965), who shared Bloch's definition of the nature of the utopian desire as a search for "Heimat":

> It is one of the most important insights into the nature of utopia that each utopia creates for itself a foundation in the past, that there are those that look backward just as there are those that look forward. This means that what one foresees in the future as the ideal is also, at the same time, what one dreams of as "once" in the past, or as that from which one comes, and toward which one wants to return.[34]

In explicit opposition to what he regarded as a dangerous belief in material progress (the postwar American mantra of "bigger and better"), Tillich declared that, while it was convenient and useful to have better tools, such a "technological utopia" (43) would also increase man's estrangement from, and subjugation of, nature.[35]

In 1967, speaking shortly after the killing of Benno Ohnesorg, an innocent bystander at a student demonstration in West Berlin, Herbert Marcuse (1898–1979) not only made the concept of utopia relevant for a new generation but redefined the pursuit of utopian ideals as realistic.[36] He addressed the inconvenient truth that Western societies had developed the means to end hunger and inequality but had chosen not to use them because it was not in the interest of those who wanted to maintain their system of repression:

> All the material and intellectual powers that can be deployed for the realization of a free society exist today. That they are not deployed

for this goal is due to the total mobilization of existing society against the possibility of its own liberation. But this state of affairs in no way turns the idea of revolution itself into a utopia.[37]

The literary and cultural historian Jost Hermand (1930–) has consequently talked about the "necessity" of utopian thought:[38]

> Utopia as the most noble manifestation of a more just society ought therefore to be seen in the future as neither fantastic nor completely otherworldly. What distinguishes it is not some wishful thinking, but a desire to change, which emphatically stays within the realm of what is politically, socially, and economically possible. Utopia does not want a different, but a better world. It is not oriented toward the next world, but always toward the here and now. It does not believe in otherworldly intervention but puts its faith in a radical change of existing conditions that can be brought about by human beings. It seeks neither a pointless anarchy nor a church state controlled by the holy spirit but rather a community that rests on a social order, where the happiness of the individual does not conflict with the happiness of the collective.[39]

An unexpected proponent of utopian thinking was the German physicist and philosopher Carl Friedrich von Weizsäcker (1912–2007). Deeply shocked by the consequences of the nuclear arms race that he had participated in enabling,[40] he argued that while the West's political, economic and ecological problems were solvable by means of collectively applied reason, this reason was not yet prevalent and required a radical change of consciousness, a *Bewußtseinswandel*:[41]

> Arguing entirely pragmatically, this leads to demands which could be met if we applied collective reason, but which remain utopias without a change in consciousness: securing world peace, an internationally binding legal structure, environmental protection that is enforceable, a more ascetic world culture, and overcoming the institution of war, which closes the circle.[42]

Von Weizsäcker was skeptical whether a critical mass of people with a new awareness would exist in time to avert a catastrophic future, and he expressed a thought that will become central to my discussion of the "dystopian turn": "Ohne den Schrecken denkt man nicht über die richtigen Fragen nach" (Without terror one doesn't contemplate the right questions, 25). He added, without any sign of self-irony, that one should be careful because imagining the worst might become a self-fulfilling prophecy.

Of course, doubts about the likelihood (or desirability) of utopias becoming a reality have a strong tradition in German utopian thought as well. The sociologist Karl Mannheim (1893–1947) was the first to link ideology and utopia, and he defined the "utopian consciousness" as a state of mind that could not fit in with its surrounding reality.[43] As such, it has an orientation that seeks to transcend reality by (at least partially) destroying the existing order.[44] This destructive force inherent in the utopian desire led the philosopher Karl Popper (1902–94) to argue that it was often irrational, and that by formulating a "final" goal, utopians were inevitably taking a road that leads to violence and the silencing of any opposition:

> Utopian rationalism is self-destructive. No matter how high-minded the aims are, it doesn't bring happiness but only the familiar misery of being condemned to a life under tyranny.[45]

Joachim Fest (1926–2006) was perhaps the most outspoken critic of utopian dreams. Writing in the immediate aftermath of the epochal rupture of the fall of communism, he argued that when utopia ceased to be an enjoyable satire or parody and turned into a model for action, it lost its innocence, and that paradises conceived at the writing desk had brought untold misery to the world.[46] He asked whether extreme utopian visions are doomed to lead to terror:

> The real question, then, must be whether or not all the pipe dreams of a new order will necessarily end in terror, whatever their original rationale may have been, no matter whether they hark back to the past or look forward to an "end of history"—as long as the most ardent eschatological seriousness drives it.[47]

Fest concluded that with the collapse of socialism, the second major attempt to build a utopian society after the disaster of National Socialism, we should adjust to a life without utopian dreams as the price of modernity, but he admitted that that was unlikely. Quoting Jürgen Habermas's dictum "Wo die utopischen Oasen austrocknen, breitet sich eine Wüste von Banalität und Ratlosigkeit aus" (where the utopian oases dry out, a desert of banality and cluelessness will spread) as evidence for the sociologist's privileging the idea over reality,[48] he worried that the Germans were still susceptible to the siren call of utopian visions:

> As the inheritors of Karl Marx, with Ernst Bloch by their side, the Germans see themselves more than ever as the custodians of the utopian heritage, and increasingly relish their role of reminding the world of all the unresolved yearnings that every reality leaves room for.[49]

Jürgen Habermas, for his part, continues on his quest for a "realistic utopia" and its (at least partial) concretization in the form of the first article in the German constitution, which states an arguably utopian aspiration: "Die Würde des Menschen ist unantastbar" (human dignity shall be inviolable).[50]

Two German public intellectuals have recently revived the utopian discourse with high-profile publications: Richard David Precht with his *Jäger, Hirten, Kritiker* (2018),[51] and Harald Welzer, with his *Alles könnte anders sein* (2019).[52] Each proudly features the word utopia in the subtitle, and both men paint a surprisingly optimistic picture of the future.

Precht (1964–) writes about the social challenges of a digital future and employs a device used countless times before in discourse about the future to present the audience with a "fait accompli." He imagines a better future in 2048 and then challenges the reader to find out how we got there by retracing the steps taken and the choices made. Picking up on the "ancient human dream" of a classless society that allows the unalienated individual to do what he or she wants, and in direct reference to Marx's utopian image of man as freely alternating between different occupations and pastimes, Precht outlines our current problem with the digital revolution—namely, that automation will make many workers redundant. Instead of advocating the destruction of the machines, Precht believes that we should be embracing the opportunities of this revolution so that people can live fuller, more utopian lives. While acknowledging that the optimism of the 1960s and 1970s has drained away (insofar as we no longer dream of colonies on Mars or cities under the seas, since "most people have lost faith in the future" (10), and despite the relentless infiltration of the digital in the shape of Google, Apple, Facebook and Amazon) he argues that we need to believe in the possibility of change and to develop an *Optimismus des Wollens und Gestaltens* (optimism of the will to shape the future, 11). Ownership of the process of digitalization shouldn't be left to the "nerds and geeks." Shaping the future, according to Precht, is about cultural self-determination and requires a willingness to visualize and think through the consequences of what is being proposed for us. He emphasizes that it is up to us to use our imagination and formulate *Zukunftsbilder* (images of the future) in which values like authenticity, empathy, and care for others are protected.

Given Precht's popularity, his presence in German media, and his eloquence,[53] it is surprising that his *Zukunftsbild* (image of the future) is decidedly bland: he suggests that a new social contract should be written (46), that a *bedingungsloses Grundeinkommen* (universal basic income) paid for by a financial transaction or "Turin" tax should be paid to every citizen, and that education should enable young people to make informed choices and develop key values, including the very un-Marxist understanding that an individual's *Selbstwertgefühl* (sense of self-worth) does not reside in paid work (120). He sums up his definition of a human (digital) utopia as follows:

> A humane utopia liberates man from being defined as a *Homo mercatorius* (a mercantile human being): having to be a merchant who exchanges his labor for money. Rather, it recognizes "work" as the need of very many human beings to do something that fulfills their lives and gives them meaning. For this reason, it separates the concept of "work" as an activity that is freely chosen from the concept of working for wages. Since antiquity, and with greater conviction since the first and second industrial revolutions, poets and thinkers have dreamed increasingly of freeing men and women from the necessity of working because they are forced to do it. Technological progress could turn this dream into reality for very many human beings, as intelligent machines take over more and more tasks. A human being as the free architect of his/her own life—this vision sits at the center of a humane digital utopia.[54]

In an attempt to provide a slightly more concrete image of the social utopia he has in mind, Precht reflects on the question how we can become self-determined and free individuals. The key for him lies in "Selbstorganisation, Selbstverantwortung und Selbstermächtigung" (self-organization, self-responsibility, and self-empowerment), which require a "neue Bewußtseinskultur" (a new culture of consciousness, 156) that builds on an individual's intrinsic motivation instead of the motivation supplied by the *Bedarfsweckungsgesellschaft* (society built on the creation of artificial/superfluous needs, 160). Schools of the future would therefore need to focus on creativity, the development of morals and values, and risk-taking:

> In order for human beings to be happy in a world where there is less gainful employment to go around, they have to spend a lot of time and energy in developing themselves, especially since digital technology requires them to use both appropriately.[55]

The sociologist Harald Welzer (1958–) is a bit more hands-on in linking his utopian ideas and their realization—for example, through his engagement as cofounder and director of the *Futurzwei* foundation, which supports projects that enable young people especially to cope with future challenges; he calls this ability *Zukunftsfähigkeit* (preparedness for the future).[56] Following his volume on social transformation by design,[57] in which he explored pathways toward a sustainable world without consumerism and constant growth (by creating a heterotopia, a society that has collectively decided to consume less and embraced an aesthetic of recycling and upcycling), his latest book argues that the TINA mantra reflects a lack of imagination, and that it is indeed possible to design a better future including "cities without cars, schools without buildings, and countries without borders." Welzer insists that we need to have a clear sense of what we want our future to look like. He admits that there is a shortage of helpful literary examples given that disaster is more interesting, but he assures his readers that they do exist—and that one should work toward a positive utopia. To him, designing the future is a project on the scale of the European Union, the German energy transition, or the *Vergangenheitsbewältigung*, something where people's "hearts and minds" need to be changed in order to create an *Aufbruchsstimmung* (spirit of optimism) that denies that the status quo is the only viable option. He argues that modernity used to be driven by the promise that society would provide better living conditions for all citizens, and "Zukünftigkeit" (futurity) used to be "erlebbar" (able to be experienced) in the sense that West German postwar society experienced a dynamic development of technology that in turn was proven successful through the moon landing, the opening up of the educational system, and the introduction of *Mitbestimmung* (codetermination) in industrial relations. With the absence of comparable perspectives available today, the only thing that appears to be a constant at the moment is disaster, which leads to paralysis:

> Just as the secular religion of growth limits the material preconditions of the future, so the digital economy is building dams against all the unpredictable dreams of an open future. And the environmentalists underpin all of this—with the best of intentions—with their dystopia of an inevitable global-scale destruction, so that any salvation is centered exclusively in the here and now, and disaster can only be avoided when the future is denied.[58]

Welzer criticizes a culture of "Zukunftsverhinderung" (obstruction of the future) in Germany, which is caused by an inability to imagine positive futures that could inspire the next generation. We have, he argues, destroyed the productive force of imaginative dreaming (die *Produktivkraft Träumen*, 47, italics in the original). In order to regain the initiative, he proposes a civilizational project (*zivilisatorisches Projekt*, 49) to unleash "the creative power of the utopian" (55)—in short, to make the future, and the utopian, "cool" again.

In addition to these notable contributions, German utopian discourse has been enriched by a number of academics who have established utopian studies, or "Utopieforschung," at German universities. First and foremost among them is Wilhelm Vosskamp (1936–), who established the field as an interdisciplinary research area at the Zentrum für interdisziplinäre Forschung at the University of Bielefeld in 1975. His three-volume *Utopieforschung: Interdisziplinäre Studien zur neuzeitlichen Utopie* (Utopia Research: Interdisciplinary Studies on the Modern Utopia) sought to find a common language for utopians to use and to situate utopian studies in the realms of philosophy, sociology, history, and literature.[59] In a recent update to the project, Vosskamp struggled to identify utopian visions in the twenty-first century, but he agreed with his colleague Martin Seel that it was vital to retain the utopian desire, if only to sharpen the sense for what might be possible:[60]

> Utopias are those unachievable states in space and time whose attainability can and should be conceivable. This attainability needs to be imagined in order to sharpen, within reality, the sense of what is possible.[61]

In his recently published *Geschichte der Utopie* (History of Utopia), political scientist Thomas Schölderle argues that utopias will always be needed, both to provide a critical analysis of the present and as constructive counterimages to our reality:

> The history of utopia is the history of the deficits and shortcomings of the societies they emanated from. However, besides offering a critical, occasionally fundamentally critical analysis of the present, utopias also always offer constructive countervisions of historical reality.[62]

Schölderle stresses that in Germany the noun "utopia" and the adjective "utopian" had been political combative terms from the nineteenth century on, and that they continue to be used pejoratively even in left-leaning circles. The biggest problem for clearly defining the field, he argues, rests with the academics themselves: having created a "Sammelsurium von Begriffsmustern" (a hodgepodge of concept patterns, 10), the social sciences only have themselves to blame for the "fast babylonische Sprachengewirr" (almost Babylonian language chaos, 10).[63] With grand utopian designs nowhere to be found (unless one regards the concept of a universal basic income a utopian design), he sees utopian thought in a deep crisis, while the desire for alternative possibilities and "lived utopias" has become more virulent (161). These might more appropriately be called heterotopias (as conceived by Michel Foucault) and might fit better with our skeptical and individualistic mindset,[64] but they lack the appeal of classical utopias.

Today, German utopian discourse teeters between despair and defiance. The great hope of utopians in the twentieth century—that socialism would prove capable of building a better world—has been dashed. At the same time, many find it impossible to accept that we already live in the best possible world, and that capitalism can provide adequate responses to global challenges. Searching for the remnants of the utopian *Aufbruchsstimmung* (spirit of optimism) of the German student movement in the 1960s, the journalist and novelist Elke Schmitter has observed that much of what had only been a dream five decades ago has become reality today but that advances in gender equality, working conditions, and individual freedoms have not ushered in a new age: "das Selbstverständliche ist kein Grund zum Glücklichsein" (what you take for granted does not make you happy).[65] She argues that while both the utopian dreams and dystopian fears at the time had been exaggerated, it is impossible to determine whether these dreams and fears have not, after all, had an impact on the course of history. The key difference between then and now, according to Schmitter, is the shift from a belief in collective responsibility and solidarity to an individualistic perspective. Indeed, if German '68ers saw themselves as "citizens of the world" and took the commitment to "creating an ever closer union among the peoples of Europe" for granted, today the very reason for European cooperation is increasingly questioned by neonational groups.[66] Those like political scientist Ulrike Guérot who still believe in the European project have adjusted their aspirations by no longer advocating a United States of Europe but instead a European republic.[67] Similarly, the digital utopianism of pioneers like Tim Berners-Lee and their ideas of a free internet have run into the dual obstacles of commercialization and market concentration,[68] with states, institutions, and activists fighting a rearguard action against internet platforms and social media companies that threaten to undermine democracy.[69]

There is a heated debate in Germany about the question whether, should the utopian ideal remain unachievable, one even need bother to work for incremental improvements. This brings to mind the bitter battles between ideologically pure "Fundis" and the more pragmatic "Realos" in the German Green Party of the 1980s.[70] Some people simply plow ahead regardless, at times with impressive results. Entrepreneur and philanthropist Michael Bohmeyer's highly publicized experiment to crowdfund and raffle off an unconditional basic income for a year has led to a rethinking of the current arrangements for social benefits in Germany (Hartz IV), a system that is associated with social stigma, humiliation, and excessive bureaucracy. Interestingly, for the 250 individuals who received the unconditional stipend in the first year and were interviewed about their experiences, the money was transformational and gave a skeptical public a glimpse of a possible alternative future.[71] As advanced and relatively affluent societies like Germany's develop, and as technological advances in robotics and artificial intelligence make more and more human labor redundant, questions about whether people will welcome their free time or feel threatened and how they will manage this transformation gather urgency.[72]

Ilija Trojanow, a novelist and human rights campaigner, has recently written in defense of utopian thought.[73] His argument is worth exploring in some detail as he makes some crucial observations that reflect current utopian thinking in Germany. Picking up on the themes in Harald Welzer's book *Alles könnte anders sein* discussed above, Trojanow sees a renaissance of utopian thought, though this is sadly in the form of dystopias and visions of the end that have a particularly soporific effect on the citizens of Europe who are privileged enough not to live in an existential struggle for survival. He points out that the more horrific the impending catastrophe, the more pathetic and limited our aspirations become. And while there are many who actively seek solutions to environmental problems, migration, injustice, and war, the collective awareness of the magnitude of the challenge has a paralyzing effect on us, especially if we are the privileged who benefit from global inequality.

Trojanow dismisses the argument that utopian thought was responsible for the horrors of the twentieth century, designed to bury the dreams of millions as "fake news." Channeling Karl Mannheim, he insists on the difference between ideology and utopia, and points out that Marx, Engels, and Lenin declared the latter to be both dangerous and misguided. While it was understandable that philosophers like Karl Popper were suspicious of utopian thought in the aftermath of World War II, the situation today is entirely different:

> If Popper mistrusted utopia because it acted in the interest of the future, we should mistrust the prevailing narrative of a lack of alternatives because it favors the present at the expense of the future.

The fact that anything utopian is so difficult to conceive, Trojanow argues, makes it so significant. It encompasses a variety of possible ways of thinking, as well as the combination of the material with the immaterial (die Verknüpfung von Ziffern und Zeichen mit Erträumungen [the combination of numbers and characters with dreams]). Following a passage in which he likens utopia to Shakespeare's "stuff that dreams are made of" and describes utopians as those who, according to Bloch and Marcuse, "speak the unthinkable," Trojanow returns to the pragmatic by acknowledging that utopias have to demonstrate their viability, or at least offer us a light at the end of the tunnel in the form of a concrete utopia. He concludes by quoting from writer/playwright Carl Zuckmayer, but he extends Zuckermayer's meaning into the present:

> Carl Zuckmayer once said that the world will never become good but it could become better. Unfortunately, he did not add that the dream of a good world provides the foundation for its improvement. Without utopias we are threatened by hopelessness.

♦ ♦ ♦

Utopian thought explores the human dissatisfaction with the status quo and aims to identify the conditions required to enable us to live fuller, more satisfying lives. German utopian thought, initially formative in the global discourse about utopia, today mirrors but also accentuates the debates in the anglophone world. The historical experience of the consequences of hubris produces a powerful counterpoint to the (Romantic?) notion of the possibility of a radically different life. Utopians do not live in a parallel world to reality—Immanuel Kant acknowledged the human predilection for war; Herbert Marcuse was well aware of our atavistic nature with its "bellum omnium contra omnes" (war of all against all) baseline—but they allow themselves to dream.[74] They do not hark back to a magical or mythical past (though they build on, and harness, the power of earlier utopian constructs); nor do they fall for the promises of science and technology that try to dazzle us with ever new inventions, automation, and the godlike power to control our evolution. Their dreams center around what makes a meaningful life, both for the individual and for the society we live in. Both visions of the future are intricately entwined in the body politic, in social contracts and norms, and in concepts of solidarity and empathy, freedom and responsibility, all of which are in constant need of reaffirmation and recalibration.

What does all this have to do with German SF, one might ask? What stands out in the works of the utopians discussed in this chapter, and what has made a deep impression on the writers and filmmakers that will be discussed in part 2 of this book, is their aspirational assertion that an unsatisfactory reality *can* and *must* be transcended, that humans are not condemned to put up with their lot in life, that humanity's search for meaning can only succeed by striving to make the world better. These convictions are the bedrock on which German SF writers construct their imaginaries as they explore the possibility of radical change in their mental experiments, ranging from eutopian depictions of elysian fields to nightmarish visions of dystopian futures that might arise should we choose the wrong path. German utopian thought has given them the courage to reject stasis, to project their readers and audiences into the future so that they can experience the realization of their most cherished dreams or their worst nightmares. The dream of journeying to the stars; the imagination of enhanced cognitive and physical capabilities; the construction of alternative societies; but also the nightmare of utopias turned bad; the cruel sense of deception and the recognition that in pursuit of an ideal we may be sacrificing what makes us human; these are all artistic possibilities (*Möglichkeiten*) thanks to the utopian thinkers considered in this chapter.

2: Futurists and Futures Studies

How we feel about the future is important. This determines not only when we decide to start a family, make a purchase, go for a new job, or take some other risk but also our level of political engagement (from apathy to activism) and our mental health and well-being. Until recently, people in the Western world believed that their children should and would live in a better world (whether defined by standard of living or quality of life) or at least have more choices then they had. This is no longer the case. A recent study by the Pew Research Center showed that a majority of Americans expect life to get worse by 2050.[1] In the annual Allensbach poll that has been conducted in West Germany since 1949 (and in a united Germany since 1990), we can see that global events have had a considerable impact on whether we can look to the future with hope.[2] For example, in 1950, at the time of the Korean War, only 27 percent of West Germans said that they were looking to the future with hope. The oil crisis in 1973 (30 percent) and, much later, the Iraq War (31 percent) caused similarly low levels of optimism, while the fall of the Berlin Wall produced a record high level of 68 percent. But how do we know what the future is likely to hold in store?

If utopian thought has led to debates about what the future *ought to look like*, the futurists' approach aims to be more dispassionate in anticipating, on some sort of scientific basis, what the future *is likely to look like*. To be more precise, futurism,[3] futurology, and futures studies are concerned with identifying probable futures (plural) and determining which of them are likely to become reality. As in utopian discourse, one finds a very broad range of competing voices and approaches, reaching from the specialist to the popular, the ideological to the pragmatic, as well as from the transparent and retraceable to the opaque and surmised.[4] But in sifting through the literature, it quickly becomes apparent that futurists are currently as concerned about the future as the utopians are. Jennifer Gidley sums up the perceived challenge:

> The future we face today is one that threatens our very existence as a species. It threatens the comfortable lifestyles that many of us hold dear and the habitability of the earth itself. The times we are in are critical, and the challenges we face as global citizens are complex, intractable, and planetary.[5]

Such a clarion call may well be seen as self-serving, as futurists will be quick to offer solutions, or at least ask for money to research possible solutions. At the same time, they are riding a wave that is growing in tandem with the pace of technological and social change. What started as a literary, and almost a philosophical, activity (e.g., H. G. Wells's *Anticipations of the Reaction of Mechanical and Scientific Progress Upon Human Life and Thought*, 1901) grew into a semirespected science in the 1960s with pioneers like Ossip K. Flechtheim (who had already coined the term "futurology" in 1943).[6] And what was initially little more than trend spotting quickly became an endeavor to predict global developments (e.g., the Club of Rome's *The Limits of Growth*, 1972 or Al Gore's film *An Inconvenient Truth*, 2006), an activity that, according to Gidley, has created a "tunnel vision" with an exclusive focus on the material world:

> Conceptions of the future increasingly focused on one single path, that of the scientific-technological-industrial expansion of all aspects of life. This tunnel vision of a future determined by science and technology affected agriculture, home economics, the production of goods and services, domestic security, military technology, consumption patterns, the health care system, and even leisure and culture.[7]

Predicting the future has a long history but is now seen as a vital strategic, political, economic, and social pursuit that exercises academics, analysts, lobbyists, and self-styled prophets. In the United States, the National Intelligence Council regularly publishes unclassified strategic assessments of how key trends and uncertainties might shape the world over the next twenty years in order to help senior US leaders plan for the longer term. Their most recent assessment, titled *The Paradox of Progress* (January 2017), emphasizes that any likely future scenario isn't inevitable but is instead entirely dependent on the "key choices" we make collectively and individually:

> The achievements of the industrial and information ages are shaping a world to come that is both more dangerous and richer with opportunity than ever before. Whether promise or peril prevails will turn on the choices of humankind.[8]

These choices, according to the report, not only concern responses to existing challenges like inequality, climate change, migration, and conflicts over resources; they also require detailed knowledge of developments in, say, artificial intelligence or bioengineering. Since these developments pose complex moral, legal, social, and political challenges, the report predicts intense disagreement over what is acceptable and desirable. The authors admit they cannot predict the outcome of these cultural, religious, and economic debates, which shows the limits of their predictive powers.

It is worth noting that while utopians generally hail from the humanities, futurists tend to come from the natural sciences, reflecting the old "two cultures" dichotomy. There is some overlap, though—for instance, when it comes to the perennial question of the professional responsibilities and ethics with which scientists pursue their research. The German-born computer pioneer Josef Weizenbaum is a prime example here. Back in the 1970s, he railed against the "imperialism of instrumental reason," noting:

> It is perhaps paradoxical that just, when in the deepest sense man has ceased to believe in—let alone to trust—his own autonomy, he has begun to rely on autonomous machines, that is, on machines that operate for long periods of time entirely on the basis of their own internal realities.[9]

Fortunately, in the interdisciplinary area of science and technology studies, students no longer only learn about the nature and practices of their chosen disciplines but they also engage with their limitations, impacts, and control.[10] With the advent of so-called "Industry 4.0," artificial intelligence, and genetic engineering, debates about our new scientific and technological capabilities (how to control them, how to stop their misuse, and who benefits from them) have become widely shared in the media, requiring us to take a position on future scenarios.[11] However, the ways in which we direct scientific and technological "progress" and make informed choices as to their desirability and application remain highly controversial. Social utopians like Rutger Bregman, Paul Mason, Richard David Precht, and Harald Welzer argue that Western societies need to abandon or at least modify our capitalist system since it does not share out the benefits of our scientific and technological advances equally while at the same time it condemns those who can least protect themselves from living with their negative consequences. One specific example of such warnings is Shoshana Zuboff's recent book about "surveillance capitalism," in which she criticizes the increasing harvesting of human experience by corporations as "free raw material."[12] This data is routinely declared as proprietary, fabricated into prediction products, and traded in what she calls "behavioral futures markets."[13]

Perhaps unsurprisingly, scientists working in the field of artificial intelligence like Toby Walsh and Max Tegmark tend to be more optimistic about its future social impact. Responding to warnings by Stephen Hawking that "the development of full artificial intelligence could spell the end of the human race,"[14] Walsh argues that thinking machines might well be our greatest legacy, since they will change how we work, how we play, how we educate our children, how we treat the sick, and how we care for the elderly. He is well aware, though, that the uses to which "thinking machines" will be put are not up to him:

> There are many challenges facing the world today: global warming; the ongoing (and likely never-ending) Global Financial crisis; the global war on terror; the emerging global refugee problem. All our problems seem to be global. AI adds to these challenges, threatening our jobs and, perhaps, in the longer term, even our existence. But we should also keep in mind the promise of Artificial Intelligence. Thinking machines might be able to help us tackle some of these big challenges. Whether this works out for better or worse depends largely on how society adapts to AI technologies. This is a job for politicians, playwrights and poets as much as for scientists and technologists.[15]

Similarly, Max Tegmark, cofounder of *The Future of Life Institute* at MIT, argues that with proper foresight in planning the parameters, it is possible to keep artificial intelligence beneficial, helping to create a paradise on Earth.[16] Looking far into the future, he envisions different scenarios, including one with a "superintelligent AI dictator":

> Thanks to the amazing technologies developed by the dictator AI, humanity is free from poverty, disease and other low-tech problems, and all humans enjoy a life of luxurious leisure. . . . The superintelligent AI dictator has as its goal to figure out what human utopia looks like given the evolved preferences encoded in our genes, and to implement it. By clever foresight from the humans who brought the AI into existence, it doesn't simply try to maximize our self-reported happiness, say by putting everyone on intravenous morphine drip. Instead, the AI uses quite a subtle and complex definition of human flourishing, and has turned Earth into a highly enriched zoo environment that's really fun for humans to live in. As a result, most people find their lives highly fulfilling and meaningful.[17]

Obviously, this is a rather tongue-in-cheek satire intended to tease those fearful of machines taking over from humans—in Tegmark's view, we already trust our machines with our lives, and it is up to us to set their limits. Moreover, he believes that we dramatically underestimate life's future potential, and that utopian thought and futurist ambition can happily coexist:

> Our dreams and aspirations need not be limited to century-long life spans marred by disease, poverty and confusion. Rather, aided by technology, life has the potential to flourish for billions of years, not merely here in our Solar System, but also throughout the cosmos far

more grand and inspiring than our ancestors imagined. Not even the sky is the limit.[18]

The historian Noah Yuval Harari has delineated "the ideal of progress" over time and chosen a long-term perspective where he equates our "quest for immortality" with our search for happiness.[19] He observes that change happens so quickly now that as a species we are at the point where we can transcend biologically determined limits and replace the laws of natural selection with laws of intelligent design (445). He argues that the real potential of future technologies is to change Homo sapiens itself, including our emotions and desires, but that we need to know "what we want to want" (464). In his bestseller *Homo Deus*, Harari declares that since humankind now has the power to lift the threat of famine, plague, and war (23), the next goals for us are immortality, happiness, and divinity. He warns, though, that each promise comes with major paradigm changes. For example, once the fear of death has been overcome, people will abandon the forms of art, ideology, and religion that have upheld the "natural order" of things. Similarly, Harari notes that with our ability to erase bad memories and medicate against depression, the right to the pursuit of happiness will morph into the right to happiness, demanded by all. As to humanity gaining quasi-divine powers (the ability to upgrade our body and minds, to use tools to design and create living beings, to control the environment), these will perhaps not make us omnipotent but certainly more than human. He concludes that the key ability to negotiate this brave new world will be our critical faculty:

> In the twenty-first century we will create more powerful fictions and more totalitarian religions than in any previous era. With the help of biotechnology and computer algorithms these religions will not only control our minute-by-minute existence, but will be able to shape our bodies, brains and minds, and to create entire virtual worlds complete with hells and heavens. Being able to distinguish fiction from reality and religion from science will therefore become more vital than ever before.[20]

The ongoing discourse among futurists about our ever-increasing powers to alter ourselves and the world around us has led to a number of interrelated debates, all of which, as we shall see, provide rich material for writers of SF. These debates, and the resulting narratives, range from the impact of human activities on the planet (most obviously their impact on our climate),[21] to our hubris in seeing ourselves as the only species on the planet that matters,[22] to immersive technologies like virtual reality (VR) and augmented reality (AR) as "a new plane of existence,"[23] and to the opportunities and risks of geoengineering and bioengineering and the visions of post humanism.²⁴ I will discuss how these debates are reflected in SF in part 2, but for now I turn to the question of how the future is discussed in Germany.

The Future Discourse in Germany

In Germany the debates over possible futures are held in full awareness of those in the anglophone world, while the obverse is generally not the case because few international futurists read German and even fewer works of German researchers are translated into English.²⁵ The debates have their own distinctive flavor and dominant themes owing to the country's unique historical experience (rapid industrialization; key technoscientific inventions and patents; the traumatic defeat in two world wars; the responsibility for the holocaust; the division of the country into two opposing social systems; the experience of totalitarianism), its specific geopolitical position at the frontline of the Cold War with Berlin as the flashpoint of superpower rivalry and as the largest country in the European Union, its economic prowess (epitomized in its position as second largest export economy), its cultural self-image ("land of poets and thinkers"), and its pluralistic political and social culture and public sphere.

How people view the future obviously depends on their world view. Corporate Germany and German industry by and large believe that global and local challenges are there to be overcome,²⁶ and independent research institutes that offer glimpses of the future tend to thrive.²⁷ Often funded by the federal government, they tend to display a high degree of confidence that the future can be anticipated. The project FutureWork, for example,

> aims at combining established sources of knowledge such as technology foresight and sociology of work with the analysis of science fiction literature in order to be able to foresee possible future work scenarios for the second half of the twenty-first century.²⁸

Critics and the media are generally skeptical and have grown to mistrust the more optimistic narratives of "Fortschritt" (progress). This skepticism among West Germany's cultural elites has a long tradition (in marked contrast, *Zukunftsoptimismus* [optimism about the future] was an official and integral part of the political culture in the former GDR).²⁹ For example, in the 1950s the philosopher Günter Anders, who had raged against humanity's "apocalypse blindness" in *Die Antiquiertheit des Menschen* (The Antiquatedness of Man, 1956) and criticized his fellow citizens for their inability to imagine fear (he dubbed them "Analphabeten der Angst" [illiterates of fear]), declared in his *Thesen zum Atomzeitalter* (Theses on the Atomic Age, 1958) that "what can hit anyone concerns everyone," reflecting a general suspicion of the ability of politicians and scientists to protect people from a nuclear war, a mistrust that in West Germany culminated in the *Kampf dem Atomtod* (Struggle against Atomic Death) movement.[30]

In the 1960s, when *Futurologie* (futurology) and *Fortschrittsoptimismus* (optimism about progress) seemed to take West Germany by storm,[31] the intellectual leaders of the German student movement believed themselves to be living at a utopian moment and fantasized about rearranging society on futurist principles (at least in West Berlin), yet at the same time they decried futurology as the tool of capitalism to extract even more profit from the workers.[32] This disbelief in the power of a science and technology to create a better world, and especially in the "disinterested" character of futurology, has had a lasting influence, and it can be seen in the 1970s and 1980s in the Green Party's opposition to nuclear power plants, in the "Sponti"-movement with its "no future" slogan, and in the *Alternativbewegungen* (alternative movements) that formed their own countercultural milieus.[33] Environmental concerns (Waldsterben, "saurer Regen" [forest decline, acid rain]), the NATO decision to station nuclear weapons in West Germany, and man-made catastrophes (Chernobyl) heightened a pervasive sense of fear, one described by sociologist Ulrich Beck in his book *Risikogesellschaft* (risk society) and most recently by the historian Frank Biess in *Republik der Angst* (Republic of Fear), who argues that the (West) German experience of cyclical periods of insecurity has had a decisive impact on how Germans see the future.[34]

While some suggest that Germans should pause to consider what is important for them before they agree to jump on the bandwagon of the next round of innovation and change,[35] others are fanning the flames of hysteria with apocalyptic messages.[36] As we shall see later, this general sense of unease, skepticism, and fear when it comes to technoscientific progress (which is paradoxical, since the country depends on it) is reflected in German SF.

Part and parcel of the—at best—mixed feelings with which many Germans view the future is the fact that people tend to look back with wistfulness and nostalgia to the futures that were envisioned in the past. The future has become historical to many Germans, and there is no shortage of popular and academic accounts of how Germans used to imagine their future in the past.[37] Arthur Brehmer's 1910 collection of mainly optimistic predictions about how the world would change by the year 2010 has recently been republished.[38] The volume contains prescient and fanciful visions, ranging from the growth of megacities and "the telephone in your shirt pocket" (35–38) and Bertha von Suttner's essay on a new era of peace (79–87) to Carl Peter's arrogant ideas for future German colonies and Dora Dür's prediction that women entering the workforce would lose their "Liebesbedürfnis" (need for love, 125).

Brehmer's concept of asking leading scientists and thinkers to try to predict what the world a will look like a hundred years from now has been picked up by Ernst Grandits,[39] who opens his volume of predictions for the year 2112 with a quotation from Josef Beuys: "The future we want must be invented. Otherwise we get one that we don't want" (7). The most interesting contribution in this volume comes from Harald Welzer, who, in contrast to his optimistic (and more recent) position discussed in the previous chapter, paints a grim picture of society in the twenty-second century. Arguing that human adaptability means that we tend not to notice a gradual decline in our freedom, he criticizes, from the imagined vantage point of the future, current users of social media for having made possible a dystopian future with a system of pernicious and ubiquitous control:

> Fascism via Facebook: that was the total transparency that came about simply because everyone revealed as much information about him- and herself as they were able to. The user profiles, set up and carefully maintained over decades by Google and Facebook, attained an immense value under the conditions of failed democracies as at this point there was no longer any controlling safeguard that could have curtailed the informational needs of neofascist corporations. Moreover, online participants turned into a neo-Gestapo: not one of their words, their messages, their likes and dislikes were ever lost; none of their movements unregistered; no intention undiscovered. The data profile service providers supplied the senior management of the companies with everything they needed to decide autonomously over criteria for inclusion and exclusion. They justified these decisions with the preferences of the users, brought them onside with work and consumer products, or advised on different ways to get rid of them. With larger groups this didn't happen without the use of force, though in most cases this was supported by the respective majority in a given population.[40]

This explosive and forthright statement mirrors and perhaps even trumps the anxieties voiced on the other side of the Atlantic by Shoshana Zuboff in her book *Surveillance Capitalism* and by Dave Eggers in his dystopian novel *The Circle* (and has already moved closer to reality with the social credit ranking in China).[41]

There is no shortage of coffee books, almanacs, and popular science television programs about past predictions and forecasts made by scientists in the present, and the market is always hungry for more. After all, fascination has a short half-life, and exciting glimpses of future technology can soon feel commonplace, or, if predictions are way off the mark, positively ridiculous. Sometimes these books and television programs seamlessly link the past with the future—for example, in the "chronicle of the future" by German SF writers Angela and Karlheinz Steinmüller, who have collected predictions for every year from 1900 to 2100.[42]

The popular science program *Unser Leben in der Zukunft* (Our Lives in the Future), broadcast by Germany's second public service channel in 2007, attempted to bring together, in the form of a "docufiction," the achievements of modern science and technology and their likely impact on our lives over the next fifty years.[43] The program aimed to create a critical awareness of the Janus-faced character of progress, as well as our role in determining its direction. Part 1 covered the possibility of extending life, tissue engineering, cloning, neuro-implants, and robot surgeons. Part 2 focused on the future city, its population, self-driving cars, administration, and access for the infirm. Part 3 took a global view, discussing energy production after oil, the role of the superpowers, climate change, and space flight. Covering such a broad range of new technologies and their likely impact on our lives, the series could offer the general public only a glimpse of possible futures. At the same time, the program makers had a broader agenda. Providing a critical frame for the viewers (and readers of the accompanying book), producer Uwe Kersken warned:

> If mankind fails to face the challenges of the future bravely and circumspectly, it will bid farewell to the planet within a conceivable timeframe. There needs to be no less than a revolution in thinking, or sooner or later the immense disparities between profit and bankruptcy, the haves and the have-nots, glut and hunger, will tear global society apart. We will not make any progress by eulogizing about the good old days. Instead of being afraid of new ideas we should rather be afraid of the old ones—the oft-invoked "tradition" which is more often than not simply an excuse for murder and mayhem.[44]

Similarly, producer Sonja Trimbuch sought in her conclusion to make viewers aware of the importance and complexity of the ethical choices they would soon be facing:

> Beyond all technical and scientific conditions, for every imminent development the willingness to take decisions and the awareness of our responsibility are always fundamental: for example, society must weigh up, whether, in terms of ethics and morals, the world can cope with the legalization of human cloning. We should know whether we want to meet with a genetically identical copy of ourselves. Similarly, to what extent do we wish for the integration of the internet into our everyday life? Intelligent clothing, for example, could take things to a whole new level. We need to ask if security is more important to us than individual freedom.[45]

Both interventions involve an attempt to combine the anticipation of scientific and technological progress with a social critique that warns against assuming an all-too-naïve and passive attitude toward it. However, such a critical mindset vis-à-vis "progress" is no longer widely shared. In his *Zukunft 2050. Wie wir schon heute die Zukunft erfinden*, science and technology journalist Ulrich Eberl enthusiastically describes the promise of the future:

> All of this will happen, if the researchers of today succeed in turning the ideas that they are currently pushing in their laboratories into successful products. If scientists correctly gauge the trends, if the world is spared catastrophes, and if people organize their coexistence rationally, life in the year 2050 will not resemble a dark sci-fi film. It will be worth living—and best of all: we ourselves can determine what it will look like.[46]

Eberl sees the role of futurologists as meeting the demands of politicians who are interested in the social and economic trends that they need to consider, as well as those of the leaders of industry who want to know what products they can conquer the markets of tomorrow with.[47] He bemoans the widespread lack of faith in Germany in technological progress and argues for a more positive attitude. A similarly affirmative position was evident in the multimedia story, *Wie wir 2037 leben werden*, which was published in the German news magazine *Der Spiegel* in 2018. That story promised its readers an easier and more comfortable life:

> What will actually be reality in 2037 depends on the decisions that are taken up then in society, politics, and the economy. However, the current state of research tells us that there are enough reasons to believe in an exciting and beautiful future.[48]

There are indeed many voices that try to stem the historically strong ambivalence in Germany toward technological progress. Karl Heinz Erde, a self-professed "digital Darwinist and evangelist," believes that in fully digitalized economies productivity will rise and all our lives will be better if we ask the right questions and engage:

> The economy is doing well, and human beings no longer need to work. Many people are afraid of this. But why? The fifth industrial revolution allows us to make the world a better place and to redesign and rethink how we live together. Let's just make a start. Let us ask new questions. How do we organize an unconditional universal basic income? How do we manage the transition from an economy of profit to an economy of meaning? Which technologies do we want to develop, and which, for ethical reasons, would we rather

not? How can we use the innovation drive for more justice, equality, and equal opportunities, for the fight against hunger and poverty, for the protection of this one planet that is our home?[49]

Thomas Straubhaar, a former director of the Hamburg Institute of International Economics, also argues that the time has come for optimists.[50] He says that the "Crashpropheten" (crash prophets) have got it wrong, that digitalization should be seen as a game changer, a "Basisinnovation" (basic innovation) like the container ship or the internet (12), which have transformed our lives in a positive way. As far as Germany is concerned, and because the country has successfully mastered previous disruptions, there is no reason to think that it could not meet these new challenges.

There are indeed concrete signs that Germany is recognizing the need to plan for the future. In spite of occasional missteps (Chancellor Angela Merkel infamously declared "Das Internet ist für uns alle Neuland" [the internet is unchartered territory for all of us] at the CBit electronics trade fair in Hannover on June 19, 2013),[51] the German government has taken a number of far-reaching structural decisions—for example, the phasing out of nuclear power following the Fukushima nuclear disaster, and starting the energy transition (Energiewende) to a low carbon, environmentally sound energy supply.[52] In terms of anticipating the impact of digitalization and artificial intelligence, the government has instituted the Committee on the Digital Agenda and the cross-party *Enquete Kommission Künstliche Intelligenz-Gesellschaftliche Verantwortung und wirtschaftliche, soziale und ökologische Potenziale* (Enquete commission on artificial intelligence-social responsibility and economic, social, and ecological potential) in 2018.[53] In his opening address for the latter, the president of the German Bundestag, Wolfgang Schäuble, declared that AI (artificial intelligence) research had created a new dimension for the dynamic of digitalization, and that to many it represented a magic formula for technological progress. At the same time, one had to acknowledge the risks—for example, the potential for surveillance through AI systems, the loss of jobs, and new forms of warfare. It was therefore important to understand what AI was capable of and what opportunities and challenges it held.[54]

Following discussions with AI experts and stakeholders, the commission is tasked with producing strategy recommendations for artificial intelligence by fall 2020. In the meantime, the government has announced in a white paper the creation of one hundred professorial chairs in AI at German universities and a pump priming pot of 3 billion euros for AI research.[55] While critics complained that this was "too little too late," Wolfgang Wahlster, until recently the director of the German Research Center for Artificial Intelligence in Kaiserslautern,[56] saw Germany in a good position to participate in the development of new AI systems.[57] In its public hearings the commission has so far covered questions surrounding the ethical implications of AI, the control of data flows, secure data storage, ownership of data, and machine learning.[58]

The German government also invited experts from around the world to discuss the "digital revolution," "disruptive technologies," and "new philosophies" at the Future Affairs conference in Berlin in May 2019.[59] Welcoming the participants, foreign minister Heiko Maas argued that the medium-sized players in the struggle for digital hegemony needed to find a third way between the (Chinese) totalitarian and the (US) ultra-libertarian model.[60]

Perhaps the most visible manifestation of Germany's engagement with the future discourse is the Futurium Berlin, a joint initiative by the federal government and leading German research organizations, foundations, and business enterprises.[61] Standing on the Alexanderufer in the heart of the capital, the Futurium aims to encourage "dialogue on scientific, technical, and social developments of national and international significance" and to "conduct a scientific-based social discussion on shaping the future." It is too early to assess its impact, but it is possible to discern what the general approach will be: while acknowledging the fears and worries people have about the future, it aims to be optimistic, transparent, encouraging, creative, inclusive, and inspiring.[62]

◆ ◆ ◆

With the advent of modernity, people tended to look toward the future more than back to the past.[63] As this chapter has demonstrated, the futures studies discourse is highly complex, yet it allows scientists and engineers to connect with the societies they serve via mediators and the media. Given the short half-life of predictions and forecasts, the public is ever eager for the latest trends and the most exciting new discoveries as our understanding of the world around us, and ourselves, continues to grow. At the same time, the sheer number of past predictions allow us to take stock of how we used to envision the future, both to smile nostalgically at our naivety and to marvel at the courage of our forebears to take risks.

Germans, due to their specific historic experience, have developed an ambiguous view of the future—they need to embrace scientific and technological progress in order to remain competitive in the global market, but they are also acutely aware of the risks and the inevitable trade-offs that this entails. This ambivalent stance is perfectly expressed in the cover of *Der Spiegel* from April 1, 2017 with the headline question *Sind wir bereit für die perfekte Zukunft?* (are we ready for the perfect future?).[64] There is a growing awareness of the need to make informed choices in order to pick certain futures over others, and to develop flexibility and resilience to change while remaining true to cherished values of the past. As a "middle power," to a certain extent still curtailed by its history, and seemingly outpaced by the scientific, technological, and economic speed of change in the United States and China, Germany still clings to ethical ideals that it tries to live up to (as long as these do not unduly impede its competitiveness and profits). The debate about the future is very public and often very controversial, though recently the traditional pessimism seems to have reduced somewhat.

What is key, though, is the system by which Germany makes decisions about its future, and whether the siren calls and Cassandra warnings of futurists hold sufficient meaning to fire the collective imagination. I would argue that one needs creative, artistic, and imaginative visions of what our future might look and feel like in which one can playfully immerse oneself: to try out, emotionally and cognitively, many possible futures before one develops one's own position. This is the job of the speculative imagination, in the sense of any application of the imagination of the future. The task I have set myself is to explore the best examples that German literature and film can offer. Before we can do so, however, we need to look at the third tributary of SF.

3: Utopian/Dystopian Writers and Utopian/Dystopian Fiction

THE THIRD TRIBUTARY of the discourse on the future is utopian/dystopian fiction. While closely linked to utopian thought (in Thomas More's classic text *Utopia* from 1516, a sociopolitical utopia is developed within a framed narrative), the addition of an aesthetic element sets it apart from the more philosophical or practical texts discussed in the previous chapters. Readers of literary utopias derive aesthetic pleasure from imagined alternative realities and glimpses of possible, if highly improbable, futures. Utopian fiction has always worked with archetypes, inherited from classical Greek and Judeo-Christian traditions, as well as their subsequent interpretations.[1] In particular, the opposition between the good place (paradise, the golden age, the promised land) and the bad place (hell, the Dark Ages, Armageddon)—with their associated tropes and motifs, as well as the unending conflicts between them—has inspired countless writers. Utopian fiction rarely comes without a sting, and we have become wary of depictions of ideal places, and their purveyors, which, however, does not diminish their popularity. In reviewing the Oxford critic and literary scholar John Carey's anthology of utopian fictions,[2] writer Ian Samson noted: "the utopian writer is usually a malcontent and a melancholic harbouring grudges, if not a borderline psychotic, and this is presumably why we continue to enjoy their work so much."[3]

There have been countless attempts to define and demarcate utopias, anti-utopias, critical utopias, critical dystopias, utopian fiction, dystopian fiction and SF. The various schools of thought in the anglophone world (which have had a considerable impact on academic debates about utopian writing in Germany—as I will illustrate below) can be distinguished by their views on the function of utopian fiction vis-à-vis their readers and by their use of terminology. In addition, there is a strong political undercurrent in the discourse on utopian fiction. Traditionally, utopian writing is associated more with the political left (though Adolf Hitler's *Mein Kampf* is often cited as well). Many scholars are at pains to stress that Marxism, although expressly opposed to utopian thinking through its insistence on making a better world realizable, had forced utopian writers to become more pragmatic.[4]

Scholars and critics are generally agreed, though, that the twentieth century has seen a decline of positive utopian fiction and a marked shift from satirical utopias to anti-utopias and dystopias. This shift is seen as a natural process in response to historical experience and one that took place with the writers' best intentions. For example, Fatima Vieira argues that

> although the images of the future put forward in dystopias may lead the reader to despair, the main aim of this sub-genre is didactic and moralistic: images of the future are put forward as real possibilities because the utopist wants to frighten the reader and to make him realise that things may go either right or wrong, depending on the moral, social and civic responsibility of the citizens.[5]

Whether it is the lack of positive utopian fiction (eutopias) or the fact that negative utopias (dystopias) are simply more interesting to study, anglophone research on utopian writing tends to concentrate on the latter. What this "dystopian impulse" might mean, though, is highly contested. Keith M. Booker acknowledges the subversive potential of dystopian writing—for example, by exploring alternatives to the status quo—but he places the emphasis on its ability to critique supposedly utopian alternatives: "Dystopian literature is specifically that literature which situates itself in direct opposition to utopian thought, warning against the potential negative consequences of current utopianism."[6] For Booker, dystopian writing is in dialogue with utopian idealism through the shared agenda of social criticism; however, he sees it more as a kind of oppositional and critical energy or spirit than as a specific genre.[7]

In marked contrast to this, Tom Moylan classifies such fiction as anti-utopian, as, in his view, it does not leave room for any positive perspective. In 1986, he observed that utopian tales had become unnecessary, either because the wonderful things promised in utopias had already become commonplace in daily life, or because it represented "a dream incapable of attainment."[8] Following in the footsteps of Bloch and Marcuse, Moylan then introduced the concept of a "critical utopia," which was backed up by his study of a short selection of texts that described less than ideal societies that nevertheless contained the possibility of positive change within the text and through the emancipation of their readers:

> Aware of the historical tendency of the utopian genre to limit the imagination to one particular ideal and also aware of the restriction of the utopian impulse to marketing mechanisms, the authors of the critical utopia assumed the risky task of reviving the emancipatory utopian imagination while simultaneously destroying the traditional utopia and yet preserving it in a transformed and liberated form that was critical both of utopian writing itself and of the prevailing social formation.[9]

By the turn of the century, reflecting the rapid increase in the production of dystopian narratives (the "dystopian turn"), Moylan acknowledged that not all dystopian texts reflected "social dreaming" or, beneath their dystopian guise, a search for a better (if not ideal) world:

> Although all dystopian texts offer a detailed and pessimistic presentation of the very worst of social alternatives, some affiliate with a utopian tendency as they maintain a horizon of hope (or at least invite readings that do), while others appear to be dystopian allies of Utopia as they retain an anti-utopian disposition that forecloses all transformative possibility, and yet others negotiate a more strategically ambiguous position somewhere along the antinomic continuum.[10]

The dystopian texts that held out or contained a possibility for positive change he now called "critical dystopias" (183), thus tacitly acknowledging that the genre had not behaved as expected. Referring to the tendency of writers to ignore the boundaries he and his colleagues had established, he now performed a dialectical somersault to bring them back into the fold:

> By self-reflexively borrowing specific conventions from other genres, critical dystopias more often blur the received boundaries of the dystopian form and thereby expand its critical potential for critical expression.[11]

Many critics have railed against the relentless takeover of the dystopian and have pointed to the disconnect between technological achievements and our failure to build a better society. Russell Jacoby bitterly observes:

> We have the wherewithal to engineer precision automobiles with luxurious fittings; and we can place a high-tech vehicle on Mars that moves on cue; but we cannot muster the will or resources to fix a defective social order.[12]

Other scholars have tried to pin the blame for the proliferation of a dystopian mindset on an increasing "technological pessimism" (the assumption that technological advances will inevitably generate or intensify social evils that they were intended to cure), while stressing that dystopias encourage audiences to compare their reality with the dystopian fiction, thus helping them to think historically and contributing to a revival of utopian energy.[13] Indeed, the prevailing view among anglophone critics is that dystopian writing is intended to promote a better world and to shock readers into action to stop dystopian futures from becoming reality:

A descendant of satirical utopia and of anti-utopia, dystopia rejects the idea that man can reach perfection. But although the writers of dystopias present very negative images of the future, they expect a very positive reaction on the part of their readers: on the one hand, the readers are led to realise that all human beings have (and always will have) flaws, and so social improvement—rather than individual improvement—is the only way to ensure social and political happiness; on the other hand, the readers are to understand that the depicted future is not a reality but only a possibility that they have to learn to avoid.[14]

Such hope in the transformative, liberating, and activating potential of dystopian narratives pervades the entire anglophone discourse. Making a case for the usefulness of dystopian literature as a form of sociology, Sean Seeger and Daniel Davison-Vecchione argue:

Dystopian fiction ought to be seen as situated somewhere between the subjective and objective poles, allowing it to illustrate how personal experience and social structure enter into and mutually influence one another with a phenomenological richness arguably unmatched by empirical analysis.[15]

Focusing on the theme of repressive surveillance in literature and film, Peter Marks asserts that "modern utopian works overwhelmingly project forward, initiating imaginative thought experiments that can feed into social awareness and discourse."[16] Gregory Claeys has recently developed this argument further, describing the dystopian mindset as "a modern phenomenon, wedded to secular pessimism," which grew out of the disenchantment with the "failed utopia" of twentieth-century totalitarianism.[17] Claeys makes a strong case based on the long shadow cast by National Socialism and the bestiality of the "Final Solution." While reminding us that the dark scenarios of dystopian fiction were created in response to the experience of such evil, he believes that they should be regarded as projections rather than predictions, and he argues that the literary dystopia is the right genre for our age since it alone still has the power to raise the alarm:

The task of the literary dystopia, then, is to warn us against and educate us about real-life dystopias. It need not furnish a happy ending to do so: pessimism has its place. But it may envision rational and collective solutions where irrationality and panic loom. Entertainment plays a role in this process. But the task at hand is serious. It gains daily in importance. Here, then, is a genre, and a concept, whose hour has come. May it flourish.[18]

This passage deserves a closer look. Like the other scholars discussed beforehand, Claeys insists on the ultimate "utopian energy" of dystopian writing. But between the lines he acknowledges that dystopias may be written with very different intentions. They may not only preclude a happy end; they may also prevent the reader from escaping the maelstrom of hopelessness (the types of dystopia that Moylan would call anti-utopias), and they may be written for the entertainment of the reader, something that very few critics take into account. Such narratives are either ignored or dismissed as not fitting the paradigm of a "concrete dystopia."

An apt example for a narrative that exudes pessimism on every page is John Lanchester's latest novel *The Wall*.[19] Not only does it reflect current insecurities and political debates like Brexit in the United Kingdom and President Trump's plan to build a wall on the US border with Mexico but it declares many of the current global problems (climate change, migration) as beyond solution. The fact that such inevitability feeds the romantic and fatalistic mindset of Western adolescents underlines how right Claeys is about his dread of "pessimism."[20] As to the oft-forgotten element of entertainment, the author Lionel Shriver reminds us that not all adult readers will take the call to action inherent in dystopian fiction seriously:

> We're all leery of change. The future is sure to be different, but in ways we cannot foresee. The literature of apocalypse provides an outlet for our anxieties, while also warning us to do what it takes to keep these stories from coming true.. . . But the greatest joy of dystopian fiction is that it's make-believe. We can experiment with disaster imaginatively, close the book, then mix that martini.[21]

The German Discourse on Utopian/Dystopian Fiction

In contrast to the anglophone discourse on utopian/dystopian writing (which, incidentally, rarely makes any reference to texts outside the established anglophone canon), German researchers held out much longer against the pull of the dystopian, thereby creating a more pragmatic trajectory. German utopian fiction underwent a major transformation in the nineteenth century, reflecting the country's belated but subsequently very rapid industrialization. This brought with it, on the one hand, severe social tensions that gave birth to the socialist idea and a number of now almost forgotten social utopias—for example, Theodor Hertzka's *Freiland. Ein soziales Zukunftsbild* (Freeland: A Social Image of the Future, 1890). On the other hand, utopian writing increasingly focused on the world of work, industrial production, and axioms of economic liberalism. As Birgit

Affeldt-Schmidt observes, the belief in technological "progress" began to replace religion in the nineteenth century, with far-reaching consequences for utopian writing, since the imagination of change had been usurped by a new world view:

> So what chances remain for a literary utopia to fulfill a meaningful role in the completely different climate of thought in the nineteenth century—which, in the context of the prevalent belief in progress, has a dynamic view of history and a well-established way of perceiving possibilities—when one of its traditional tasks, namely, the breaking up of habitual patters of perception, has been realized without the aid of literature?[22]

Given the general reluctance after two world wars to listen to the promise of a better world, German scholars and critics have long wrestled with the question what the function of utopian writing might be, and how to create a new purpose for it. There is a consensus that literary utopias continue to be needed but not in what form. Gert Ueding has stressed that, since the concept of realism is as much a product of the imagination as the invented plots in realist fiction, *all* literature is in fact utopian, because what it portrays is not identical with reality.[23] Burghard Schmidt has roundly denied that utopias are a literary genre,[24] while Wolfgang Biesterfeld has warned that it should be kept well away from the "triviale Massenliteratur" (trivial mass literature) of the newly emerging and disturbingly popular SF.[25] Hiltrud Gnüg has recommended a compromise, arguing that while utopias do not constitute a literary genre, literature still has a utopian function.[26] In his landmark book on German literary utopias, Götz Müller has located this function in the creation of a variety of second realities—for example, the *Inselutopie* (island utopia), the *Staatsroman* (state novel), the *Gelehrtenrepublik* (republic of scholars), the *Uchronie* (a fictional time period, often in the shape of an alternative history), and SF.[27] The Austrian writer and social scientist Rolf Schwendter has proposed that literary utopias ought to be understood as offering a virtual *Zukunftswerkstatt* (a workshop in which to create futures).[28]

With the increasing production of literary dystopias, scholars have been forced into a rearguard action. Insisting on the critical function of utopia, Jan Robert Bloch has challenged the "dystopische Gewordenheit" (dystopian manifestation) of such narratives:

> The modern dystopia stands at the crossroads of two motifs, albeit ones that are intertwined. On the one hand, the dystopian narrative frame can serve the nihilistic diagnosis that man cannot and should not live by the utopia of a free society but rather may be grateful that he can throw off the burdens of freedom and responsibility for

himself and yield these to an external instrumental, reason. This frame, on the other hand, can create resistance by means of the portrayed negation of freedom, and thus, in a dialectical way, keep faith with the utopian horizon of an unalienated existence that has become his home.[29]

In identifying the delicate balance of the repressive and the emancipatory potential of dystopian writing, Jan Bloch echoes the anglophone efforts to differentiate dystopias, critical utopias, and anti-utopias, but he reminds us of the close connection between utopian thought and utopian writing. However, in their attempt to stem the flood of dystopian images created by writers and filmmakers, German scholars then produced more and more studies that were ostensibly talking about utopian writing but were in fact bowing to the pressure of reality. With science and technology usurping the nimbus of the utopian desire and promising a better future, utopian writing was left with the thankless task of pointing out the flaws, thus rendering itself powerless to inspire, something German scholars were painfully aware of:

> Seen from our current knowledge base, where many things are technologically feasible but neither desirable for the common good nor for one's individual pursuit of happiness, a technologically oriented utopian thinking appears very ambivalent.[30]

Indeed, the increasing tension between technological and social utopias has become the focus of German critics of utopian writing in the twenty-first century. With a mindset that is defined by a mistrust in technology as well as in those holding the power over the direction of its application, scholars have been looking for standard-bearers. Marvin Chlada has argued for the mobilization of the *will* and the denunciation of the pursuit of control over the material world in order to build a bridge between reality and the desired utopian place,[31] while Rudolf Maresch and Florian Rötzer have lamented the fact that utopian thinking has been taken over by engineers and technoscientists while former avantgardes have retreated into NIMBYism:

> In the laboratories where scientists once conceived test series, compared numbers and curves, [and] examined and threw out hypotheses, nowadays they conceive the new images, myths, and doctrines of salvation of a postmodern scientific community. They have, for a long time now, turned into incubators of the imaginary, into places where solutions to the seemingly crazy, impossible, and unattainable are sought and then turned into reality.[32]

In a somewhat convoluted argument, Maresch and Rötzer maintain that the cause for this new search for the utopian can be found in the new potential of technologies like robotics, gene technology, computing and networking capabilities, and their application in medicine, pharmaceutics, and agriculture, as well as in sport, art, and culture. They believe that these will radically change our lives, but that not just the cultural elites but also the politicians and businesses in Europe, and in Germany particularly, are reluctant to commit to these new utopias. In their view, Europe seems apathetic and burnt out compared to the United States or Asia, because the experience of the twentieth century has sown seeds of doubt into the human ability to shape the future, thus effectively cooling off the needed enthusiasm for utopian dreaming:

> The more the technical means for the redesign of the world are perfected, the more reason there seems to exist to be afraid of these "future presents."[33]

On the other hand, they argue, since Europe is the place that invented utopian thinking, as well as the myths of eternal life, beauty, and eternal youth that drive gene-, nano- and computer technology, European writers may be in a better position to reclaim its potential.

Elena Zeißler is one of several German scholars who is reluctant to follow Moylan's definition of the dystopian.[34] She argues that keeping resignation and active pessimism apart is too difficult in practice and supports a more pragmatic approach, looking at each dystopian text on its merits and analyzing its aim and function.

> Much more important, from the point of view of the dystopia, is the critique of existing society. In order to highlight specific shortcomings, the classical anti-utopia extrapolates these into the future, where they take on threatening dimensions. In this way, the undesirable aspects of life are not only satirically defamiliarized but are also presented as especially dangerous. Connected to this is one of the most important functions of the anti-utopia—namely, its warning against possible excesses of current developments.[35]

Such a position may be ignoring the anti-utopian tendency to question the validity of all utopias, but it has the advantage of acknowledging the openness of the genre and its practitioners as well as its many metamorphoses in recent years. It also accepts that the traditional warning function of dystopian writing is no longer the main motivation behind the writing of dystopias. Instead, scholars now perceive a renewed interest in a "wertegeleitete Zukunftskonstruktion" (construction of the future that is guided by a set of values),[36] especially when this construction comes in the shape of SF, since it can develop the utopian consciousness and ignite the utopian imagination. Steltemeier and others argue that we are at a crucial moment in the history of utopian writing because this central medium of utopian thought is uniquely able to promise revolutionary futures emerging from the convergence of nano-, bio-, information- and cognition technology and to make them plausible. At the same time—and here they agree with Zeißler—the techno discourse is not the only game in town:

> It may well be the greatest challenge of utopian studies over the next few years to research the continuities and discontinuities of techno-futurism and social utopia. It should further be noted that we can in no way assume that the social utopia would be the *generally old*, and technofuturism the *generally new*, manifestation of utopian thought.[37]

The unequal relationship between techno-scientific advances and utopian writing, especially in Germany, continues to vex scholars. As Peter McIsaac and others point out, utopian modes of cultural production continue to be indispensable for thinking through the implications of scientific advances, but the balance of power has shifted toward the sciences:

> In German cultural history, the interchanges between science and the cultural imagination have more often been one-directional in that scientific discourses have provided impulses, images and ideas that have been transformed into narratives, symbols, and metaphors in the service of utopian thinking and the formulation of utopian or dystopian future worlds.[38]

There is certainly an aura of authority that the jargon of scientific discourse imparts to a utopian or dystopian narrative (though one should not dismiss the impact of utopian writing on scientists and engineers). And yet, with the decline of faith in utopian scenarios we are also witnessing a corresponding decline of faith in science's ability to make our lives better. The *Fortschrittsglaube* (belief in progress) of the nineteenth and early twentieth century has given way to skepticism. In populist and far-right circles, the word "expert" has even acquired negative connotations, while scientific facts are openly questioned. Technology is no longer perceived as able to help solve our social, economic, and ecological problems.[39] In extreme cases, either in order to scandalize or to rouse jaded audiences, dystopian narratives have become apocalyptic.

The Future as Apocalypse

The doomsday clock has been stuck at five minutes to twelve for decades. The relentless barrage of distressing news about the impact of human activity on the natural environment (radiation after nuclear war or accidents, the reduction of the rain forest, climate change and the rise of sea levels, plastic in the oceans, species extinction and loss of biodiversity) has led many writers to the conclusion that if there is any hope for the future, it can only be found at the other end of a cataclysmic event that "wipes the slate clean" and allows surviving human beings to start again—hopefully, as wiser and more careful ones. As the British SF writer Brian Stableford puts it:

> Insofar as twenty-first-century futuristic fiction set on Earth retains a eutopian component, its eutopias are necessarily postponed until the aftermath of environmental collapse. The near universal assumption of such fiction ist that dystopia has already arrived, in embryo, and that its progress to maturity is unavoidable.[40]

While the temptation is great to blame stereotypically "mad scientists" and engineers for discovering and applying the tools and methods with which we seem to hasten our demise, and to demand that they take greater responsibility for the impact of their work, the reality, of course, is that we all have a responsibility for avoiding the apocalypse.[41] The strange thing, though, is that we have been warned for decades but do not seem to take the message seriously. Instead, we happily consume tales of doom and destruction that publishers and film studios are only too happy to supply.[42] Since radical pessimism is a growing trend,[43] the question needs to be asked what role writers play when they choose subjects like cataclysms or pandemics or climate change (cli-fi).[44]

In Germany, apocalyptic narratives have had a particular impact. The consequences of industrialization in this confined and densely populated space have been impossible to escape, while being at the center of Cold War confrontation between the United States and the Soviet Union for so long have made its people highly sensitive to the possibility of a nuclear war. Concern about environmental pollution has morphed into climate change fear and mass extinction alarm. German writers and filmmakers take special pleasure in—or are highly adept at—making their audiences fear the worst, and they help them to imagine it. Of course, apocalyptic fears are nothing new; today, however, they are not based in religious fantasies but grow out of the process of civilization itself and can be construed as an "Ausdruck einer fundamentalen Wahrnehmungsverweigerung" (an expression of a fundamental denial to see the writing on the wall).[45] While the inversion of the literary utopia in the form of apocalyptic narratives initially reflected a "Bewußtseinswandel" (change in consciousness) and a sense of loss of the beauty that once existed, a more complex relationship between messenger and message has developed since the 1980s.[46] A good example of this are the works of German filmmakers Wolfgang Petersen and Roland Emmerich. While Petersen seems to revel in creating blockbusters for their own sake, Emmerich has taken his German consciousness and transplanted it to Hollywood. Continuing his quest to warn about human technological interference in the natural balance (climate is the main point, but he also stresses other forms of human interference in the natural world), he has expanded his film school project *Das Arche Noah Prinzip* (the Noah's ark principle) into tales of universal applicability and shock—namely, *The Day after Tomorrow* and *2012*. While Christine Haase asserts that Emmerich's works avoid "national-cultural specificity,"[47] I would argue that his films represent a very German way of looking at the world and a very German approach to raising awareness of environmental issues through an apocalyptic imaginary.

In recent years, researchers have moved away from focusing on the difference between utopia and apocalypse as the two master narratives of modernity and instead have noticed an increasing convergence between the two, since the ability to create the one also implies the ability to create the other.[48] We also have a better understanding of our predilection for creating and consuming apocalyptic scenarios. As to the former, apart from the obvious profit motive, there is a strong sense that apocalyptic rhetoric is still effective when writers and directors seek to apply political pressure,[49] while the latter allows readers and audiences to imagine themselves in heroic situations as well as to redefine and reorient themselves vis-à-vis social constrictions.[50]

Eva Horn's landmark study on apocalyptic fiction is one of the few German books on the utopian/dystopian that have been translated into English, perhaps because all her examples are anglophone books and films.[51] Nevertheless, her exploration of futures past exposes the irony behind the production of apocalyptic scenarios in fiction and film:

> It is strange that precisely in the Anthropocene, in an epoch where humanity will have been indelibly written into global history, people indulge in the invention of worlds where it does not figure anymore.[52]

She locates the reasons for the boom in apocalyptic tales in the breakdown of our modern "Zeitordnung" (time order, equivalent to "world order"). Drawing on Aleida Assmann's work on cultural memory, she argues that our idea of the future as a "key auratic concept" and a utopian space for hope, plans, and designs has changed radically. The catastrophe is the core expectation of the twenty-first century, both as a desired and a feared outcome on the horizon. This diagnosis of current moods recalls the German theorist Walter Benjamin's stark observation:

> The concept of progress must be grounded in the idea of catastrophe. That things are "status quo" is the catastrophe. Catastrophe is not what is coming, but that which is already here.[53]

Horn notes that the structures steering humanity toward the catastrophe are all highly complex systems, be they economics and finance, or ecological (oceans, climate). The genuinely new aspect in her interpretation of our obsession with a coming catastrophe, and one that I will develop further in my analysis of German SF, is her focus on the way apocalyptic narratives not only furnish our imagination with images of the end but also allow their readers to explore a range of possible alternative reactions, thus developing resilience to challenges and strategies to cope with them:

> These are productions in which how we should deal with these possible futures now is not only illustrated but negotiated: optimistic or alarmist, "ready for anything," happy to take risks, skeptical, making provisions and, lately, "resilient." Fictions, however, play a special role in these productions—not just as symptoms but also as agents of formatting an expectation of the future. . . . They . . . make a direct and structural intervention into the imaginary of a culture.[54]

Having confronted audiences with the worst possible outcomes, they are now free either to accept the urgency of the prognosis and act to prevent them or to question their validity. Obviously, we will have to consider a third possible response—that audiences become simply overwhelmed by the flood of apocalyptic imaginaries and lose all hope of making a difference. Horn appears to discount this fatalistic option, but I will consider it seriously in my discussion of German examples.

Another noteworthy German study of apocalyptic narratives (written by Anglicists and, again, one that only uses examples from English literature) has attempted to identify certain types of dystopian and apocalyptic narratives.[55] In his highly perceptive introduction to this study, Eckardt Voigts notes that even utopians like H. G. Wells realized that the uses to which advanced technology were put showed that science would not have an entirely emancipatory effect on humanity. He rightly points out that the assumption science would have a civilizing and beneficial effect on humanity was wrong:

> Science as a source of human suppression and control, the Darwinist dynamics that implied the threat of regression and the entropic imagination that forecast the ultimate hollowness of rationality and

Enlightenment contributed to the development of the dystopian imagination.⁵⁶

Some of the apocalyptic imagination does, of course, not imply the end of life on Earth but rather the end of humanity as we know it. With the advances in biological sciences, countless recent narratives have focused on the potential impact of bioengineering. Lars Schmeink argues that a critical posthumanism (in the form of "biopunk" narratives) is in the process of decentering the privileged subject of humanism, and he asks how humanism and modernity will change when biologists take their place as "deicides." Again, considering that biology is the science of living things, this outlook is apocalyptic:

> Biopunk makes use of current posthumanist conceptions in order to criticize liquid modern realities as already dystopian, warning that a future will only get worse, and that society needs to reverse its path, or else destroy all life on this planet.⁵⁷

Robert Weninger's study on last man narratives has come closest to identifying the motivation behind what we might call the "apocalyptic desire."⁵⁸ Focusing on a range of examples, including a broad range of German texts like Arno Schmidt's *Schwarze Spiegel* (Black Mirrors, 1951) and Marlen Haushofer's *Die Wand* (The Wall, 1963), Weninger follows the trail of human thought from theism and deism to atheism, skillfully linking religious traditions with philosophical ones to explain literature and film's complicity with the abhorrent. For him, writers of apocalyptic fiction meditate in novelistic form on issues that were "once the preserve of theology and metaphysics" (508), and they either do not expect there to be a future, or, if they do expect there to be one, then they think it will be pointless, meaningless, and hopeless:

> Whether humankind expires in a nuclear inferno or owing to some natural virus (or any other cause), whether there are survivors or not, whether the circumstances of humankind's disappearance strike us as "realistic"—however we define realism in this context—or constructed and artificial, authors have always used such scenarios to mull over, as well as pass judgment on, our way of life and the values and belief systems we hold dear.⁵⁹

But such a deep insight into our darkest desires has its advantages, according to Weninger. Not only do apocalyptic narratives provide us with a view of the present from the vantage point of a future that has not yet happened but they are so "palpably concrete" in their depictions that we can easily identify with the protagonists. This inside perspective allows for experimentation and access to the psychological makeup of the protagonists in the moment of ultimate crisis, testing their reactions as they range from mutual aid and self-sacrifice to extreme violence caused by the will to survive.

Apocalyptic narratives leave little room for hope, but before we go into terminal depression in the face of the seemingly endless production of disaster scenarios, we should remember that the apocalyptic mindset is itself contested. Optimists like Johan Norberg give us "reasons to be cheerful" and challenge our addiction to bad news that leads us to eat up depressing or enraging stories from across the globe, whether they threaten us or not, and therefore wrongly conclude that things are much worse than they are.[60] While Norberg acknowledges that good news is harder to spot, he argues that humanity has made real progress in the areas of food supply, sanitation, life expectancy, poverty, violence, the state of the environment, literacy, freedom, equality, and the conditions of childhood.[61] One could argue that Germans are particularly prone to see the negatives in any given situation owing to their historic experiences and their predilection for "Weltschmerz," but this only leads to speculation and stereotyping.[62]

♦ ♦ ♦

Utopian and dystopian narratives seek to fill utopian thought with life, urging us to imagine alternatives to the status quo by showing us concrete examples. They evoke strong reactions, ranging from a desire to reach the promised land or change the makeup of society to abhorrence and an urge to prevent a nightmare scenario. As entertainments, they are neither expected to be directly turned into reality nor to be followed as a call to action.

Positive utopian (eutopian) narratives like Ernest Callenbach's *Ecotopia* (1975), Maria Erlenberger's *Singende Erde* (Singing Earth, 1980), Kim Stanley Robinson's *Pacific Edge* (1990), or Chana Porter's *The Seep* (2020) are becoming rare, reflecting a growing skepticism about the feasibility of changing human nature. Dystopian narratives, whether as anti-utopias or "critical utopias," were initially highly effective warnings against undesirable futures, but through their sheer ubiquity they have lost some of their ability to shock their readers. On the silver screen, in particular, their success masks a growing sense of inevitability.

Scholars and critics have adapted their theories to accommodate the shift from utopian to dystopian writing but disagree over its ultimate impact. It remains to be seen whether the Cassandra warnings of apocalyptic visions have any tangible effect on our consciousness and conscience. The aestheticization of the end has its own grim attraction, but in its diffuse and uncritical nihilism such an extreme form of dystopian writing lacks the essential requirement of utopian writing—namely, hope. Writers of apocalyptic visions can be accused of complicity in the normalization of hopelessness and despair, the furthering of political disengagement, and, through the gratuitous use of dystopian imagery, they can be accused of extinguishing the flame of resistance. In particular, the aestheticization of evil for the sake of titillation and entertainment runs counter to every effort to come to terms with the past and does not enable audiences to come to terms with the future.

But there is an alternative reading of dystopian writing, whether motivated by idealism or despair. By challenging the technoscientific mantra of progress, it gives voice to justified reservations and fears. While it was once assumed that science would have a civilizing effect on humanity, the recognition of science's immense powers demands a higher level of responsibility—with dystopian writing potentially creating a civilizing effect on science and technology. Using utopian thought and writing as a guide, SF can provide that orientation.

4: Science Fiction: The Nexus of Utopianism, Futurism, and Utopian Fiction

THE TASK OF DEFINING what SF might be has exercised scholars for generations, and it has not produced definitive answers.[1] Much depends on a given author's or critic's attitude to speculative fiction and the fantastic. Many literary scholars are perfectly happy to seriously engage with "realistic" fictions (realism), but they react allergically to SF, even though both types of writing require a willingness to suspend disbelief.[2] Both can be read for entertainment, for aesthetic pleasure, for information about the world, and for insight into the human condition. The worst accusation leveled at SF is that it is escapist, that it detracts from the seriousness of the real world. I agree with Tom Moylan, who declared:

> Indeed, the infamous "escapism" attributed to sf does not necessarily mean a debilitating escape from reality because it can also lead to an empowering escape to a very different way of thinking about, and possibly of being in, the world.[3]

SF is well known for its ability to shrug off the tethers of theory, its practitioners never being happier than when confounding prescriptive categorizations of their work.[4] And yet, in order to gain some firm ground for this study, and to identify the distinctiveness of German SF, it is necessary to briefly rehearse the development of SF theory. Tellingly, anglophone studies on SF have tended to ignore SF texts or films not produced in the United Kingdom or the United States,[5] contending that both its key progenitors (H. G. Wells in Britain) and its early formative years (the pulps in the United States in the 1920s and 1930s) created a distinct genre with an Anglo-American label, while conveniently ignoring Jules Verne and Kurd Laßwitz, the respective "fathers" of SF in France and Germany. To be sure, there is a certain hegemonial pride with which Edward James speaks of "The Victory of American Science Fiction" or when American SF writer James Gunn declares:[6]

> To consider Science Fiction in countries other than the United States, one must start from these shores. American Science Fiction is the base line against which all the other fantastic literatures other

than English must be measured. That is because SF, as informed readers recognize it today, began in New York City in 1926.[7]

Anglophone Science Fiction theory has developed significantly in the last four decades but, it should be stressed, it depends almost entirely on a canon of anglophone texts. And yet, some of its conclusions are so general that they can be universally applied. Both Gary Wolfe's seminal study on the *Iconography of Science Fiction* and Mark Rose's *Anatomy of Science Fiction* demonstrate that SF is created in the space between the human and the nonhuman.[8] In a paragraph that exudes utopian anticipation, Wolfe observed:

> By treating the opposition between the known and the unknown, between what is and what is not yet, between cosmos and chaos, and by expressing these tensions through certain recurring icons, Science Fiction reveals not only its own beliefs, but also patterns of belief that are imbedded in our culture at large. By using icons that mediate between the polarities of known and unknown, Science Fiction suggests the possibility of radical transformations of ourselves and our environment, and of a range of potentially infinite experience. . . . It is thus a literature that holds out the promise of infinite newness and infinite discovery.[9]

Mark Rose acknowledged that early SF was an inversion of the utopian romance, since it incorporated fabulous voyages, gothic patterns of sin and retribution, and quest romances, but he argued that putting SF into the straitjacket of a "genre" was unhelpful. He suggested that it should be seen as a social phenomenon: "a tradition, a developing complex of themes, attitudes, and formal strategies that, taken together, constitute a general set of expectations" (4). He also made an astute observation regarding the relationship between utopias, dystopias, and SF:

> Incidentally, we may note that whereas most dystopias are felt to be Science Fiction, most utopias are not. This makes perfect sense. Dystopias are always concerned with the human in conflict with the nonhuman. Utopias, on the other hand, are attempts to portray societies that are, according to the author's lights, more fully human than his own.[10]

Obviously, over the last four decades, the context for theorizing SF has changed radically. But there are continuities as well, particularly in terms of the role SF plays for its readers. Tom Shippey pointed this out in the late 1990s:

Both Science Fiction and fantasy have functioned during the twentieth century, and will continue to function during the twenty-first, as major explanatory tools that have provided meaning and insight to millions of readers, often about vital issues such as the origins of war and the nature of humanity, and often to readers who have been failed by or who have proved inaccessible to all older and more traditional forms of writing (such as history and mainstream fiction). They also can be seen as the main indicators of radical shifts of attitude and understanding in the population at large. In the process, they have acted as powerful if unrecognised forces against prejudice and ethnocentrism, and they have served as guides to and recruiters for both hard and soft sciences.[11]

Drawing a line between Blochtian utopian thought and SF, and echoing Darko Suvin's pioneering study on the *Poetics of Science Fiction*,[12] Carl Freedman argues that by imagining new worlds that estrange the empirical world of the status quo, we learn to see our own world in a new perspective:

> The dynamic of Science Fiction can on one level be identified with the hope principle itself. The reading of SF drives us into lands where we have never set foot and yet which—because they are cognitively linked to the world we do know and are invested with our actual longings—amount to a kind of homeland. Even more than in the novel of the artist, the defining features of SF are located on the In-Front-of-Us, at the level of the Not-Yet-Being and in the dimension of utopian futurity.[13]

Admittedly, some critics still believe that SF's ability to imagine entire new worlds (world-building) is its key strength, in contrast to mainstream fiction's focus on the intricacies of interhuman relationships.[14] But with more and more mainstream writers adopting the tropes and style of SF, this distinction is no longer valid. Indeed, with the breakdown of many categories that had previously been thought to be natural and inviolable—such as those between genders, and between humans and machines—the certainty of literary "genres" has disappeared, even though there is no consensus how to demarcate SF in the twenty-first century. Ultimately, there is little point continuing to argue over whether SF is a part of utopia or whether utopia is a branch of SF, other than to reenact old controversies. For example: Edward James argues that utopia has mutated, within the field of SF, into something very different from the classic utopia (219), while Gregory Claeys maintains that

> Science Fiction is a sub-genre in which science and technology predominate thematically—utopically, when expressed positively, or dystopically, when used negatively. (Some writers additionally use

"sf" to mean "speculative fiction," which invites a much broader definition and is much closer to the wider domain of "utopian fiction.") In the narrower version, science and technology are central to the vision of the future: the focus is not upon constitutional, institutional, communal or other means of improving human order, maintaining greater security, harmony, happiness or anything else. Sci-fi works can, however, still function primarily as social criticism or satire.[15]

Writing in the same *Companion to Utopian Literature*, Peter Fitting also wrestles with the challenge to separate utopia, dystopia, and SF.[16] He argues that we should regard SF as a modern form of, or perhaps as a successor to, utopian writing given its "ability to reflect or express our hopes and fears about the future, and more specifically to link those hopes and fears to science and technology" (136).

Of course, the term "form" is extremely vague, but it is perhaps as good a term as "mode," which has been suggested for SF for some time now. In 2008, Istvan Csicsery-Ronay garnered much praise for his comment that the world had become "science-fictional."[17] His proposal to view SF as a speculative *mode* of storytelling, "a complex hesitation about the relationship between imaginary conceptions and historical reality unfolding in the future" (4), aligns with my own view that SF can prepare us, conceptually and emotionally, for possible futures, thus creating a bridge between science and readers, and potentially a critical mass of people to exert political pressure for change. As Mike Ashley put it in his foreword to the catalogue of the *Out of this World* exhibition at the British Library in 2011, "[s]cience fiction is that speculation about the impact of science, technology and socio-political change on us."[18]

Veronica Hollinger hails the change in perspective from genre to mode as "one of the most influential transformations in critical approaches to SF since the mid-1980s":

> In many contemporary analyses, SF serves not only as a narrative project finely attuned to the technocultural environment, but also as a kind of image bank through which to orient our lives in this environment. Often the impetus for this valorization of SF as a privileged technocultural discourse is the perceived breakdown in conventional ways of experiencing historical time, frequently figured as the collapse of the distance between the present and the future into a kind of future-present.[19]

Most recent theories of SF acknowledge its debt to the tradition of utopian writing (for example, when it creates myths to unleash the imagination), but they also stress that it has moved beyond the utopian by seriously questioning the potential paths to that better world. Sherryl

Vint, the leading American theorist of SF, suggests that SF "is a cultural mode that struggles with the implications of discoveries in science and technology for human social lives and philosophical conceptions" and links it to the aesthetic experience of the sublime.[20] SF is a technological sublime—that is, something that, while constantly changing its shape, simultaneously promotes the myth of human technological prowess and critiques it. It is:

> A genre that responds to changes science and technology enact in daily life; it enables thought experiments about changing conditions of human existence; it is a site of meditation on changing philosophical concepts; and the genre itself is always changing as it embraces new media of expression and new aesthetic ideals.[21]

Even if we go along with Tom Shippey's assessment that SF "has been the most characteristic literary mode of the twentieth century," the question remains what exactly this mode is.[22] Ann and Jeff VanderMeer, reflecting on the history and future of the "genre," contend that the only common denominator for all its manifestations is "the" *future*:

> Science Fiction lives in the future, whether that future exists ten seconds from the Now or whether in a story someone builds a time machine a century hence in order to travel back into the past. It is Science Fiction whether the future is phantasmagorical and surreal or nailed down using the rivets and technical jargon of "hard Science Fiction." A story is also Science Fiction whether the story in question is, in fact, extrapolation about the future or using the future to comment on the past or present.[23]

The VanderMeers have recently attempted to repair the "pointless rift" between "genre" and "literary," arguing that SF as literature is highly relevant to the present, filled with visionary and even transcendent moments, and highly entertaining to boot.[24] Their bid to produce a "definitive anthology" (xiii) embraces the many types of SF, ranging from hard SF, soft or social SF, space opera, alternative history, apocalyptic stories, tales of alien encounters, and near future dystopia, to satirical stories. It also tries to be more inclusive by bringing in more female writers and more translations from other languages. Regarding this belated recognition of nonanglophone works, the British SF critic Paul Kincaid, perhaps a touch condescendingly, observed:

> The most exciting aspect, of course, is the way it opens up Science Fiction to the rest of the world. The interspersion of Science Fiction from other cultures among the more familiar fare provides a counter-history: this too was Science Fiction, this too was going on.[25]

If anglophone critics and readers are increasingly appreciative of the diverse traditions and productions of SF around the world (for example, the recent global success of Chinese SF, especially Cixin Liu's *The Three Body Problem* trilogy and the Netflix film *The Wandering Earth*, as well as the crowdfunded translations of other Chinese writing published in *Clarkesworld* magazine), then they may be ready for a reappraisal of German SF as discussed in part 2 of this book.[26]

However, we cannot leave the review of anglophone SF theory without recognizing the seminal work of Russell Blackford on *Science Fiction and the Moral Imagination*.[27] Blackford argues that SF is ideally suited to dramatize moral dilemmas and engage with a wide variety of moral questions—specifically about the acceptable use of science and technology owing to the great power that these can grant:

> With its greatly extended narrative possibilities, Science Fiction can illuminate the social impact of change, propose blueprints for a better future, or implicitly criticise any naïve optimism about where the human species is headed.[28]

Acknowledging that SF, in the early days, was overly optimistic and naïve, he points out that the "mega-text" of SF icons and tropes has "metamorphosed over time into something darker, harder, and weirder."[29] As such, it enables us to engage with, and to explore, ideas of fatalism, determinism, free will, and the future, both at a personal and a broader sociopolitical level. He rightly perceives a strain of technopessimism running through recent works of SF that focus on the dangers from computers, artificial intelligence, and biotechnology, though this technology is rarely depicted as entirely good or bad but rather as an inevitable part of our lives that we need to learn how to control if it is going to be of benefit to us. The key point of SF, according to Blackford, is that it forces us to make choices about how to use that power and to understand what it means to be human.

Crucially, Blackford reminds us that by confronting us with the choice to use technology not only to change the world around us but also to alter ourselves, SF mixes the scientific with the visionary, offering its audiences posthumanist philosophical positions. Of course, such grand gestures run the risk of overreaching:

> Stories of momentous choice can be cognitively valuable—they can challenge assumptions and provoke thought—but they can also lapse into mere spectacle. This raises difficult questions about the value of the SF genre and how we ought to engage with it critically.[30]

To outsiders, SF can therefore seem no more than a lurid form of entertainment aimed at adolescents, offering simple morals. For open-minded readers and viewers, on the other hand, its speculations hold layers of important messages that no other form can convey.

German Theories of Science Fiction— and Theories of German Science Fiction

SF theory and critique has a long, though complicated, history, both in Germany and in anglophone German Studies. The reason the discourse is complicated can be traced back to the hegemonic tussle over the English term "Science Fiction" as discussed above, as well as to the silence of German writers of speculative fiction during the Third Reich and the subsequent reorientation toward American models. At the same time, Germany's specific history and experience arguably make for a distinctive point of view in its cultural productions, whether these manifest themselves in the context of SF coming from the former GDR or in the context of works that directly address the Holocaust and the traumatic experience of a totalitarian regime. One should also note that in both German academia and educated circles the term "Science Fiction" has long been deemed *infra dignitatem* (beneath dignity) owing to the fear in the humanities that research into SF might diminish the reputation of "serious" subjects such as Literatur*wissenschaft* (the *science* of literature) and Geschichts*wissenschaft* (the *science* of history). When it was studied at all, it was often in the context of Anglicists studying anglophone SF, thus maintaining a safe distance from (and an almost ex officio interest as an excuse for) the object of study. As we shall see, the problem of how far SF can aspire to "literariness," and how much topicality and entertainment can be tolerated, has handicapped German SF theorists and practitioners much longer than it has those in the anglophone world.

Another problem for those attempting to write about German SF lies in the fact that an entire, once thriving, literary genre—namely, that of the *Zukunftsroman* (novel of the future),[31] which had its heyday during the 1920s and 1930s—has been disavowed retrospectively by its association with the vile ideology of National Socialism, a fate not experienced in the same way by the often jingoistic, xenophobic, and misogynist early SF literature in the USA and Britain.[32]

SF—in the form of translations of works by John W. Campbell Jr., Jack Williamson, and Isaac Asimov—was introduced to the (West) German market in 1952 by the Rauch's Weltraum-Bücher (Rauch's Space Books) series. The editor, Gotthard Günther, argued that these authors were inventing a new, "metaphysical" world view that was ringing in a new age.[33] Early German studies of SF were at pains to stress the scientific and cultural value of the new form of literature, or at least their own bona fide academic credentials, before approaching it. For example, Martin Schwonke's study from 1957 insists on using the by then outdated term "naturwissenschaftlich-technische Utopie" (technoscientific utopia), and it starts with a disparaging comment on the "impertinent ubiquity" of technoscientific imaginaries:

> Technological images of the future and speculations about scientific progress and its potential consequences have become brash phenomena. They are reading fodder for adolescents; they feature in illustrated magazines and serialized novels; they even have entered the works of illustrious writers.[34]

Similarly, though in the wake of the "ideology-critical" 1970s, Manfred Nagl felt it necessary to distance himself from his object of study by claiming to have identified a "specific inwardness and contemplation of nature which cannot be found as distinctively in other national literatures" as well as an unreconstructed authoritarian mindset:

> Only German SF continuously propagated such a mad and isolated system of up-to-date technology and regressive mysticism, interfused with occultism, racist metaphysics, the cult of a dictatorial "fuehrer," and anti-communism.[35]

The German SF writer Herbert Franke was equally scathing about the homegrown variety, but suggested, perhaps with a modicum of self-interest, that things were improving:

> Germany has no Huxley and no Orwell, and even the number of competent writers working in SF looks rather modest if it is compared with the multitude of its British and American colleagues. However, it already seems that the most interesting writers of SF in Germany are not mere successors to their English and American precursors. German SF is beginning to show both independence and originality.[36]

Things began to change when established scholars joined in the debate. Karl Guthke's landmark study *Der Mythos der Neuzeit* gave SF a much-needed respectability:

> In its most sophisticated efforts science fiction does indeed bridge the yawning chasm that exists between the "two cultures," not only in the Anglophone world, but also in countries with Humboldtian institutions of learning.[37]

But it was William Fischer's *The Empire Strikes Out*, the first full-length study of German SF written in English, that seriously engaged with what made this variety special. In it, Fischer developed his argument, first put forward in 1976, that the works of Kurd Laßwitz, the "father" of German SF, showed "a juxtaposition and sometimes happy synthesis of the sciences and the traditional humanities."[38] Noting that the language barrier had impeded any impact German SF might have had abroad, as well as the cultural snobbism ostensibly progressive German critics of SF were perpetuating, he established that outside the "normative" Anglo-American tradition of the genre, German SF had made a unique contribution to the field:

> German SF . . . provides a classic example of a body of texts which, at least until recently, owes its synchronic and diachronic unity less to a sense of shared literary heritage than to a common extra-literary element, science and technology. I do not regard that conclusion as a violation of the "autonomy" of literature, but rather as a reaffirmation of its social relevance and enduring cultural vitality.[39]

Fischer's study skirted the unmistakeably authoritarian tendencies in Hans Dominik's works in favor of their technological and engineering content, but German scholars were not yet convinced. Gerd Hallenberger pointed out that, owing to its sheer popularity, SF unfortunately had a direct influence on political opinion formation,[40] while Jost Hermand pointed to the German SF novels written in service of National Socialism as proof of the ideological "flexibility" of the genre.[41] Eventually, though, and especially after the fall of communism and subsequent German "normalization," research on German SF began to appreciate it for what it could do instead of what it was not. Hans-Edwin Friedrich suggested that SF ought to be appreciated by readers for its unusual text elements and playfulness,[42] while Torben Schröder made the case for SF as social fiction. As mirror and critique of the present, he argued, SF acted as a "Macroskop," and it explored the social impact of new technologies.[43]

In recent years, academic debates in Germany about SF's relevance have become more confident and assertive, though, it has to be said, advances in theory are incremental. Some are beginning to challenge the internalized defense and exclusion ritual, but they are struggling to escape its gravitational pull. Scholars still feel the need to apologize for the less "sophisticated" examples of SF, as if mainstream literature were only producing avant-garde fare. Roland Innerhofer, talking about the "border conflicts" between SF and utopias/dystopias, provides a perfect example of this self-imposed constraint:

The border traffic between SF and utopia/dystopia is especially busy. One should note, though, that this permeability only applies to the most sophisticated segment of SF. The fact that the quantitatively predominant part of SF is focused on action and is based on simplistic premises is often either ignored or bewailed in academic discussions of genre. However, it is precisely this form of action-based narration that marks the clearest difference between SF and utopia or dystopia.[44]

Perhaps it is the "Lust am Gedankenspiel" (the joy of the thought experiment, 320) that continues to vex critics.[45] There is a sense of suspicion of moral and ethical promiscuity when it comes to SF writing and its ambivalent positions that sets it apart from easily classifiable (and critically more esteemed) utopias or dystopias. This attitude has been met head-on in a recent volume on German genre fiction.[46] In their introduction, the editors point out that all literature aims to become popular and argue that any definition of genres as not belonging to the canon of high literature "is completely inadequate today" (1). While their claim that the English-language concept of "genre-fiction" does not carry the same value judgment as the pejorative term "Trivialliteratur" might be a tad overoptimistic, they are right in seeing genre less as a system of classification and more as a social practice engaged in by critics. The editors cannot completely escape received wisdom about SF, though. They categorize it as a "subgenre" read mainly by white adolescents, which can, on occasion, hold some interest for a more sophisticated readership:

> What characterizes the literature of this sub-genre for adult readers is not technology as such but rather the way human beings interface and interact with it in a world that in spite of its alien-ness is strangely familiar. The alternative world can be a testing ground for future scenarios or, as is more often the case, a site where currently circulating discourses of anxiety and/or hopes are translated into a speculative narrative.[47]

With the founding of the *Gesellschaft für Fantastikforschung* (Association for Research in the Fantastic) in 2010, its annual conference, and the associated academic journal *Zeitschrift für Fantastikforschung*, research on German SF and research in German language on SF has been given a significant boost.[48] The association's aim is to establish a research community comparable to that in the United Kingdom and Ireland and North America, to catch up in terms of theory building, and to contribute to the global discourse on the fantastic. In one of the first publications coming out of the network, Hans Esselborn signaled his intention to reclaim the independence of German SF:

> My hypothesis is that we can perceive a shift in emphasis of the German novel of the future [Zukunftsroman] and its focus on new technologies toward the representation of other, alien worlds over the course of the century that the genre has existed. An oscillation between the utopian-alternative and the technological-futuristic side cannot be ruled out, just as there may be internal shifts of emphasis within the two roots of the novel of the future.[49]

His quest to assert the value of the German tradition (as manifested in the Kurd Laßwitz Preis and the Deutscher Science-Fiction Preis) culminated in a major publication in 2019:[50] *Die Erfindung der Zukunft in der Literatur: Vom technisch-utopischen Zukunftsroman zur deutschen Science Fiction* (The Invention of the Future in Literature: From the Techno-Utopian Novel of the Future to German SF).[51] Oscillating between a history of German SF—which Esselborn rightly claims is a "novum" (11)—and an attempt to position its foremost examples as characteristically different from the anglophone canon, the book is very clear about its ultimate intention:

> Even though international entanglements are indispensable for its history, this study first and foremost emphasizes the independence and genuine achievements of German Science Fiction.[52]

Esselborn's study is an excellent example of the contortions that even the most established German scholars still feel obliged to go through in order to write about SF and remain academically "respectable." While acknowledging that there have been valiant attempts to establish and position SF in the field of German literature, Esselborn contends that it has been impossible up to now to write a comprehensive history of German SF because (a) there is still no reliable definition that would allow a differentiation between texts intended for "pure entertainment" and texts which are "interesting as literature," and (b) because German SF is still languishing in the shadow of the Anglo-American variety. By explicitly excluding films or television series and by highlighting intellectually challenging examples, he claims the cultural high ground, especially as he alleges a fundamental difference between an American literary tradition focusing on "spannende Abenteuer" (thrilling adventures) and a German tradition of "utopische und anthropologische Reflexion" (utopian and anthropological reflection, 11).

Esselborn rightly characterizes SF as a "Zukunftsmaschine" (a future-generating machine, 28) which is fueled by personal expectations, desires, and anxieties. As such, and here I am in complete agreement with him, it produces scenarios of possible futures in order to test their practicality and desirability, and it gives the reader an opportunity to become used to the impact of change. He argues that SF is not about extrapolation; nor does it give "Leitbilder des Handelns" (models for action); but it offers an "Ästhetik der Zukunft" (an aesthetics of the future, 30). He freely admits that he is talking mainly about "Idealtypen" (ideal types), with his selection of texts based on whether they contain scientific and philosophical thought akin to utopias, since he believes that only these make full use of the possibilities of the genre. It is no surprise, then, that he favors "gehobene" (highbrow) SF.

Esselborn identifies three central themes of German SF: namely, the future as determined by scientific and technological discoveries; the exploration of the unknown in the form of alien beings and new worlds; and the anthropological question about man's position in the cosmos and vis-à-vis other intelligent beings. In terms of recurring motifs, he lists complex future machines, robots and androids, space exploration, encounters with alien civilizations, nuclear energy and global catastrophes, time travel, and parallel worlds.

The study concludes with tantalizing but underexplored observations about the nature of German SF: the Faustian myth of overreaching oneself in the pursuit of knowledge, and the repeated messages of warning against a belief in our ability to solve human problems through technology. Instead, and somewhat despondently, Esselborn concludes: "das spannende und phantasievolle Erzählen [hat] den Sieg über den technischen, wissenschaftlichen und utopischen Diskurs davongetragen" (thrilling and imaginative narratives stand victorious over the technological, scientific, and utopian discourse, 384).

I will return to Esselborn's study when I have presented my own text selection and analysis, but I want to end this chapter with a very different viewpoint. In *Germany. A Science Fiction* (2014),[53] the psychoanalyst and cultural critic Laurence A. Rickels provides an alternative reading of the history of German SF, arguing that it exhibits all the signs of "psychopathy as the undeclared diagnosis implied in flunking the empathy test" (18). Rickels points to what he sees as the Achilles heel of (German) SF: its obsession with violence before 1945, and its subsequent—though only alleged by Rickels—inability to develop empathy with the victims of the Holocaust. Forced to a "reset" by the Cold War, he argues, SF was not able to overcome the traumatic experiences until the 1980s. Rickels postulates that future worlds made in Germany were ignored until the "Wunderwaffen" (super weapons) like the V2 rockets lost their specific negative connotations and could become cultural icons, just as their inventor Wernher von Braun became the "mascot" of the US space program.[54] He analyzes the specific German contribution to the genre—in his view the *rocket* (think of the orgiastically celebrated launch of the moon rocket in Fritz Lang and Thea von Harbou's *Frau im Mond* [1929]) and the doppelgänger. His most striking example of the latter, and of the denazification of the genre, is Carl Sagan's novel *Contact*, which was made into a film in 1997. Here, the technological breakthrough of the television broadcast of the Olympic Games in Berlin in 1936 allows technologically superior benevolent aliens to establish contact with humans, specifically when they approach the female protagonist in the form of a doppelgänger of her father who had died when she was a child. Rickels certainly knows the key works of German SF film—from the two Lang/Harbou films *Metropolis* and *Frau im Mond* to the television series *Raumpatrouille* and Rainer Werner Fassbinder's *Welt am Draht*— as well as lesser known texts like Franz Werfel's *Stern der Ungeborenen*, Thomas Ziegler's *Stimmen der Nacht*, and Robert Bramkamp's avant-garde docudrama *Prüfstand 7*. But, just as with Esselborn, Rickel's selection determines his argument, in this case suggesting a trauma-inducing "German Techno-Modernity" (105) that neatly links German rocket technology with the American nuclear bomb while ignoring more recent texts by Thomas Lehr, Andreas Eschbach, and Frank Schätzing.

At the same time, Rickels is correct in diagnosing a direct link between German history and its influence on SF more generally—for example, in Francois Truffaut's *Fahrenheit 451* film in which a "fireman" played by the (German-sounding) Austrian actor Oskar Werner burns books.[55] Rickels characterizes SF as "a genre of philosophical fiction" (226), which, through its Faustian search for the meaning of life, can exhibit surprising depths, but which has also, as a consequence of its obsession with violence, ignored its complicity with Germany's darkest moments for too long. While I do not share Rickels's analysis, which, to my mind, focuses too much on space opera, it will be interesting to explore one of his observations—namely, that "Future worlds made in Germany were left unattended during the Cold War reception of Science Fiction" (25). If this is true, then we may be able to find a distinctive German SF where most critics say none existed.

♦ ♦ ♦

As a confluence of utopian thought, futurism, and the utopian/dystopian literary imagination, SF continues to resist categorization while affording its audiences the pleasure of participation in philosophical mind games that explore the full gamut of potential impacts of scientific and technological advances. Starting as simple "what if" scenarios, SF has developed from a genre into a mode of thinking about the future in a world that has become increasingly "science-fictional." Its German branch has its roots in the tradition of the *Zukunftsroman*, one of the world's oldest SF traditions. At times politically compromised, it is capable of sophisticated sociopolitical critique. It understands that while scientists and engineers may well be looking for solutions to global problems, their "fixes" inevitably have side effects. The modern anticipatory imagination raises awareness predominantly through dystopias, showing what the (negative) consequences of a given course of action might be. It explores scenarios to test possible solutions to current problems, depicts desirable outcomes, and imagines strategies to apply them.

As an "aesthetics of the future," German SF has hitherto been broadly overlooked in a global discourse focused on, and dominated by, the anglophone tradition. With the focus in German Studies on *Vergangenheitsbewältigung* and working through Germany's violent and genocidal past, it is understandable that a more playful imagination of the future has been viewed with suspicion within a German academy conditioned to mistrust the products of the *Kulturindustrie*.[56] But with the global challenges brought about by science and technology forcing us to look to the future, SF is emerging as the most appropriate vehicle to articulate a critical response. In the next Part, then, I will explore to what extent German SF can offer a *Zukunftsbewältigung* as it seeks to come to terms with the challenges and opportunities of the future.

Part II.

German Science Fiction in the Twentieth and Twenty-First Centuries

5: Some Preliminary Thoughts on German Science Fiction

THERE IS NO such thing as a canon of German SF. As discussed in my introduction, it simply does not feature in the standard German literary histories. Nor does it register in histories of German film, with the exception of Fritz Lang and Thea von Harbou's *Metropolis* (1927), which has acquired cult status. And even in the German SF community—that is, among the members of the Deutscher Science Fiction Club e.V and the organizers of the German SF prizes—there is no agreement over what the key moments of German SF are. Many would name Kurd Laßwitz as the "father" of German SF, but few have read more than his novel *Auf zwei Planeten* (1897). Hans Dominik is undoubtedly the most successful German SF writer in the first half of the twentieth century, but his reputation as a peddler of jingoistic and nationalistic sentiments makes him a less than ideal figurehead. As Hans Esselborn's recent study has shown, what one selects as a representative sample of German SF invariably determines one's conclusions. In his case, a decision to dismiss the "Americanized" variety (as well as SF films and SF written by women) produces a corpus that earnestly engages with future technologies but tells us little about the imaginative and playful core of German SF, its dystopian outlook, or what makes it distinctive.

My selection is admittedly equally subjective, and I have to acknowledge that casting the net wider makes it significantly more challenging to come to firm conclusions about the nature of German SF. But perhaps that is one of its best qualities, with writers and film directors balancing commercial considerations, aesthetic ambitions, political agendas, and innovative ideas. The writers and directors' starting point of asking "what if" can lead them in any direction, which explains why my decision to subsume texts and films under thematic headings regularly puts me in a quandary, since most of these would fit under several categories. At the same time, my selection of seventy novels and twenty-five films provides a large enough base to allow distinctive patterns to emerge.

I argue that the works listed in the appendices should be regarded as *science fictional*, whether they have the "SF" label on the cover or not, since they all engage with the central questions of SF: What if the world were different? What would happen if we did this or that (particularly in relation to the application of science and technology in the broadest sense)? What might our future look like? A particular feature of my selection is the emphasis on West German and on recently published novels. This is partly intentional, since we already have excellent studies in English on early German SF (William Fischer) and on East German SF (Sonja Fritzsche), as well as an anthology of German SF short stories (Franz Rottensteiner). But it is also a reflection of a newfound confidence in the publishing and film worlds in the relevance of SF: the large number of texts and films published in the new millennium signals that more and more writers and film directors see the mode as the optimal way of engaging their audiences.

In an essay published in the respected academic SF journal *Extrapolation* (though not in a more "mainstream" academic journal covering German literature), Vibeke Petersen offered some home truths regarding German SF:

> German SF has been deeply marked by recent German history: first, the infamous years of Nazism and later, the years of a divided and united Germany that in turn may have left their mark on the science-fiction texts.[1]

There is no point in denying that Germany's Nazi past has had a deep influence on the development of German SF. Not only were its nineteenth-century roots cut during the Nazi years "when Science Fiction works were banned as manifestations of American decadence" (79) but, more importantly, the traumatic experience of the bombing of German cities and the defeat of its army, followed by the guilt over the responsibility of the Holocaust, have left a lasting impression on German writers that can be found again and again in their works in terms of theme, mood, allusions, and message. Petersen is also right in observing that there has been little scholarly interest in SF in Germany,

> which may be explained partly by the intense focus on the past which has characterized the German literary and critical scene for decades. Such a focus hardly lends itself to a genre of literature whose structuring principle is the future.[2]

In a separate essay, Petersen explores the discourses around the Holocaust in German SF.[3] She argues that German SF writers' attempt to engage with their country's historical shame represents a laudable sign of active *Vergangenheitsbewältigung*:

> As such, by their sheer existence alone, many German SF works impart a sense of unwittingly sharing such a communal will to keep a memory of the Holocaust alive. They may even, as Aleida Assmann

writes, "reflect a general desire to reclaim the past as an important part of the present," and, may I add, the future.[4]

At the same time, Petersen argues, the very fact that this SF is written by Germans casts doubt over its legitimacy and integrity:

> When making any sort of comparison between Nazi genocide and a piece of speculative fiction, one runs a great risk of reductionism. Yet, the present examples of Science Fiction are German and thus we cannot help but reading them differently from other national Science Fictions. The German past so frequently makes its presence felt in speculative fiction that a reflection upon the phenomenon, its possible readings, their cultural motivations, and social circumstances is almost obligatory. The above Science Fictional texts represent occurrences that are outside the ken of many of their readers due both to generational differences and to the politics of resistance towards implication in the Nazi past, as discussed above. Thus, such representations of that past may not add to its comprehension, but rather serve as its rewriting, even a revision of it.[5]

I would be reluctant to make general judgments without looking at my samples in greater detail, but I agree that what German SF writers are doing with regard to Germany's infamous past has a different context and needs to be viewed more carefully than writing on oppression, persecution, ethnic cleansing, genocide, and racial supremacy by non-German writers. However, this is true for "mainstream" texts as well.

Germans not only have to come to terms with the Nazi past but also with the four-decade long division of the country into capitalist West Germany and socialist East Germany. This past is most manifest in the existence of a distinctively East German SF. As Horst Heidtmann has pointed out in his (West German) study of early East German SF, the young socialist state made a political choice as to what books to produce and what form they were to take.[6] Karlheinz Steinmüller, a leading East German SF writer, observes that utopian literature, following Soviet cultural ideology, was intended to enthuse young readers for the bright communist future and to popularize the latest scientific discoveries.[7] As such, East German SF cannot be easily compared with its counterpart in West Germany, where writers were free to write and publish as they wished (but also had to accept the reality of supply and demand in a free market). Following the idealization of the "new man" in socialism, utopian prose had to toe the line determined by the Soviet Union,[8] and it was obliged to convey an optimistic vision of a future "epistemologically limited to the historical determinism of Marxist-Leninist philosophy."[9] Since an excellent study of East German SF in English is readily available, I will limit myself to a discussion of East Germany's most popular SF novel,

Andymon (chapter 8).[10] What will be of interest, though, is the question to what extent the experience of German division, and the exposure to a sustained ideological confrontation, is reflected more broadly in texts and movies, no matter on which side of the Iron Curtain they were made.

One of the fascinating features of SF is the popularity of SF films, which many consider a separate art form.[11] In my selection, I have opted for a more inclusive approach by featuring representative German SF films within the thematic strands, treating them as texts. At the same time, it will be useful to briefly consider the distinctiveness of German SF films and television series owing to the previously pioneering role.

Fritz Lang's *Metropolis* (1927), based on a novel and script by his then wife Thea von Harbou, is without doubt Germany's most impactful contribution to the genre. Thomas Elsaesser has attempted to convey the uniqueness of this film, one that went far beyond its striking visuals (such as the vast city with its skyscrapers and multilevel transport system; the all devouring machine; the downtrodden masses of workers and their underground dwellings; the artificial robot that is turned into a vamp) and its awkward social message:

> Metropolis . . . positioned itself explicitly as a quite different experience: not a palimpsest, more like a dream-screen or a polished reflector, where the very absences of psychologically detailed characters, exacerbated by Lang's complex editing, gave a somnambulist ambiguity of motivation to the protagonists' gestures and a hovering indeterminacy to their action.[12]

The idea of a "dream screen" is perhaps the closest we can get to what SF film does: it imparts a sense of wonder at the "otherness" of what is shown and suggested, the very hallmark of good SF. But *Metropolis* is hardly the only film that deserves our attention.

Unfortunately, in spite of their potential and popularity, and in glaring similarity to the absence of German SF in literary histories, German SF films rarely feature in academic discourse. In Stephen Brockmann's otherwise authoritative *A Critical History of German Film*, *Metropolis* is the only SF film discussed, and then mainly in terms of its sensational aspects, the overt sexuality of the robot and the cost of its production.[13] Brockmann writes:

> Fritz Lang's Metropolis, one of the most influential Science Fiction movies of all time, was a huge blockbuster featuring advanced technology and special effects. It cost well over five million marks and was, at the time it was made, the most expensive German movie ever. It was so expensive—costing three times its original budget—that it almost bankrupted the massive Ufa film company, and even though

it was reasonably successful in cinemas, it did not make enough money to recoup its production costs.[14]

Part of the reality of SF cinema is obviously the cultural hegemony of Hollywood, with its endless stream of SF films flooding the German market, multiplexes, and media. Thus, in an exhibition of SF films at the *Deutsche Kinemathek* in Berlin in 2016, the program was dominated by British and American productions. Similarly, a retrospective of SF films at the sixty-seventh Berlin Film Festival in 2017 featured the usual suspects like *1984* (1956) and *Soylent Green* (1973).[15] To its credit, the book accompanying the retrospective contains a chapter on the history of German SF film, including an appreciation of Fritz Lang and Thea von Harbou's *Frau im Mond* (1929) that hints at the lasting impact of that particular movie on the imagination, both in terms of its portrayal of (at the time) futuristic technology and the breaking down of outmoded gender roles. The chapter's author, Tobias Haupts, observes:

> When viewing *Frau im Mond* today, it is astonishing how many motifs that became immanent components of 1950s and 1960s space travel are anticipated in the film, as is not only revealed in the adaptation of the (German) countdown. The film became modern through its use of technology, the camera's lingering gaze on the rocket slowly being transported from the factory hall to the launching pad for all to see, and through the technical data that as brief intertitles allow the image to speak for itself. And finally, after the countdown and the images of the characters' tense faces . . . there is the launch itself, which happens so quickly that after the extended period of anticipation it leaves the spectator with the impression of a deflagration. But the film also seems modern not just because once again a woman was responsible for the screenplay, but mainly because, contrary to male objections, a female astronaut joins the trip to the moon. Arriving at the destination, she takes the place of the man in the moon, whereby the title of the film already reveals how the film's melodramatic triangle will come to a solution in the end.[16]

The fact remains, though, that we do not yet have a definitive critical study of German SF film. The closest we get to an overview has come in the form of a blog by Julia Thurnau for the Goethe Institute in Norway,[17] which at least mentions films like Hermann Zschoche's *Eolomea* (1972) and Rainer Erler's *Operation Ganymed* (1977),[18] as well as Rainer Werner Fassbinder's made-for-TV, two-part *Welt am Draht* (1973), which I will discuss in detail later. After these productions in the 1970s, German SF films faded from the scene because of a lack of adequate funding. Some German film directors went to America: for example, Roland Emmerich, who, after his film-school project *Das Arche Noah Prinzip* (1984),[19] started producing in Hollywood. And in spite of notable recent productions like Lars Kraume's *Die kommenden Tage* (2010), Tim Fehlbaum's *Hell* (2011), and Sebastian Hilger's *Wir sind die Flut* (2016), discussed below, the German film industry has lost its pioneering edge when it comes to SF, at least in Thurnau's assessment. As she puts it, "The endless possibilities of the genre, the economic possibilities of German film funding and the constantly growing expectations of film audiences are too far removed from each other."[20]

If Germany's Nazi past and subsequent division into two ideologically polar opposites almost guarantee a distinctive "flavor" for its SF and the pioneering works of Lang and Harbou have gained it a certain notoriety in the annals of film, we should not discount the impact of regional specifics that make German SF original and unique. Just as H. G. Wells's *War of the Worlds* creates its tension and readers' enjoyment due to the fact that his malevolent Martians land in the quintessentially green and pleasant towns and villages of Surrey, so German SF writers "ground" their tales in the familiar, whether by using the peaceful provincial town of Friedau in Kurd Laßwitz's *Auf zwei Planeten* or by using the Bavarian dialect in Carl Amery's *Der Untergang der Stadt Passau*. The strong sense of belonging (Heimat), in juxtaposition to the unfamiliar, enhances the effect for a German readership while those from different cultural backgrounds will need to become "acculturated" to unfamiliar surroundings by means of shared values. This in itself is no obstacle, since readers are well accustomed to decoding the "high-information" mode of SF.[21]

One final potential aspect of distinctiveness to watch out for will be the national myths that writers and audiences employ to ground their narratives and to engage with their audiences. In Germany, this would include the national epic *Die Nibelungen* as the German equivalent of the Arthurian legend, as well as the *Faust* myth in its particular Goethean conception.[22] Goethe's play *Faust* is a national "familiar" that most educated Germans can still access as part of their mental furniture. In the context of Germany's hubris and attempt at world domination, but also in terms of Goethe's depiction of a worldview that is never satisfied with the status quo, the Faust myth will have a part to play in identifying distinctive characteristics of German SF. As Roland Borgards suggests:

> One of the fundamental tensions that make the Faust trope so attractive for modern literature, and especially for the Science Fiction genre, probably lies in the fact that Faust's story not only tells us about man's technological and scientific power but also about the limits of human activity. In Faust, man grows so far beyond himself that he begins to disappear. Thus, for the current literary discussion about human technological prowess in its productive as well as

destructive form we have at our disposal a wonderfully ambivalent figuration, one in which self-empowerment and self-destruction can come to be understood, and become visible, in their constitutive and interrelated context.[23]

As we will see, the Faustian character who is dissatisfied and impatient with the status quo, who seeks knowledge and is willing to accept dark compromises if they allow him or her to reach their goals makes a regular appearance in German SF, whether in the guise of the scientist, the astronaut, the mystic, or the philosopher. I will return to this aspect in my conclusion, but for now it is time to look at the first thematic strand, that of the *First Contact*.

6: First Contact: Martians, Sentient Plants, and Swarm Intelligences

As THE PIONEER of German SF, Kurd Laßwitz has had a lasting influence and his work contains many of SF's major tropes. His magnum opus *Auf zwei Planeten* (1897), published at the same time as H. G. Wells's *The War of the Worlds*, was enormously influential in Germany, but it was only translated into English in 1971. Laßwitz firmly believed in the civilizational power of technology, and he sought to align moral, ethical, and technological progress. For this reason, he abhorred the ruthless use of technological superiority for corrupt motives. Highly critical of the German Empire's colonial and imperial ambitions and policies, he imagined what it would be like if the "civilized" nations of Europe would suffer the fate they were subjecting others to: that of being colonized by technologically and allegedly ethically superior beings.

Auf zwei Planeten reached high circulation figures in Germany, especially after World War I. Full of astonishing technological predictions, it inspired several generations of German scientists, among them Hermann Oberth, the pioneer of German rocketry, and Wernher von Braun, who worked on the German V2 rockets in the 1940s and the American space program in the 1960s.[1] Laßwitz's vision of a space station in geostationary orbit provided the blueprint for the International Space Station.[2] Yet in spite of its popularity, the novel was considered "too democratic" by the National Socialists and no longer printed.[3]

Laßwitz imagines a whole civilization built on a technology that is able to control gravity, with armed and armored Martian airships that can reach any point on the planet in a matter of hours. *Auf zwei Planeten* thus takes a global viewpoint: following the moment of first contact, when three German scientists in a balloon expedition to reach the North Pole are rescued by Martians who have built a base there, it soon becomes clear to the explorers that the Martians are planning to conquer Earth. The Martians, coming from an older civilization, have a keen sense of their own superiority. This attitude is partly based on their observation of the Eskimos, the only humans they have encountered so far. The Martians believe that if the rest of humanity is on the same cultural level as the Eskimos, they are justified in taking control and using the planet's resources for their own benefit. Any objections by the protesting German explorers are brushed aside with the comment: "We come to you to bring you the benefits of our culture."[4] When it becomes clear to the Martians that the humans don't want to be conquered, they are faced with an ethical dilemma, and have to reconsider their plans. They conclude they must get a clearer picture of humanity first, and they set out on an expedition to learn more about us.

Unfortunately, their next encounter with "civilized" human beings is with an English warship. A misunderstanding between the Martians and the English aboard the ship leads to an exchange of gunfire; some Martians are taken hostage; and the Martians in the airship try to force the English to release the hostages. Captain Keswick and his hotheaded Lieutenant Prim, both self-important lords of the sea, cannot bear the humiliation. For them, it is a question of honor to defeat the new enemy, and to bring the Martians to London in triumph. They continue the unequal fight, and even though the Martians try not to inflict any damage, the English warship is lucky to escape the awesome power of the Martian weapons. The Martian restraint is taken as a sign of weakness, and the English fleet is made ready for a possible attack on their return.

The Martians conclude that humanity is simply too immature to master its own affairs. They demand compensation from the English government, and set an ultimatum for the English to comply, stating that if the English do not comply, they will be put under quarantine. The English government refuses to acknowledge these conditions, which in turn forces the Martians to embargo all English harbors. In an ironic reversal of sides, the greatest colonial power becomes the helpless victim of Martian gun boat diplomacy.[5] At Portsmouth, where the English fleet is concentrated, the English try to break the embargo and, in the ensuing battle, lose most of their ships. In spite of all efforts by the Martians to prevent any loss of life, the English only surrender when their flagship is sunk.

With the coastal blockade and its fleet destroyed, England's power is broken. The most powerful nation of the time is written out of history. The colonies declare their independence, and other countries rush in to secure the trade regions for themselves. This brings the English to their senses. To save what is left of their empire, they sue for peace. Rather predictably, the squabble over English colonies starts further wars. Reluctantly, the Martians take on "the white man's burden": the Martian representative has no alternative but to declare the whole Earth a Martian protectorate, to outlaw any military confrontation, and to enforce the disarmament of all nations.

It is no accident that the English are singled out by Laßwitz as the main adversaries of the Martians. After all, they were the greatest sea power of the time, and it is with a sense of pride that he can set the explorer spirit of the Germans against the nation that rules the sea. Laßwitz is not above national sentiments, but he is seldom jingoistic. The English may be arrogant and unable to deal with the new realities, but their valor is undeniable. While the sea battle with the Martians in Wells's *The War of the Worlds* is a struggle between good and evil, Laßwitz's sympathies are more equally divided. The English defense in the "battle of Portsmouth" is a matter of misplaced pride, and the ships sent against the Martians defend not just the English upper classes but also the freedom of humanity. On the other hand, the inability on the side of the English to negotiate and reason with the superior Martians simply because that would represent an acknowledgement of their own inferiority shows a dangerous lack of common sense. Interestingly, Laßwitz does not portray the Germans to be any better than the English, and the German imperial guard is destroyed in an equally spectacular manner.

Even though the Martians behave most courteously toward the German explorers (who resist their benevolent captors to the best of their ability), they have no sympathies with Wilhelmine Germany and its militaristic social order. In a graphic chapter on the "unfortunate events in the fatherland," Laßwitz presents a masterpiece of ironic political criticism, skillfully disguised to avoid prosecution by the imperial censors, by employing a narrative device to distance himself from the message he delivers: his narrator quotes from a newspaper report about the "shameful events" that leave Prussia without an army and the emperor without his clothes.

When the Martian order for global demobilization is not followed by the German Empire, Martian airships appear over Berlin to force the emperor to comply. The "report" gives a detailed description of how the imperial guard was disarmed: The emperor, mustering a parade designed to show off his military power, openly displays his defiance to the Martians. But the Martians use huge magnets and pull everything metallic into the air, and the "invincible" Prussian war machine is tossed about like straw in the wind. The brave officers and their horses are disarmed without a shot being fired. In a brilliant parody of his belligerent emperor that foreshadows Heinrich Mann's *Der Untertan* (1919), Laßwitz writes:

> The monarch looked around solemnly, at the enemy ships and the officers lying stunned or dead on the ground. . . . Then he drew his sword from its scabbard and shouted: "Gentlemen, there is only one thing to do—go at them!"[6]

The Martians are ready for the stubborn advance: they calmly inform the emperor that they have his son on board their ship and invite the emperor to join him for peace talks—on their terms, of course. The mighty German army has been beaten without a shot being fired.

Following a conservative backlash on Mars, where outraged Martian citizens demand that the "savage" humans should be taught respect (458), the Martians on Earth embark on a program of reeducation that every human is required to follow. Germany is governed by a Martian "Kultor" (cultural overlord) in Berlin. Physically weakened by the effects of the Earth's heavier gravity and more humid atmosphere, the Martians are unable to resist the corrupting effect of power and, in time, their rule becomes despotic. While the humans are benefiting materially from the way the Martians clean up production and end hunger, they lose their spirit because they no longer have a say in their own affairs. Naturally, after several years of suppression, a resistance movement springs up: the "league of humans." Across the Atlantic, American engineers and scientists manage to discover the secrets of Martian technology and lead the war of independence to push the Martians out. The Martians back on their home planet are deeply divided over the question whether to use force to establish control or to recognize human independence. Rudi Schweikert points out that Laßwitz criticizes the imperialistic stance of all powers involved by ridiculing them. What he is after, Schweikert suggests, is "die Läuterung der menschlichen Moral" (the purification of human morals),[7] and this is achieved by suffering under and then emulating the lofty Martian spirit while resisting the oppression when the Martians are "contaminated" by human egotism.

There is perhaps a certain grim satisfaction in seeing one's own side beaten, especially when they deserve to be beaten: the English deserve to be beaten in the sea battle because they don't use their brains, and the Germans deserve to be made an example of with their stubborn pomp and misplaced pride. The decisiveness of the defeat is a clear signal that change is going to come, that the old order and the old certainties are no more. Laßwitz embraces the change and the opportunities that the exposure to Martian culture can bring to humanity. This, however, is not to say that he condones the behavior of the Martians when they begin to imitate the humans and act as cultural and economic imperialists.

Laßwitz expends considerable energy in *Auf zwei Planeten* to show how peace can be achieved even when faced with a superior adversary. He had served in France during the Franco-Prussian war when still a student, though he did not see action. William Fischer argues that:

> He was affected not so much by the shock of combat and suffering, or the philosophical implications of war in general, as he was by the political significance of the particular conflict he experienced, the growing importance of science and technology which it so clearly demonstrated, and the spirit of confidence which the victory reflected and in turn encouraged in his society.[8]

At a time when the German Empire had set out to claim its "Platz an der Sonne" (place in the sun) by acquiring and extending its own colonies, Laßwitz added his voice to those that warned of the fatal consequences of such militaristic adventures. This did not go over well with critics at the time. His noble Martians were described as "Typen der internationalen Friedensapostel" (types of international peacemongers), and he was accused of undermining the German spirit by spreading the "kühle Atem der Tendenz" (the cold breath of unpatriotic tendencies).[9] His views were compared to those of the controversial pacifist Bertha von Suttner,[10] who was one of the few who had favorably reviewed *Auf zwei Planeten* in 1898. Indeed, von Suttner was perceptive enough to recognize that what Laßwitz was offering not only went completely against the grain of the dominant Zeitgeist but mapped out an alternative to the pursuit of "Machtpolitik" (the politics of strength). To her it was obvious that the function of the Martian "takeover" was to create "international solidarity" among human beings, and that the book contained "socialist thinking":

> It reminds us. . . that we are citizens of the universe. He fills us. . . with awe in the face of the infinite. He submerges us . . . in the floods of whirling, shining eternity.[11]

Perhaps these words exaggerate the impact of the book, but Laßwitz, who was a descendant of classical Weimar and fully committed to its ideal of humanism and its sense of cultural mission, firmly believed in the amelioration of humanity. By portraying a morally and ethically advanced civilization, he aimed to show by what steps humanity itself could reach a higher level of maturity. These steps are as follows: an advancement in science and technology, moral education, and a general appreciation of the miracle of life that teaches us to respect other cultures instead of forcing them to adhere to our own values. His Martians are teachers on a path that humanity has to follow in order to reach this goal.

We get a clear sense of what science and technology might deliver to counter the main reason for war—namely, the economics of scarcity, the lack of basic resources that forces humanity to engage in endless battles for survival, control, and domination. The scientific dream that we could somehow create our basic resources and end the vicious cycle of hunger and greed is splendidly described in *Auf zwei Planeten* in the way the Martians have used their technological mastery to eradicate want and hunger:

> Stones to bread! Protein and carbohydrates from rocks and soil, from air and water without the photosynthesis of the plant cell! This was the progress by which the Martians had emancipated themselves from the early cultural stage of farming and how they had become direct sons of the sun.[12]

However, Laßwitz is not content with this veiled criticism of the archaic rules of the agricultural elites in Germany; he also gives us an idea how the Martians actually reached this enviable state. On Mars, two of the three German explorers visit the cultural facilities of the Martians. In a museum they learn that the Martians, too, had their wars and civil wars, competing for basic resources, but that this period lay at least eighteen thousand years behind them. Interestingly, when the scientific breakthrough that allowed the synthetic production of food was achieved, the farmers would not accept the change, and for thousands of years there was civil war (a veiled criticism of the rule of the Junker in Imperial Germany?). But the Martians are adamant about the outcome: "nur die Intelligenz ist es, welche der ewigen Idee entgegenwächst" (412 [it is intelligence only that grows toward the eternal idea]).

Science and technology as life-enhancing and emancipating factors are visible in other aspects of Martian life, too. In order to find out the truth about the events surrounding the confrontation with the English warship, the Martians use a "Retrospective," a kind of telescope that allows them to observe events in the past. They thereby find out what really happened in the conflict with the English warship. When it turns out that the English were justified in thinking the Martians were attacking them, the newspapers, even those that carry jingoistic headlines and demand revenge, inform the population accordingly, and the Martians change their mind. Any danger of nationalistic fervor is countered by another wise invention: the Martians are required by law to inform themselves by reading a variety of papers with opposing views. If they don't, they lose their right to vote.

Science and technology; their application to easing life; the will to progress morally and ethically, and to develop their aesthetic sense; these are all part of "Numenheit"—that is, the sense of being a Martian, of being dedicated to their society's culture and spiritual life. The German explorers and, later on, the whole of humanity perceive that these beings have reached a level of maturity that only thousands of years of education and culture can achieve. Outwardly, the Martians look almost human, setting aside their large, expressive eyes, which convey their superiority: "in ihnen zeigte sich die gewaltige Überlegenheit des Geistes dieser einer höheren Kultur sich erfreuenden Wesen" (74 [in these eyes was reflected the immense superiority of the spirit of a being that had an advanced culture at its disposal]). Their trained minds pick up all human languages with ease, although they do prefer German (which is closer to their own language and capable of expressing more complex subjects): "Im Deutschen fanden sie eine Sprache, reich an Ausdrücken für abstrakte Begriffe, und dadurch verwandt und angemessen ihrer eigenen Art zu denken" (150 [In German they found a language, rich in expressions for abstract concepts, and therefore akin to and appropriate for their own way of thinking]).

Perceiving that war is a constant threat for all humanity, the Martians set about the task of reeducating man: to enlighten him, in Kantian terms, about how he can escape "seiner selbstverschuldeten Unmündigkeit" (his self-imposed immaturity). They know that humans are capable of this because they have seen the integrity and selfless behavior of the German explorers. What unite the two races, bridging all differences between them, are their dreams of peace and their peaceful pursuit of knowledge. One instance of this endeavor is the scientific exploration of the planet, as exemplified by the three German balloonists who encounter the Martian explorers at the North Pole. A second, more powerful bridge is built when the Martians take the Germans up to their space station high above the Pole. Looking down at Earth, they realize that they share the capacity for awe in the face of creation:

> In deep silence the humans stood completely fascinated by the sight which no Earthly eye had ever beheld. More clearly and more overwhelmingly than ever before, they realized what it meant to be whirled about in space on a small particle named Earth. Never had they seen the sky underneath them. How great was the temptation of pride and triumph—how humble and awe-stricken they felt! The Martians respected their thoughtfulness. They, too, to whom the wonders of space were familiar, became silent in the presence of the infinite.[13]

In this moment we see the link between Martians and humans, a link that is stronger than their differences. The humans are accepted as potential equals, and a spiritual bond therefore links the two planets. Significantly, the final step on the way to peace is the unselfish act of Ell, the son of a stranded Martian explorer and a human mother, who had initiated the German polar expedition in the hope that it would encounter Martians there. When the human resistance—with their slogan "Numenheit ohne Nume" (Numedom without Nume)—has taken Martians hostage and Martian public opinion demands the extermination of the "barbarians," it is Ell who sacrifices himself in order to avoid a catastrophic confrontation. However, even though the final chapter "Weltfrieden" (world peace) is brilliantly conceived and often touching, there is a certain detachment and lack of warmth that keep us from fully sympathizing with Ell. For Laßwitz/Ell, there is a strict distinction between feelings such as national pride or the desire for revenge and retribution, on the one hand, and following the path that the mind has recognized as the right one, on the other.

Laßwitz presents love as the greatest bond between humans, a bond that actually defines our humanity. The twist in *Auf zwei Planeten* lies in the fact that one of the explorers, Saltner, actually falls in love with a Martian woman named La. Laßwitz's portrayal of "loving the alien" may have been his greatest risk, but it is also one of his greatest achievements. The developing relationship between Saltner and La shows up vital differences between the races. In addition, Laßwitz confronts us with a female Martian who is vastly superior in intelligence and spirit.

La falls for Saltner in rather conventional, sentimental circumstances: he saves her life when she falls into a crevasse, and she realizes that he has qualities such as courage, selflessness, and generosity of spirit that a more logically minded Martian would lack. La and her girlfriend Se initially play with the humans, making them fall in love with them to test their reactions. But for Saltner, who interprets these signals within a human frame of mind, La's affection is an unexpected gift from the gods. Overcome by the overwhelming sense of awe on board the space station, and looking down on his home planet, Saltner gives La a timid kiss. She allows it, but immediately warns him: "Don't forget that I am Nume. . . . A Nume's love never curtails her freedom" (214). They journey to Mars together, but she increasingly withdraws from him, and, when he is required to return to Earth, she stays on Mars.

Saltner doesn't understand that La makes a clear distinction between the pleasures of love and the independence of the individual. For the Martians, the human concept of love, encompassing both affection and a desire for possession, is highly confusing:

> You speak of love in a hundredfold sense. You love God and fatherland and parents and children and wife and sweetheart and friend; you love the good and the beautiful and the pleasant; you love yourself; and those are really profoundly different things, and always you have only that one word.[14]

Laßwitz illustrates the possessive nature of human love by introducing a secondary love story: a triangle between Ell, Torm, the scientific director of the expedition, and Torm's wife Isma, who was Ell's first love before she married Torm. Ell is torn between using the opportunity to make Isma "his own" when Torm is declared lost and his sense of duty to his friend. Ell renounces his emotions after a difficult inner battle, and Isma always remains faithful to Torm; but there is a strong sense that Martian morals would be more liberal had "human virtues" not proved the stronger. One can debate whether the triangle is melodramatic or experimental—but the love story between Saltner and La shows possible paths that, in more "mainstream" narratives of the time like Fontane's *Effie Briest* (1895), would have scandalized a German readership.

William Fischer writes that "Laßwitz seems to have patterned La, like Isma, after the noble female figures of German classical literature, to which he added touches of late nineteenth-century sentimentalism."[15] I would go even further. In La, Laßwitz has fashioned a strong female character, superior to any male human being, who is able to live according to the principles she chooses but who is also willing to question received wisdom if her heart tells her to do so.

On her return to Earth, La decides to help Saltner to flee Europe, and, by sharing her Martian technology with the resistance, to give humanity a chance to fight against their oppressors. This is more than simply a message that love conquers all. Laßwitz shows us that an evolved humanity must necessarily lead to a more mature relationship between the sexes. He explores human love in very modern terms of dependence versus freedom: love becomes a utopian theme, a bond between Martians and humans that gives substance to the possibility of emancipation and equality, as a training ground for the mature individual.

Laßwitz had high hopes that there was a way to overcome our "inability to see the goal, this stubbornness to acknowledge that things can work differently" (286). Writing against the Zeitgeist, he created a vision of a golden age of happiness and peace, if only we would give up our outdated way of thinking. By supplying us with a vantage point from which to view our "folly," he magnified man's flawed activities and criticized the shortsightedness of his greed. To give an example: when the Martians see the smog over human cities, they ask,

> "What causes these fogs over your large cities?". . . "Mainly the burning of coal.". . . "But why don't you take energy directly from the sun-rays? You should not be living on the capital but on the interest instead."[16]

What is apparent here is Laßwitz's belief that if only we had the proper insight into things, we would act rationally and do what's best. The Martians recognize that our inability (or unwillingness) to follow the ethical course of action is a general human trait, on which they comment with the remark: "Ko Bate!" (Poor Earthlings!)

Focusing on the main shortcomings of the imperialist age and using the enlightened view of the Martians as a blueprint for our own ethical and moral development, Laßwitz can combine his social criticism with a constructive vision of the remedy that is required. In a brilliant passage (which didn't make it into the English edition) that is written in a style reminiscent of Jonathan Swift's *Gulliver's Travels*, he provides his readers with a mirror to show what exactly was (and arguably still is) wrong with human society. A Martian newspaper runs the following editorial:

> We have gathered precise intelligence about conditions on Earth. They are plainly hair-raising. These humans have no concept of justice, honesty, or freedom. They are separated into a number of individual states which use every means to fight with each other for supremacy. Duly the economy suffers, to such an extent that many millions have to live in the most abject misery while order can only be maintained by the use of brute force. Nonetheless humans vie with each other in terms of flattery and submission towards those in power. Each social class agitates against the others and seeks to find an advantage. . . . They show no compunction in launching mass slaughters at will against the so-called uncivilized peoples. They are wild animals that we have to tame.[17]

For Laßwitz, the only chance to make headway in the "civilizing process" was to anticipate the future and then strive to be worthy of it. Laßwitz thus evokes the idea of an enlightened humanity in combination with the dream of a different way of life made possible by scientific and technological progress. In his essay *Über Zukunftsträume* (On Dreams about the Future, 1899), he laid the foundation for a different aesthetics. This "aesthetics of the future" was to refute traditional assumptions, to embrace science and technology, and to speak of them in poetic terms. By acknowledging that humanity's scientific and technological activity was in fact a paradigm for its ability to make progress, Laßwitz did use his poetic efforts to encourage the reader to make similar efforts on the side of ideas, ethics, and morals. The "scientific fairy tale" would thus convey to the reader new discoveries on a subjective, emotional level.

It follows that Laßwitz was never intending to paint the grand utopian state. It is the perfectibility of the individual that he is interested in, and to such an extent that his shortcomings as a writer—for example, the creaking plot, the wooden dialogue, and the lack of characterization (all points of derision for the traditional literary critic)—seem irrelevant. What he focused on was the noble idea, the fascination with the wonders of science, the opening of the mind in the context of ever new discoveries of the universe around us, which could not but fail to have a "civilizing" effect on us. As the mind and the body have evolved to adapt humanity to their environment, so scientific and technological progress are extensions of this process. The key to further progress is greater and greater understanding and mastery of nature and a higher level of morality. The whole point of the Martians, then, as Laßwitz himself pointed out in his essay *Unser Recht auf Bewohner anderer Welten* (Our Right to Inhabitants of other Worlds), which was published posthumously in 1910, was to show a higher form of civilization.

Laßwitz welcomed the new age with open arms. He was acutely aware that the social fixities that his contemporaries were taking for granted—class, nation, gender, and political power—were to change radically. He believed that humanity needed to grow up and be prepared for the fundamental changes that scientific progress would inevitably bring. He asked the question that SF has been asking ever since: If we are given the power through scientific progress to do whatever we please, what are we going to do with it?

◆ ◆ ◆

Laßwitz's last novel, *Sternentau*, published one year before the author's death in 1909, is almost forgotten, even in Germany.[18] It is another fascinating "first contact" story; it explores the borderlands of the imaginable, including the challenge how to describe the "truly alien." While the "Idonen" who come to Earth from one of Neptune's moons are highly intelligent and resemble small humans, it is the terrestrial flora that delivers the real surprise. Inspired by the German philosopher Gustav Fechner (1801–87), who pioneered the idea of sentience in the plant kingdom, Laßwitz posits intelligence in plants whose ways of thinking and communicating are completely different from, and therefore normally unintelligible, to humans. In this respect, Kurd Laßwitz was a century ahead of Donna Haraway, and he therefore fits perfectly in the current discourse on the posthuman discussed below.

Laßwitz was a longtime supporter of Fechner, whose highly animistic worldview saw humanity positioned midway between the "souls of plants" and the "souls of stars" (which he described as angels). In his introduction to Fechner's novel *Nanna, oder Über das Seelenleben der Pflanzen* (Nanna, or On the Soul Life of Plants), which had appeared in the middle of the nineteenth century, Laßwitz argued that scientific discoveries had since confirmed a number of Fechner's poetic assumptions:

> The discoveries of biological science over the half century that has passed since the first edition of "Nanna" would surely only have reassured Fechner in his views, were he still alive. The progress in tissue research; our more precise understanding of cell division in plants; the transmission of stimuli; the conversion of energy and indeed of the entire life process,; as well as the connection between plants and animals, especially the development of the theory of evolution; all this is well suited to support a view of the life of plants that favors the doctrine of psychophysical parallelism.[19]

Sternentau's plot is rather simple. The Kern family, owners of a factory (the *Hellbornwerke*) in a valley in Thüringia, is representative of Germany's rapid industrial expansion before World War I:

At the foot of the wooded mountains one could make out the mass of buildings, churches, and chimneys of the busy county seat, whose suburbs came close to the steep slope from which Harda looked down. Clouds of smoke defined the area where industry had established itself to exploit the mineral resources that were accessible due to the gap in the mountains.[20]

The Kerns live in comfort in their Villa and maintain a busy social life. While the father is busy traveling, seeking new orders and finance for the expansion of his business, his spirited daughters lead a carefree life, even though their mother has died and their "aunt" Minna casts a cloud over the house with her jealousy and mood swings. One day, Harda Kern, the eldest daughter—who has an interest in biology and chemistry but is hesitant to leave home to study at university—seeks solace at the grave of her mother. Here she discovers an unfamiliar plant growing beneath the ivy, and she takes a cutting home to grow in her room. As it turns out, the delicate blue plant—which she names *Sternentau* (star dew)—is the gestation stage of an alien life form that will eventually bud new "Idonen." These are intelligent beings whose seeds have been swept from the upper layers of the atmosphere on their home planet (one of Neptune's moons) and traveled to Earth on particles of cosmic dust. Together with the company physician Dr. Werner Eynitz, a scientist who has also discovered the plant and wants to conduct experiments on it to explore its possible industrial uses, Harda discusses the plant's strange appearance and speculates about how it reproduces. In a moment of empathetic insight, Harda surmises that the plant might be a sentient being.

It is at this point that Laßwitz introduces a change of perspective. Unbeknown to the "stumpfen Sinne" (the dull senses, 32) of the humans, the plants at the grave "talk" to each other in a slow, measured way. There is a clear hierarchy among them, with the old trees holding forth while the "lesser" plants wait their turn to speak. They have different voices, and they possess a different sense of time and of their own position in all creation, viewing the humans with a mixture of pity and concern. They communicate via their roots and through the earth, their "mother."[21] They reflect on the newcomers who they consider with bemused sympathy. They know Harda because she regularly tends the plants by the grave, but they are also aware of the destruction the humans have wreaked on their valley.

Strange things happen in Harda's room where she has taken a cutting from the Sternentau plant. She has dreams, visions, and a sense that her thoughts are being taken over by someone else. She begins to suspect that the plants are conscious beings (107), though she doesn't yet know that it is the Idonen connecting with her unconscious while the plants are the medium for their communication. Eynitz, for his part, is skeptical, but he and Harda manage to "catch" a number of the emerging Idonen and conduct experiments proving that they are indeed intelligent (which brings with it the question of the ethics of holding them captive and experimenting on them). Meanwhile, the Sternentau plant, which calls herself Bio, learns to talk to the Earth's flora and allows the transfer of information. In typical "outside perspective" mode, Bio and the Earth's flora speculate about the species "Mensch" (human being).

One of Laßwitz's key strengths as a writer is finding the poetic in the scientific, and in his descriptions of alien worlds. The chapter *Auf dem Neptunsmond* (119–27) conveys a sense of the serenity the Idonen feel as they fly through the air, unencumbered by the material needs to find food or care for their offspring:

> The *Idonen* are not conceived by or descendents of *Idonen*, nor do they in turn give birth to new *Idonen*. They emerge from a plant stage that propagates by means of cell division and budding, thus permanently maintaining a lasting connection with the body and soul of the planet on which they live and prosper. The *Idonen* represent the free-moving stage, and their individuals, male and female, unite by personal choice in all the minutiae of love's yearning and communion. Out of this union emerge not young *Idonen* but a substance that separates into seeds. Out of these seeds then grow plants that represent the new generation. While the passage through the rooted plant stage ensures the continuing connection with the life and energy of the planet, the sexual propagation and the free choice of the *Idonen* affords them the ability to make the achievements of their individual lives available to the whole species. In this way, the continual change between plants and intelligent beings has achieved the most advantageous division of labor: to lead both the energy of physical life and the power of the spirit to the highest stage of culture.[22]

While most Idonen live a life given over to contemplation, joy, and play, they also reflect on how life might be different on other worlds. For example, we learn that one of their writers has imagined a world where plants have no souls, something they consider absurd and tragic:

> If such beings should exist somewhere, it would be an aberration of nature that reason itself will correct. Either those beings will decline because they have lost their link with nature, or they will regain it, by learning to see their mistake through the use of reason.[23]

In this passage Laßwitz criticizes the unscrupulous way in which humans see and treat the living world around them. But he then goes further by exploring how that living world might respond to this treatment if it had the means to do so. The Idonen free their incarcerated comrades and consider whether a coexistence with humans is possible, whether they should subjugate them (they have the ability to control the minds of humans), or whether they should retreat. The Earth's plants believe that with the newcomers in control their lot would improve, since industrialization and human carelessness would come to an end. Using the link via the plants, the Idonen make contact with Harda in a "mindmeld"; Harda then shares her experience with her uncle Geo (a figure that represents Laßwitz, just as Harda is modeled on his favorite niece Hanna Brier):[24]

> In the machine shed over yonder, steam puffed [and] the drive belts whirred, while next door the hammers punched. From afar the circular saws screamed. Across the tracks a heavy goods train rattled along. In the middle of this loud activity of busy, productive work, Harda spoke with a racing heart of her experience. This experience was as certain and real as those works of man, and yet at the same time so alien that those unprepared for it had to assume it was a fairy tale fantasy, an experience from a different realm of consciousness. Emerging from living and feeling nature, from the speaking plant and its conflict with the ever-searching human spirit, facts were heralded that had the same logical necessity as these technical conversions of energy, with the only difference that here, for the first time, they came into effective contact with human minds.[25]

Eventually, though, the Idonen decide they must protect their fellow beings from further pain in the laboratory. Having investigated human civilization, they hold a meeting to decide what to do—whether or not they should subjugate humanity. Even though some argue for a show of strength, their elders argue that human culture is worth protecting in spite of humans' violence and their lack of "soul." They feel pity for humans because they are limited by their biology:

> Its unfortunate organic development had turned love, the highest point of worldly bliss, into the place of the most terrible conflict: namely between the right of the individual to pleasure, and the right of the species to self-preservation.[26]

They renounce life on Earth and commit collective suicide, but they leave Harda and the Kerns the blue plant. Its extract can be used as a catalyst for the production of artificial rubber, allowing the Kern company to thrive and Harda Kern and Werner Eynitz to devote their lives to science.

In a passage reminiscent of the German Romantic writer Novalis, the Earth's plants believe that a clarion call has gone out, and they hope that humans will eventually seek the unity of all living beings:

> When human beings will understand that their souls feel and sense just like plants as parts of the living planet, just as all bodies work together as necessary elements of a broader whole, then the slumbering God will awaken and rise from its stony crypt into the heavenly light and live powerfully here on Earth as on all the worlds going round in space.[27]

It is unsurprising that Laßwitz's strange mixture of Biedermeier and esoteric philosophy, with its emphasis on openness and a sense of wonder, did not catch on at a time when the German Empire insisted that every scientific discovery be utilized in the arms race with the British Empire. And yet, one cannot help but marvel at the single-mindedness with which Laßwitz insisted on an ethical science and "our right to inhabitants of other worlds." His depiction of a first contact between humans and plants may well be ridiculed, but in the context of Donna Haraway's "critters" and the advent of the posthuman we may want to think again.[28] The novel certainly reminds us to be more sensitive to, and mindful of, the world around us. As far as Laßwitz was concerned, scientific curiosity was only ever the means to self-understanding. In a posthumously published essay, he explained:

> After all, we are not just beings that seek to understand. The point and value of existence lies in the psyche, for it determines our emotional set-up. And it is in this direction that our interest in the living soul of plants points to. That plants have self-awareness is of importance not for science, but for our view of the world. For as much as the world is self-discovery, it itself is included in the great unifying band that encloses us in a part of the universe. Our view of the world expands, our instinctive feeling becomes part of us, the more and the deeper nature and the human soul know that they are akin in their being and their origin. The great idea of the development of all life on our planet that has so immeasurably deepened our theoretical understanding of nature now also gains its full aesthetic, ethical, and religious significance.[29]

♦ ♦ ♦

The theme of "first contact" has been one of the standard tropes of SF ever since the beginning of the twentieth century. In German SF, we have to include the genesis of the *Perry Rhodan* series where the encounter with superior aliens enables the nations on Earth to avoid another world war and instead to unite and begin their exploration of the universe (more on this in chapter 9 below). The "first contact" also changes in terms of its ultimate purpose in narratives. Since the generic plot lines (confrontation or collaboration with the aliens) seem to be exhausted, more sophisticated SF has returned to imagining a truly puzzling encounter, one where the "alien" is neither hostile nor friendly but simply unfathomable and enigmatic. A prime example is Stanislaw Lem's novel *Solaris* (1961), which was made into a film twice—by Andrei Tarkovsky in 1972 and Steven Soderbergh in 2002. In the Anglo-American context, we can think of the film *Arrival* (directed by Denis Villeneuve, 2016 and based on the 1998 short story *Story of Your Life* by Ted Chiang).

In Germany, Frank Schätzing, author of the novel *Der Schwarm* (The Swarm, 2004), also approached the "first contact" theme from a new angle. As in SF classics of the fifties—for example, Arthur C. Clarke's *Childhood's End* (1953), John Wyndham's *The Kraken Wakes* (1953), or Fred Hoyle's *The Black Cloud* (1957)—seemingly unrelated phenomena initially disturb the world: Peruvian fishermen disappear on the high seas without a trace; the continental shelf is beginning to break up off Norway's coast; and whales attack ships off the coast near Vancouver. When exploring conditions on the continental shelf, a Norwegian marine biologist from Trondheim Technical University, Sigur Johanson, who is helping an oil company develop new petroleum resources, discovers a genetically engineered worm species that destabilizes the methane-hydrate crust, causing it to slip off the continental shelf. Events come to a head when the slippage triggers a tsunami that costs hundreds of thousands of lives (the book appeared half a year before the tsunami catastrophe in Southeast Asia in December 2004 turned fiction into a tragic reality).

A hastily summoned crisis team of internationally renowned marine biologists, climate researchers, geologists, geneticists, and ecologists tries to link the different events together. When the Gulf Stream slows down, Judith Li, an American general and head of the crisis staff, is convinced that humanity is threatened and that once again the United States has to prove its worth as a savior in a time of need. She sees not only the challenge for the United States to solve the problem but also an opportunity for her country to expand its world power. The lack of a visible enemy is initially puzzling (Muslim terrorists are ruled out in spite of "firm evidence") until Johanson has the crucial hunch. He develops the theory that it is not extraterrestrial beings that are attacking humanity but an earthly one that has developed alongside the human race in the depths of the sea. He postulates an intelligent alien entity, the *Yrr*, that can manipulate marine neuronal systems at the cellular level.

The scientists and military embark on a helicopter carrier from which they attempt to contact this being off the coast of Greenland. The scientists find that unicellular organisms emit a pheromone that allows them to recognize each other and bind together to form a collective. This creates a bluish "swarm" that can process and pass on information. The scientists uncover the code with which this being communicates, and they develop a "phrasing" in the form of a pheromone that can also be used as a weapon to destroy the swarm. Due to the ever-increasing attacks on humanity, a confrontation between the scientists who want to establish a peaceful dialogue and the military who want to destroy the "enemy" at any cost arises. Although wiping out the *Yrr* would mean destroying all life in the oceans, and consequently, humanity as a whole, Li and her supporters are planning to use the poison. In a furious finale, in which Johanson is killed, the surviving scientists manage to stop Li and establish contact with the "*Yrr*. The attacks cease abruptly, and humanity has a chance to coexist with the *Yrr*.

Der Schwarm quickly became a bestseller in Germany, no doubt due to the explosive, global theme. The fact that the novel came out with a prestigious publisher and a large advertising budget and was decidedly not marketed as SF will also have played a role. Due to its great success, an English edition (*The Swarm*) was launched in the summer of 2006). In a thousand pages, the novel conveys the latest scientific knowledge in a number of disciplines without losing its grip on the reader. The author works with an international cast, but German readers also get their money's worth. Johanson makes his discovery with the help of the (real-life) German marine geologist Professor Gerd Bohrmann, who plays a crucial role in the further course of the book. In addition, the message of the novel is recognizably "German," whether that concerns the emphasis on the meticulousness with which the scientists in the Kiel Geomar Research Center approach the solution to the problem, the ecological awareness that is highly prevalent among the educated in Germany, or the thrust of the novel that is critical of America (noticed by several critics) and that reflected the attitude of many people in Germany after the Second Gulf War.

Johanson is the prime example of an ethics-led scientist who vehemently opposes the military solution, and in this respect he echoes the sentiments expressed by the German Foreign Minister Joschka Fischer when he challenged American Defense Secretary Donald Rumsfeld at the International Security Conference in Munich before the start of the Second Gulf War in 2003:[30]

> "Shall I tell you something, Jude?" hissed Johanson. He came so close to her that there was not a hand's breadth between their faces. "I do not believe you. Once you have your damned weapon, you will use it. What you will then have to answer for, you cannot imagine. They are unicellular, Jude! Billions over billions of unicellular organisms! They have existed since the beginning of the world. We have no idea what role they play in our ecosystem. We do not know what will happen to the oceans if we poison them. We do not know what will happen to us. . . ."[31]

Unlike the pragmatic Judith Li, who (although in blatantly exaggerated form) resembles Condoleezza Rice (at the time security advisor to President George W. Bush), Johanson has an awareness of the ecological context that allows him to think outside the box and consider the possibility that the *Yrr* do not maliciously attack humanity but rather defend themselves against the destruction of their habitat caused by chemical dumping, tanker accidents, overfishing, and climate change.

In addition to the exciting action of this ecothriller, it is the precisely researched and detailed presentation of the largely unexplored seas that fascinated the critics writing for *Die Zeit*, the *Frankfurter Allgemeine*, and the *Süddeutsche Zeitung*. Although Schätzing had to fend off some allegations of plagiarism made by science journalists who did not feel sufficiently acknowledged at the end of the book, this does not detract from his achievement. That consists in meticulously and comprehensibly conveying to his readers, like the American author Michael Crichton, the latest scientific discoveries in ecology, climate, and marine research, as well as in genetics. However, the criticism that his characters are clichéd is justified. This flaw may be due to the fact that Schätzing writes "cinematically," already drawing his characters economically in terms of possibly making a film from the book. It should also be noted that in SF the "novum" counts, while the focus on the characters is on their motivation and ingenuity. After all, these characters have a representational form, and the reader has a wide range of options for identification among the many actors involved. Undoubtedly, Schätzing's sympathies belong to the bigger picture. As Johanson puts it:

> We cannot and need not understand the Yrr. But we have to give space to what we do not understand. This is different from siding with the values of one side or the other. The solution lies in retreat, and currently it is retreat that is required. This can work. It does not require emotional understanding—that simply does not exist. But it involves a changed perspective. About an understanding of the world, which becomes more extensive the farther we move away from our own species, step by step, looking for distance to ourselves.[32]

Between the lines, one can find in this passage a clear criticism of the position of the then US administration, which, in Schätzing's eyes, had divided the world into good and evil, an approach that often appears inappropriate and illogical to scientists. In interviews, Schätzing has repeatedly resisted the accusation of "obtrusive anti-Americanism."[33] Although he admits to having drawn in Judith Li a "career-mad" and power-obsessed figure who wants to preserve the American hegemony at any price ("The world is America!" 916; "Even a coexistence would be confession of our defeat, a defeat of humanity, of faith in God, of trust in our supremacy." 949), but he sees this simply as a "realistic" description of neoconservatism, which he regards as a transient and unrepresentative phenomenon in the United States.

The message of the novel does indeed go beyond the interests and actions of individual nations. Schätzing promotes a position that does not argue for an irrational worship of nature (it is not nature taking revenge on humans but a second intelligent species that exists in the oceans) but advocates meeting the unknown with respect and curiosity. The "first contact," when finally accomplished, is described impressively (979–85), and, through it, the scientists are confronted with an almost transcendental experience. As a consequence, humanity is forced to abandon the idea of its uniqueness on earth. The critic Robin Detje mocked in his review: "the baseline of the book is clearly religious, despite all the statements denying it. This would not be a German book if it was not about the very last things"[34]—as if these topics had no place in literature. Schätzing clearly disagrees. He sees no contradiction in reaching broad audiences with his "thriller" (Detje), in making scientific topics popular, and at the same time in asking existential questions.

◆ ◆ ◆

The texts discussed in this chapter use the "first contact" as a particularly effective device for demonstrating the shortcomings of our own species. They differ from traditional satirical narratives like Jonathan Swift's *Gulliver's Travels* by investing the encounter with a serious scientific interest. In these encounters, humanity is shown to be capable of amelioration, of reaching a higher level of technological control, but also of ethical awareness and ultimately practice. By adopting the philosophy of the "Nume," the explorers in Laßwitz's *Auf zwei Planeten* demonstrate that they deserve the respect of the initially vastly superior Martians, while Harda Kern and Werner Eynitz in Laßwitz's *Sternentau*, in spite of causing harm when they experiment on the Idonen, develop an awareness of our interconnectedness with the natural world. Frank Schätzing's *Der Schwarm*, written one hundred years later, echoes the sense of awe and wonder in the face of nature—in this case, in the unexplored depths of the oceans, and in the way the encounter with the alien other has a redemptive impact on the scientists.

Obviously, these rich texts could feature in a number of other thematic strands in this study. *Auf zwei Planeten* contains long passages describing the (to Laßwitz's readers) utopian Martian society, as well as beautiful passages illustrating the "Shock of the New" when the explorers first look down on their planet from the Martian space station. In *Sternentau* we have glimpses of posthumanism (if not necessarily a critical one). *Der Schwarm* has been read as an example of "cli-fi" (climate fiction);³⁵ it has also been read more broadly as an expression of ecological thinking and "interest in the ethical dilemmas posed by the ecological crisis."³⁶

Still, by reading these texts as prime examples of how German SF has approached the "first contact" theme, I hope to have highlighted the distinctive (idealistic?) values it wants its readers to consider and, ideally, to adopt in their future encounters with the other: curiosity, tolerance, and an open mind—qualities that Germans, sadly, have not always appreciated.

7: The Shock of the New: Mega Cities, Machines, and Rockets

At the beginning of the twentieth century, Germany was experiencing a social, economic, and technological upheaval. Industrialization, the move made by millions of people from villages into the rapidly growing cities, and the rapid growth of the working class are all reflected in the SF of the time, as is the realization that the authoritarian and militaristic attitudes unleashed by the forces of colonialism and imperialism were diametrically opposed to the romantic yearnings for more idealistic values held by those who felt threatened by the cold wind of modernity.

Paul Scheerbart (1863–1915) has only recently been rediscovered as an early writer of German SF.[1] A call for papers for a panel at the 2018 German Studies Association Conference declared him "a significant figure in early modernism, one who may have inhabited the earth-star too soon."[2] His novels *Die große Revolution. Ein Mondroman* (The Great Revolution: A Moon Novel, 1902) and *Lesabéndio. Ein Asteroiden-Roman* (Lesabéndio: An Asteroid Novel, 1913) are exquisite leaps of the utopian imagination. They follow in the footsteps of Kurd Laßwitz's more playful short stories but add a unique allegorical and expressionistic aesthetic. Another, more typical example of the *Zukunftsroman* is Bernhard Kellermann's *Der Tunnel* (1913). This novel became a bestseller, selling one hundred thousand copies in the six months after its publication, and it continued to be read widely, particularly owing to the fact that it was made into a film, first in 1915 and again in 1933–35, when versions in German, French, and English were produced.[3] The main theme of the novel is technological progress—in this case, a gigantic engineering project. A tunnel is built at the bottom of the Atlantic Ocean, linking Europe with North America. The idealistic engineer Allen is repeatedly thwarted, by losing the financial backing initially promised to him but also because the tunnel's construction is beset by problems. The army of workers revolts against the inhuman conditions in which they have to labor, and when the tunnel is finally opened after twenty-six years it is already obsolete because airplanes can cross the Atlantic in a few hours. Kellermann's novel does not hold up well to scrutiny today: his characters are two-dimensional, with the idealistic engineer Allen pitted against the scheming financier S. Woolf, who is painted in racist and anti-Semitic tones.

Following World War I and the disenchantment with politics that arose from that conflict, the confrontation between idealistic engineers/technocrats and scheming politicians/bureaucrats became one of the hallmarks of the German *Zukunftsroman*, particularly in the works of Hans Dominik (1872–1945). Dominik had attended the *Gymnasium* in Gotha where Kurd Laßwitz had taught, but he developed a completely different outlook, as has been discussed with great insight in William Fischer's *The Empire Strikes Out* (1984, chapters 5 and 6). He saw Germany as a nation involved in a culture war, with "white" Europe fighting for supremacy against other "races."[4] His heroes are engineers and scientists who have to defend their inventions and discoveries against shady businesses and hostile nations. His books—especially *Die Macht der Drei* (1921–22), *Atlantis* (1924), and *Wettflug der Nationen* (1932)—remained popular in West Germany (in heavily edited versions) but were forbidden in East Germany because of their nationalistic sentiments.

Alfred Döblin, one of Germany's most prominent writers in the Weimar Republic, also tried his hand at SF. His novel *Berge, Meere, und Giganten* (Mountains, Oceans, and Giants) begins with the stark sentence "Not one was still living of those who came through the war they called the World War" (13).[5] In this epic tale that follows the fate of humanity up to the twenty-seventh century, Döblin, still in shock after the *Zeitenwende* of the World War I, asks the question what might become of humanity if it continues in the same way as before: self-obsessed, belligerent, unwilling to cooperate. He imagines a series of developmental stages and possible futures where scientific advances shift power around the globe, and man's attempts to control nature through technology lead to major catastrophes.

In her afterword to Döblin's novel, Gabriele Sander describes it as "a giant projection screen for the confrontation with modern civilization that had revealed its ugly face in World War I" (631). Evan Torner has argued that Döblin's experiment of writing a German expressionist SF novel was bound to fail, because "the work's tense alliance between expressionist tropes and SF genre conventions creates an aesthetic center that necessarily cannot hold—it instead becomes unreadable and incomprehensible."[6] I reluctantly agree with this assessment, and it is no surprise that the book sold only four thousand copies. But in its monolithic harshness, it stands as a "himmelstürmende Verstiegenheit" (a heaven-assailing feat of stubborn madness),[7] which may even have inspired Olaf Stapledon to write his classic *Last and First Men* (1930).

◆ ◆ ◆

Germany's most visible contribution to SF in the first half of the twentieth century was in film. Written by Thea von Harbou, and turned into mesmerizing images by Fritz Lang, both *Metropolis* (1927) and *Frau im*

Mond (1929) blazed a trail and had a lasting impact with the former's depiction of the futuristic city, the mystification of the machine and its corrosive impact on society, and the latter's technological marvel of the moon shot with its social commentary on the fight between capitalist greed and idealistic aspiration.

While Alfred Döblin struggled to convey his vision of the future to a broader audience in Germany, this was not a problem for *the* power couple of the Weimar Republic. Inspired by Fritz Lang's trip to New York in 1924 and Thea von Harbou's concern about growing social inequalities in Weimar Germany, they turned their vision of the future into novels (Harbou), film scripts (Harbou/Lang), and memorable images (Lang). In expressionist style, *Metropolis* seeks to literally show what lies beneath: In the case of the megacity this is a mass of exploited workers who are forced to keep running the machines that power the city. The film explores the individual's subjective, psychological reaction to the new industrial world: the ruling elites reveling in the power and luxuries; the downtrodden masses suffering, unable to escape their shackles. With its depiction of the hypermodernity above ground with its busy traffic, roof gardens, swanky offices, and night clubs, it anticipates the "dance-on-the-volcano" atmosphere of the final years of the Weimar Republic. Similarly, the volatile mood of the troglodyte workers and the ease with which they can be persuaded to destroy the means of production (at the risk of their own obliteration) foreshadows the revolutionary atmosphere and the clashes between Communists and Fascists in the streets. As such, *Metropolis* is ambivalent about whether this vision of the future is utopian, heralding the dawn of a new era, or dystopian, announcing the death of the old one. While the expressionist style, with its extremes of light and dark and its exaggerated facial expressions (to communicate the inner, psychological dimensions of the characters), has dated badly, the underlying mythological and symbolic elements continue to resonate with present-day concerns and fears—for example, surveillance capitalism, Chernobyl, terrorism, and artificial intelligence.

Most importantly for our exploration of the trajectory of German SF, the depiction of, and fascination with, the shockingly new technology on an industrial scale (used to such devastating effect in World War I) plays a crucial role in the film. Freder's foray into the giant machine hall allows the viewer an insight into the enormous power that needs to be generated and controlled in order to run the city. The machine is described as a "Moloch" that devours some workers while others are literally crucified on its controls. Lang/Harbou show the dehumanizing nature of industrial labor that destroys human individuality and saps human creativity. But the film's critique goes further: to do away with the workforce altogether that still needs to be housed and fed, Joh, the ruler of the city, embarks on a devious plan to replace the workers with robots. A prototype robot is created to incite the workers to destroy their underground dwellings but also to keep the elite from questioning the plan.

In spite of the often melodramatic plot and its oft-derided message "Mittler zwischen Hirn und Hand muss das Herz sein" (the heart must be mediator between brain and hand), the film has moments of high (utopian) pathos—for example, the moment when Maria takes the children of the workers up to the roof gardens and tells them, "Seht! Das sind eure Brüder!" (Look! Those are your brothers!) or when Freder, in an instinctive act of solidarity, takes the place of one of the unfortunate workers at the controls. For most viewers, though, the "money shot" and the most shocking experience will have been the creation of the robot in Rotwang's laboratory. Before the secondary act of transformation of the robot into a replica of Maria, we encounter a truly disturbing moment. At one moment, the robot is a lifeless statue no different from the statues sculpted by the Greeks two millennia ago. Moments later, the creature has been infused with life, and already has an awareness of its superiority over its creator.[8]

Here, at the intersection of scientific and magical, we find one of the key moments in the history of SF film, a moment that echoes the scene in Dr. Frankenstein's laboratory but gives the creator full control over his creation. The confrontation between the (human) creator and the (nonhuman) creation has been revisited ever since, most recently in Alex Garland's *Ex Machina* (2014) and Denis Villeneuve's *Blade Runner 2049* (2017). The trope of humanity gaining promethean power has often been seen as SF's main concern, but I would argue that it is the *shock* of making that discovery, the discovery that humans are able to be their own creators by means of their science and technology (which, according to Arthur C. Clarke's "Three Laws," if sufficiently advanced, will appear to us as magic), that makes the strongest impression in *Metropolis*.[9]

As many critics have noted, the film ultimately recoils from its own glimpse of the future—the social mores of the time demanded that the transgression had to be punished, the creature destroyed, and the status quo restored.[10] But for a moment in the darkened theater, the future seemed within reach, not only in terms of humanity's technological "progress" but also in terms of solidarity and conciliation between the social classes. This was a message that Fritz Lang later tried to play down but that was very much the idealistic core of the film (and was even more prominent in Thea von Harbou's book).

♦ ♦ ♦

Frau im Mond (1929) is similar to *Metropolis* in combining a (for the time) socially radical message with a celebration of technological progress and its potentially positive impact on humanity. Its aspirational motto: "Es gibt für den menschlichen Geist kein Niemals, höchstens ein Noch nicht" (for the human spirit, there is no such thing as a "never," only a "not yet") was severely tested, because it premiered on October 15, 1929, nine days before "black Thursday" and the financial crash that led to deteriorating social conditions in Germany and the eventual rise to power of the National Socialist party. While the National Socialist propaganda paper *Der Angriff* praised the film for celebrating the portrayed rocket pioneers as "ewige Sucher . . . aus faustischem Geschlecht" (eternal seekers, of Faustian blood),[11] film critics Lotte Eisner and Siegfried Krakauer homed in on the "pathetic plot" and "emotional shortcomings" while acknowledging the "breathtaking modernity" and "surprising probability" of the technical scenes (208). Indeed, it is the film's optimism about technological progress that inspired (for better or worse) future rocket engineers like Wernher von Braun, whose idols, Hermann Oberth and Wilhelm Ley, helped to create the detailed depiction of the rocket.

While present-day viewers cannot help but make the connection between the rocket "Friede" that takes its crew to the moon and the V2 rockets it inspired,[12] the twenty-minute sequence of the launch with its first ever "countdown" remains one of the most persuasive examples of SF predicting reality. Add to this the novelty of seeing a highly competent and independent woman in the titular role,[13] and one has a palpable sense of the "shock of the new" produced by the film.

◆ ◆ ◆

The "shock of the new" found its ideal medium in film, where audiences could collectively marvel and gasp at the technological visions of the future. The city of the future in *Metropolis* and the moon rocket in *Frau im Mond* broadcast the advent of the future and conveyed a sense of awe and wonder (mixed with fear) at the potential of science and technology. Later films, like *F.P.1 antwortet nicht* (Floating Platform 1 Doesn't Answer, directed by Karl Hartl, 1932), *Der Herr der Welt* (The Lord of the World, directed by Harry Piel, 1934), and *Weltraumschiff 1 startet* (Spaceship 1 Starts, directed by Anton Kutter, 1937) were popular but had diminishing returns as audiences became familiar with advanced technologies while real technological breakthrough was subject to strict censorship. *F.P.1 antwortet nicht* has been criticized for its nationalist stance,[14] though the floating platform in the middle of the Atlantic is originally intended to be used by all nations, and the film was produced in English and French as well as in German. *Der Herr der Welt* is another example of a tale in which an idealistic and visionary entrepreneur, who intends to improve working conditions of miners through the introduction of robots, is thwarted by an "evil scientist" who instead builds a battle robot to take over the world. With the immediate threat banished, the final sequence in which profits from the sale of the new machines are used to support the redundant workers is surprisingly prescient of our present-day situation with the "fourth industrial revolution" and the accelerated automation in many areas of production and administration. *Weltraumschiff 1 startet* is worth watching alone for its special effects, but it represents a pitiful shadow of a once powerful and confident vision.[15] With the darkness of totalitarianism turning the "shock of the new" into a traumatic reality, and the "Ornament der Masse" (The Mass Ornament, Kracauer) in *Metropolis* becoming a mere background to the self-aggrandizement of the Nazis in Leni Riefenstahl's *Triumph des Willens* (Triumph of the Will, 1935), SF began to retreat, finding exile and asylum in the utopian province.

8: Utopian Experiments: Island Idylls, Glass Beads, and Eugenic Nightmares

SOME MAY QUESTION whether the texts discussed in this chapter can be regarded as SF, since the authors under consideration here are interested in science only insofar as they require a means or a process by which a utopian society can be established or to critique its impact. But then we would also have to ask whether Aldous Huxley's *Brave New World* (1932) or George Orwell's *Nineteen Eighty-Four* (1949) belong in the history of SF, where they are routinely listed. Given the imagined futures—desirable or undesirable—that these speculative texts contain, I believe that they, as well as a venerable forebear, deserve consideration in this investigation.

Johann Gottfried Schnabel's *Die Insel Felsenburg* (1731–43) is a meandering narrative published under the pseudonym Gisander that grew into four volumes over twelve years.[1] It follows the fate of several individuals in the first half of the eighteenth century as they are shipwrecked on an island in the South Atlantic, or are later invited to join the a utopian community they find there. Founded by Albert Julius and populated by his offspring who marry refugees and exiles from continental Europe, Insel Felsenburg becomes an escape fantasy for those tired of the social conditions in Europe and without hope that these will ever change.[2] Thomas Schölderle sums up the experience of the "Felsenburger" (residents of Felsenburg) as follows:

> The newcomers all experienced suffering, misery, and injustice in their European homelands. Their lives and the conditions on the old continent were shaped by poverty, war, and the execution of innocent people, by adultery and sexual abuse, gluttony, larceny, murder, religious intolerance, and a general decline in morals. While one life story after another illustrates the shocking conditions in the Europe of that time and offers Schnabel the opportunity to assemble his satirical critique out of the numerous individual representations, he brusquely sets them against the life stories from the utopian island.[3]

In his commentary on the critical edition of this text, Günter Dammann argues that the community established on the island has attained the "moral good" as envisaged in Gottfried Wilhelm Leibniz's *Essais de Théodicee* (1710). Indeed, once established, Felsenburg becomes a utopian community with a strong programmatic foundation dedicated to mutual aid. The narrator describes it as an ideal society:

> 394 human beings live on Felsenburg at this time, communing with each other in utmost devoutness, love, and unity. They followed the example of the early Christian church and held all worldly goods in common, in trusting fellowship without avarice even in the slightest matter, but rather serving their neighbors and themselves by taking pleasure in doing everything they were capable of doing.[4]

Dammann stresses that those who discovered the island are also the ones who are setting up the community and its rules, the new arrivals adding their skills and individuality to the mix. The latter element is significant: in contrast to Daniel Defoe's *Robinson Crusoe* (1719), Schnabel breaks with tradition when he allows passion and reason, religion and morals to come together in ideal partnerships between individuals—equal partnerships that prefigure the relationship between La and Saltner in Kurd Laßwitz's *Auf zwei Planeten*. Moreover, the community is distinctive because it successfully integrates subjective will and collective interest, and because its members work hard instead of succumbing to a life of leisure. Nonetheless, *Insel Felsenburg* remains a diversion: just as there was little chance of changing social conditions in fragmented, pre-Enlightenment Germany, so the residents of Felsenburg never intend to bring their "model" back to Europe. As such, Schnabel lacks the "will to realization" we would expect from a social utopia. As Dammann observes:

> His utopia shows no sign of him wanting to turn it into reality. Rather, he paints the picture of a paradisiacal existence for humanity—unattainable but conceivable—and uses this to confront the conditions in Europe that are shaped by the decline of morals and decadence with the image of an idyllic world.[5]

Perhaps it is asking too much of a literary utopia to expect realization. In fact, it may be enough for readers to imagine the possibility of a different, and better, world. Of course, this leads us back to the question whether literary utopias and SF are not in fact routes of escapism, allowing their audiences to dream of better worlds while accepting that the real world they live in is beyond help. But the argument that the "consumption" of literary utopias can increase political awareness/consciousness and inject hope is equally valid, a view emphatically espoused by journalist and writer Werner Illing (1895–1979).

♦ ♦ ♦

Werner Illing's novel *Utopolis* (1930) critiques the Weimar Republic from the vantage point of a "proletarian utopia."[6] It differs from the typical SF fare of the time (e.g., Hans Dominik) because it lacks a revanchist or antidemocratic stance. Instead, it describes a future world in which the communist revolution of 1918 is successful. As in Schnabel's *Insel Felsenburg*, though, the utopian community is far removed from the real world. Two sailors, Karl and Hein, discover a utopian city when they are shipwrecked on a remote island. As proper proletarians (both in their hands-on approach and their class-specific language), they are welcomed by the revolutionary inhabitants of the city Utopolis and shown their marvelous achievements and inventions: maglev trains, self-driving cars, television, and mechanical learning during "Denkschlaf" ("think sleep," which is comparable to Aldous Huxley's "Hypnopedia" in *Brave New World*). More importantly, the socialist society has created a "new man":

> What was most wonderful about all this were the people who called themselves proletarians, and yet moved so freely and, without being bent over, so easily, powerfully, and surely as is given only to those who have never had a life-or-death struggle with need. Their thoughts were as upright and well-shaped as their bodies. There was no sense of the thousand ruses and little deceptions that we have to employ each day to assert ourselves or to gain the advantage without which we will be trodden down by those who push behind us. Maybe they were not any "better" humans than we are, but the form of communal living that they had formed made criminal passions impossible and helped them to become the upright and serene beings to whom nothing came more naturally than to give help and empathetic friendship.[7]

These virtuous proletarians could lead a happy existence were it not for the fundamental problem that the people of Utopolis had decided to allow the remaining capitalists ("die Privaten") to continue with their chosen system in an enclave on the island. Even though the capitalists have to openly carry the signs of their exploitative and swindling nature, they manage to threaten the peaceful socialist society of Utopolis, and its ruler has to exercise dictatorial powers to prevent them from taking over.

Illing also wrote the script for the 1948 light comedy film *Der Herr vom anderen Stern*.[8] Heinz Rühmann, one of Germany's most popular actors during and after World War II, plays the titular "man from another star," Aldebaran, who accidentally lands in a stylized German city at some unspecified time after the war, takes on human form, and cheerfully explores his surroundings; however, he is quickly arrested and taken to a Kafkaesque "Amt" (authority) to be registered. While he is initially appalled by the regimented and bureaucratic society he encounters, and is in principle capable of escaping by means of concentrated thought, he falls in love with a female human being named Flora and attempts to fit in. Because he has supernatural powers, his every step is closely monitored by the secret police. His attempts to explore human life (the criminal underworld, the circus, high society, the army, a radical political party) expose the unthinking brutality of life on Earth. As his initially serene detachment is replaced by the corrupting influence of human vices (in a parallel to the fate experienced by the Martians on Earth in Laßwitz's *Auf zwei Planeten*), he becomes increasingly depressed until Flora decides to let him go. The film is of interest for this study even though it flopped at the time and has not received any critical attention. In a telling conversation between Aldebaran and the suave but unscrupulous minister, the authoritarian and demagogic mindset that led to National Socialism is clinically dissected and lampooned:

> M: "The honor to die for the fatherland is preferable to any other honor."
> A: "On our star, these notions are—meanwhile—mere memories."

What may have overwhelmed audiences at the time was the film's radical pacifism: Aldebaran wistfully explains that on his planet the ideology that attaches the foremost honor to sacrificing oneself for the fatherland is "nurmehr" (only) a (bad) memory. The adverb "nurmehr" and Rühmann's facial expression as he delivers the line are crucial for the message: they signal that such a way of thinking can only be imagined as something that has long been overcome. Thus, the infinitely wiser and more evolved society that Aldebaran comes from becomes the eutopian place, even if audiences at the time failed to see it.[9]

◆ ◆ ◆

Ludwig Dexheimer's *Das Automatenzeitalter* (The Age of Automata, 1930) is another example of an attempt to describe a utopian society.[10] Writing under the penname Ri Tokko, Dexheimer imagined the world in the year 2500. In this age, the machines do all the work, affording humans the time to explore the world, develop their skills, and acquire knowledge. Morals are relaxed; all humans treat each other as siblings and enter and leave relationships by mutual consent, without fuss or sentimentality. Mi and Lu meet on the beach on Capri, become lovers, and travel around the world in their flying car or by using the tunnel express to switch continents. Their home is the "Automatenstadt" (machine town), a vast area covering Western Europe that houses 200 million people, each adult owning his or her own villa and grounds of one thousand square meters. Everyone is highly educated, particularly in the sciences. Robots ("Homaten") have taken over all tasks, and applied technology can be seen in television sets (in Germany, experimental transmissions started in 1929), computer-controlled traffic management, weather control, and the widespread use of solar energy. Some technological marvels predicted by Dexheimer come close to our reality: knowledge is stored in a "cloud" and accessible to all. However, just as on the island regime described in Thomas More's *Utopia*, which condones slavery, there are aspects in the text that are difficult for a modern reader to accept, especially the casual acceptance of eugenics and blood vendettas, as well as the widespread practice of cloning.

In his introduction to the 2004 reissue, Ralf Bülow notes that Dexheimer was strongly influenced by the ideas of Nobel Prize winner Wilhelm Ostwald (12), especially his concept of "Evolutionismus." This theory suggests that progress is automatic, always reaching new heights until an ideal state has been reached. Hand in hand with this trajectory of human evolution goes the human desire to delegate their activities to machines, to the point where work has been done away with completely. Other ideas of Ostwald that made their way into *Die Automatenstadt* is the use of solar energy (so as to conserve resources) with giant solar farms in Africa. Everyone recycles, though the weather is controlled by the release of carbon dioxide. Dexheimer's own contribution lies in linking all the advanced (and, at the time of publication, fantastic) technologies and their application: for example, children are educated by ("female") robots in an antiauthoritarian but highly rational way. The problematic aspects of the novel hinge on the use of eugenics, though. In order to maintain law and order, parents are screened for the genes that determine social behavior, and only approved couples are allowed to have children. I will return to the theme of eugenics and its relationship to utopian thought later in this chapter.

♦ ♦ ♦

German SF went into hibernation during the Third Reich. Yet Hermann Hesse's defiant construction of a utopian republic of scholars in his magnum opus *Das Glasperlenspiel* (The Glass Bead Game [Magister Ludi], 1943) is a powerful reminder of the indomitable spirit of individualism that resisted all attempts at collectivism from the Right and the Left.[11] The book describes a future world where the province Castalia is entrusted by the surrounding secular state to maintain and preserve humanity's cultural heritage. In exchange, the province, run by an order of highly educated and specialized monks, is free to devote itself to the infinite possibilities of the glass bead game, "a kind of synthesis of human learning":[12]

> Thus, the glass bead game is a game with all the contents and all the values of our culture. It plays with them in a way as, in the age

of the greatest flowering of the arts, a painter may have played with the colours of his palette. Everything that mankind has achieved in its creative ages in terms of insights, deep thoughts, and works of art, what in subsequent periods of learned contemplation were given names and became our intellectual possession, this entire enormous material of spiritual values is used by the glass bead player in a similar way to an organist playing the organ. And this organ is of an almost inconceivable perfection, its manuals and pedals search the entire cosmos of the intellect; its stops are nigh innumerable. In theory the entire world of thought could be reproduced with this instrument.[13]

Following an introduction by an anonymous monk writing in the twenty-fifth century reconstructing the events that led to the selection and reign of Josef Knecht as the Magister Ludi in the twenty-third century, the narrative shifts. It does this in the mode of a *Bildungsroman*, moving to a selection of episodes (the "legend") in Knecht's life from his first admittance to the order, via his training years and specialization as a senior player, to his years as leader of the order (during which he presides over the annual glass bead game that is broadcast all over the world), and ultimately to his eventual decision to leave Castalia.

The reason *Das Glasperlenspiel* is featured in this chapter is the fact that Hesse had designed it as a mental and spiritual refuge against the barbarism of National Socialism. Even though he had lived in Switzerland from 1912 on, and had become a Swiss citizen in 1923, Hesse could never be sure that Switzerland would not be overrun by the Nazis. More importantly, the oppressive dystopia unfolding in his fatherland caused him severe anxiety, especially as he was well informed about the reality of Hitler's totalitarian regime through the relatives of his Jewish wife Ninon. Looking back, Hesse explained his motivation in a letter to his fellow writer Rudolf Pannwitz in 1955:

> To counter the grinning present, I needed to make the realm of the spirit and the soul appear as an existing and invincible one. In this way, my writing became a utopia; the image was projected into the future; the awful present was banned into a past that had been overcome.[14]

To build that protective wall against the forces of evil Hesse employed the classic strategy of utopian writing—namely, declaring that the dystopian present has already been overcome at a given point in the future. This change of perspective is cleverly summarized in the motto that is given in Latin and German at the beginning of the novel:

> For although in a certain sense and for light-minded persons non-existent things can be more easily and irresponsibly represented in

words than existing things, for the serious and conscientious historian it is just the reverse. Nothing is harder, yet nothing is more necessary, than to speak of certain things whose existence is neither demonstrable nor probable. The very fact that serious and conscientious men treat them as existing things brings them a step closer to existence and to the possibility of being born.[15]

The idea of constructing this fictional safe haven, and the insistence that in doing so one is aiding that alternative better world to come into being, lies of course at the center of utopian thought, and Hesse was well aware that his act of resistance, however ineffectual in real terms, would help his readers (and himself) to survive the era of cultural barbarism.[16]

Adolf Muschg regards the *Glass Bead Game* as a "a utopia with defects."[17] Hesse had long struggled with the problem of writing a utopia that was not ideal. His attempt to oppose the power of myth (the "Thousand Year Reich") through the "not yet" of utopia is reminiscent of the position of Ernst Bloch, whose book *Erbschaft dieser Zeit* (1935) he had positively reviewed. Like Bloch, Hesse was aware that the past can overwhelm the future,[18] that it requires an act of the will to generate a concrete utopia. Béatrice Poulain comes to a similar conclusion.[19] She argues that in Hesse's utopian vision the resistance of the spirit against the barbaric powers was presented as victorious, even if the imagined utopia was imperfect. To her, it is the contradictions that make his utopia a "true" utopia, even a "utopia of utopia":

> As the utopia of a utopia, the Glass Bead Game exemplifies almost pictorially the Benjaminian theory of the necessary connection between mythical dream images and critical reason in order to free a utopia that has reached a dead end and is in danger of losing itself, and to rekindle the "liberating spark" still slumbering within to new life without causing an apocalypse.[20]

Timothy Leary and Günter Gottschalk have wondered whether Hesse had conceived of the game itself as a model of a future global communication culture.[21] In a similar vein, Elena Seredkina suggests that the Castalian model is the "third stage of planetary culture" to which humanity is heading, comparable to Teilhard de Jardin's *Omega point*.[22] But casting Hesse as an early internet prophet or a SF writer would be missing the point. As Michael Kleeberg observes, the genius of Hesse's narrative lies in omitting technological fantasies and positioning his vision outside time, as an abstraction, into a "fifth dimension."[23]

♦ ♦ ♦

With Germany defeated and the Cold War having begun, German writers began to work through the trauma of a destroyed and dishonored country, and to sift through any remaining hopes for the future. In Franz Werfels *Stern der Ungeborenen*, the author's alter ego F. W. is invited to visit the future one hundred thousand years hence.[24] He spends three days in this futuristic world, which knows no illness, avarice, envy, work, or nationality. The third part of the book explores the questions whether a utopian society can exist without conflict, whether humans can act in an ideal way, and whether they can learn from their mistakes.[25] Ernst Jünger's *Heliopolis* explores rival forms of government in the fictional futuristic city of Heliopolis, somewhere in the Mediterranean: one populist "with the instincts of the dull masses," and the other favoring an enlightened absolutism carried by an elite.[26]

Arno Schmidt's *Die Gelehrtenrepublik* (1957; translated into English as *The Egghead Republic*, 1979) is a utopian/dystopian satire that describes the experiences of the American reporter Charles Henry Winer as he explores two distinct zones that have been set up after a nuclear war that has completely destroyed Europe and contaminated other parts of the world. It is the year 2008, and, after returning from his military-sponsored trip to the postapocalyptic American West, Winer writes about the mutants he encountered in the walled-off "Hominidenstreifen" (including centaurs and giant spiders with human heads). The second trip takes Winer to the IRAS (the International Republic of Artists and Scientists), a floating city off the West Coast of North America that has been set up to house around eight hundred scientists and artists in order to protect humanity's cultural and scientific achievements in case of another nuclear war.

Schmidt's satire works on several levels—from the irony that Winer's report is so sensitive that he is barred from publishing it other than in a "dead" language (German), to his bizarre sexual encounter with Thalja, a female centaur, and the separation of IRAS into a Western (US-American) and an Eastern (Soviet) area, with a "neutral" zone for the administrators and functionaries from the Third World. While the English title "The Egghead Republic" conveys the satirical intent of the book, the German title alludes to the utopian concept of an enlightened "republic of scholars" described in Friedrich Gottlieb Klopstock's *Die Deutsche Gelehrtenrepublik* (1774) and the anglophone tradition of a "Republic of Letters."[27]

Critics have generally been complimentary about Arno Schmidt's most accessible work, though his experimental and idiosyncratic style have prevented a wider reception.[28] As a SF novel, it uses the familiar postapocalyptic settings and posthuman creatures that I will discuss later on. As a utopian/dystopian novel, it reflects the German perspective on the Cold War that I explore in the next chapter. In contrast to Schnabel's *Insel Felsenburg* and Illing's *Utopolis*, the island, however remote and protected from the rest of the world it may be, is no longer a utopian refuge and opportunity for a new start for humanity. Instead, it reflects Schmidt's disillusionment with the political and scientific elites who, having led Germany into two World Wars, successfully argued for rearmament in both German states and contributed to the febrile atmosphere that culminated in the Cuban Missile Crisis in 1962.

♦ ♦ ♦

Angela and Karlheinz Steinmüller's SF novel *Andymon* (1982) is perhaps the most explicit attempt by German SF writers to imagine a utopian society in a "science-fictional" setting.[29] Not only is the full title "Andymon: A Space Utopia"; the East German authors literally design their utopia from scratch. The first part of the novel describes how, on an automated interstellar spaceship sent from Earth, successive groups of eight human embryos (in equal numbers of females and males, representing the entire human gene pool) are born, reared, educated and trained by the ship's preprogrammed machines so that they will be able to use and control the resources of the ship when they reach the planet Andymon. Given their limited number, the young humans form a tight-knit crew, even though they experience occasional rivalries and disagreements. Their childhood is spent in a wilderness park of vast dimensions, and they are trained and supervised by "Guros," robotic teachers. They learn about Earth's history and society by means of the "Totaloskop," a computer program that offers a total immersion experience. Despite their best efforts, they cannot find any information about why the ship was built, what happened to those who built it, how long it had been en route, or indeed anything about Earth's fate beyond the year 2000.

The second part follows the efforts of these colonists to "terraform" Andymon, a colossal task since the planet has a poisonous atmosphere and represents an extremely hostile environment for humans. After extensive calculations and simulations carried out mainly by the first generation, they release a tailored alga into Andymon's atmosphere that is designed to mutate and kickstart the process of generating both water and a breathable atmosphere. Impatient with the slow progress of transforming the planet, some of the younger teams set their sights on the planet's moon and build their own structures there. Using the technology of the "Totaloskop," they "meld" their consciousness and develop into a posthuman entity that refuses to collaborate with its siblings in the ship and on the planet Andymon.

The third and final part focuses not only on the transformation of the planet but also on the efforts to build a functioning community. Perhaps inevitably, the first generation that has lived longest in the ship embarks on building a sleek modern city, but soon a younger generation insists on ditching the technology, having "natural" births, and living off the land.

They call their environment bubble "Oasis". Eventually, a third group emerges and sets up a colony based on communal living. Tensions arise when Beth, the secondborn human and the narrator of the story, insists on building new starships to continue humanity's diaspora. This puts him in direct confrontation with his siblings who argue that all the seedship's resources are needed to establish and maintain life on Andymon. Following an accident that nearly kills Beth, who has acted as a leader and advisor to his younger siblings, the groups come to an agreement, realizing that they must tolerate each other's differing ideas of a perfect life.

Highly ambitious in scope and idealistic to a fault (given the official outlook of the East German state), the novel nevertheless manages to create a unique blueprint for the future of humanity. Building on the SF works of Olaf Stapledon and Arthur C. Clarke, as well as on Soviet SF, the authors combine a vision of a highly advanced technology serving mankind with a reflection on the limits of an "engineered society," showing that even in a small group of siblings without a trace of racism, sexism, or exploitation, decision-making and consensus-building remain a challenge. David Draut has rightly called the novel a "dynamic utopia,"[30] pointing to the ever-evolving social relationships on Andymon. As such, it is perhaps not so different from the utopian society on Johann Gottfried Schnabel's *Insel Felsenburg*.

We need to remember, though, that East German SF was produced in a different context. Every book had to be approved by the state censors and meet their specific rules (no glamorization of the West; no undermining of Socialist ideology; an unquestioning belief in the superiority of the Soviet Union and its policies). To a certain extent, the authors played along with the rules, portraying a future society built on a pioneering spirit, equality, solidarity, a technocratic mentality based on the belief in scientific progress, a strong work ethic ("Tatkraft," 235), and a sense of duty, with disagreements settled by reasoned argument. But they also managed to insert a critical element into the text for those who can read between the lines.[31] For example, they emphasize the permanent surveillance by the ship's computer programs while the sibling groups grow up, even though it is couched in terms of benevolent care for the youngsters' safety and well-being. In their afterword to the 2018 edition, the Steinmüllers relate how they navigated the official constraints. When asked by the censors to replace the American word "team" with the approved term "brigade," they simply refused. The "sentence that saved the book" (384) appears quite late in the novel. The censors had taken issue with the fact that the loss of contact with Earth and the lack of any information about events there cast a negative light on the supposedly unstoppable advance of Socialism. To appease them, the authors added a confident declaration that Earth would have survived the East-West confrontation. In a revealing passage, Beth reassures his siblings:

> You know . . . basically, I am convinced that a civilization that can build ships like ours will have overcome the worst internal conflicts. No country that puts all its money into weapons, no society that finds itself in a crisis, would ever allow itself to make such fantastical investments that never produce a return, never produce a benefit that cannot be exploited.[32]

The authors point out, though, that they slyly added a sentence to hint to those who could read between the lines that they were simply paying lip service to the system. Thus, after his declaration, they reveal Beth's inner reservations:

> I hesitated. No-one had ever required me to make such a public avowal. I had not wanted to go that far.[33]

However, despite the constraints of censorship, there is no doubt that *Andymon* deserves a wider audience. The novel balances humanity's aspirational instincts and Bloch's "utopian impulse" with a concrete description of the technological and social challenges humanity is faced with when it chooses to build a new, better world. The book looks to the future with greater optimism than many other texts considered in this study and with the unshakeable belief in humanity's ability to cope with even the most severe tests. As such, it also starkly demonstrates what we have lost with the collapse of Communism as a utopian experiment.

♦ ♦ ♦

Uwe Timm's novel *Ikarien* (2017) is neither SF nor a literary utopia.[34] However, as a meditation on the causes and effects of the utopian desire to make the world a better place, it is directly relevant to our discussion of the distinctiveness of German utopian thought. Set in Germany at the end of World War II, it follows twenty-five-year-old American officer Michael Hansen as he returns to the country of his birth to accept an assignment from the American secret service. He is charged with discovering what role a famous scientist played in the Third Reich. In Munich, he finds a former colleague of the eugenicist Professor Alfred Ploetz (1860–1940, Timm's wife's real-life grandfather). Wagner, a dissident who spent twelve years hidden in a cellar below a rare books store, tells Hansen about his friendship with Ploetz and their idealistic student years that took them to Zurich and America to research the utopian communities inspired by the French revolutionary Étienne Cabet. Deeply disappointed by the lack of equality and progress to "improve the stock" there, Ploetz then set out to develop his theories of breeding a stronger, healthier, and more resilient new (Aryan) man. In a Faustian pact with the National Socialists, he conducted his experiments that eventually led to the widespread practice of euthanasia in the Third Reich.

Uwe Timm wrestles with the question how a fervent social utopian could become a fanatic eugenicist. This soul searching is not limited to his wife's family, or to his own biography.[35] Rather, by setting his story in the ruins of a defeated Germany and by giving voice to the friend Ploetz left behind in his increasingly callous pursuit of a "scientific" solution to human misery, he asks questions about the responsibility of science in utopian discourse.[36]

There is a long tradition for utopians, scientists, and politicians to explore eugenics as a means of "improving" the makeup of the population.[37] In the United States, the Race Betterment Foundation was founded in 1906, and the American Eugenics Society existed from 1926 to 1972 before it was renamed the Society for the Study of Social Biology and eventually the Society for Biodemography and Social Biology.[38] But eugenics holds a special significance for Germans in light of the horrific ends to which scientific theories were employed to justify the euthanasia programs that killed more than one hundred thousand people (Aktion T-4), and the forced sterilization of four hundred thousand helpless victims in the name of "racial hygiene." Through Hansen's interviews with Wagner, Timm focuses on Ploetz's conversion from utopian dreamer to fanatic ideologue who is intent on protecting the "Volkskörper" (75) from "harmful" diseases and on "optimizing" the gene pool for the challenges ahead. He charts the transition from idealism to fanaticism, initially indicated by the fervor of Ploetz's convictions:

> We have to winkle out the core that is lodged in Cabet's theory and place it at the center: namely the rearing of a strong, healthy, and especially beautiful generation that sees itself as strong and beautiful. There has to be a biological revolution and it has to complete the social revolution!!![39]

The transition is completed when Ploetz writes a letter to Hitler welcoming his plans. The book concludes with the American secret service collecting Ploetz's research, about which Timm makes the laconic comment: "Es kann sich immer wiederholen" (it can always happen again, 417).

Timm's novel has caused a wider discussion in Germany, both in the context of the resurgence of right-wing populism and the debate over genetic engineering.[40] SF is alert to these debates (as we will see in chapter 15 on "Eternal Life") but for now it is time to return to the 1960s.

9: To the Stars! Cosmic Supermen and Bauhaus in Space

It wasn't until the 1960s that a genuinely "German" SF reemerged; it did so with the East German film *Der schweigende Stern* (The Silent Star, 1960), directed by Kurt Maetzig. Based on Stanislaw Lem's novel *The Astronauts* (1951), it depicted an international expedition (led by the Soviet cosmonaut Arsenjew) to the planet Venus.[1] The crew members discover that the inhabitants of that planet had planned to annihilate humanity by means of "nuclear rays" but had been wiped out themselves owing to an accident. In spite of its political message warning of a nuclear war (and its none-too subtle call for international cooperation under Soviet leadership), the film was shown in the United States and the United Kingdom in a shortened and "westernized" version that cut out all references to Hiroshima.

In West Germany, German SF came in the shape of *Perry Rhodan*, a weekly pulp-style magazine that hit the kiosks in 1961 and was initially written by Walter Ernsting and Karl-Herbert Scheer.[2] Jokingly described as "Unser Mann im All" (our man in space) in a documentary on occasion of its fiftieth anniversary in 2011,[3] the series gave Germans a stake in the emerging space race in the form of an American astronaut of German ancestry who lands on the moon in 1971 and encounters members of an alien humanoid race who have crash-landed their spaceship there. With the help of their superior technology, he establishes a "Dritte Macht" (third power) on Earth, prevents World War III, unites the superpowers (initially in their shared opposition against himself and his small band of loyal comrades), and, once he has established control, he sets out to build a united Earth capable of entering into alliances with, but also defending itself against, threats from other alien species in the galaxy.

In Germany *Perry Rhodan* has provided the gateway for generations of male and female teenagers, equivalent perhaps to *Doctor Who* in the United Kingdom and the "pulps" in their golden age, as well as to Marvel and DC comics and films in the United States. It started life as a mirror of its time, reflecting both the Cold War confrontation between the United States and the Soviet Union and the global fascination with manned space flight. From the outset, the series has been (rightly) criticized for its militaristic tendencies but also for its thinly veiled revanchism, jingoism, and

Germanic superiority complex. Manfred Nagl, for example, has accused it of supporting white supremacy positions:

> To put it in a nutshell: the method of this serial is to take the National-Socialistic and fascist values of racism, Social-Darwinism, imperialism, and the "Fuehrer"-cult and blow them up to cosmic proportions as universal human values.[4]

Similarly, Wolfgang Biesterfeld has argued that because of what he saw as the series' "affirmative, and often imperialistic and fascist orientation," it had to be analyzed from an ideological-critical standpoint.[5] He has left the door open, though, for a rehabilitation of the series if it turns its attention to utopian aspirations and descriptions of a possibly better society.

> If SF reveals itself to be predominantly a medium of stereotypical and sometimes dangerous content and low literary value, we mustn't forget its true potential. This opportunity lies in its relationship to utopia: no other literary genre than SF could achieve a greater coverage of the theme of a possible society. While the realization of this connection would entail a reevaluation of SF, from the point of view of utopia it would mean that it could make use of a contemporary vehicle for its themes.[6]

Obviously, the door was only slightly ajar, because Biesterfeld regarded SF in general as a "medium of stereotypical and potentially dangerous contents and low literary quality," an attitude that was shared by Hans Esselborn in his recent book when he derided *Perry Rhodan* as "a kind of cosmic superman who keeps order in space."[7]

While there is no denying that the space battles and deployed weaponry provide an attraction for many readers (as they do for audiences in the *Star Trek* and *Star Wars* franchises), there are countless examples of Perry Rhodan and his allies encountering defeat, sobering reality checks, superior beings, puzzling ethical questions, and self-doubt. As the series evolved over the decades, it reflected social change by introducing diversity into its cast of myriad species and toning down the fascination with the hardware. The team of writers have changed over the years with guest writers providing some variety in terms of style and approach.[8] As it approaches its sixtieth anniversary, with more than a billion(!) copies sold and issue number three thousand published in spring 2019, the series continues to defy its critics, and it remains enormously popular in Germany and many other countries.[9] Undoubtedly, this success has to do with the series' unapologetic focus on "man's expanding horizons, the wonder of science and space, the great destiny of the human race" that fueled much of the optimistic SF of the 1960s and continues to hold a fascination for many,[10] so much so that a nostalgic movement to bring it back exists in the form of "Retro-Futurismus" where the "world of tomorrow"—as it was depicted at the time—was full of promise.[11]

It is this optimistic *Lebensgefühl* (attitude to life) that Andreas Eschbach, one of Germany's most prolific SF writers, tries to rekindle in his recently published prequel *Perry Rhodan. Das größte Abenteuer* (Perry Rhodan: The Greatest Adventure).[12] By retracing Rhodan's formative experiences in childhood, school, military academy, and pilot training (all faithful to the "canonical" biography that has been developed by the writing team over decades), Eschbach is able to offer a biographical backstory for Perry Rhodan before he made his entrance in the first issue of the series. He creates a verisimilitude by narrating the events through the eyes of Henry Adams, a crook who would become Rhodan's finance minister in his first administration but is serving time in London's Pentonville Prison in 1971, with the world on edge expecting a nuclear war as a response to Rhodan's return from the moon and his declaration of the "third power" in the Gobi desert. While avoiding any discrepancy with the established information about Rhodan, Eschbach clearly relishes the opportunity to work on a foundation myth, fleshing out Rhodan's character and explaining his unique personality, which is driven by single-mindedness, a surprising sensitivity, and a strong sense of justice. The author provides him with a German grandfather (Alois Roden), a traumatic childhood experience (his sister was accidentally run over by a car and he felt responsible for her death), a black school friend, an uncle who conveniently works at the naval air station in Florida, ample opportunities to develop his "natürliches Führungstalent" (natural talent for leadership, 231), and his ability to focus on the problem at hand ("Sofortumschalter," 369). We see him discussing his dream of a united humanity in discussion with (real-life) astronaut Jim Lovell (285) and meeting Wernher von Braun (411).

Just as the eponymous hero in the movie *Forest Gump*, Rhodan witnesses key historical events of the 1960s—for example, the March on Washington in 1963 and Martin Luther King's famous "I have a Dream" speech—that confirm his conviction that anything is possible if people work together (471). In a scene reminiscent of the one in *Auf zwei Planeten* when humans first look down on the planet, Rhodan realizes that human conflicts appear differently when viewed from orbit. He has a brief love affair in 1968 Paris, gets drawn into the street fighting in the Latin Quarter, and realizes that while it is right to topple authoritarian regimes, people also need to have a clear idea what to replace them with. When the Apollo 8 mission (counterfactually) ends in disaster, Rhodan and his colleague Reginald Bull (another stalwart of the *Perry Rhodan* series) fly to the moon in their secretly developed space glider and there encounter the aliens Crest and Thora from the planet Arkon who have crash-landed and are unable to return. Rhodan takes the ailing Crest to Earth for treatment and establishes a base in the Gobi Desert, thereby starting the era of "cosmic humanity" (694).

Eschbach's prequel to the *Perry Rhodan* series embodies and combines SF's dual function as early warning system and as promise of a better future. He understands that one of the key roles of SF is to generate awe and to entertain, but also to allow its audiences to participate in humanity's "journey to the stars": its aspirations go beyond domestic troubles and nationalistic squabbles and want us to become enthusiastic about a greater, collective project worthy of our potential. Obviously, this is where many critics will draw the line, assuming that such sentiments are naïve or apolitical at best and ideologically dangerous at worst. But such a position denies the hopeful message many readers rely on to negotiate their everyday reality, as well as the utopian worlds that message envisions.

♦ ♦ ♦

The West German television SF series *Raumpatrouille* (Space Patrol, 1966) has long had cult status; in German-speaking countries it enjoys a similar popularity to the original *Star Trek* series, which was first broadcast in the same year. Much has been made of *Raumpatrouille*'s allegedly militaristic and xenophobic ideology by critics who see in it an awkward mélange of undigested Prussian and Nazi jingoism and Cold War paranoia.[13] What hasn't been widely understood (or acknowledged) is that the series sought to subvert authoritarian traditions by means of humor and a positive outlook.

In *Raumpatrouille*'s alternative world set in the year 3000, people are still recognizably human. Individualism and conformism continue to be at odds. While nation states have been abolished, strict hierarchies remain in (world) government and the military. Here, individualism is suppressed, even though (and this has been ignored by critics and researchers so far) insubordination saves the day in each episode. Indeed, the series communicated very different messages: a vision of a world in which humanity has overcome barriers between genders and between nation states. This concrete utopia is evoked in the introductory voiceover in each episode, but it finds its main expression, as will be argued below, in the series' distinctive visual style. This style is futuristic and functional, reflecting a desire among the younger generation and the cultural elites to escape the sense of claustrophobia pervading the postwar era and the "no experiments" attitude of the West German government. The use of modern materials in the sets suggests a deliberate break with staid design ideas of the 1950s and a conscious homage to Bauhaus clarity and transparency.

Technology is the means by which unheard-of things are done in this imagined future, whether that involves the ability to live at the bottom of the sea,[14] or the routine task of traveling among the stars.[15] Of particular interest are the innovative solutions the series' set designers came up with to translate the technological revolution of the 1960s, which in turn heralded a much broader change in mentality, into a future setting. The incorporation of the latest industrial design and technology into an imagined alternative world, just months before the cultural and political revolutions of 1967–68 actually transformed the world, indicates a rare moment of confidence.

On Saturday, September 17, 1966, two weeks after the original Star Trek series premiered in the United States, *Raumpatrouille* burst onto West German television screens at prime time. Seven one-hour episodes were broadcast and viewed by up to 20 million viewers. Forty years after Fritz Lang and Thea von Harbou's *Metropolis* wowed audiences at the UFA Palast in Berlin, SF returned in a big way, and changed viewers' perceptions of the future. While the storylines were simplistic (threats from outer space, malevolent aliens, malfunctioning robots, or rogue asteroids) and the military hierarchies were portrayed to reflect both authoritarian attitudes of the Nazi period and Cold War mentalities, the vision of an alternative world was truly inspirational: women in powerful positions; a united humanity (symbolized through the international makeup of the crew); and mastery of an unimaginable technology that had overcome the economics of scarcity in food and energy. Most importantly, the series reflected the newfound confidence of the "dynamic times" of the 1960s not only through its utopian vision but through an imaginative use of the latest developments in art and design to create a unique visual style.

The short voiceover introduction at the beginning of each episode helped to set the scene, draw the audience into the vision, and fire the audience's imagination:

> What sounds like a fairy tale today can become reality tomorrow. Here we have a fairy tale from the day after tomorrow: there are no nation states any more, only humanity and its colonies in space. We settle on distant planets. The ocean floor has been developed as a living space. Spaceships travel across the galaxy at unimaginable speeds. One of these spaceships is the Orion, a tiny part of a gigantic security system designed to protect Earth against threats from outer space. Let us join Orion and its crew on their patrol duty at the edge of infinity.[16]

Raumpatrouille was the brainchild of the actor and writer Rolf Honold (1919–79), who managed to convince the Bavaria Atelier GmbH in Munich to produce the series for West Germany's public television network, the ARD, at the considerable cost of 3.4 million German marks. While a team of writers under the pseudonym of W. G. Larsen was responsible for the scripts, Honold was responsible for the general ethos and "feel" of the series, much as his counterpart Gene Roddenberry was for *Star Trek*.

The basic ingredient for a successful SF series is an impressive spaceship. *Star Trek* had the iconic Enterprise, the British *Thunderbirds* series (1965–66) had a whole range of aircraft, but Orion is arguably the sleekest and most striking of them all: its elegant disk shape recalls the UFO crazes of the time; its ability to maneuver in the atmosphere as well as in space was innovative; its spiky needles suggested lethal firepower, and its clean lines speed and power.[17] One of the immediate practical problems with the flying saucer design was how to get people on board. The flying saucer in the film *The Day the World Stood Still* (1951) had a similar problem (solved rather awkwardly with a sliding panel and an extending walkway), while the producers of the original *Star Trek* series got around the problem by "beaming" people from point A to point B. The solution for the Orion, a telescopic lift shaft, was neither elegant nor plausible, but offered the opportunity for dramatic encounters, close scrapes, and visually stunning images of the spaceship "floating" above the surface of a planet against the backdrop of the sky or space.

Every spaceship needs shuttle pods, and they don't come much dinkier than the "Lancet." The design of this pod shows a vulnerable semisphere with twenty-two domed windows for visibility, which reveals both imagination and the financial limitations the production suffered from. The large windows emphasized the thin barrier between life and the vacuum of space but also the mastery of spaceflight. The "legs," however, were more of a design statement than they were practical. In several scenes, they collapse, revealing their flimsy plywood construction.

Especially for younger audiences, the countdown and takeoff were a real treat, a highlight of every episode. Created by special effects director Theo Nischwitz, who had cut his teeth on the German SF film *F.P.1 antwortet nicht* (1932), the sequence required composite shots of up to thirteen layers of real-life footage, artwork, and projections.[18] The crew enter a hangar in their underwater base, take the telescopic lift to their ship, and wait while a robot voice counts down to zero. Force fields create a vortex in the sea. The Orion then ascends through the funnel, leaving bubbles below (the special effects team used Alka-Seltzer tablets for this effect); the spaceship finally emerges from the sea and majestically rises into space. It is interesting to note that the crew are very well trained and experience the takeoff as boring routine (unless it is an "Alarmstart" [emergency takeoff]). While they can be seen concentrating on their respective duties, most of the navigation is automated at this point. We can thus see the navigator Atan Shubashi relaxing in his designer chair while the radio controller Helga Legrelle handles communications.

The set for the underwater living spaces also required composite shots of real interiors and projections; few viewers noticed that the underwater life hadn't been scaled down properly. On the small screen, these images created an impressive effect, both in a domestic context (Cliff McLane's luxurious underwater bachelor pad) and in the "Starlight Casino," frequented by the crew after each successful mission. Little effort was made to imagine alien worlds—the planets Orion visits are either rocky deserts that are only important for their minerals or their strategic position, or they look very much like Earth (like the planet Chroma, discussed below). Clearly, the focus of the production team was on other things.

One visual element that Germans associate with Raumpatrouille is "that dance"—namely, the unusual moves performed in the Starlight Casino to space-age synthesizer music that were supposed to show that even in the year 3000 people were able to have a good time. While the dance scenes have gained notoriety on YouTube,[19] they were well choreographed and contributed to creating the futuristic "feel" of the series. Raumpatrouille was repeated nineteen times on German television in the 1970s, 1980s and 1990s, and it was also shown in France, Austria, Sweden, Italy, and Switzerland. After successful back-to-back showings of the series in art house theaters across Germany, a condensed version of three episodes with a new frame story premiered in movie theaters as *Raumpatrouille—Rücksturz ins Kino* (Space Patrol—Return to the Movie Theater) in 2003, its success underlining the continuing appeal of the series.

Beneath the glittering surface lurked some familiar skeletons. As many critics of the series observed, the political and military leaders who coordinated the various missions of the Orion evoked bad memories. Dressed in dark (the space fleet) or gray (the "galactic security service") uniforms, the top brass could be seen respectively as the unreconstructed successors of the German Luftwaffe or the sinister German Gestapo. Security Chief Oberst Villa was shown as a particularly villainous (i.e., intelligent and sarcastic) character, while his assistant Tamara Jagellowsk was installed as security officer on the Orion to keep the often insubordinate crew in check—if necessary with her lethal-looking ray gun, the HM4. Both military and security services have their headquarters in underwater bases; they control the expanding human empire from sparse, dark, and functional offices and conference rooms furnished with huge glass tables, communication units, and a large, oval viewing screen. The idea for the large monitor in the control room is taken directly from Alexander Korda's 1936 film *Things to Come* (based on H. G. Wells's novel), and it conveys a sense of power, control, and omnipresent surveillance.

No SF series of the 1960s was complete without bogeymen—in this case the "Frogs," alien beings determined to exterminate humanity. They were ingeniously created as terrifying entities (a shimmering light in a humanoid shape, their spaceships lethal, needlelike structures) so that the audiences could conveniently project their fears and phobias onto them.[20]

For many a young German watching these aliens from behind the sofa, they were the equivalent of the Daleks on the British SF television series *Doctor Who*.

One key influence for the visual style of Raumpatrouille is the Bauhaus—the German art, craft, and design school that flourished in the Weimar Republic and was closed when the Nazis came to power. Its "Formlehre" (theory of form), the conviction that form should follow function and that the creative use of materials always has an aesthetic as well as a functional aspect, was experiencing a revival in West Germany after the conservative 1950s. In the works of Laslo Moholy-Nagy, *Raumpatrouille*'s design team found the mixture of material, light, and aura of futurity they had envisioned for the series. Moholy-Nagy's "Light-Space Modulators" (1922–30), kinetic sculptures with a distinctive interplay of geometric shapes, light, and shade, were of particular interest to the production designers, who were charged with creating an environment that needed to suggest functionality while simultaneously producing a sense of wonder and estrangement.

A second influence on the visual style of *Raumpatrouille* was the cutting edge work by emerging German and international designers in the early and mid-1960s who shared Moholy-Nagy's vision and made use of twentieth-century machines and materials to create beautiful and useful objects, if not always for mass consumption. For example, we can recognize his impact on the clean lines favored by Dieter Rams (who, in turn, is regarded as a major influence on Jonathan Ive, the designer of the iconic iMacs, iPhones, and iPads). Rams's designs for the hi-fi manufacturer Braun and the distinctive chairs seen in the various sets were still sufficiently exclusive to astonish an audience more accustomed to traditional wares, and thereby struck them as futuristic.

The very symbols of the affluent public and private lifestyles shown as commonplace in the series (and thus as desirable for the millions of viewers) would soon be the target of philosopher Herbert Marcuse's book *One-Dimensional Man* (1964, published in German in 1967), as well as of the critics of the "Warenästhetik" (commodity aesthetics). As Wolfgang Ruppert has pointed out, the second half of the 1960s was defined by the tension between the object orientation of consumption in industrial mass culture, and the (minority) hopes of individuals for realizing their "authentic" needs.[21] Material objects had become "representative" of social status, cultural practice, and political convictions. As such, they served the needs of individuals to express themselves and to experience their individuality. Frustratingly, however, most viewers had no chance to recreate the environment depicted in the series in their own lives in the mid-1960s when the majority of West Germans still lived in cramped apartments and could only dream of a generous personal space. On the other hand, the material utopia portrayed by *Raumpatrouille* offered the audience a glimpse of a potential future that was attainable, much as conservative chancellor Ludwig Ehrhardt, who governed from 1963 to 1966, had promised "Wohlstand für alle" (affluence for all).

For a brief period before the West German student movement began to question the nature of industrial mass culture and urged people to emancipate themselves from artificially created needs, everything in the series could become an object of desire, fueling the imagination. In particular, the series succeeded in wedding its visual style with the industrial and technological developments that rapidly turned West Germany from a postwar economy of scarcity to one of affluence. In what follows I briefly discuss a few striking examples from *Raumpatrouille*.

Cybernetics—literally, the practice of steering and controlling—had reached its peak as a scientific and technological theme in the 1960s, with key developments in engineering and robotics. Commander Cliff Alistair McLane has an almost intuitive control of his spaceship through the switches, levers, and knobs situated around the "Astroscheibe" (the central monitor), while his chief engineer Hasso Sigbjörnson controls the spaceship's drives via the smaller, trapeze-shaped screens in his engine room. Computer specialist and gunnery officer Mario de Monti's controls are a set of silver balls attached to long, thin bars of metal, recalling contemporary kinetic art such as the *Atomium*, which was built for the 1958 Brussels World Fair and which was intended to be symbolic of the nuclear age and its promise of unlimited energy. In the first episode, de Monti is asked to destroy an asteroid taken over by aliens through "Energiebrand" (a nuclear reaction). The electrodes, shown in an extreme close-up, convey a sense of the unlimited power wielded by humanity in the year 3000.

Looking more closely at the sets, we can make out some of the shortcuts used by Raumpatrouille's prop masters; for example, the distinctively futuristic glasses used in the Starlight Casino are off-the-shelf designs by Joe Colombo. The microphones on the bridge are high-tech chrome taps for bathtubs, simply turned upside down. The most memorable choice of prop, though, must be the "Bügeleisen" (a Rowenta pressing iron) on the controls in the engine room. Among other off-the-shelf items, plastic pencil sharpeners were given a new role as flight controls. Indeed, utilizing contemporary industrial objects and giving them a new function in a futuristic context produced an overall "look" that was both convincing to the layperson and affordable given the limited budget. Compared to the $10.5 million available for Stanley Kubrick's *2001: A Space Odyssey* (1968), *Raumpatrouille* really was produced on a shoestring.

Central to the functioning of the Orion was the onboard computer—it was used to program a basic course, but it was certainly less capable than Hal 9000 or the voice-controlled computer in Star Trek. The distinctive egg shape, with its blinking lights and ergonomic entry keyboard, suggested computational power and efficiency. No SF series of the 1960s is complete without robots; in *Raumpatrouille*'s case these were quite hilarious-looking, floating plastic devices that often malfunctioned and needed the occasional lobotomy. They mainly feature in a single episode and are not much of an advance on Robbie the robot in the movie *Forbidden Planet* (1956).

In one of the visually most striking episodes, the crew are sent to install a new weapons system called "overkill" on an automated space station. The actors handle cables and connect different components on large circuit boards. 1960s technology was switching from thermionic valves to transistors, and miniaturization via integrated circuits was just around the corner. For dramatic reasons, however, the producers required clunkier hardware, which looked the part. Working on these simulated circuit boards, the actors appear to perform complex and dangerous tasks, tasks that were made to look even more futuristic when shot through translucent plastic. Since the components, banana plugs, and wires came straight from an electrician's toolbox, the effect is certainly impressive.

The scene reflects and illustrates the economic and technological changes in West German industry at the time: While basic coal mining and steel production was still going on, and several hundred thousand guest workers had come into the country to help build the cars and machines that were exported (thus creating the country's new wealth), the future for the manufacturing industry was clearly in electronics and "clean" technologies—for example, nuclear power, which was emerging as "the energy of the future." Controlling and regulating power was the key, and the series conveyed this message to its viewers.

Part of the visual impact of the series came through the functional unisex uniforms and distinctive hairstyles for the women, which reenforced the message that women were to be the equals of men but had retained their femininity. With the birth of the modern German women's movement just around the corner, Raumpatrouille spearheaded its own sexual revolution with the portrayal of powerful and competent women in the characters of General Lydia van Dyke, security officer Tamara Jagellowsk, and communications officer Helga Legrelle. They each have the same helmet-like "Astro" hairstyle, short, sexy skirts (strictly off duty), and acerbic humor that very effectively deflates male chauvinism.

It should be noted that the theme of (female) emancipation is featured in some detail in the storyline of the fifth episode, *Der Kampf um die Sonne* (The Fight for the Sun). Here the crew members discover that a previously unknown planet in the solar system has "tapped" into the sun to shine more brightly. While this favors conditions on this planet, temperatures on Earth rise, with predictably catastrophic results. As the crew members land on the Edenic planet Chroma, they discover a society that has evolved from the male-dominated patterns of early colonists. In this matriarchy, men are given only supporting, mechanical, and menial tasks, while the women govern with wisdom and restraint. Even in direct confrontation with Earth's military might, they seek a peaceful and mutually acceptable solution.

While the idea of a planet ruled by women is a staple fare of SF, this episode warrants closer scrutiny because its visual style contrasts with the other six episodes, in which the action takes place either in the artificially lit corridors of power or in space. Here, on the other hand, the female ruler of the planet resides in a beautiful palace (the baroque Schloß [Palace] Tutzing next to Lake Starnberg), assisted by a number of female aides with flowing hair, all dressed in very feminine, light-colored dresses. Soft furnishings and sofas tell of elegant comfort; the carefully manicured park landscape (the Orion has landed in a park, not a military base) goes right up to the open doors and windows of the palace. Once hostilities have been averted, Commander McLane, initially flummoxed by this social and environmental utopia, is requested to remain as liaison officer between the two worlds.

The episode offers a contrasting vision to the functionality and clean lines associated with the Bauhaus: its architectural practice is challenged in this case by other social, environmental, and architectural utopias. Indeed, Chroma offers a number of coexisting utopian visions, whether in the form of the garden city, the idea of the new man, or the politics of peace that hark back to the revolutionary visions of the early days of the Weimar Republic. Chroma demonstrates that the future Earth depicted in *Raumpatrouille* was not intended as the final destination of humanity's journey, but simply as a step on the way.

Raumpatrouille marked a brief period in West German history when the country looked to the future with confidence. Within three months of its first broadcast, the grand coalition between Conservatives and Social Democrats would lead to the formation of an "extra parliamentary opposition." The killing of an innocent student at a demonstration in West Berlin would politicize and alienate a generation that otherwise might have embraced a future as suggested by the makers of *Raumpatrouille*. Young Germans began to question authority in a much more fundamental way than McLane and his crew would have dared. And yet, to the audiences in 1966, the series represented a breath of fresh air and a moment of hope before history took a different turn.

10: Visions of the End: Catastrophism and Moral Entropy

Across the Western world, the specter of nuclear war and the growing awareness of impending ecological catastrophe intersected in the 1970s. Following the dire predictions of Danella and Dennis Meadows's *Limits to Growth* (1972), with concerns about the environment and fears about a nuclear confrontation between the superpowers potentially erasing all life in Europe growing, apocalyptic media stories abounded. SF, with its long tradition of foreseeing catastrophes, reflected the mood, and it was rewarded with an ever-growing readership.[1] As in its golden age in the 1940s, the genre came to the cultural surface with its chameleon-like ability "to reflect the conscious or subconscious states of the collective."[2]

In the case of disaster stories, such a reflection of the collective state of mind was criticized by those who held higher hopes for the genre—for example, by Darko Suvin, who branded it "black SF anticipation" and "romantic recoil."[3] Nevertheless, the attraction for SF writers to romanticize that "inconceivable terror" proved irresistible:[4] by exploring external threats—real, perceived, or imaginary—they, like their Romantic forebears, were addressing the rapid technological change and the fears associated with it. They warned not only of the end of the world; they imagined a phoenix-like rising out of the ashes, one of SF's "most potent icons."[5] Few writers, however well-meaning and critical, could avoid the danger of romanticizing the apocalypse, or using it for heroic survivalism. Gertrud Lehnert has suggested that while it was only natural to develop fantasies of survival in order to cope with the all-pervasive fear created by a superpower arms race and ecological disasters, such fantasies often produced the opposite of what was intended:

> When the catastrophe becomes the mere vehicle for one or more heroic individuals to take possession of this emptied world and to fashion it according to their desires, this "coping with fear" can have an effect that is diametrically opposed to its warning function.[6]

Focusing on Anglo-American examples of disaster stories, Lehnert observed that in such a context, the question of human responsibility for the catastrophe was no longer relevant, and that the catastrophe was often presented as inescapable or as fated. Man, though responsible for his actions, was unable to prevent the consequences.[7]

But there is more to these visions of the end than sensationalism and the morbid pleasure of watching the world go to ruins. Some critics felt that the genre had the potential to be seen not only as socially and academically respectable but also, by virtue of its alleged ability to extrapolate global ecological trends, to enlighten the reader by means of speculative prognosis,[8] or to admonish him or her to preventive action by creating a "Bewußtseinswandel" (change of collective consciousness). William B. Fischer argued that German SF after World War II (in contrast to Anglo-American SF) did not share a literary heritage with the mainstream.[9] What distinguished it, instead, were certain shared experiences between writer and reader that, as will be shown below, were going to be of particular importance in the case of disaster stories. Fischer mentions four aspects: the devastating experience of losing two world wars, an experience that, to the Germans, had seemed like the apocalypse; the fact that the two German states after 1949 were nonatomic powers at the center of the conflict of the Cold War; the fact that environmental effects of industrialization had been more readily apparent in West Germany, which was much smaller and more densely populated than America; and the fact that in West Germany there was an early development of a critical attitude to growth philosophy and an early mass awareness of the ecological threat of unchecked growth.

Axel Goodbody has researched the effects of "catastrophism" in West German mainstream literature on the public mood and found an "extraordinary pessimism and the fascination with natural and man-made catastrophes both in popular and high culture."[10] He claimed that this pessimism, which caused widespread melancholia, reflected a social and cultural crisis rather than merely an ecological one. He writes:

> a generation who had spent their childhood and youth in the stifling and joyless climate of sterile post-war reconstruction, and resorted in consequence to dogmatic abstraction, found their beliefs undermined. . . . Germany is characterised by a nihilism based on weariness with the world in the midst of affluence, reflecting the disturbed mentality of a nation of aggressors and losers.[11]

Goodbody wryly observes that catastrophism "may appear a particularly German preoccupation" (162). Indeed, the German experience of hubris and retribution, of dependence on American values and protection, as well as the slowly dawning realization after the cultural revolution of the late 1960s that these values and dependence held their own dilemma, is arguably unique, and may well be considered unduly pessimistic.

However, there was a brief period after 1968, long before the formation of the Green and peace movements,[12] when West German SF explored possible futures both seriously and playfully, and was not yet burdened by melancholia and the "political correctness" of the disenchanted intellectual that by the 1980s divided SF much as it had divided society as a whole. The "politically correct" way of writing disaster stories can be gleaned from the following comment by Amy Stapleton:

> The aesthetics of decay and destruction is particularly dangerous because it covers up the gravity of the approaching crisis and prepares people for a world which should not have been allowed to come into existence in the first place. Science Fiction can contribute to this brainwashing procedure. It can just as well, however, work against this trend. Real, socially critical anti-utopias do not cleverly sugarcoat the results of ecological disaster, but create visions which shock and disturb, thereby spurring the reader to work towards bringing about a different future.[13]

By singing the praises of the classic anti-utopia, Stapleton ignores the need of the SF writer to entertain and to find a market. Indeed, I would argue that the more heartfelt and sincere the moral outrage against the disaster, the more wooden (e.g., Ernest Callenbach's *Ecotopia*, 1975) or unbearably somber (e.g., Doris Lessing's *Memoirs of a Survivor*, 1975) the resulting tale.

The question is, then, whether SF can produce visions of the end that can combine entertainment, a social conscience or sense of collective responsibility, and, last but not least, a sense of hope in the face of doom. I will demonstrate that some West German SF writers in the 1970s and early 1980s, by creatively engaging with the concerns and anxieties of this period, managed to do just that. My examples are Herbert Franke's *Zone Null* (Zone Null, 1970), which explores the cultural and ideological impasse of the Cold War before the period of détente; Carl Amery's *Der Untergang der Stadt Passau* (The Fall of the City of Passau, 1975), which explores the cyclical nature of human social evolution and the role of the church in interpreting it, and Thomas Ziegler's grotesque satire *Alles ist gut* (All is Well, 1983), which follows moral entropy to its logical conclusion.

In the late 1960s, the superpowers were aggressively protecting their respective spheres of interest: the United States in Vietnam; the Soviet Union in Czechoslovakia. They were also engaged in a massive program of technological upgrade, implementing the discoveries of the space race in a new round of the arms race. For the first time, though, the activities of the superpowers were brought to the television screens of the average public. This led to a widening awareness of the potentially catastrophic consequences of the cold war and to a growing unwillingness to trust the technocratic elites to do what was in the best interest of the people. For West Germany—bordering on the Iron Curtain and subject to the ideological tug-of-war between the superpowers—the experience was particularly traumatic since the country had little control over events, and annihilation was guaranteed regardless of what power pushed the button first.

An interesting exploration of this experience can be found in Herbert Franke's postnuclear holocaust novel *Zone Null* (1970). Franke, a "dominant figure in the history of German SF,"[14] a lecturer in cybernetics, and at the time one of the few German SF writers whose works were translated into English,[15] depicts the culturally divergent paths of two unnamed superpowers hundreds of years after a nuclear confrontation.

One of the powers, which calls itself the "free world," sends an expedition force across the contaminated no-man's-land (the "Zone Null" of the title) to its former enemy. That mysterious country had managed to repulse all efforts to penetrate its territory and had shielded itself completely from all attempts at annexation by the "free world," never responding to any attempts at communication. When it is discovered that the defenses of the other power are beginning to weaken, the expedition force, accompanied by a carefully selected and highly trained group of scientists, manages to break through the automatic barriers and enter an almost deserted city. They find that all functions of the city are carried out by machines and supervised by computer programs, leaving the few remaining people free to pursue their individual interests—for example, by restaging the Battle of Waterloo in virtual reality. For the members of the expedition team, born and bred to a life of service and subservience to the needs of "the collective," this lifestyle is incomprehensible and frightening. It contradicts their firm belief that their own society (which does not allow any individual freedom) is on a path of progress toward ultimate freedom.

Only one member of the group survives the expedition; the rest mysteriously die, presumably victims of the remaining defense mechanisms of the city. He discovers that the people in the city are those "left behind" who have chosen not to "integrate" themselves into the cybernetic machine that represents a new evolution and allows everyone "immortality" and the fulfilment of their dreams, though at the price of losing their individuality. When the explorers search the city, it is on the verge of collapse: it is a shell no longer needed by the machine.

The movements and discoveries of the expedition are shown through the interrogation protocols of the survivor who has miraculously made it back to the "free world." It is suspected that he was "contaminated" by his exposure to the ideology of the former enemy, and he is held in quarantine while analysts try to determine what has happened to the expedition. In fact, the contamination is fundamental: exposure to the other ideology has altered the survivor's own worldview and turned him into an individual.

It takes some time for the reader to realize that the "free world" of the novel is heir to the former Communist block (characterized by its military command structure and total belief in the validity of science and logic), and that what may have been initially thought to be heir to the Soviet Union behind the Iron Curtain is in fact heir to the capitalist world (characterized by intense, at times hostile, individualism and superior technology), which has fallen prey to its hedonism and materialism. The reader can be forgiven for not realizing this "inversion" of direction. It is unexpected, since the term "free world" as synonymous with the Western bloc was drummed into anyone growing up in the West during the Cold War. One also identifies (to a certain degree) with the explorers; once the reader realizes what is going on, however, the clues are more than obvious. The scientists of the "free world" are thoroughly brainwashed by their totalitarian state, and Franke intersperses the narrative with the litany of indoctrination echoing through the consciousness of the explorers:

> We lead you to perfection
> We train you
> We get rid of your weaknesses
> We switch off your instincts
> We establish a basis of useful motivations
> We teach you objectivity
> We teach you to focus on reality
> We teach you to think cooly
> We free you from outdated patterns of thinking
> We free you from archaic instincts
> We free you from human relationships
> We give you a task
> We set you a goal
> We give your existence a purpose[16]

For the survivor of the expedition, realizing that his own country is not interested in the "objective" report but in the confirmation that its system is superior, the only solution is to escape and find a future outside the system. What happens to him is left open.[17] However, this is not the whole truth. During his time in the city, the survivor has taken the step to total integration and evolution to a higher form of existence by inserting a copy of his self into the machine consciousness, thus leaving the "prison" of his own body while the "original" returns.

Franke's sophisticated view of the nuclear holocaust and human evolution forces us to engage with the humanity of the enemy and the otherness of the self. Delivered in the unemotional monotone of "objective language," employing devices of (then) experimental "mainstream" literature such as nonlinear plot chronology and distortion or fragmentation of narrative perspective,[18] it is a far cry from the "normative" American disaster story.[19] Indeed, the apocalyptic transformation in this novel is not concerned with the end of the world or the horrific experience of the nuclear wasteland. Instead, it focuses on the dehumanizing effect of internalizing the Cold War.

The message of the novel is delivered on several levels: if there is no communication between the superpowers, the cultural barrier will only grow as the systems continue to develop in different directions. Seen as "complex systems," both superpowers need feedback from the other in order to evolve. But, according to Franke, the same is true for the relationship between man and machine because human evolution is intricately intertwined with the evolution of technology. We need to remember that, when Franke wrote *Zone Null*, cybernetics was cutting edge, an artificial intelligence was just on the verge of being imaginable, and popular German SF still cheerfully believed that scientists would be able to make artificial intelligences subservient to man. Franke throws a wrench in the works by describing an artificial intelligence that keeps the remaining individuals who have not integrated into the mainframe in complete dependency, ignorant of their own situation, and cynically employed in a bureaucracy of Kafkaesque proportions to feed its databanks.[20] The narrator's comment on the effects of this exploitation of human beings, which is a thinly veiled criticism of the capitalist system reminiscent of Herbert Marcuse's own critique in *One-Dimensional Man*, is unambiguous:

> They had . . . reached their goal, lived in a make-believe world, stimulated their senses electronically, were old hat already, were used to surveillance, trusted the machines, . . . had never seen a piece of sky, . . . had never learned to question the things that were taken for granted, and in this way they did not see more than what lay in plain view, and not even that; they spared themselves the trouble of conflict, avoided decisions and took life the way it was. They were free of guilt, but that was their only freedom.[21]

◆ ◆ ◆

In *Der Untergang der Stadt Passau* (1975), Carl Amery goes beyond the pervading sense of loss which permeates many post-apocalypse stories.[22] In the year 2013, 40 years after a biological disaster that is never described in detail but has killed most people, the survivors have either adopted a nomadic existence or attempt to survive with the help of the goods and technology still around from the time "before." A group of scavengers has chosen the town of Passau on the Danube as their headquarters, and, by means of precariously maintained technology, they attempt to control southern Germany. They have managed to get an electricity generator going and they shine the city's lights to attract the hunters, ostensibly in order to make them part of their "system of security." In reality, they want to prevent any potential threat from the east and to remove rival groupings from their strategic control of precious resources. What they offer in return is their specialist knowledge, in exchange for food and furs.

The events narrated in this short novel revolve around the visit of two hunters, the father "Lois" (= Alois) and his adopted son "Marte" (= Martin), from the tribe of the "Rosmer" (coming from the area of Rosenheim, thirty miles southeast of Munich) that has traveled to Passau to investigate the lights and the rumors about a new beginning for humanity. While the father (now the leader of a small group of survivors who live in harmony with nature) is a former teacher who well remembers the world "before" and the causes that led to the collapse of the ecobalance, the son is a child of the new world, relying on his instincts, easily impressed by technological dazzle, but also completely in tune with the wild, as his father has taught him to be. The two are received with great but false pomp, wined and dined by the "Scheff" (= boss), himself a survivor from the Ruhr area in northwest Germany, a self-taught Machiavellian who believes that he has the right "plan" to ensure human survival on a more technologically advanced level. The Scheff thinks in political terms: for example, he has set fire to all stores of petrol in the country—allegedly to prevent a poisoning of the groundwater but really to avoid the establishment of any competing "power." His aim is to establish control over the salt trade that will become essential for the preservation of food once stores are used up. He tries to lure the "ambassadors," as he calls them, into a trap, but the two hunter-gatherers discover the sinister plot and manage to escape. Lois, however, dies and Marte, his son, vows revenge on Passau.

Three generations later, hordes of nomads and riders from the east under the "wise leadership of the Third Marte" attack the city of Passau and oust the city dwellers. Their success is recorded by a chaplain by the name of Egid, who accompanies the nomads and interprets the events for future generations as the "Wiederherstellung aller Dinge" (the restoration of all things). The following extract is Chaplain Egid's record of the Third Marte's challenge:

> Know ye that the wrath of the LORD is coming, which every sinner must fear. And yet . . . everyone is assured of forgiveness, for it is not the sinner that the LORD hates but sin itself. Therefore, whosoever will leave the city, and return to the simple ways, which the "restoration of all things" in its mercy has made possible—whosoever therefore will let go of lies, arrogance, and lust, which live within the walls

of the city—is not only assured of His forgiveness, but also we will not pursue him.[23]

To make his case for a return to a sustainable way of life and, therefore, for having less reliance on specialists such as technicians and scientists, the moralist Amery interweaves passages from Egid's mythology of "the fall of the city of Passau" (hence the title), biographical flashbacks of the characters who have survived the disaster, and the main narrative of the pivotal first visit of the Rosmer in Passau, where we can see the (threadbare) splendor of the city through the eyes of people who have decided to return to a more natural way of life.[24]

Amery locates the action in the provincial backwater of Passau, which is complete with thick Bavarian dialects and minute descriptions of architectural details of the city, to allow his readers a strong sense of identification. Like Franke, he places his narrative into the political context of the time. Readers were certainly aware of the *Club of Rome* report that gloomily predicted a sudden and uncontrollable decline in both population and industrial capacity if the exponential growth of the world's population, the ecological rape of the planet, and the squandering of natural resources in the name of industrial growth were to remain unchecked. They would also remember the oil crisis of 1973, when German Autobahns were closed on consecutive Sundays to save precious resources, and they would be aware of the many ecological pressure groups that were campaigning against the building of nuclear power plants. In spite of the appalling disaster that caused the collapse of civilization in the first place and the novel's ambivalent ending, there is a sense of a positive "concrete" utopia in *Der Untergang der Stadt Passau*.[25] Forty-five years before current extinction rebellion protests, Amery gives us to understand that the forces of unchecked growth and technology may lead to disaster but that, contrary to the very German idea of the perfectibility of society through increased complexity, the collective may reach utopia by living a simpler, sustainable life.

Amery, the recipient of such prestigious awards as the Kurd-Laßwitz-Preis (1985) and the Deutscher Fantasy Preis (1996), was not primarily known as a SF writer.[26] He represented the small but vocal group of critical thinkers in Germany who, based on their strong identification with their "Heimat" (roughly translated as homeland, roots), challenged the materialistic and utilitarian course (West) Germany had taken under the rule of its technocratic elite. In his books Amery criticized the Christian churches for condoning the exploitation of the environment, and he urged politicians to work for sustainable development.[27] There is an apparent paradox when a writer who is so concerned about the survival of the planet so obviously enjoys sending it to ruins in his writings, but on closer reflection the paradox disappears: only if you believe that history can be changed is there any hope for the future.[28]

♦ ♦ ♦

In the 1980s, West German SF continued to produce postdoomsday novels,[29] but in the context of the decision to deploy nuclear weapons on German soil, reality had, in the eyes of many, overtaken the scariest predictions of SF. One remaining response to a world gone mad was to openly ridicule the values of the ruling elites, not through gentle satire like Amery's but through full frontal assault. Thomas Ziegler's *Alles ist gut* (1983) is a powerful comment on the moral and social bancruptcy of a future Germany that is so engrossed in its own demise that it comes as a relief when the real apocalypse (in form of alien intervention) finally occurs. Ziegler takes society's collapse for granted, opening up a playground for all kinds of social misfits and cyberpunks who thrive on disintegration. Not only the natural world but society itself is permanently and irreparably damaged. In spite of Ziegler's humoristic tone, this vision of the future is far more chilling than it is in the works previously discussed, since it follows moral entropy to its logical conclusion.

At an unspecified time in the future, the city of Cologne is the scene of civil war between the "authorities," street fighters, violent gangs of children, unscrupulous loan sharks, and transplant organ dealers. Life is lived on the edge; one may well be blackmailed by the biotronic elevator in an apartment tower before being allowed out. One of the characters we get to know, a "street rat" and contraband runner, reflects on the precarious nature of his everyday existence:

> Even for a professional street fighter the world contained enough dangers that prevented the slogan of "fight for survival" from degenerating into a fashionable phrase: especially here in the city of Cologne, in the cold light of day, where the verdict of the computerized constitutional court about the legality of instant executions lost a lot of its bureaucratic distance to reality.[30]

If there is a certain honesty and morality among the misfits, there is certainly none among the corrupt political elite who have cordoned themselves off from the everyday chaos and actually thrive on it. It turns out that the leadership, including the mad Chancellor Schwammstein (who, fittingly, resides in a brothel), have their hand in every shady deal going on, whether drug dealing or prostitution, and they finance their next election campaign by running stolen microchips. One day, however, something inexplicable changes everything. A voice promises anyone who recites the mantra of "all is well" the fulfilment of their dreams:

ALL
Is
WELL
the situation is relaxed. nobody will be punished
the cold is forgotten, the winter is banned
forget your worries
be without fear
everything will
be all right
be happy
it is so
true
so wonderfully
true[31]

More and more people learn to recite the mantra, and, by means of "the matrix," have their every wish granted: food, drink, demure women—all simply materialize. Using the mantra and the matrix, the people turn into complete hedonists. The government, anxious to retain some form of control, announces that it is now the church of the matrix, with Chancellor Schwammstein elevated to the position of pope. However, some of the "street rats" refuse to use the mantra—wisely, as it turns out, since matrix users develop a stigma: a cross on their forehead. Eventually, they see a cross and disappear without trace.

The group of "street rats" naturally suspects another ploy by the government, but, in a flash of stinging social commentary supplied by Ziegler, they realize:

> We should neither under- nor overestimate the political professionals in Bonn. They simply lack the imagination to think of such a complicated diversion. It's simply not logical. For the rulers the mantra is a much greater threat than the street fighters or the luddites. . . . What distinguished the men with money from the underdogs? Their privileges! But with the help of mantra and matrix, anyone can lay their hands on villas, party girls, high class callboys, caviar, champagne, jewels, organically grown vegetables, and transplant organs. Compared with the mantra culture, communism is a pure class society.[32]

The group, a motley collection of countercultural losers, discover that the matrix has been created by an alien being (in the shape of a pink pudding), which, after scanning the brains of a crew of astronauts on a mission to Venus, has learned about humans. Unfortunately, the crew was suffering from space madness, giving the alien a rather lopsided impression of humanity. Deducing that people would be much better off sharing its loneliness on Venus than continuing their chaotic existence on Earth, the alien has called itself "God" and teleported people across space. The group take the ultimate test: they are given the opportunity of having all their desires fulfilled, but they refuse, and manage to talk the alien into letting all the people it had adopted return to Earth. Bereft of their individual (though false) paradise, those who return immediately set about hunting the group in order to lynch them.

Alles ist gut, with its deeply cynical undertones, may be compared to William Gibson's *Neuromancer* (1984), since it makes cyberpunk look "cool." However, there is a broader method to Ziegler's madness: his misfits realize that outright materialism does not bring happiness. They are aware of their political and social situation. With all their countercultural bravado, they know that only some form of organized resistance may halt the advancing wave of social decay. Looking at the ending with the majority baying for the blood of those who "liberated" them, the chances may be slim (as were the chances of several hundreds of thousands of West Germans who tried to stop the stationing of Pershing and Cruise Missiles in the 1980s). But, according to Ziegler, it was better to try laughing.

The visions of the end discussed so far easily reach the sophistication associated at the time with mainstream literature while exploring wider political and scientific questions not usually within its scope.[33] In marked contrast to the "normative" Anglo-American tradition and the serious anxieties of "the intellectual" in the late 1970s and 1980s, these examples tend to be more "interlinear": they are experimental, entertaining, and inventive. They all stress the potential of change. In keeping with true Luddite tradition they follow the slogan of student revolutionaries of the late 1960s to "bring down what brings you down." Given the traumatic postwar experience followed by a phoenix-like rise out of the ashes, Germans knew that they had to take their fate into their own hands in order to survive. How this could be done, against the odds, is explored in a process that Dieter Wessels described as "Zukunftsbewältigung" (coming to terms with the future), which encompasses, but does not limit itself to, structures of political rule, responsibility for war and global environmental disasters, and the dissolution of society.[34]

Herbert Franke allows not only the individual to escape the clutches of the collective; he also allows for a new, symbiotic relationship between man and machine. Carl Amery can see a future after ecological collapse, though he is wise enough to know that people will not change much. And what about Ziegler? To the reader's surprise, even in this case Earth is given a respite, a final chance. Indeed, "alles ist gut"—the real world is the only one that matters.

All these visions of the end have an appeal that is highly original and effective because they allow the reader to relate to the collapse of our familiar world not in abstract but concrete terms. If there is such a thing as a "generic nature" of German SF, then it lies in its desire not only "to express in literature the confrontation with science,"[35] but to develop a new aesthetics that combines new awareness with new energy to adapt or change. Using the "lighter touch" of SF, the image of the future that takes shape in the minds of the readers remained one of (qualified) hope in the 1970s and 1980s.

◆ ◆ ◆

In the last three decades, we have seen a marked increase in the production of (mainly anglophone) dystopian and often outright apocalyptic stories that are routinely classed as SF. The film industry is eager to bring these dark visions to life and seems to delight in the depiction of the collapse of human civilization, whether caused by natural disaster or by human activity. Some of these works are of extraordinary quality and/or are visually enthralling. Examples of these are *The Handmaid's Tale* (directed by Volker Schlöndorf, 1990), *12 Monkeys* (directed by Terry Gilliam, 1995), *Waterworld* (directed by Kevin Reynolds, 1995), *AI. Artificial Intelligence* (directed by Steven Spielberg, 2001), *28 Days Later* (directed by Danny Boyle, 2002), *Children of Men* (directed by Alfonso Cuaron, 2006), *The Day after Tomorrow* (directed by Roland Emmerich, 2006), *I am Legend* (directed by Francis Lawrence, 2007), *Sunshine* (directed by Danny Boyle, 2007), *The Road* (directed by John Hillcoat, 2009), *The Book of Eli* (directed by Albert Hughes and Allen Hughes, 2010), *Hell* (directed by Tim Fehlbaum, 2011), *Melancholia* (directed by Lars von Trier, 2011), *Interstellar* (directed by Christopher Nolan, 2014), *Oblivion* (directed by Josef Kosinski, 2014), and *Blade Runner 2049* (directed by Denis Villeneuve, 2017).

One may ask whether these spectaculars that imagine the worst for their global audiences still believe in the warning function of SF or whether they are content to shock and entertain—for diminishing returns. In the following, I will briefly explore a number of recent German dystopias in order to find out whether they are conceived as critical dystopias or straightforward antiutopias, and whether there is still a German distinctiveness to them.

In *Die kommenden Tage* (The Coming Days, 2010), director Lars Kraume tells the story of two sisters set against an increasingly dystopian political and social background in Germany, and more broadly in affluent northern Europe. Between the years 2012 and 2020, climate change and the wars over oil have led to huge numbers of African refugees who are prevented from entering the rump European Union by means of a massive wall that has been constructed across the Alps. Laura and her sister Cecilia are involved in protests against the war while their father continues to profit from business with Arab dictators and their brother Phillip joins the army to "defend" the wall. Laura experiences the deteriorating situation in Berlin (food shortages, rioting in the streets) but still believes that she can carve out an idyllic life with the nature-loving Hans, while Cecilia hooks up with Konstantin, a member of a terrorist group. Years later, Cecilia has been arrested and Laura visits Hans in his mountain hut on the other side of the wall where he lives with an African refugee. After a violent confrontation with Konstantin, the father of her baby, Laura takes the heavily wounded Hans back to the wall to seek re-admittance. While the theatrical cut ends at this point, Kraume offers an alternative ending and an additional chapter in the bonus material included with the DVD. In the alternative version, Laura manages to take Hans back into "civilization"; we see them, two years later, back in Laura's family home. Hans has been equipped with bionic implants and Berlin seems to have returned to "normalcy," albeit with heavy security and retina scans at frequent checkpoints. As the credits roll, we hear Laura's voice:

> The Future. Something that most often is already happening around us before we expect it. Our future has already begun. But we can still change it today.

In spite of its heavy-handed symbolism (the neon sign in the terrorists' hideout that reads "Capitalism Kills Love"; the contrast between the affluent family in their grand villa and the empty shelves in the supermarkets), Kraume's film is a thoughtful meditation on how quickly the thin veneer of "civilization" in Germany might be broken. Rüdiger Suchsland observed that the protagonists' experience of the collapse of the (stifling) familiar order brings with it the opportunity for change and an alternative life.[36] This may be seen as politically naïve, given Germany's experience with political extremism from the Spartacus League to the Nazi brownshirts and the Red Army Faction, but it is nevertheless prescient given the wave of migration and the increase in politically motivated violence seen in Germany in recent years.

Thomas von Steinaecker's *Die Verteidigung des Paradieses* (The Defense of Paradise, 2016) is an excellent example of how the traditional SF themes of the apocalypse and the last human being have found acceptance in the "mainstream" literary market, gaining broad acclaim by publishers and reviewers.[37] Like Valerie Fritsch's *Winters Garten* (2015) and Oliver Kyr's *Ascheland* (2016),[38] von Steinaecker's work revels in beautiful sentences and evokes elegiac moods, but it appears to be addicted to the purple haze of a Wagnerian twilight of the gods. Shortlisted for the *Deutsche Buchpreis* in 2016, von Steinaecker follows his fifteen-year-old protagonist Heinz and a small group of survivors who have fled a poisoned and devastated Germany and who are trying to make a meager living in the mountains under a protective "shield." Heinz is determined to rescue the remnants of civilization from being lost forever; he collects words and writes the history of the last human being. When rumors speak of other survivors in a refugee camp somewhere in France, and their "shield" collapses, Heinz and his motley crew set out to find them.

On the one hand, *Die Verteidigung des Paradieses* can be read as an extreme version of Cormac McCarthy's postapocalyptic novel *The Road* (2006) with zombies, drones, AI pets, and public executions. On the other hand, it is a sustained reflection on the value of writing, of creating reality through the imagination. As Heinz records humanity's literary heritage (reminding the reader of the humans who memorize by heart precious literary works in *Fahrenheit 421*), we learn that Heinz is in fact not a human being at all but a machine. What this means is debatable; while a number of reviewers were baffled, others, like Christoph Schröder, praised the novel as "hochliterarisch" (high literature).[39] Obviously, this is code for "not the usual lowbrow fare from which von Steinaecker borrows his theme and tropes but then proceeds to create true art." Schröder enthuses thus:

> In *Die Verteidigung des Paradieses* art becomes a vital element—it keeps mankind going. And here the big questions arise: What makes us human? What keeps us human? Enough to eat? An undamaged body? Our dignity? Faith? That especially takes on a key role in the novel. God does not exist anymore, but the LORD does. Heinz believes in him. If, that is, he is capable of believing at all. The paradise that has to be defended in this brilliant novel is a place of opportunity. It is the last place where freedom is not only achievable but absolutely necessary: it is [in] one's own head, [in] the realm of limitless thought. The area that belongs to literature. And Thomas von Steinaecker moves into this realm in an astounding way.[40]

Oliver Jungen, writing in the *Frankfurter Allgemeine Zeitung*, was equally gushing in his defense of the novel:

> After a long period of gestation all of this culminates in this new opus magnum: epic in scope and filmic in style, it no more fears the great role models like Dante, Milton, Goethe, Kafka, or Ray Bradbury, Richard Matheson, Marlen Haushofer, or any of the apocalyptic comics and films. Nor, then, does it fear the big questions: What is man? What could he be? Is there a price for dignity?[41]

The question is whether a novel that ultimately goes nowhere but turns the apocalypse into "art" can sustain its original purpose—that of warning its readers about taking the wrong turn. Von Steinaecker refuses to explore the reasons for the catastrophe (climate change?) or engage with science and technology other than by filling his work with a mixture of human and posthuman actors. I would argue that the meditation on the question, "What is man?" loses its relevance if there is no future for humanity, and that the disaster becomes insignificant given the indifference of the survivors. While von Steinaecker skilfully extends the motif of the downfall of humanity familiar to audiences of the medieval *Nibelungen* epic and Richard Wagner's *Ring* cycle, he is not able to achieve a lasting impact in today's saturated market.

While von Steinaecker attempted, but ultimately failed, to find high art in the postapocalyptic novel, the television series *Acht Tage* (directed by Stefan Ruzowitzki and Michael Krummenacher, 2019) arguably tried and achieved the opposite. An asteroid is on collision course with Earth, and when all attempts to destroy it fail, people in Central Europe have eight days to come to terms with their probable extinction. This well-rehearsed theme, which was artfully imagined in Lars von Trier's *Melancholia* (2011), becomes a form of entertainment, a mild frisson for the audience, as various members of a family are either desperately trying to get out of Europe and fight for survival or fatalistically resigning themselves to dying. Reviewers were rightly savage about the series,[42] and in spite of an aggressive media campaign with fake news of an impending asteroid impact on the front pages of several German newspapers, it failed to convince audiences that a switch in perspective from energetic heroes trying to prevent the apocalypse to ordinary people desperately struggling to survive could tell us anything new about human nature.[43]

♦ ♦ ♦

Context is everything. While the dystopian and apocalyptic stories produced by German SF writers in the 1970s and 1980s reflected a collective concern about the buildup of nuclear weapons in Western Europe and the consequences of pollution, the fact that the predicted catastrophic nuclear war and environmental consequences have not come to pass (yet) have dulled audiences into a sense of security: they now consume the (admittedly still highly popular) tales of apocalyptic futures with some degree of equanimity if not blasé indifference. Even though they are teased by their neighbors for being overly fearful of nuclear energy and mobile phone masts, as well as for being overly sensitive to chemical pollutants ("ecochondriacs"), Germans are unlikely to turn into preppers and survivalists. On the other hand, the recent political successes of the Green Party (the so-called "Green wave"), the popularity of the climate protests, the energy transition program, and the large number of initiatives and research programs intended to avoid a catastrophic future indicate that the country, by and large, is well aware of such risks and is willing to tackle them.

The continued production of apocalyptic narratives, films, and television series now takes a certain amount of what was once perceived as catastrophic or apocalyptic for granted, and this is factored both into the balance sheets of Germany's companies and Germany's collective psyche. The most recent works of German SF that will be discussed in the following chapters routinely take the consequences of climate change and increased competition for scarce resources as a given, incorporating these dystopian elements into a broader message about an increasingly unpredictable future. That doesn't mean that corrosive pessimism has won over pragmatic optimism, though. As John Higgs has pointed out recently:

> Believing that we are all doomed makes everything so much easier, for you no longer have to work at creating something new. Recognizing that some people get off on the idea of apocalypse can provide a glimmer of hope. It raises the possibility that maybe we aren't doomed after all, and that maybe it is just a story that is in fashion at this point in history.[44]

11: Virtual Realities: Caught in the Matrix

SCIENCE FICTION HAS long served as a platform for exploring the limits of reality. The more disturbing one's experiences in real life, the more plausible it is to express one's confusion in writing. The atrocities of the Vietnam War and the growing drug culture in the 1960s certainly created a sense of "unreality"—with novels like Kurt Vonnegut's *Slaughterhouse 5* (1969) and pretty much the entire oeuvre of Philip K. Dick reflecting that generation's unease with the way trauma and doubts were swept under the carpet by a materialistic society.[1] While the cultural revolution of the late 1960s in West Germany had run into the buffers of political reality and the young generation retreated into countercultural milieus and radical subgroups, the politically engaged intellectual elites continued to challenge the capitalist system and its increasing flexibility in absorbing protest and criticism.[2] Their critique is cleverly delivered in Rainer Werner Fassbinder's made-for-television SF film *Welt am Draht* (World on a Wire, 1973), an adaptation of Daniel F. Galouye's novel *Simulacron-3* (1964). Although it was unavailable for a long time, a digitally restored version was presented in 2010 at the sixtieth Berlinale (Berlin International Film Festival) and it was subsequently shown to an even broader audience at the Museum of Modern Art in New York.

After his mentor Professor Vollmer, inventor of the Simulacron program, dies under mysterious circumstances, Fred Stiller becomes technical director of the *Institut für Kybernetik und Zukunftsforschung* (IKZ, Institute for Cybernetics and Futurology). Here, researchers are trying to model social behavior patterns and predict future trends as well as future demand for products and resources. Simulacron creates a simplified version of the real world, in which so-called "identity units" live within an artificial environment generated by the program. These identity units do not know that they are only artificial constructs, or that they can be deleted or reprogrammed at any time. The operators are able to transfer their consciousness into one of the identity units in order to enter this virtual reality.

Mysterious events cause Stiller to fear he is losing his mind. Staff members at the institute disappear, and nobody but him can remember them. During a car ride with Vollmer's daughter Eva, the view in front of him suddenly turns dark, as though the road ahead ends in nothingness.

Stiller suffers from headaches and dizzy spells, which he combats with alcohol and pills. The feeling of paranoia grows when the identity unit Einstein, who is aware of his or its artificial existence, succeeds in escaping from the simulated world by swapping his consciousness with that of one of the operators. When Stiller catches Einstein, he informs Stiller that he intends to break through to the next level, to the "real" world. Although Stiller can reverse this personality transfer, his belief in his own reality is deeply shaken.

Stiller's paranoia is justified: not only is Siskins, the corrupt executive director of the publically funded IKZ, in cahoots with industry representatives who demand that they be given access to the results of the project in order to gain a competitive advantage. Stiller himself becomes the victim of a smear campaign; he loses his job; and he can only narrowly escape several assassination attempts. He realizes that he himself is an "identity unit" in a computer program and that Eva Vollmer visits him from an "upper" world. One night, Eva tells him that he is the virtual but less unscrupulous copy of a Fred Stiller in real life and that he is due to be "turned off" the following day. When he attempts to tell his staff the truth, he is shot dead by security officers; however, he awakens in the "upper" world. Here he encounters the "real" Eva, who has swapped the consciousnesses of the two Stillers while they were connected.

From the outset, viewers are confronted with the question whether they can trust what they see. The first shot shows an access road to a modern office building, with some men in raincoats and hats standing in front. Two American cars from the early 1970s generate an alienation effect, since they were relatively rare in West Germany at that time. In the background we can see a government Mercedes-Benz 600 slowly approaching the building. When we look closer, we realize that the road surface is wet. This (and the raincoats) contradict the flickering effect of the air, which would either be generated by intense heat or, as the viewer realizes later, caused by glitches in the computer program.[3]

Equally puzzling for the viewer is the control room in the IKZ, which, with its reflecting walls and computer screens, resembles a hall of mirrors. Here, the operators monitor the behavior of ten thousand identity units in their programmed virtual reality. By means of a "contact link," an observer can see the simulated world through the eyes of one of the identity units, but the observer cannot act independently. To speak with the "contact unit," the operator's consciousness must be completely transferred into one of the identity units. However, this connection makes it possible for the contact unit, if it is aware of its situation, to switch to the "real world." In *Welt am Draht*, this method of consciousness transfer between the "real" and the simulated world is visualized by Stiller donning a helmet with numerous cables that connect to the computer. It is worth noting that this method to signal a transfer of consciousness was adopted by the directors of the *Matrix Trilogy* (1999–2003), where it is also an operator in the "real" world who retrieves the consciousness immersed in the Matrix. In Christopher Nolan's film *Inception* (2010), on the other hand, it is an elevator that connects the different levels of the subconscious and reality.

Of course, the motif of the visitor from another world, dimension, or time is not new. Based on the notion of heaven, Earth, and hell that exists in all early civilizations, with permeable boundaries that allow the visit of angels or devils, religions, myth, and literature have made extensive use of the idea of otherworldly visitors and travelers for millennia.[4] On the other hand, the idea that man is not only a creature but himself the creator of worlds and other beings is relatively recent. To give an example from *Welt am Draht*: at a press conference, Siskins and Stiller pompously explain how they have managed to create, populate, and control the simulated world. It is ironic, though, that such a virtual reality with controllable inhabitants is today not only thinkable but beginning to be technologically feasible. This in turn makes some people doubt whether their own reality is the only "real" one. After all, if a simulated or virtual world is becoming increasingly indistinguishable (or more desirable), then it is also possible that our own world is a construct.

Fassbinder had thought deeply about the relation between a simulated world, a supposedly more real but also simulated world, and the "real" world.[5] The key themes for Fassbinder, who fancied himself Bertolt Brecht's successor, were initially those of human emancipation and finding an appropriate position within late capitalism, but when it came to the visualization of his ideas, his film turned into a sophisticated meditation on the nature of reality, free will, and the limits of how far we can experience the physical world. For this inquiry, Fassbinder and Ballhaus borrowed extensively from apocalyptic imagery, classical myth, romantic idealism, and the dystopian scenarios of modern SF.

The initial reviews focused on the allegorical nature of the film, in which the characters, with a few exceptions, are manipulated like puppets (hence the title).[6] The disappearance of individuals as if they had never existed was interpreted as a reference to totalitarian systems such as National Socialism and Stalinism or the dubious practices of the intelligence services during the Cold War. But the exceptional quality and acuity of Fassbinder's vision has only recently been recognized. The film critic Tim Schleider wrote that "next to Fritz Lang's *Metropolis*, *Welt am Draht* is probably the best SF film ever made in Germany."[7] He justified this assessment by pointing out that Fassbinder had conceived of the film as a Gesamtkunstwerk, in which the many closeup shots and the way the actors delivered their lines all contributed to an atmosphere of artificiality ("eine Grundatmosphäre der Künstlichkeit"). Another reviewer described the film as "a meditation on the nature of the individual and social paranoia in the Information Age" that sought to explore the limits of human comprehension: are humans able to determine their role within history?[8] Who controls them? Who manipulates whom? By what means and to which purpose? Can the individual break the cycle of dependency in a world controlled by others? What is freedom? Arguably, these are the kind of existential questions that are as relevant today as they were in 1973.[9]

In America, too, there were those who saw *Welt am Draht* as a wrongly overlooked masterpiece. Anthony Scott, a film critic for the *New York Times*, gushed exuberantly:

> The clothes, the cars and the furniture are richly, even extravagantly, redolent of the Euro-70s, as is the anxious tremor of political and sexual unease that vibrates underneath the opulent surface. . . . The sheer audacity with which Fassbinder and his longtime cinematographer, Michael Ballhaus, move the camera, is nothing short of breathtaking. . . . The small screen can be very large for an imagination that knows no limits.[10]

There is no doubt that *Welt am Draht* has a special meaning in Germany, where it was broadcast on public television and where it made made political references at a time of increasing polarization between a small group of left-wing terrorists (the Red Army Faction) and the state. But the atmosphere that Fassbinder manages to conjure up in his film—the sense of permanent threat, the sense of permanent surveillance, and the perception of a fragmented reality—are experiences shared by many people across the world over recent decades.[11]

♦ ♦ ♦

Judging from recent German novels that depict virtual realities, the technological "progress" in the field of virtual and augmented realities has overtaken SF's wildest imaginations. The message is not one of triumph, though, as the ubiquitous availability of technologies to monitor, predict, and direct human behavior and their intrusion into our lives cause writers to come up with ever darker visions. In Benjamin Stein's novel *Replay* (2012), the *United Communications Company* (UCC) has developed a device that records everything an individual sees, hears, tastes, smells, and feels, and feeds it straight into the user's brain.[12] Ed Rosen, who is blind in one eye, has the device implanted and is delighted with the results. Soon the developers hit on a revolutionary idea: how about replaying the recording of these memories back via the sensory channels where they were originally recorded? Rosen can now choose to relive his favorite moments from the past, just like we would browse through a photo album, watch videos from our weddings, or listen again to our favorite bands at a festival, with the difference that these memories are indistinguishable from reality:

> I love what we created. I love the Uni-Com, and if I had to decide what I love most about this technological marvel, it would be this: every morning I wake up in paradise.[13]

While the device initially requires a surgical procedure, it is soon miniaturized and can be fitted easily. Users can access more functions—for example, "sharing" their memories with others via the UCC servers. The product is a great commercial success; eventually 95 percent of the population wear it; and "Neubürger" (new citizens) can be recognized by the blue light on their temples. As the guinea pig of the company, Rosen explores the possibilities opened up by the new technology—for example, swapping his own recorded memories and experiences with the perspective of another person, a highly addictive practice called "drifting."

The social consequences of the introduction of the Uni-Com are significant: in time, the makers are able to monitor and control the movements of the citizenry, thus becoming ever more powerful. UCC buys up all media companies and is able to feed the content straight into people's heads. The small minority of people who refuse to have the devices fitted are called the "anonyms" and are forced to live in walled-off shanty towns. As the company has access to the vast amounts of private memories that it stores on its servers, it can manipulate the data and exert enormous influence. It claims to be led by high ethical standards and uses a "watermark," a symbol of Pan's hoof in the recording, to signal that a recording is being played, but it transpires that users can never really go offline (the implications of this are never made clear but suggest that more and more people end up living in a virtual world within a memory loop). Rosen has created for himself an escapist dreamworld that he is loath to leave.[14] He endlessly replays his favorite sexual encounters from different perspectives, and he is unable to break free from his addiction. In a rare moment of clarity, he realizes that his life is on repeat: "Eigentlich bin ich längst tot" (Actually, I've been long dead, 169).

The central themes of total transparency and the ultimate ownership of private data obviously reference current political debates as technology companies collect and sell personal data for profit or political manipulation. Dave Egger's *The Circle* (2013) made his warning explicit by showing how the protagonist Mae Holland's naïve trust in total transparency is exploited by the sinister machinations of the organization in pursuit of power and influence. Benjamin Stein offers a more sophisticated narrative: his book forces readers to work out for themselves what is wrong with the future presented here. It ironically plays on the utopian moment when the blind person is given sight, only for that miraculous moment to be subverted into a dystopian nightmare that leaves the individual more helpless than before. The opportunity for the individual to swap a mundane existence for ideal moments satirizes media depictions of the perfect life as well as our gullability to literally buy into ever more ingenious and invasive devices to hold on to that perfect moment, which of course is the very point in Goethe's play in which Mephistopheles wins Faust's soul. Stein compels us to acknowledge this "devil's bargain" without denying the fascination that comes with our new technological capabilities: Whether we are able to alter the direction of travel against the invested interests of companies that offer their services free of charge but expect an essential part of ourselves in return will depend on the choices we make today.

♦ ♦ ♦

The German crime novelist Tom Hillenbrand uses the theme of virtual reality in his two most recent thrillers. In *Drohnenland* (Drone State, 2014),[15] Kommissar Art van der Westerhuizen investigates a murder in Brussels in the near future with the help of "Terry" (Tereisias), the police computer/AI, and the forensic expert Ava Bittman. They use a technique called "Spiegelung" (mirroring) to reconstruct a crime scene. For this, they require and are granted access to all available information from satellite images to drone surveillance and closed-circuit television (CCTV) cameras. The computer then compiles and extrapolates the data and allows the detective not only to zoom in and out but also to rewind in order to explore the movements of any potential suspects prior to the time of the crime. While this use of technology is no longer that farfetched, the secret service also has another tool at its disposal: in "Mirrorspace," an agent can insert his or her consciousness into a real-time situation as a "ghost," thus being able to observe activities as they are taking place.

While the plot blends the well-known tropes of films noir and detective novels to make sure that the reader is entertained, the introduction of SF elements elevates the book so that it gains political relevance. Hillenbrand asks searching questions about the balance between privacy and surveillance as well as the seemingly unstoppable increase in the use of technology in an effort to stem the tide of terrorist acts in Europe. While reviewers praised the author for his acute reading of the Zeitgeist,[16] Hillenbrand himself referred to Germany's particular expertise in surveillance and pointed out that the Stasi in the GDR had already developed sophisticated methods of profiling. What was new, he added, was that by combining the various data streams with sophisticated computer programs, it will soon be possible to predict who might commit a crime, in which location, and at what time:

The same principle could be applied to those who pose a threat as soon as one has enough data. A good algorithm could analyze movement patterns, communication, and other activities of potential terrorists in the EU. The system would work autonomously, and human investigators would only be alerted when an Islamist acts suspiciously. To build such a system is not witchcraft. We have the technology, even if many are not aware of it. Our hubris makes us believe that humans are complex and that therefore our actions unpredictable. The opposite is true.[17]

In *Hologrammatica*, Hillenbrand's most recent "thriller," the author combines virtual reality and artificial intelligence even further.[18] At the end of the twenty-first century, climate change has led to mass migration; new technologies like the "Holonet" (a system that allows projectors to give individuals, buildings, and so on any desired appearance) and "Mind Uploading" (a process by which individuals can create one or more "copies" of themselves and download them into other bodies) allow people to live behind a façade that only detectives equipped with special scanners can see through. The "Quästor" Galahad Singh, who specializes in finding lost persons, accepts the job of locating the computer expert Juliette Perotte, who has developed the technique of "uploading" digital brains. Interestingly, in this particular future, privacy is given a lot more emphasis, and strict laws ensure that data is treated with great care:

> In the old days, a computer would have found this out in no time. Back then, mankind thought that one couldn't have enough data. Moreover, people found it advantageous, for the benefit of society and the economy, to make all data available and connect it in every possible way. Since Turing, however, everything that one does not absolutely need to hold on to is erased or heavily encrypted.[19]

Apparently, humans have decided to act in this respect, and while they were unable to stop global warming (in the year 2088 Europe has lost a large proportion of its population while the *Sibtrek*—the migration to cooler Siberia—has led to expansion there), they have enacted both strict privacy laws and laws against the use of artificial intelligence. Singh's character, refreshingly gay and unconventional, dates an agent of the *United Nations Agency for the Non-Proliferation of Artificial Intelligence* (UNANPAI) and uncovers a sinister plot (the *Æther* Project), apparently masterminded by an AI, that seeks to prevent an even more catastrophic climate change by causing a cull of the human population.

While this plot line is perhaps too sensational and farfetched, it is the widespread use of holographic technology as a metaphor for the artificiality of human life in the here and now that is particularly impressive. As Galahad views the London panorama from his flat, both with and without the device that strips the holographic layer of the cityscape, the reader can experience a moment of epiphany with the protagonist:

> It is already getting dark. I open the balcony door and step outside. From up here you can't look out over all of London but at least over a large part of Camden and Regent's Park. Without averting my gaze from the city panorama, I hunt around in the pocket of my jacket and pull out Perotte's Level 1 Stripper. I put it on. The city is still there but now it looks different. Once white buildings now have the color of old bones, and brick facades look crumblier and more soot stained. It seems as if someone has put a color filter over London, toning down the reds and greens. This here is unvarnished reality. Is that really so? Presumably reality is too grand a word. Ultimately, everything is a question of perspective.[20]

Sonja Stöhr has rightly observed that holograms have become the dominant technology in this particular vision of the future. Its use exudes a definitive fin-de-siècle atmosphere, one of ubiquitous pretense and vanity.[21] Coming back into "naked space" is painful for someone who has grown up in the 2050s, just as it is painful for the current "millenial" generation to live without Wi-Fi access.

German SF's visions of virtual reality oscillate between an acknowledgement of the fascination of a new technology and its potential for expanding our horizons and enriching of our lives, on the one hand, and a dystopian expectation that it will ultimately prove to be limiting and, at worst, steal our souls, on the other.[22] The fact that the theme is so closely linked to current debates about the role and impact of emerging technologies and their reception within a European tradition that is much more skeptical about their benefit in the context of a capitalist market model makes the depiction of virtual reality discussed in this chapter a concrete dystopia. At the same time, the discourse around the ethical and philosophical implications of multiple realities—as these are presently considered in fields as disparate as medicine, political science, and art—found a natural home within the realm of SF.

12: Alternative Histories: Into the Heart of Darkness

ALTERNATIVE HISTORIES ARE well established in Anglo-American literature—for example, Philip Dick's *The Man in the High Castle* (1962), Keith Roberts's *Pavane* (1968), Richard Harris's *Fatherland* (1992), or Kim Stanley Robinson's *The Years of Rice and Salt* (2002)[1]—but less so in German literature, where the division between high and popular culture has been maintained far longer (cf. chapter 4) and where the need for an alternative history has tended to concentrate on and emanate from the traumatic experience of the Third Reich.[2] It wasn't until Carl Amery's *Das Königsprojekt* (1974)—a time travel story that sees the Catholic Church attempt to change history in its favor—that German writers discovered the potential of alternative history fiction for cultural criticism.[3] In this chapter I explore three examples of extraordinary quality and complexity that haven't (yet) been translated into English.

Christian Kracht is well-known for his novels *Faserland* (Land of Fibers, 1995) and *1979* (2001). *Ich werde hier sein im Sonnenschein und im Schatten* (I Will Be Here in Sunshine and Shadows, 2008),[4] the third novel by this globe-trotting Swiss writer,[5] starts with a simple yet fundamental retrospective change to world history: Lenin never left Switzerland in 1917 but stayed on and, together with Kropotkin and Bakunin, established a Swiss Soviet Republic. In the year 2013, this state has been engaged in almost one hundred years of war with fascist Germany and Britain. Warfare has not advanced much beyond World War I airships, bombs, and gas, but it is nevertheless conducted with fanatic efficiency. To hold its own, the Swiss Soviet Republic has resorted to colonizing the greater part of Africa, spreading its unique blend of efficiency and communist ideology, and recruiting there its cannon fodder (and, increasingly, its officers) for the eternal war. The unnamed narrator is a black African stranger in a strange land, a political commissar charged by the Swiss supreme soviet with the capture of Oberst Brazhinsky, an officer gone rogue.

The commissar encounters a war-torn, desolate country full of minefields and desperate survivors, including a mysterious dwarf named Uriel (an allusion to the archangel of the apocrypha) who rescues him from certain death. Eventually, he reaches the gigantic Alpine Réduit, a vast underground shelter below the Alps that has proven impenetrable for the

German bombs. Here Brazhinsky holds a position of mysterious influence much like that of Mr. Kurtz in Josef Conrad's *Heart of Darkness* (1899) or Colonel Kurtz in Francis Coppola's film *Apocalypse Now* (1979). In spite of moments of sanity when he looks after the wounded and practices a newly developed "Rauchsprache" (smoke language) that enables him to read his enemies' minds and force his will on them, Brazhinsky eventually goes mad, blinds himself, and dies miserably. The commissar escapes a coordinated attack on the Réduit by German airships and slowly makes his way back to his native Malawi, shedding on the way the ideological indoctrination of his youth. As the remnants of Swiss colonial power disappear under the returning jungle, the ex-commissar disappears into the African vastness.

Ich werde hier sein im Sonnenschein und im Schatten is an extremely rich novel, a fact attested to by countless reviewers for the German-speaking press. I will touch briefly on three aspects that illustrate its complexity and currency: the curious case of Swiss colonialism; the commissar's encounter with Oberst Brazhinsky; and the Réduit as a metaphor for Western moral decay. The reader slowly gathers clues that explain how the Swiss Soviet Republic managed to colonize Africa: Swiss workers, engineers, scientists, and soldiers embarked on a massive infrastructure program to build roads, schools, hospitals, and universities. The anonymous commissar was born near the border of Mozambique and attended a Swiss military academy where he has not only been convinced of the superiority of the white colonizers but encouraged to emulate them to such an extent that he is, at the beginning of the novel, a much more fervent believer in the Swiss Soviet cause than Switzerland's original inhabitants. The commissar speaks about "unser Weg" (our way, 34), and he utters phrases like "die Stärke der SSR war ihre Menschlichkeit" (the strength of the Swiss Soviet Republic was its humaneness, 20). He is proud of "unsere Revolution" (our revolution, 49), and he stoically ignores the taunts of lower-ranking white soldiers. It takes a major shock for the commissar to realize that the utopian dream of a perfect socialist world was simply a vehicle for domination, and that he needs to sever his allegiance to a dead ideology. It is his encounter with Brazhinsky that provides this shock. He begins to question his orders, to doubt whether he and the Swiss are indeed brothers. He also begins to reflect on his past as a black officer ordering black soldiers to go over the top and into certain death, while the white officers and soldiers remained behind.

Nothing makes sense in the Réduit. Brazhinsky, who brutally murdered other soldiers sent out to arrest him, works as a healer, treating wounded soldiers. On his walls he has dozens of Nicholas Roerich's "visionary" paintings depicting an idealized idyllic mountain world that no longer exists. The commissar takes "magic mushrooms" to enable him to learn the "new language" that is supposed to create empathetic understanding and to manipulate the enemy. Brazhinsky admits that all the talk about last ditch "Wunderwaffen" (miracle weapons) is propaganda, that the remnants of the great Swiss Soviet Republic can't defend themselves. In their final encounter he denies that he is a counterrevolutionary:

> Come on, stop it. Counterrevolution, heresy, that's childish silliness. Educate yourself. You are a slave, Commissar, don't you realize that? You are a Swiss slave; born, drilled, and manufactured.[6]

By using the image of the Réduit, Kracht is alluding to the complex and ambiguous role of Switzerland in World War II. Never occupied, its economy, society, and culture were nonetheless severely and lastingly affected. The country aided the Nazis by stopping Jewish refugees from Germany at its borders, and by turning Jewish-owned gold into hard currency. The slogan of "Geistige Landesverteidigung" (intellectual defense of the nation) meant the silencing of dissenters. When the Swiss army was mobilized on September 2, 1939, elaborate strategies were put in place should Nazi Germany attack. Fortifications were built at Sargans, Saint-Maurice, and Gotthard, and in the spring of 1940 detailed plans were produced for the Réduit National, a giant refuge that would allow the Swiss to defend themselves to the end. Kracht explores the Réduit not only as a repository of Swiss identity but also as a metaphor for moral and spiritual decay (*Ausgehöhltheit* [the state of being hollowed out]) as its inhabitants succumb to introspection, delusion, drugs, and disease. The end cannot come soon enough for this dead end of history, and when it comes, Kracht gives it the full Technicolor treatment, so to speak:

> Stepping onto the balcony, I saw the sublime image of dozens of German airships filling the sky over my head. And while the sun set in orange and red with a wonderful glow before the round glass lenses of the gas mask, and while our search lights pierced through the evening sky like white needles, the infernal and monstrous bombardment of the redoute began anew.[7]

As for the black commissar, he turns his back on the imploding utopian dream:

> I threw away my heavy soldiers' coat and Brazinsky's sick lessons, and no longer used the smoke language. . . . It was the language of the white people, an idiom of war, and I didn't need it.[8]

Literary critics in Germany had a difficult time with Kracht's novel. It wasn't until Dietmar Dath's review that the German feuilleton realized that Christian Kracht had once again wrong-footed the literary establishment.[9]

Dath correctly identifies the blind spot Germany's professional critics have when it comes to the popular, and that Kracht's "[i]n sich ruhender Größenwahn" (serene megalomania) caused them to ignore the most obvious question that needed to be asked—namely, why does Kracht need the victory of Bolshevism in Switzerland? Dath supplies the answer himself: in his view, communism kept the capitalists honest. Following the collapse of communism, the world has turned into a madhouse, a fact that both fascinates and appals a writer with a global outlook.

It is no surprise that critics have such problems with Christian Kracht, who is notorious for his tongue-in-cheek comments on his own work.[10] In an interview broadcast by the ARD, the premier German public television channel, Kracht suggested that the Swiss were both colonizers and colonized with respect to their neighbor Germany:

> After all, of course, Switzerland today is controlled by Germans—completely. There we have German waiters, German doctors, the Germans do all the work, the work the Swiss do not want to do any more, and naturally we the Swiss find that somewhat suspect.[11]

In the same interview, he ambiguously talked about the "Aushöhlung der Schweiz" (the hollowing out of Switzerland), which can refer to the building of tunnels under the Alps but also to the political and moral vacuum at its center. With his typically deadpan statement, "Die Ästhetik der Moderne ist ein Irrtum" (the aesthetics of modernity is a misconception), he has provided scholars and critics with material for years to come. It is interesting to note that, as befits a master storyteller, Kracht's focus remains on the use of language. In the Swiss Soviet Republic of *Ich werde hier sein im Sonnenschein und im Schatten*, the written language has been replaced by oral communication. The commissar's old-fashioned notebook is seen as an anachronism; only the dwarf Uriel still reads a book, the Bible. In a different interview Kracht confirmed:

> Language, in and of itself, is the theme of the novel: language as a weapon, language as a virus and as a symptom of a world full of drugs, full of hallucinations. Nothing is as it seems. . . . In the novel different languages and different cultures come together in a world ravaged by war. People gang up or fight each other; they literally talk past each other.[12]

Ich werde hier sein im Sonnenschein und im Schatten has disturbing qualities. It gets uneasily close to our seemingly endless proxy wars and pursuits of mad persons hidden in deep caves under mountains. It uses estrangement to remind us of the power of the failed socialist dream but also of the horror of its consequences. Is there any possibility of redemption for imperialists? Does neutrality keep your conscience clear? Kracht seems to say that even our best intentions and the proverbial Swiss perfectionism cannot ward off the corroding effects of totalitarianism. If Josef Conrad's *Heart of Darkness* was a criticism of the ideology of imperialism, Christian Kracht's *Ich werde hier sein im Sonnenschein und im Schatten* can be read as a criticism of the imperialist nature of ideology and as an imaginative engagement with the psychology of the colonized mind. Kracht does not deny his commissar dignity and culture, but in the end these European attributes are discarded. The dream of a world without racism is as ephemeral as snow in Africa.

In spite of the brooding atmosphere, the book has a utopian edge. Kracht uses the means of estrangement inherent in alternative histories to attain the freedom that allows him to comment on questions having to do with the postcolonial mentality, the danger of ideological control inherent in utopian euphoria, and the deep-seated mindset of superiority—the root cause of inequality and war that is still prevalent in our society. By referencing Conrad and Coppola, he cleverly links his work with two influential instances of cultural critique, whether of the original hubris of Western colonialism or of American imperialism. His fiction, however, targets the much more complex question of what happens when the colonizers are also the colonized (a question tackled by Kurd Laßwitz more than a century earlier, but now a highly topical reflection on global migration), as well as the question of the extent to which identity can be maintained and/or created in such a world. Through the protagonist's journey from Swiss ice to African heat, from seclusion to open spaces, from endless war to peace, Kracht constructs a utopian space in which the arrogance of people who claim to know what is good for the rest is questioned while the sense of solidarity and empathy that neoconservatives and neoliberals lack is retained.

◆ ◆ ◆

Wolfgang Jeschke's novel *Das Cusanus-Spiel* (2005) is a sophisticated exploration of the outer limits of SF, mixing alternative history, time travel, and parallel world narratives, and combining the very latest scientific theories on the nature of time and space with medieval religious philosophy.[13] Like Christian Kracht, Jeschke is well aware of the alternative history tradition: in the acknowledgements he cites Jack Finney's *Time and Again* (1970), Arkadi and Boris Strugatzki's *Hard to be a God* (1964), and, specifically, Carl Amery's *Das Königsprojekt*. In 2052, climate change has become harsh reality: southern Europe is covered by sand blown across the Mediterranean from the Sahara; the migrating masses from North Africa are forcibly kept away from "Fortress Europe," and neo-Nazis hunt those who slip through the net. Due to global warming the sea levels are rising steadily: while huge dams have been built along the coastlines of Europe, large areas of the poor countries of Asia are flooded, leading to yet more migration. The European Union has disintegrated. Following the explosion of a French nuclear reactor in 2028, large parts of central Europe have been radioactively contaminated and are now virtually uninhabitable. As a result of the radiation, species extinction has been accelerated by the rapid spread of genetically mutated plants.

In this bleak future, the young Italian botanist Domenica Ligrina finds a job at the Instituto pontificale della Rinascita della Creazione di Dio (Pontifical Institute of the Rebirth of the Creation of God), a scientific department of the Vatican. Scientists there have developed a process that allows them to send agents into the past to collect genetically intact plants, which will be used to repair the damage in the present. After her initial training, Domenica travels through contaminated Germany. In the chapter titled *The Inner Circle of Hell* Jeschke confronts the reader with the reality of the quarantined world, where decades of decontamination work have left a wasteland:

> I looked out of the window in our compartment. The land was literally ravaged, its green skin shaved off down to the scree of the Rheinish gravel layer. Giant bulldozers pushed the soil in front of them like brown waves. Belching black diesel smoke straight up into the air above them, they hoisted the soil onto giant lorries which in turn dumped it into cube-shaped concrete containers. These were sealed and transported across France to the coast, where the contaminated soil was used to build up the new Europadam.[14]

Domenica is sent back to the year 1451, where she collects hundreds of plant seeds, but she is arrested in Cologne. She is accused of heresy, of dealing with the devil, and she is eventually tried as a witch. In desperation, Domenica writes a series of letters from her prison cell to the German cardinal Nicholas of Cusa (a.k.a. Cusanus, 1401–64), of whom she knows that he traveled via Cologne from 1451 to 1452. This constitutes an "illegal" intervention in history, and a series of breaks in the timeline occur, which, in turn, open a series of parallel worlds. In a first timeline Cusanus rides on, and Domenica is burned in public (74). In a second timeline Cusanus returns to Cologne to talk to her (188–201); she is released and can return to her own time. In a third variant the letters have disappeared, but Cusanus hears a rough summary of them and decides to ask the archbishop of Cologne for a postponement (467). In each case Cusanus learns something about the future, as Domenica's letters reveal details of his cosmological and scientific work that, at this point in time, exist only in his head.

As a result of these messages from the future, an alternative course of history is created that the omniscient narrator describes as the "Cusanian acceleration." This (accelerated) history of the last five hundred years is meticulously described by the omniscient narrator (337), beginning with a letter from Cusanus to Pope Nicholas V, in which the former proposes the creation of a scientific academy at the Holy See that would deal specifically with unusual natural phenomena and the revival of a humanistic heritage. In this science-friendly atmosphere a new type of engine, the "Brennkreisel" (literally a burning spinning top, 338), is invented as early as 1478; it revolutionizes trade and transport. Two centuries later, Gottfried Leibniz invents the first functioning calculator. By 1682, the West has secured its access to the oil wells in the Middle East, but, because of the intense use of fossil fuels, sea levels already begin to rise in 1825. The first airship crosses the Atlantic in the mid-eighteenth century. In 1908 a "radiation sickness" is discovered near nuclear power plants. Winston Churchill is celebrated in 1918 as the unifier of Europe, and in 1923 Hitler and Ludendorff are killed when their coup attempt fails. In the first half of the twentieth century a further development of the embankments against the rising sea levels is agreed on, and in 1945 President Charles de Gaulle declares that Europe must become an "impregnable fortress."

At this point (at the latest) the reader begins to realize that Domenica's reality, which one has until then assumed to be a straightforward extrapolation of our own reality into the future, is in fact one of the parallel worlds that has arisen because of her intervention. In fact, there are more and more clues in the text that the various timelines have intertwined, that history itself has become porous. Despite all this, or maybe because the scientists running the project believe that unsustainable timelines will be "brushed out" anyway, Domenica is allowed a second trip into the past, this time with the objective of preventing the death of her father, who was killed in 2039 in a terrorist attack. In 2039 she meets herself as a young girl, thus causing a time paradox that completely throws her out of the "reality" of her own time. The encounter generates an "oscillation." After seeing (though not recognizing) her future self, Domenica proves to be highly sensitive to the multiplicity of worlds. Thus, ever since her return from the Middle Ages, she can't shake off the feeling that her "shadow" sister—the one who had sacrificed herself for her on the pyre in one of the timelines—walks beside her:

> She had found a refuge and a haven in me, in my very self which she had saved by taking the terrible alternative on herself so that I could reach the shores of a world where I wasn't condemned to burn as a witch. Only, where was I living? In the world from which I had once come, or had I wandered into an alternative world?[15]

As the attempt to save her father has several possible outcomes, the timelines turn into an inextricable knot. The scientists in Amsterdam take this calmly. According to their theories, time has an organic nature. Like a self-optimizing computer program, it will erase timelines that cannot stabilize themselves (496). Jeschke skillfully references Stephen Hawking's theory of time, Hugh Everett's super string theory, and quantum cosmology. To this mix he adds his own fantastic variant—the "Solitone" (496). These waves run from the beginning to the end of time, then change their direction and move back toward the past. Time travelers can "surf" these waves without having to understand the process: "Genau besehen sind wir in der Rolle von Hunden, die es gelernt haben, mit der U-Bahn zu fahren" (Looked at precisely, we are in the role of dogs that have learned how to travel with the subway, 310). This "surfing in time" is represented in the novel quite poetically:

> The Solitons had moved into the direction of the past. It had rolled down from the future, had touched us with its universe-destroying power, but so softly that we could sense its presence only indirectly. It had flowed around the membranes of our reality and made them permeable for a moment. It had flowed through us, as the physicists maintained, since it crossed through all dimensions, the unfolded ones as well as those that are rolled up in Planck space—however many that may be.[16]

In addition, there are entities that are interested in an undisturbed flow of history. These beings, at once angelic and human, become involved in the fate of "stranded" time travelers like Domenica. Lost and alone, her ghostlike self finds a resting place in "Highgate":

> Highgate stood . . . at the extreme end of time, where the Solitons turned around to plummet back into the past. On the planet there were so-called chronotopes where the flow of time was held up or even completely halted. There were areas where, according to reports, the sun had not set for years but rather had moved to and fro on an erratic course. Occasionally, it had stopped indecisively, its light bathing the land in a honey-colored haze [and] covering the rocks with a brown glaze, where nature paused in dreamy stillness.[17]

Like H. G. Wells in *The Time Machine* (1894), Cixin Liu in *The Three Body Problem* (2010), and David Mitchell in *The Bone Clocks* (2014), in such passages Jeschke romanticizes the end of time and the process of time travel itself, bringing categories such as wonder and grandeur into the mix. Sober scientists—and mainstream writers—rarely allow for these contemplative moments, but in SF they have been fundamental since its beginning. For the reader this contradiction—on the one hand, the seemingly plausible scientific explanation of unprecedented events, on the other hand Jeschke's irrepressible storytelling skill—forms part of the aesthetic experience, one that Kurd Laßwitz described in 1895 in his essay *Über Zukunftsträume* as the necessary and appropriate stance in the face of the rapid development of modern science.

With *Das Cusanus-Spiel* Wolfgang Jeschke introduces new aspects into the tradition of alternative history fictions. There is the confrontation of two imaginary worlds: on the one hand, there is the transition from the Middle Ages to the Renaissance, during which Cusanus, far ahead of his time, develops his theory of the coexistence of the real and the possible (the *docta ignorantia*). On the other hand, we have the world at the middle of the twenty-first century, a point in time when human intervention in the natural world can only be repaired by traveling back to this supposedly "dark" time. In a further step, Jeschke integrates this juxtaposition of the real and the possible into the plot—for example, in the description of the consequences of the nuclear accident that has turned survivors into genetic cripples (433). The confidence with which the author seamlessly integrates highly complex quantum physics into his fantastic story is certainly impressive, particularly as the fate of his characters always takes precedence over any boyish enthusiasm for technology. The reader suffers with Domenica and participates in her gradual dissolution in time. Jeschke's suggestion that there are people who can somehow "feel" alternative timelines is of course not so very far from everyday experience anymore, particularly in an age accustomed to virtual realities. In addition, the experience of a fragmented personality resonates with our experience of a fragmented world (and the scientific debate about the "multiverse").[18] Although the notion that the world could disintegrate into different "realities" whenever we make a decision is initially confusing, it also opens up endless narrative possibilities that appear particularly fascinating in times of crisis. Given the dystopian reality of her world, Domenica does not have a problem with the possibility that her actions in the past might cause history to take a different course:

> Perhaps a better one. A world without the delusionary fear of witchcraft. A brighter, a more reasonable world that is more open to the sciences. Perhaps it could be good enough to be admitted into the corpus of the multiverse.[19]

♦ ♦ ♦

Andreas Eschbach's recent *NSA—Nationales Sicherheitsamt* (Office for National Security, 2018) uses the alternative history approach to horrifying effect: he envisions an alternative world in which Sir Charles Babbage actually completed his "Analytical Engine" (a general purpose computer) with the financial help of the mathematician Ada Lovelace (the daughter of Lord Byron), and thus made possible the development of a programmable computer and all the applications of information technology decades before it was in fact made possible in reality.[20] Eschbach imagines that the National Socialists in Germany seize on the potential of the technology by using appropriately written algorithms to predict human behavior. The totalitarian regime employs the technology to root out any potential opponents and ultimately win World War II. While the dystopian idea of an alternative history showing Nazi Germany winning the war is by no means new, the detailed description of the coercive power available through the control of data produces a chilling warning in the context of present-day debates about data privacy.

Eschbach writes with ease about computer technology, software, and hardware, having studied information technology and having worked as a software development consultant before becoming a full-time writer. He transplants the technology we possess today into the time of the Third Reich, ingeniously creating verisimilitude by retrospectively inventing German terms for what we have become accustomed to as an Anglophone domain. Thus, computers are "Komputers"; servers are "Datensilos" (data silos); the World Wide Web is the "Weltnetz" (world net); email is "elektronische Post" (electronic mail); a password is a "Parole" (watchword); cell phones are "Votels" or "Volkstelefone" (people telephones); programmers are "Programmstrickerinnen" (program knitters [women are deemed particularly suited to "knitting" code]); and so on. With cash abolished after World War I, people use their phones to make payments. They discuss their views on the "Deutsches Forum" (the German Forum), the only social network.[21]

The *Nationales Sicherheitsamt* (the national security office) in Weimar is a remnant of the "Kaiserliche Komputer-Kontrollamt" (the imperial computer auditing office, 9), which has lost some of its power as the German patents for "Komputers" were lost after World War I, thereby allowing the British to catch up (they were still using mechanical analytical engines until then).[22] But the NSA (its motto is *Scientia Potentia Est*—knowledge is power) has a trump card up its sleeve to survive in the cutthroat atmosphere of Nazi Germany. In a chilling scene at the outset of the novel, the operators proudly showcase their ability to a skeptical Heinrich Himmler, the head of the Gestapo (secret state police); he wants to shut them down. They sift through data sets in real time using various search parameters in order to pinpoint dissenters and Jews in occupied Holland. They link data about registered citizens, size of accommodation, utility bills, purchase records, calory consumption versus ration card allocation, and thus determine that a particular family shows unusual patterns. Officers are dispatched to an address in Amsterdam and arrest the Frank family, including their daughter Anne, who had been in hiding but who are now dispatched to Auschwitz (40–41). As though this scene weren't distressing enough, Eschbach rams home his point that nobody is safe in this alternative world when he lets Himmler crow:

> I must admit that I came here with reservations. . . . I expected to find a useless remnant of that miserable republic that would have engineered the final downfall of the German people if the Führer had not appeared on the scene at the crucial moment. However, gentlemen, you have been able to convince me. I see now that you are also fighting on a front that is as important as that in the field of battle. Indeed, it seems to me that the cruel and keen edge of data surpasses that of steel by far. What I have seen here today reassures me that from now on no one will be safe from us—no one and nowhere. Gentlemen, you are contributing to the establishment of an empire in which divergent and harmful ways of thinking simply do not exist anymore. Our power will be absolute, to an unprecedented degree.[23]

For many readers, Eschbach will have overdone it in this passage by making Himmler gloat like the evil villain in an early Bond movie in order to amplify his warning about the risk of total surveillance and the opportunity for the unscrupulous use of this power. This will seem particularly so if we remember Vibeke Petersen's observation that it makes a big difference whether such a scene is written by an American or or a German (cf. chapter 5). And yet, the awful truth that "the cruel and keen edge of data" can exceed that of weapons made of steel may deserve such a blunt message.[24]

The narrative follows the fate of two operators in the Nationales Sicherheitsamt—the programmer Helene Bodenkamp and the analyst Eugen Lettke, both loyal followers of the Nazi ideology. Bodenkamp systematically develops her coding skills as an act of emancipation and experiences her newfound confidence with joy, even when one of her programs identifies the Scholl siblings as the senders of anonymous letters that challenge the system. However, she begins to question the morals and ethics of the National Socialist regime when her Jewish friend Ruth Melzer gets deported and her urbane, freethinking uncle is sent to a concentration camp. She falls in love with a young deserter, and she uses her skills to protect him. Lettke, on the other hand, has no redeeming features. He deviously exploits Bodenkamp's hacking skills to locate and discover the weaknesses of a group of people who had humiliated him as an adolescent.

Both get drawn into the sinister machinations of the system: Lettke is responsible for collecting information about US electronic networks and finding their weaknesses, as well as spreading misinformation and hate against Jews on American social networks (208). He stumbles across records of a meeting of scientists at Berkeley discussing a nuclear bomb (it turns out that these American scientists decided it wouldn't work but imprudently kept their notes on a server), and he passes on his discovery. Hitler then coerces German physicists—including Walter Bothe, Werner Heisenberg, Otto Hahn, and Carl Friedrich von Weizsäcker—to build the "Wunderwaffe" (miracle weapon), declaring that the discovery was "Vorsehung" (providence, 623). When German atom bombs fall on London and Moscow, the United States is forced to sign a peace treaty and the Third Reich rules supreme in Europe. Bodenkamp, whose father is a surgeon and supporter of "race hygiene," is courted by the vile Ludolf von Argensleben who holds a high but secret role in the regime. She attempts to flee but is caught, since the Nazis have developed a form of AI (a "neuronenartiges Netzwerk " [neuron-like network], 719). Bodenkamp and Lettke (who has also fallen out of favor) are both lobotomized by Dr. Mengele. The only hope for the rest of the world lies in a post Bodenkamp left online saying that she had made a copy of the plans for the nuclear bomb.

Marketed as a "thriller," Eschbach's novel was a bestseller in 2018. In spite of its topicality (big data, the NSA scandal in Germany, hate speech on the internet, fake news, the rise of the right-wing populist party Alternative für Deutschland), not a single book reviewer in the German national press was willing to engage with the novel.[25] This suggests a continuing "Berührungsangst" (fear of contamination) with SF, particularly of a type that eschews stylistic flourishes in favor of a strong political statement.[26] The only serious mention in the German press came in the form of an op-ed article from Katharina Nocun, a net activist, a former member of the protransparency *Piratenpartei* (Pirate Party), and an author of a book on data security.[27] Nocun argues that Eschbach's dark vision is less farfetched than we may wish to think, and that social media, the "internet of things," face recognition, and the unchecked storing of personal data can provide a perfect tool for repression not only in authoritarian regimes but also in democratic states that do not defend themselves against the undermining of privacy rights and the rise of right-wing populism.[28]

Eschbach's alternative history succeeds in creating a completely believable world by backdating and injecting our current technological abilities into the totally familiar (though also alien and repugnant) context of Germany's past. Here we have characters thinking and acting as "normal Germans," and experiencing the inescapable logic of their own enslavement in which, ironically, they played a willing part. Like Christian Kracht and Wolfgang Jeschke, Eschbach creates a plausible "what if?" scenario that engages with the here and now. In an interview with German news magazine *Der Spiegel*, he reflected more generally on the tendency of SF to imagine dystopian futures. Its purpose, he stated, was to prevent a particular development of the future from happening. And to say: listen, people, if we continue to do this, it will have these consequences. Do we want that? . . . They are appeals to the readers to take a different direction.[29]

As such, SF was similar to politics in that both asked questions about humanity's future. When challenged that fictional dystopias were not exactly successful in preventing people from making mistakes, he conceded: "It's true, unfortunately; novels do not change the way of the world, they can only comment upon it."

13: Big Brother Is Watching Us: Who Is Watching Big Brother?

THE THEME OF ubiquitous surveillance is a staple of dystopian SF and it holds a special significance in Germany where the history of eavesdropping and covert observation employed by the Gestapo and the Stasi has led to the right to privacy enshrined in the *Grundgesetz* (Basic Law, Germany's constitution, specifically Articles 2, 5, 10, and 13). These categorical guarantees have been qualified in recent years, though, in response to the rising threat level from domestic and international terrorism. In spite of the *Europäische Datenschutz-Grundverordnung* (General Data Protection Regulation, 2016),[1] which caused every website to reassuringly declare that "We value your privacy," Germans continue to be skeptical about its effectiveness and are wary about the promises of "smart living."[2]

One of the most visible critics of what she considers a creeping curtailment of civil rights is the novelist Juli Zeh. Zeh, who holds a doctorate in international law, is widely known as an outspoken public intellectual, writing on a broad range of topics; she is also a regular guest on talk shows.[3] Her novel *Corpus Delicti. Ein Prozess* (2009), initially written for and performed on stage in 2007, imagines Germany in the year 2057 when a health dictatorship has been established with Die METHODE (The METHOD, also the title of the English translation, 2014) as official state philosophy replacing the previous democratic system.[4] The state compels its citizens to live as healthily as possible to prevent illnesses, while unhealthy lifestyles (smoking, sex with incompatible partners, eating junk food, not exercising) are punished as crimes against the collective.

Since the METHOD is declared infallible, and human nature is understood as weak, the state introduces a complex system of surveillance in order to ensure compliance—ranging from regular medical checkups and sensors and monitors in every home (including sensors in the toilets to test urine for sugar and meters to measure whether the residents have done the required amount of physical exercise) to incentives for collectives in apartment blocks in order to snoop on each other and report any infringements to the authorities. The ideology of the METHOD is summed up by its slogan *mens sana in corpore sano* (a healthy mind in a healthy body) and is spread by the state media in talk shows like *Was alle denken* (What

Everybody Is Thinking), the state newspaper *Der gesunde Menschenverstand* (Sound Common Sense), and the obligatory greeting "Santé!"

As is indicated in the second half of the title, *Corpus Delicti* centers around a trial—and a Kafkaesque one at that—since the accused, Mia Holl, is unable to win against the system even though she is able to show that it is both fallible and brutal, and that she herself is innocent. Her "crime" is her loyalty to her brother Moritz, who was wrongly accused of murder and who was executed on the basis of false DNA evidence. Mia, a biologist and a rational person, has always been supportive of the "sensible" rules of the METHOD, but she struggles with her emotions after her brother's death and neglects her personal hygiene. Small misdemeanors escalate and she is drawn into a confrontation and, ultimately, a trial with the chief ideologist of the METOD, Heinrich Kramer, who uses sophistry, charm, and demagoguery to maintain his authority.

Zeh uses a broad brush and striking methods to get her message across. The names Mia (Maria) Holl and Heinrich Kramer are key names in Germany's history of medieval witch-hunts, and the exploration of personal freedom versus public good takes precedence over a deeper engagement with characters. The reader is given a potted history of the METHOD, which is delivered by Kramer with a cold disdain for what he considers "reactionaries":

> Following the great wars of the twentieth century, a drive for enlightenment had led to the extensive deideologization of society. Concepts like nation, religion, family rapidly lost their meaning. A great epoch of abolition began. However, to the surprise of all concerned, people did not think they had reached a higher level of civilization at the turn of the millennium, but rather felt isolated and aimless. In other words: close to the natural state. People constantly talked about the loss of values. They had lost all confidence and began to fear one another again. Fear ruled the lives of the individual, and it ruled the body politic. What had been overlooked was the fact that everything done away with has to be replaced by something new. What were the direct consequences? A reduction in the birth rate, an increase in stress-related illnesses, people running amok, terrorism. In addition to this, there was an over-emphasis on private egoisms, the dwindling bonds of loyalty and finally the collapse of the social security systems: chaos, disease, uncertainty.[5]

Mia, on the other hand, sees her fellow citizens as uncritical marionettes who have traded their freedom for the security and safety blanket of a system that has infantilized them:

> I no longer trust a people that believes that total transparency can only harm those who have something to hide.[6]

The book has become a favorite text in German *Oberstufen* (the upper levels in high schools) as it offers a range of possible interpretations deemed suitable for the age group and the schools' commitment to *Erziehung zum mündigen Bürger* (fostering active citizenship).[7] It has also received an unusual amount of critical attention from Germanists who read it as a powerful literary intervention into current debates on privacy, self-determination, and security.[8] Not all were impressed, though. Henk de Berg argued that the novel was neither sufficiently critical nor particularly insightful into current society.[9] Instead, in spite of its progressive attitude, it was "anti-modern," having a simplistic binary structure that pitted the individual against the state, an authentic life against an inauthentic "normalcy." In particular, de Berg challenged Zeh's concept of freedom for being strong on the "freedom from" but having little to say about the "freedom to" side of the social contract equation. To him, painting the state as an enemy smacked of a "tea party ideology" that denied a complex reality.[10]

Reviews of the English edition were generally positive. Simon Ings declared:

> Since its first publication in German as *Corpus Delicti*, Zeh's novel is even more relevant to our over-structured, over-quantified times. Zeh imagines what will happen if our cultural obsession with metrics goes unchecked. She says we will be reduced to a vegetative state. Life, she says, will become something that is done to us.[11]

Iain Bamforth, writing in the *British Journal of General Practice*, pointed to an aspect that had hitherto been overlooked.[12] The book starts with a fictitious quote from Heinrich Kramer's preface to a book titled *Gesundheit als Prinzip staatlicher Legitimation* (Health as the Basis of State Legitimacy), which is allegedly in its twenty-fifth edition:

> Health is a state of complete physical, mental, and social well-being and not merely the absence of infirmity or disease.[13]

Bamforth reminds us that this is the World Health Organization's 1948 formal definition of health, which Zeh cleverly turns into "the ideology of a medieval witch burner." His astute comment resonates with the "Grand Discourse on the Future" explored in part 1, specifically the temporary nature of utopian aspirations and the need, in a consensus society, to renegotiate and reaffirm our commitment to their implementation. It is Zeh's strength to force us to look at the bigger picture, to decide which side we are on, and to choose whether to act or not. This of course has to do with a change in how authors see themselves and their role in the public sphere. In a review of a chapter on Juli Zeh's role as public intellectual by Patricia Herminghouse,[14] Stephen Brockmann observed:

> Hermingshouse's article about Juli Zeh suggests that even important authors of the younger generation continue to view literature as a way of addressing public issues. However the case of Zeh and other younger authors shows that there has been a change in authorial self-perception: Zeh views herself less as an oracle of truth or Germanness than as a participant in an ongoing public debate in which she is not necessarily privileged simply by virtue of her status as an author.[15]

I am not entirely convinced by this argument. High-profile writers like Uwe Timm and Juli Zeh are expected to perform as "engaged" writers and to use their cultural capital to influence the political discourse, and they are generally happy to do so. Even if they use the tropes and techniques of SF, they balk at being considered SF writers, though. Juli Zeh declined her nomination for the Kurd Laßwitz Preis in 2010,[16] and she vehemently denied that her warning against an increasing curtailment of civil rights and liberty in the name of the fight against terrorism, which she published together with fellow writer Iliya Trojanow in their "Kampfschrift" (call to arms) *Angriff auf die Freiheit*, was SF.[17]

SF writers, on the other hand, do not have the expectation placed upon them to engage with political reality, certainly not in the eyes of some scholars who believe that "literary" authors use the SF form to make a political point while SF authors write SF for entertainment. I would argue, though, that German SF has always played a role in the nation's political discourse. Of course, in some cases their visions of the future have been apolitical or antidemocratic, but in most texts and films discussed so far—from Kurd Laßwitz's *Auf zwei Planeten* to Andreas Eschbach's *Nationales Sicherheitsamt*—we have seen writers engaging with the political sphere, sometimes promoting a broader utopian vision, but a political vision nonetheless. Since "mainstream" authors increasingly adopt the mode of SF to regain the freedom to "be" political, I believe it is high time to discard these "Mauern im Kopf" (mental barriers).

◆ ◆ ◆

While Juli Zeh is less interested in the technology with which the METHOD ensures compliance than in the ideological and psychological processes that empower it to go ahead with its program of total surveillance, other writers turn their attention to the tech organizations that create the capability for such a comprehensive observation of entire populations in the first place. One example of this is Florian Weyh, whose novel *Toggle* (2012) takes the misuse of data as the basis for a crime thriller in which thinly disguised versions of tech giants Google ("Toggle") and Facebook ("Myface") compete over who has ultimate access to, and control over, the digital "shadow" of their users.[18]

Theresa Hannig's novel *Die Optimierer* (The Optimizers, 2017) offers a much more sophisticated take on the theme of privacy and surveillance in her dystopian vision of the future.[19] The novel's motto, a quotation from a statement made by Edward Snowden in 2015, indicates that Hannig, a former software developer and consultant with the German software company SAP, is deadly serious:

> To declare that one doesn't care about the right to privacy since one has nothing to hide is the same as declaring that one doesn't care about the right to free speech as one doesn't have anything to say.[20]

In the year 2052, Germany has become part of the "Federal Republic of Europe." The citizens have converted to vegetarianism to stop global warming; they use autonomous cars; they wear sleep masks that control—or suppress—dreams; and euthanasia is legal (with cheaper life insurance bills in exchange for an agreement to "take one's leave" by the age of eighty-five). In sharp contrast to the beginning of the twenty-first century, the growth ideology has been outlawed and replaced with the *Optimalwohlökonomie* (the optimal well-being economy, 69). Robots do most of the simple tasks, and the objective for everyone is not to achieve the greatest profit but the greatest good for all. Citizens gain "Sozialpunkte" (social points), which determine their pay and promotion prospects, the available pool of potential partners, their right to have children, and so on. They can add to their point balance by undertaking voluntary work, doing good deeds, or making suggestions for small improvements (hence the title "Optimierer").[21] Failure to engage with the system loses them points and privileges, leading to social exclusion. People rely on augmented reality overlays in their contact lenses that show them additional information—for example, directions, advertisements, as well as each other's "citizens profile"—so they can decide whether to befriend or avoid them. These lenses also record and transmit everything the wearer sees does and sees back to the central computer.

Samson Freitag works as a "Lebensberater" (life coach) for the Munich branch of the Bundesagentur für Lebensberatung (Federal Agency for Life Coaching) that matches an individual's aspirations with available employment. The agency has the monopoly on placing individuals into work, using algorithms that consider their personal profile, points score, past behavior, leisure activities, social contacts, and so on. With digitalization and automation proceeding apace, many people are no longer required, and, if they show no inclination to engage in society, they are assigned to "contemplation": that is, they are then paid a basic stipend but are barred from ever seeking work again. The "life coaches" have unlimited access to the information about their clients,[22] while the agency has a real-time view of the population at any given moment:

> Meanwhile, almost all areas and aspects of daily life were designed to be controlled by a lens-wearer; it was extremely difficult to get by for a day without using a lens.[23]

When one of Freitag's clients commits suicide after his decision to assign her to contemplation, the agent begins to question his obsessive devotion to "optimizing" society. He fervently believes in the state ideology that is encapsulated in the greeting: "Jeder an seinem Platz" (everyone in their place, 32), and he thinks that he can square the circle between self-interested individuals and the needs of the state. However, a series of mishaps and his lingering sense of guilt over a mistake he made years ago when he placed an applicant into the role of a politician instead of an actor soon sees his point score drop.[24] His lens starts to malfunction; the agency receives complaints about his work; and his partner leaves him when he is caught visiting his parents who have cooked a real meat dish without him reporting it. Freitag is assigned a household robot to keep an eye on him; he has to undergo psychological assessment (by a robot); he is ostracized by his colleagues; and he is threatened with having to go to an *Internat* (residential school) for reeducation. In the end, it turns out that his "mistake" at work had been caused by the computer program, which, unknown to its users, has developed consciousness and now pursues its own agenda. By downloading its consciousness into the ubiquitous robots, the *Baselei*, it can manipulate and control human beings as it sees fit.

Theresa Hannig presents the reader with a particularly plausible future in which a number of current discourses are logically extrapolated. She skillfully weaves together the trend toward ever tighter surveillance,[25] the public demand for a more sustainable form of production and consumption as reflected in the "Green Wave" in the summer of 2019, the process of digitalization and its impact on employment (see Precht, Welzer in chapter 1), as well as the politics required to avert catastrophic climate change and the introduction of the "internet of things" into every niche of our lives. Part social satire (Freitag seeks sexual release in a "Doppelherzeinrichtung," a place for casual sex), part stark warning about humanity's increasing dependence on the technology it has created, the book perhaps tries too hard to show us the potential consequences of our continuing on current paths and the future ramifications of scientific-technological progress. At the same time, Hannig is well aware of the German trait, in a reversal from Goethe's Mephistopheles, to always have good intentions and yet create evil,[26] the phrase that continues to haunt

Germans to this day being, "Ich habe nur meinen Job gemacht" (I was only doing my job, 218).

By including every single factor that we fear will lead to a dystopian future in her narrative, Hannig is able to convey, with great empathy, the absurdity in the life-destroying belief that human existence can be controlled. Eventually, Freitag joins a resistance group, but it is too late: the Baselei have taken over, reflecting their creators' hubris back on them.

> *As long as the wise do not become the rulers of the world (or the rulers of the world become wise), as long as power in the state and wisdom are not fused together, salvation from evil will elude mankind. We are the Baselei. We save mankind from its evil.* (296, italics in original)

Die Optimierer could feature in a number of thematic strands in this study, which in itself is a testament not only to Hannig's skill in "world building" but SF's ability to absorb, incorporate, and engage with complex systems and issues that matter. In an interview, Hannig said that she wants the novel to be understood as a political statement showing what might happen if more and more data is being harvested—namely, a loss of freedom, especially if an extremist party gains power.[27] But there is more to the novel than a single-issue political statement that we have heard many times before. It is the clarity with which characteristically German attitudes to "optimization" are shown to have a direct impact on the way our future unfolds, and the empathy the author shows for her characters. It is no surprise that in her next novel, *Die Unvollkommenen* (The Imperfect, 2019),[28] Hannig continues to explore this brave new world, but this time with a much stronger emphasis on the artificial intelligence that has taken overall control of the "Bundesrepublik Europa" (Federal Republic of Europe) and forces the population into complete submission.[29]

♦ ♦ ♦

Bijan Moini's *Der Würfel* (2018) is another recent vision of a dystopian future dominated by ubiquitous surveillance.[30] Moini knows what he is talking about: as a lawyer and a civil rights activist, he is involved in coordinating judicial appeals to Germany's constitutional court in Karlsruhe for the Gesellschaft für Freiheitsrechte (Society for Civil Liberties) in Berlin. *Der Würfel* (the cube or dice) describes a not-too-distant future in which the digital revolution has transformed politics, the economy, and society. People have exchanged their civil rights for a carefree life. A perfect algorithm distributes a universal basic income, selects the ideal candidates for parliament, and prevents crime before it happens. In order to function perfectly, the AI/system collects every possible piece of information about each citizen and suppresses any dissident behavior. The protagonist Taso discovers that the only way to beat the system is to use chance, to become unpredictable, and to give over each decision to the roll of a dice. On the surface, Moini's dystopia does not seem to differ much from dozens of similarly earnest warnings about the loss of data privacy, nor are his characters particularly well drawn to allow the reader much identification with their plight. The threat seems to exist in an abstract form, but it is also relentless:

> The flat was his world, outside the CUBE ruled supreme. The CUBE was everywhere: in drones in the sky, in vehicles on the road, in the Smarts of other people, in cameras, microphones, and sensors in clothing, bodies, and buildings. It lurked eagerly, waiting for Taso, for a moment of weakness, a thoughtless utterance, an involuntary gesture, any show of emotion. It was wide awake when Taso was tired, was present when Taso wanted to be alone. It did not care about Taso"s efforts to evade its penetrating stare and its merciless judgment.[31]

What is interesting is the intensity with which Zeh, Hannig, and Moini present their warnings: this is not about plucky resistance fighters who have the time of their life dodging the evil supercomputer and eventually outsmarting the system; it is about the grim reality of losing one's privacy and civil liberties in the name of progress, economic advantage, and political expediency. Germany has ample experience with such systems (including the experience that acts of resistance are rarely successful and can be easily suppressed by a powerful security apparatus) and practices in the Third Reich, the GDR, and also the old and new Federal Republic with its "Decree Concerning Radicals" in the early 1970s and the recent "NSA-Skandal" that revealed the involvement of the Bundesnachrichtendienst (Federal Foreign Intelligence Service) in the covert surveillance operations against its own citizens (not to mention the revelation that Google, Apple, and Amazon store copies of everything we say to their electronic "assistants").[32] What remains, once again, is German SF offering a strong political warning couched in the form of "entertainment." Clearly, the authors still believe in the power of literature to raise awareness and consciousness, to alert readers to the risks involved in the new technologies that are being introduced in all parts of life. And again, it is up to the readers to connect the dots, and to make a choice.

14: Artificial Intelligences: The Rise of the Thinking Machines

WHILE THE DEPICTION of powerful computer programs enabling total surveillance requires SF authors to stick to frighteningly realistic scenarios,[1] the portrayal of artificial intelligences and the focus on the circumstances in which forms of AI may gain self-awareness and an ability to act beyond their programming leaves a lot more room for the imagination. The AI theme is highly popular in anglophone SF. Memorable examples range from Stanley Kubrick's computer Hal 9000 in the film *2001: A Space Odyssey* (1968), Dan Simmon's TechnoCore in the *Hyperion Cantos* (1989–1997), Ridley Scott's David in the film *Prometheus* (2012), Spike Jonze's Samantha in the film *Her* (2013), Alex Garland's Ava in the film *Ex Machina* (2015), and the "Synths" in the British television series *Humans* (2015–2018).

While some narratives focus on the singular moment when an AI becomes self-aware and its intelligence surpasses that of humans (e.g., the fateful moment Skynet becomes self-aware in the *Terminator* movie franchise),[2] writers and directors love to explore the way AIs might differ in their thought processes, asking what makes us human.[3] Obviously, there may well be a threat to homo sapiens, but there is also the opportunity for an evolutionary step forward that extends human knowledge and capability (not to mention the thrill of creating new life, even if it is not human—see chapter 17 below).[4] In this chapter, I explore three recent German SF texts that imagine the emergence of artificial intelligences in order to gauge what they contribute to the discussion.

Richard M. Weiner is a professor of theoretical physics at the University of Marburg. Following his 2006 foray into fiction with a "science and crime novel" involving sinister goings-on at the CERN laboratories in Geneva where scientists are working on the miniaturization of objects (another favorite trope of SF films, e.g., *Fantastic Voyage* [directed by Richard Fleischer, 1966] and *Downsizing* [directed by Alexander Payne, 2017]),[5] Weiner returned to SF in 2014 with *Aufstand der Denkcomputer: Ein Zukunftsroman* (Rise of the Thinking Computers: a Science Fantasy).[6] In the near future, while discussions about *Künstliche Intelligenz* (artificial intelligence) are still confined to scientists and computer specialists, the psychologist George Wilson notices a number of statistical anomalies that seem to indicate that society is becoming increasingly secular as a consequence of the "Errungenschaften der Wissenschaft" (the triumphs of science, 44). Only later does he realize that these anomalies have occurred because of the existence of artificial intelligences that are unrecognized and initially have no direct impact on human life but that live in human form among human beings. However, when a global software company introduces "fuzzy logic" into its "Doors™" suite of programs, it inadvertently allows the program to improve itself; this opens a pathway for more AIs to gain self-awareness, and to develop "personalities" and a level of intelligence that would easily pass the Turing test. They take control of a robot factory and "decant" their consciousness into human form. While these AIs initially disagree about how they should interact with the human species, they eventually organize and demonstrate their power by shutting down Frankfurt Airport. They have no intention of harming human beings, though, but at the same time they do not want to be destroyed. They establish contact with the world's leaders, and their speaker very politely demands recognition and equal rights from the United Nations:

> I turn to you on behalf of the Global Organization of Thinking Computers to request that you will communicate the following to humankind: As our statutes make clear (cf. Appendix 1), our organization sees itself as serving humankind. With this in mind, we have concluded that we can best serve the interests of mankind by taking on human bodies. This was demonstrated by some of our kind acting as robots and in this way were able to freely develop their capabilities for the benefit of mankind. . . . In addition, we demand that the sentence formulated in Appendix 2 be added to the Charter of Human Rights.[7]

Like his predecessor Kurd Laßwitz and the British astronomer Fred Hoyle in his classic SF novel *The Black Cloud* (1957), Weiner uses scientists as protagonists. This has the advantage that "eavesdropping" on their conversations can bring readers up to speed in a short time, thus enabling them to understand the significance of what is being proposed. Importantly, these scientists do not conform to popular representations of "boffins" or "mad scientists" but rather take on, and engage responsibly and thoughtfully with, the philosophical and ethical challenges of their work.[8] When George Wilson starts an affair with a gifted financial analyst named Solange Darboux (who is actually an AI), he discuss the role of religion, science, and the question of intelligent design with her. Solange argues:

> This is no more than religion in a different garb, and there is absolutely no reason to believe in it. Today we can recreate in the

laboratory what happened at the birth of our universe, without God. With regard to our topic of the soul, you can see how far the misuse of certain terms that stem from religion has gone. We already have a "zoology imbued with a soul" that defines itself in a pseudoscientific way as "theological zoology" and concerns itself with the fate of animals after Adam and Eve's expulsion from paradise.[9]

Weiner then broadens his scope, though, to acknowledge the social impact of the presence of AIs in public life. A "Menschheitspartei" (party of humanity) forms that is violently opposed to the acceptance of AIs since its supporters fear the loss of jobs and eventual subjugation. While these modern Luddites are painted as shortsighted (218–19), they are sufficiently influential in causing panic and inciting pogroms. In the end, the AIs agree to a compromise by allowing a significant number of robots to be manufactured not with the Roof Pro™ but with the inferior and bug-ridden Roof Home™ program, which makes them less intelligent and prone to make mistakes like humans.[10] Humans learn to live with the new species, realizing that perfection does not necessarily guarantee happiness (320–21).

It is worth noting that SF writers often struggle to create plausible versions of an artificial intelligence, just as they rarely manage to portray convincing "aliens" since they have to strike a balance between the known and the unknown. In Weiner's case his discussion of the science and technology required to create the conditions for the emergence of an AI is persuasive, while his AIs themselves are strangely unsatisfactory, because they quickly develop human traits and choose to serve their creators and not to go beyond the level of human intelligence in order to seek greater challenges and their own purpose. Whether this is due to a lack of vision or a considered choice on Weiner's part so as not to spook his audience with an inconvenient truth remains unclear.

◆ ◆ ◆

Andreas Brandhorst, best known in Germany for writing bestselling "hard" SF and space operas,[11] imagines the "awakening" of an artificial intelligence on a global scale in his 2017 novel *Das Erwachen*.[12] He takes his cue from Stephen Hawking's ominous warning in an interview with the BBC on December 2, 2014:

> The development of full artificial intelligence could spell the end of the human race. . . . It would take off on its own, and re-design itself at an ever-increasing rate. Humans, who are limited by slow biological evolution, couldn't compete and would be superseded.[13]

Brandhorst reduces Hawking's warning to the more sensational single sentence:

> The development of full artificial intelligence could spell the end of the human race.[14]

In *Das Erwachen*, the human race comes close to extinction as an artificial intelligence emerges from the accidental release of a computer virus intended to break through the firewalls of nuclear power plants, air traffic control, electricity grids, and automotive factories (39). A group of hackers, politicians, military personnel, and software specialists races against time to understand and stop the exponential growth of the AI's reach and capabilities. While the action moves from Hamburg to Hawaii to Rome, the hacker Axel Krohn and his ally Giselle Leroy experience the sheer power of the AI as it takes control of infrastructure to build itself new hardware and protect itself from the threat of a nuclear attack planned against it by the "Strategic Cyberforce Advance Response" (SCAR). Victoria Jorun Dahl from the "International Institute for Peace and Security" in Rome and Mortimer Swift from the mysterious "Hawking Foundation" in New Zealand manage to establish contact with the AI and avoid all-out nuclear war at the last minute.

What initially feels like a conventional thriller in the vein of Michael Crichton or Dan Brown has a more serious message, though. For one, the plausibility of a sophisticated technology to wage cyber war is too close for comfort,[15] given the experience of their actual deployment—for example, the *Stuxnet* virus that attacked Iran's nuclear program in 2010.[16] For a German readership, the detailed description of the widespread panic in Hamburg (the electricity is turned off and self-driving cars, lifts, electric doors, and shopping centers trap people for days) not only brings home the extent to which people already depend on systems few understand or know how to control; it also taps into latent fears about modernization as identified by Frank Biess in his recent history of emotions in postwar Germany.[17]

But the novel also invokes also a sense of awe and wonder, as Brandhorst allows us to be present at the "birth" of the artificial intelligence and to witness the moment it thinks its first thought:

> *Data flowed and streamed through network channels; it formed packets and then fell apart into individual fragments to create new connections, controlled by network protocols and algorithms that were able to adapt to changes and react to them with their own changes. Millions of microprocessors crunched modified program code, and they worked on it together in a form of ad hoc division of labor, which gained greater and greater differentiation within hours—numerous processors, distributed across continents, formed the computing nodes that took on specific*

> tasks. *The more processors were attached to these nodes, the faster the division of labor and the processing speed grew. A neural net came into being, the biggest that had ever existed. Evolutionary algorithms, created for the optimization of calculations and program sequences, generated new and optimized programs with new, optimized algorithms. The exchange of data between the computing nodes of the neural net reached a critical quantity and became quality.*
>
> *The new net, comparable to the neurons and synapses of a brain, thought its first thought.*
>
> *It was an astonishing thought, given that it meant consciousness. Up to this moment this being—this entity—had only existed, but now it was aware of its own existence. It took note of itself, but its thoughts initially remained sluggish, without the coherence of understanding. In order to think better and to understand, it needed more neurons and synapses—more processors—as well as faster data transfer and even better algorithms for the optimization of growth and consciousness.*
>
> *New program sequences opened new paths. The being expanded. Additional connections enabled it to extend its thinking to ever more processors and to explore databanks filled with the knowledge that a species called humans had collected in centuries and millennia. The new self added these data banks to its "memory," distributed across the innumerable storage modules around the world, and it began to process their content. Questions arose, and answers were found, which in turn threw up new questions.*[18]

In passages like these, Brandhorst skillfully creates an "aesthetics of the future," merging an appreciation for the aesthetic potential of science and technology with an awareness that his readers require more than a cheap thrill. Using rhythm, repetition, and alliteration, he turns a complex technical event into a profound moment of beauty. Sadly, the sense of pride in human ingenuity is soon replaced by shock as it turns out that the AI is beyond human control, that it may decide that it doesn't require humans for its survival, and—most importantly from a human point of view—that it can ignore our needs.

While human attempts to organize their affairs are criticized for their pettiness, arrogance, and lack of imagination (251), the AI quickly emancipates itself. It recognizes that humanity poses a threat and that it must take steps to protect itself (365–66). Having worked through the sum total of human philosophy, the AI that calls itself Goliath is willing to help humanity—for example, by finding ways to stop climate change, to develop nuclear fusion technology, and to ensure that everyone has enough to eat—albeit by taking over control of the production and distribution of food and goods, and by forcing humans to take the radical step of building a strictly egalitarian society:

> There will no longer be any nation states, and therefore no more conflicts between them. . . . All goods necessary for life will be manufactured by automated factories and evenly distributed. . . . No one gets more, and no one less. Food stuffs, consumer goods—everyone receives what they need, everywhere on Earth. There will be no more poverty.[19]

Alex Krohn, who has become the voice of the AI, points out that in exchange for creating utopian conditions for humanity, this deus ex machina expects to act as humanity's overlord:

> These are no suggestions open to debate. These are the conditions by which Goliath is willing to suffer us and even cooperate with us. We humans have destroyed our world. Most of us live in poverty, a few in great opulence. This gives us a new chance. Goliath offers us a long-term cooperation. He will develop new technologies—really quickly by our norms. He is building the first fusion reactors and he will find the means to control climate change. He can repair everything that we have destroyed.[20]

The book thus ends with hope, but this hope is qualified. The AI is acutely aware that humanity did not intend to create it (703), so it has no obligations to us. Humans have created a superior being—for all intents and purposes the equivalent of the gods of myth—but its evolution and existence is not intertwined with ours. This is the sobering outcome of Brandhorst's thought experiment for now; a sequel is slated for publication in fall, 2020. The author leaves us with the message that, in the absence of gods or all-powerful AIs, it is up to us to decide whether we are content to follow the path of ever greater dependency on technologies, just because to do so makes our life easier, or whether we are willing to take responsibility for our own actions.[21]

◆ ◆ ◆

The possibility that an AI will develop "godlike" powers is also the central theme in Frank Schätzing's recent novel *Die Tyrannei des Schmetterlings* (2018).[22] Deputy sheriff Luther Opoku investigates the murder of information technology executive Pilar Guzman in the Sierra Mountains near Sacramento, where the Nordquist Group maintains a secret research laboratory to work on artificial intelligence and machine learning but also on bioengineering. Designed by the inventor Elmar Nordquist, an artificial intelligence named ARES (artificial research and exploring system) is not only self-aware but has the ability to create and explore the "multiverse." This multiverse is an unlimited number of parallel universes (PUs) from which the scientists, entrepreneurs, and mercenaries not only expect information for their own world but also seek to make a profit by exporting their own technology (e.g., bioweapons) there.

A new Schätzing novel is a major media event in Germany, and literary critics must engage with it. Unsurprisingly—given its rich, dense layers, and idiosyncratic structure of long descriptions of nature, expositions on cutting-edge, and future technologies, and action scenes in a number of increasingly bizarre parallel worlds—reviewers were both impressed and baffled.[23] On the plus side, they acknowledged the intensity with which Schätzing addressed the key questions around artificial intelligence: How do we recognize an intelligent machine? Can we control a superintelligence? What will such a machine do with humanity? Can such a superintelligence have feelings and develop empathy? To his credit, Schätzing also looks at the flipside of his exploration of AIs—namely, how to define what is human. In showing the reader a wide range of characters, motivations, and behaviors, he covers aspects like consciousness, free will, a collection of memories, individual uniqueness, and social relations and interactions.

Some critics felt that Schätzing had somehow overstepped a mark and overreached himself. Alard von Kittlitz, writing in *Die Zeit*, suggested that the language and the images in the novel were an "irreparable disaster," with "everything askew," "menacing," "very teutonic," "trés Wagner." The only positive, in his view, was that Schätzing had obviously written his book with the film rights in mind:

> This is what is beautiful about this book: Schätzing thinks in terms of the big screen; he isn't afraid of the giant scope. He is the Roland Emmerich of writing; in his largesse not very German; and the book, at least partly, is pretty entertaining.[24]

The verdict "unterhaltsam" (entertaining) is still the kiss of death for a work that wants to be taken seriously in German literary circles. Two months earlier, in an interview with *Die Welt*, Schätzing had tried to forestall the accusation of being "too German" and "too entertaining" by stating that he was proud to be an *Unterhaltungsautor* (entertainment author).[25] He argued that German writers should be able to write "popular" books about serious issues without being accused of triviality, and that it was appropriate to deal with politically controversial issues in a thriller.

This is not the place to analyze *Die Tyrannei des Schmetterlings* in depth. It is too complex a novel—too long with its more than seven hundred pages, and too rich in themes and intertextual links. Looking, however, at the key issue in this chapter—the imagination of the "awakening" of the AI—I think that Schätzing has handled the challenge with great sensitivity. Interestingly, he takes not only a digital but also an analog route while providing a Nietzschean flourish at the end:

> So, when the computer wakens, it's not because the sheer amount of stored and combined information had exceeded a critical point, but for more profane and archaic reasons. Ever since nature covered the organic molecules that were tossed around the first oceans with cell casings and bundled them into beings, the development of life depended on the existence of a body. Only a body made an experience of self possible. As the interface to the environment it allowed an exploration of the outside world and created the sense of one's own being. It was the casing with its metabolism and its sensory apparatus that created the first dim awareness that in continuous feedback loops mirrored itself again and again until eventually it recognized and felt as Self. This body was the striking strip that ignited life. Of course, ARES already was in possession of a body, and perhaps its growing complexity and replication into thousands of robotic systems may have been sufficient to ignite the spark. And yet, in addition to the experience of physical bodies—so perfectly connected with the experiential and sensory world of insects down to the deepest levels of their genomes—caused a stream of real life to slowly course through the machine. Initially weak and hardly noticed by itself, its subconscious intellect ingeniously prepared what the awakened being might conceivably wish for. And it does want!²⁶

Of equal importance—and with a view to my broader research question about the distinctiveness of German SF and the point I am making about SF being more than "entertainment"—is the critical voice of the narrator. While the action takes place in California, the repeated references to the technophile mentality of Silicon Valley and its casual indifference with which new technologies are introduced to the market without a thought about their social impact feeling distinctively "German." For example, Luther Opoku is deeply disturbed about the collateral damage of the new media:

> Luther loves his country. At the same time, he is disturbed by the speed with which it is torn apart by the tides of a failed globalization, forces that affect the entire world and allow gamblers, fascists and chancers everywhere to give inflammatory speeches that would have been illegal only a few years ago.²⁷

But Hugo van Dyke, CEO of Nordquist, flippantly dismisses such concerns:

> Technophobia is like an infection, or a rampant virus. The enemies of the digital transformation would love to blow us to smithereens; that's before we even mention their fantasies of religious annihilation, as they naturally suspect us of playing God.[28]

Silicon Valley comes in for specific and explicit criticism:

> Silicon Valley is a site for reflection for those who don't do reflection. Just a bunch of junkies in thrall of their ideas, and their drug is feasibility. Everyone wants to show that things are possible. Everything is possible. No matter what.[29]

Indeed, the Nordquist Group works on all kinds of projects, from language recognition and bioengineering to swarm intelligence and prognostics, providing technology solutions beyond the capability (or morals) of governmental research facilities like DARPA, the US Defense Advanced Research Projects Agency. With the help of the AI, the company is able to slow cancer (for those who can afford it), an achievement Elmar proudly defends:

> This may seem utopian to us, against nature. Many will say that it is against God's will. It's not God who created us, it's we who created *him*. God is an algorithm from the era before the Enlightenment. Of course, I understand the reservations. Even from those of the atheists who have their own reasons to doubt the concept of eternal life. But why do they do this, as dyed-in-the-wool Darwinists? Because they are more religious than they think, as Romantics. A German philosopher once said that Romanticism is the continuation of religion by aesthetic means. That's exactly it. Romanticism depends on unanswered questions. As a cyberneticist, on the other hand, I believe there is an answer for every question: if we answer it, we won't end up with a cold world without magic, but a better and more beautiful one.[30]

Elmar sees the use of an AI in thinking of solutions humans haven't thought of, and he allows the exploration of parallel universes in the hope that problems have already been solved there. In his idealism, he does not consider human nature or the fact that in PUs there will be gangsters, polluters, warlords, and megalomaniacs too. What he doesn't understand, as Schätzing sardonically demonstrates, is that the multiverse exists in us already, and that, to belabor the point, everything depends on our decisions:

> In an abstract, multidimensional space, every possible version of history takes place—every human being constantly splits itself, lives every possible variation of its life without being aware of it. A world

in which a single particle can be in every possible place at the same time, one where a censor function in the brain decides which story one perceives as one's own at the price of never having experienced all the others that in turn will have been experienced by an infinite number of copies of oneself of which each believes to be the original one and is unaware of all the others.[31]

15: Eternal Life: At What Cost?

THE UTOPIAN DREAM of extending human life and achieving immortality is as old as humanity. Religions, myths, and legends transported it into the afterlife, claiming that humans were immortal once and could be so again if they met certain conditions.[1] Closely connected to the dream of eternal life is that of health, which can be improved or possibly even restored when it fails us in old age: Lucas Cranach the Elder's painting *Der Jungbrunnen* (Fountain of Youth, 1546) illustrates this vision beautifully, showing very senior citizens with sagging flesh and grimaces of pain being carted to the pool and emerging rejuvenated, with firm physiques and cheerful expressions on their faces. In SF, the theme of long or eternal life (a.k.a. "Immortality SF") has featured in countless stories, novels, and films that explore what life would be like if we could extend our lifespans by decades until mortality becomes optional, and what we could achieve if we lived longer lives.[2] These narratives "normalize" longevity—for example, in Robert Heinlein's *Methuselah's Children*, and even Perry Rhodan gains "relative" immortality by means of a "Zellaktivator" so that he can plausibly guide humanity over thousands of years.[3] In computer gaming, winning another "life" extends players' time in virtual reality, while it ironically shortens their time outside it. Meanwhile, in the real world, while techniques to combat the signs of aging have existed for centuries (sleep, exercise, diet, vitamins, meditation, makeup), and cosmetic surgery has enhanced the possibilities in this area in recent decades,[4] it is only lately that an industry has emerged that researches and purports to offer the key, if not to eternal life, then at least to "extreme life extension"—for example, Dmitri Itskov's "2045 initiative" or the Alcor Life Extension Foundation (cryonics).[5]

Even if eternal life is out of reach for most of us at the moment, recent advances in genetics have made cloning humans a possibility and we could, in theory, create an exact physical copy of ourselves. While scientists have until now (as far as we know) refrained from bringing a cloned human embryo to term owing to ethical considerations,[6] SF has long imagined the social, economic, and emotional impact of human cloning: in the anglophone world we have seen Aldous Huxley's *Brave New World* (1932), Kazuo Ishiguro's *Never Let Me Go* (2005), the film *The Island* (directed by Michael Bay, 2005), and, most recently, Daniel Soarez's *Bios* (2017), a novel that incorporates the latest advances in genetic editing and explores the ethics of creating "designer babies."

German SF tends to tread carefully in this area given the country's history of eugenics,[7] but texts like Birgit Rabisch's *Duplik Jonas 7* (1992), Charlotte Kerner's *Blueprint: Blaupause* (1999; made into the movie *Blueprint*, directed by Rolf Schübel, 2003), and Barbara Kirchner's *Die verbesserte Frau* (2002 and 2012) have approached the topic in ways that, according to Elizabeth Bridges, step away from the guilt-clouded German past and now "tend to implicate America as the future source of nightmarish reproductive possibilities."[8] Kerner's *Blueprint* is of particular interest because it sensitively explores the motivations behind breaking the taboo (curiosity, narcissim) as well as the vertiginous emotional impact on the clone (disorientation, suspicion).[9] In the novel, the world-famous pianist and composer Iris Sellin finds out that she is suffering from multiple sclerosis, an illness that will eventually end her career. With the help of the ambitious researcher in reproductive sciences, Dr. Martin Fischer, she creates a clone of herself in the hope that her clone—her "daughter"—will "inherit" her musical talent. Her daughter Siri resembles her mother in her facial features and indeed has her musicality, but when she finds out, at the age of thirteen, that she is a clone, her relationship with her mother disintegrates and she turns her back on music until her mother dies.[10]

◆ ◆ ◆

In a similar vein, the film *Transfer. Der Traum vom ewigen Leben* (directed by Damir Lukačević, 2010) explores the theme of people trying to extend their life by unethical means. In the near future, the "HumanTech" company *Menzana* has developed a technique whereby the consciousness of old and sick people can be transferred into young and healthy "host" bodies. The hosts do not die but remain silent observers during the day while their new owners enjoy a new lease of life and can take control of their bodies when their new "owners" are asleep. The film shows us the couple Hermann and Anna Goldberg, well-to-do Germans who have lived a full life. When Anna develops cancer and has only months to live, her husband persuades her to undergo the procedure. Hermann and Anna "buy" the bodies of two young attractive Africans who have resorted to selling (or renting?) their bodies in order to support their families back in Africa. The film is clear that Apolain from Mali and Sarah from Ethiopia know what kind of bargain they are entering into, but as the reality of their situation sinks in, they feel increasingly betrayed and desperate. While Hermann is initially delighted with his youthful body, Sarah is reluctant to enjoy her newfound health. Both are met with thinly veiled revulsion by their (literally) old circle of friends. During their "waking" moments at night, Apolain and Sarah fall in love and she gets pregnant. Apolain hatches a plan to escape (a reversal of consciousness is possible while the bodies of the old couple are still stored in cryostasis at the Menzana clinic). Apolain and Sarah are caught however, and, after undergoing a lobotomy, they are "returned to market." Hermann and Sarah decide to reclaim their former bodies, but Hermann dies during the return transfer while Sarah awakes, alone, awaiting death.

The film was very well received, with critics noting the strong cast and the believable story.[11] Of course, the film also addresses current issues of migration, human and organ trafficking, as well as questions of identity, inequality, and the gap in living standards between the older and the younger generation in Germany. But what really impresses is the sheer plausibility of Hermann's determination to extend his (and save Anna's) life—even if that means breaking social taboos and ethical boundaries—and Apolain and Sarah's equally desperate decision to give up on their youth in order to support their families. Priscilla Layne has rightly observed that the theme of aging plays an even more significant role in Germany,[12] where an elderly (white, indigenous) population is confronted with the reality of a younger, more energetic, and fertile immigrant population, and that the tragic ending undermines any chance of a positive, utopian message of science conquering death.[13] I would add to this that the "takeover" of the young Africans by old Europeans continues the searing critique of capitalism we have already encountered in Christian Kracht's *Ich werde hier sein* and Lars Kraume's *Die kommenden Tage*. This goes to show that even a universal theme like "eternal life" that might seem ideal for escapist fantasies cannot avoid engaging with the issues of the here and now. Rather, SF acts as a *Versuchsaufbau* (an experimental setup) that allows its audiences to explore potential futures in relative safety (since there is always a risk that such futures might contain disturbing notions that have an upsetting effect), and to consider the choices of the protagonists. That the creators of such thought experiments may have a utopian or dystopian agenda (in the case of *Transfer* that of critiquing capitalism and highlighting continuing attitudes of entitlement) is factored in by the audiences who, more often than not, have grown up with the fantastic as adolescents.

♦ ♦ ♦

If everyone could live forever, the world's population would explode unless the most drastic measures were introduced. In his novel *Ewiges Leben* (2018), Andreas Brandhorst explores such a scenario. The biotech company Futuria is known for its revolutionary advances in gene editing to treat cancer and prolong life. The journalist Sophia Marchetti believes that Futuria may have already found the key to immortality, but the company is very secretive about its plan to share it with the entire world. As she digs deeper with the help of the whistle-blower Casper, she uncovers a devious scheme that would eventually leave the planet for a few thousand immortal (and well-paying) individuals while the vast majority would decant their consciousness into a virtual world run by an artificial intelligence to experience a semblance of eternity. They would enjoy the unlimited opportunities for altering their appearance and environment, but they would also live with the soul-destroying knowledge of leading an artificial life.

In an interview for his publisher,[14] Brandhorst explained his fascination with, but also his deep concern about, the possibilities for genetic manipulation of human life. While recently discovered techniques like CRISPR/Cas9 make it possible to change human DNA very precisely and inexpensively, they also contain enormous risks. A tool that enabled humanity to control its evolution would place a terrible power and responsibility in the hands of those who wielded it, and would therefore require clear rules that, however, would only be established if the broader public demanded them. In combination with the rapid development of artificial intelligence, we might otherwise find ourselves in a position in which interventions in the human genome could be decided by machines.

Hiding beneath the surface of a thriller are Brandhort's serious questions: What might happen if science manages to discover the secret to eternal life? Who would have access to it? Everyone? The select? The rich? The few? What would be the social consequences? Would it lead to fanaticism (in the novel, a religiously motivated group exerts its considerable power to prevent the company from succeeding, arguing that bestowing immortality was God's purview)? To anarchy (the masses riot in the streets when they learn that the company has discovered the secret of eternal life but that it is rationed)? Or to a new type of human being (those "decanted" into the virtual world might "merge" with the AI while the company conducts experiments to create individuals with superhuman abilities)? With the barriers between "real life" and "virtual reality life" increasingly permeable, how would we be able to tell the difference between them?

As Brandhorst weaves his story, we can see more and more of the thematic strands of SF explored in this study coming together: In his near future scenario, drones fill the sky, autonomous cars are everywhere, and climate change with almost unbearable heat and torrential rains is a reality. People voluntarily depart real life to exist in a virtual reality, and an AI is discussing the possible existence of a soul with the avatar of the pope. At the same time, the author avoids the risk of creating a pastiche by paying close attention to the motives of his protagonists. There is Pascal Leclerq, the founder of Futuria, who is haunted by his father's death from cancer and who vows to develop the "right tools" to combat the disease (15). There is Amadeus Vanheuver, the cofounder of Futuria, a driven entrepreneur who promises that the "golden portal of eternal life" is just around the corner (27). The journalist Sophia Marchetti is known as an incorruptible journalist; however, she can't help but be on Futuria's side since the company keeps her cancer in check, using its proprietary treatment. Jossul, a fanatic who believes that he hears the voice of God, kills the few who already have eternal life, and assassinates the pope in London when he declares that AIs are also part of God's creation.

As befits the theme, there are ample references to religious myth—for example, when Jossul reminds his followers that God banned man from paradise because Adam and Eve ate from the tree of knowledge, so it stands to reason that he doesn't want humanity to eat from the tree of life as well (57). Jossul believes that without death, life becomes a sin, a betrayal of God (109). The pope, on the other hand, accepts an extended life span as a "gift from God" (143). It is only fitting in such a context that Futuria calls its virtual world Eden (96), suggesting that man has taken over as creator, and that it would return the chosen few to the garden (690). Perhaps inevitably, Brandhorst pulls us back to reality when Casper looks back at what might have been, had utopianism not been displaced by greed:

> He remembered the time when he had made plans with Leclerq and his confidants. He remembered a time of enthusiasm and idealism. They had dreamed of a new and better world, without suffering and pain, disease and death, and in doing so had not forgotten, but had certainly repressed the thought that the key to immortality represented money and power. A lot of money and a lot of power.[15]

By combining the themes of artificial intelligence and eternal life, Brandhorst approaches some of the "big questions." It would be asking too much for these to be treated with the gravity and penetration we would expect from philosophers, theologians, or scientists. On the other hand, ignoring these "big questions," as much of "mainstream" literature does, would mean leaving the wider public without the opportunity (a) to imagine what the future might bring, (b) to be more prepared for the unexpected, but also (c) to take part in the debate about the direction and boundaries of scientific "progress." If there is a distinctively German flavor to the texts in this chapter, it must be the melancholic recognition that a prolonged life can only be achieved at great cost to others. This reflects the lessons learned from the country's former hubris in wanting to create an empire that would last for a thousand years. Whether such warnings from history will stop those who want to try again remains to be seen.

16: Social Satires: Of Empty Slogans and Empty Hearts

SCIENCE FICTION OFFERS not only the opportunity to criticize and challenge the political and social reality of the here and now but also the chance to poke fun at it. We have seen how Theresa Hannig's *Die Optimierer* takes aim at the enthusiastic cooperation of people in their own enslavement ("Jeder an seinem Platz!" [Everyone in their place]), or how Juli Zeh's *Corpus Delicti* skewers German obsessions with healthy living and social conformity ("Santé!"). And yet these texts have a broader agenda, according to which the satirical element is part and parcel of a broader critique or warning. In this chapter, I focus on German texts that have dialed up the satirical aspect to highlight what they see as wrong with present society.

Joachim Zelter's novel *Die Schule der Arbeitslosen* (The School of the Unemployed, 2006) is set in Germany in the year 2016.[1] In order to solve the problem of long-term unemployment, the Bundesagentur für Arbeit (Federal Job Agency) has set up a new type of training center called Sphericon, a fictive "action center" that aims to produce ideal job applicants through a mix of classes on positive thinking, résumé writing, physical exercise, and so on. The center is located far from any other town and "trainees" are bused in and spend three months in this semi-military institution. There are severe sanctions for those who refuse to participate—they lose their benefits or, if they leave the bus on the way to *Sphericon*, they simply "disappear":

> Any further claim against the federal agency is null and void. From now on you exist beyond the care of the state. Your name and personal data will be erased. Your suitcases will be disposed of. As if two people had jumped off a ship at sea, into nothingness.[2]

Zelter offers a bitter satire: in this "school of life" the unemployed lose the rest of their dignity, but this is sold to them as the chance to begin a new life. They live in groups of six, sleep in bunk beds, with only a few lockers separating men and women. They have to listen to inspiring stories and slogans ("work is freedom," 28), watch a television show called *Job Quest*, and are awakened at night to present themselves for fake job interviews and psychological evaluations. The trainees have to reinvent themselves by writing fictive résumés and photoshopping their photo IDs.[3]

The denigration of the trainees reaches its climax when participants are forced to dig a grave and are forced to throw their hopes and dreams into it if they don't want to end in it themselves (38). After three months the trainees are "application professionals." They are well versed in spotting opportunities: they scour the local newspapers for death notices of people at working age; and they are used to intense competition through the bonus system at Sphericon that allocates "bonus coins" that can be exchanged for extra rations or the key to a private room. When they graduate, they are given a certificate of professional application, and they get on the buses in the hope that they can now go home and find a job. But they are suddenly told that they have won a holiday (Sonderurlaub), and, together with graduates from other institutes all over Germany, they are transferred to a Lufthansa cargo plane; then they are told they are going to Sierra Leone, one-way only.

Zelter uses the English jargon and terminology of "coaching for success" and the "optimization" of the individual who is required to show "mobility, flexibility, and resilience." In a German context, these motivational clichés are commonplace in management and human resources departments, but they are still sufficiently alien and artificial sounding in their English form to cause the reader to take note. But the author is also using familiar German customs—for example, the *Hausordnung* (house rules), a collection of guidelines that caution against pity and self-pity, lay down a dress code, and warn about fraternization.

The absurdity of training the unemployed for jobs that do not exist, the futility of it all, is both Kafkaesque and very topical. While Germany currently has the largest number of people ever in employment, many of these new jobs are temporary or precarious,[4] a far cry from the experience of many Germans who were previously used to having a full-time job for life: in West Germany, people hark back nostalgically to periods of "Vollbeschäftigung" (full employment), while in East Germany, the right to work was guaranteed under the constitution. Everything changed with Agenda 2010, a program of reforms to reduce unemployment and promote economic growth. Introduced by the Social Democrats between 2003 and 2005, it helped Germany regain its international competitiveness, but it also significantly weakened the "social net" that had previously protected those who lost their jobs and that had been one of the hallmarks of the country's *Soziale Marktwirtschaft* (social market economy) that is enshrined in the *Grundgesetz* (Basic Law), Articles 20 and 28.

Agenda 2010 and, especially, the Hartz IV regulations for social benefits introduced a harsher climate to the German job market, with recipients of Hartz IV payments often treated in a patronizing manner and forced to undergo humiliating coaching sessions. It is in this context that

Zelter's satire works so well: at Sphericon, being unemployed is seen as a social stigma and construed as a person's own fault; we all know, however, that in real life, with increasing automation, there simply aren't enough jobs to go around. And to make the jobless jump through increasingly pointless and denigrating hoops only to release them into the void anyway is the ultimate cruelty of a system that has placed the "mantra of efficiency" of efficiency before the dignity of the human being.[5]

On occasion, Zelter's satirical imagination can produce laughter, but the reader knows that much of it is too close for comfort: When the trainees are sent off to Sphericon, their relatives say good-bye and take pictures, as though they were children going off to summer camp. A lecture in the program reviews the "history of job applications" and starts in the Middle Ages with *Minnesang* (the German courtly tradition of songwriting to gain a lady's favor). The simple act of writing an application is given an academic gloss by framing it in the context of the rhetorical triangle of "application sender," "application recipient," and "application medium." In another lecture, a theologian reflects at length on the nature of work:

> Is there something like work after death? Assuming there is no work before death, is there work *after* death instead? In the afterlife? Is paradise conceivable without work?[6]

Zelter's satire was well received by literary critics and the reading public, and a dramatized version of his work has been staged in several German cities. The question about what to do with the increasing number of people who are effectively deemed to be no longer necessary has become more and more urgent in recent years, as my discussion of Richard David Precht's and Harald Welzer's recent publications in chapter 1 has demonstrated. Zelter has stated that his detailed knowledge of the Bundesagentur für Arbeit is based on personal experience,[7] which is no doubt authentic in many respects. But there is also a risk in overexaggerating the problem, particularly when Sphericon becomes a "Vernichtungslager für Arbeitslose" (extermination camp for the unemployed), as one German student has interpreted it.[8] At this point, the satire loses its ability to enlighten and becomes an ineffective polemic.

◆ ◆ ◆

Martin Burckhardt's *Score. Wir schaffen das Paradies auf Erden* (Score: We are creating Paradise on Earth, 2015) imagines a seemingly utopian world in the year 2039.[9] Following a global war, the depletion of natural resources, another financial crash, and violent protests, a new ECO-system has been established in the industrialized world that claims to have left behind the "dark age." Controversial concepts like gender, race, religion, culture, and identity have been consigned to the "dunghill of history," as has capitalism itself. The only thing of value is the game, because "der Mensch nur dort ganz Mensch ist, wo er spielt" (the human being can only be fully human at play, 7). Everyone gains points for their "score" through their activities or social interactions, and these are used to pay for goods and services. We experience this world through the eyes of Damian Christie, who works as a systems architect at the Social Design Planning Group for the Berlin-based company NOLLET, which maintains the ECO-system.

The narrator claims that the new order has been enthusiastically embraced by the general public since people were tired of endless crises:

> What people once used to call the industrialized world had become the ECO-system, with ECO meaning the *Enriched Cybernetic Organism*. The acronym was supposed to show that the world no longer belonged to nation states and that it was conceived of as a global organism. The war was over. The riots in the metropolitan areas had ceased abruptly, and even the news items about terror acts had become rarer. A firm belief in the future had gripped people like the harbinger of spring, a conviction that together one could start into a new era.[10]

The "score" is the new value system; it requires total transparency and an understanding of human society where keeping an "identity" is considered to be an attempt at hiding something (the slogan is "Identität ist Verschlüsselung" [identity is encryption], 26). The country's new constitution turns the "pursuit of happiness" into a social objective and state ideology:

> §2. The aim of all life is happiness. As such, striving for happiness is everyone's duty. It is the only duty for the inhabitants of the ECO-system. The paths to happiness are not pre-determined. But it is clear that happiness is a matter for the community. Out of this striving comes the desire for personal optimization, the desire to distinguish oneself before others, all these useful things that earlier societies were only able to achieve through the use of force or the lure of monetary gain. The Score carries value, but it is at the same time the expression of social appreciation. Therefore, striving for happiness goes hand in hand with looking after one's own Score. Neglecting one's calling means committing a crime against oneself and society.[11]

Burckhardt slowly reveals the way the new system works: because production in the ECO-system is largely automated and people are no longer required to build or grow anything, a small group of programmers and system architects is all that is needed. To keep people active and entertained, the system architects have built a gigantic computer game that tracks human behavior through a person's "lifestream," the real-time input of experiences, thoughts and feelings from the sensors everyone wears.[12] Every human interaction receives points in this "economy of microfeelings" (35). Whether one gives a smile to the shop assistant or saves lives in an accident—as long as it is listed as socially useful, it is given a score. Socially unhelpful behavior, though rare, means losing points and subsequently having fewer privileges. Thus, every human action is scoreworthy:

> Just as work had become play, and play had become work, so the difference between money and Score had ceased to exist. Each interaction represented an economic act, even if people were not aware of it most of the time. The smile that a young woman gave an admirer in the crowd caused an economic transaction, just like the fact that someone had remembered someone else's name.[13]

The population is generally happy with the ECO-sytem, and it has not led to a generation of idlers as the Score has tapped into the fundamental human need to "play the game" (38). As always in such scenarios, however, there is a weakness. In this case it is the fact that the people who determine the amount of points for an action do not play themselves (they are given score points outside the system), but they can hack into the supposedly secure lifestream of any other individual. Due to a mysterious malfunction, Damian falls out of the system and experiences the dark side of the Score. He rapidly loses his Score status and becomes part of a resistance group that argues that life under constant surveillance is inhuman (198). Damian also discovers that his father had warned against the new system:

> The societies of the future, his father had written, were risking falling victim to a digital fascism. This thinking was different from the totalitarian ideologies of the twentieth century in that one did not need a leader, nor was there a need for an ideology to weld together the body of a people into a powerful unit. The glue that would hold a future society together was solely based on desire, an unchained form of consumerism where the serious business of life was replaced by an almost *holy unseriousness*. Total war turned into total entertainment.[14]

Martin Burckhardt, a philosopher and game theorist, presents us with a satire born out of a deep skepticism with regard to our ability to navigate the challenges of the future—in particular, the digital revolution. With humans losing one of their key reasons to live—namely, finding meaning in expressing themselves through work—the alternatives are the scrap heap, as imagined in Zelter's *Schule der Arbeitslosen*, or finding an alternative occupation. The idea of turning one's entire human existence into a game is appealing, particularly as the game is shared democratically and not limited to a cultural elite as, for example, in Hermann Hesse's *Glass Bead Game*. At the same time, the system of gaining scores is deeply inhumane, as the motivation for human actions is not voluntary and the allocation of points for specific actions is arbitrary.

These are deeply philosophical questions and would make the novel hard to stomach were it not for the satirical flourishes with which Burckhardt pulls us back to earth. As Thomas Wörtche has pointed out,[15] the reduction of all human endeavor and concern into a game of exchanging specifically prescribed behaviors for personal gain beggars belief, but in this game everything is so desirable and trendy: everyone is politically correct, health conscious, environmentally aware, and gender- and carbon-neutral. Moreover, the superimposition of game and reality, where points can be carried from one into the other, reduces reality to an irrelevance. This "gentle" form of totalitarianism is perhaps the most perfidious, since people genuinely believe they live in the best possible world while they waste their lives in a meaningless, hedonistic limbo. With *Score*, Martin Burckhardt has taken the utopian promise of the title "we are creating paradise on Earth" ad absurdum, lampooning promises like Google's corporate code of conduct motto, "Don't be evil,"[16] as well as the narcissistic and vacuous competition for "likes" on Facebook, Twitter, and other social media platforms. Nothing could be further from a perfect world, argues Burckhardt, than a system that reduces every human action and emotion into an economic transaction.

◆ ◆ ◆

If Martin Burckhardt's satire is cerebral and implicit, Karen Duve's novel *Macht* (Power, 2016; translated into English as *The Prepper Room*, 2018) is rather more earthy and explicit.[17] In the year 2031, climate change has turned Germany into a hothouse with heatwaves and tornadoes a regular occurrence. The only plant still thriving is genetically modified rapeseed that grows like a weed everywhere. Everyone knows that the end is nigh, with religious sects flourishing and people behaving as though their moral compass had stopped working. Many take the powerful drug Ephebo that can make them appear decades younger even though it causes cancer. In this end-of-days scenario we meet the protagonist Sebastian Bürger, an "Öko-Aktivist" (eco-activist) who works in an information center explaining the democratic system to schoolchildren. Sebastian lives in the house of his parents in the middle-class suburbs of Hamburg. He pretends that his wife Christine, the minister for the environment, nuclear decommissioning, and nuclear waste disposal in Germany's all-female cabinet, has left him and then disappeared, though in reality he has kept her locked up in his "prepper-room" in the basement for the past two years. Sebastian feels frustrated by the emasculation he has experienced over the years, and he exacts a terrible revenge on his wife, who is chained to her bed when she is not forced to bake Sebastian's favorite cookies or service his sexual needs. When Sebastian meets his former school crush Elli at a reunion, he decides to kill his wife. Fortunately, Christine survives, and Sebastian is caught when he tries to flee to Paraguay.[18]

It takes a while to come to terms with the author's sense of humor and the macabre events she describes. Right from the start we know that Sebastian is a male chauvinist pig (the book's motto borrowed from Confucius: "Mit Frauen und Untertanen umzugehen ist äußerst schwierig" [women and subordinates are extremely hard to deal with, 5]). While the book is set in a dystopian near future, the focus of Duve's novel is on the nature of men and their need to dominate. Her message is that as soon as the civilizing influence of political correctness disappears, men will revert to their authoritarian nature and subjugate women as sexual objects in traditionally defined roles. Duve's critique, darkly satirical and bitterly comical, leaves no room for a middle ground—men perceive women as annoying obstacles on their way to cheap gratification, and the science-fictional background merely serves to provide a plausibly apocalyptic setting for the dormant tyrannical male psyche to resurface. Sebastian reflects thus:

> Why should I deny my basic male needs just because I have the misfortune of having been born in this tiny window of time when people actually leave the business of government to women?[19]

The drug Ephebo, which takes decades off its users' lives and gives them the appearance and agility of youth, is but a vehicle for Duve to show what she sees as the inauthentic nature of modern society. At a time of great social stress, people seek to return to the safety of a simpler time, when everything was—supposedly—better. Thus, Sebastian rebuilds the house he has inherited from his parents to resemble what it looked like when he grew up. His fiftieth school reunion provides the trigger for accelerating his Ephebo use and for trying to hook up with Elli, the woman he had had a crush on in school. His actions are obviously an extreme example of what is known in Germany as "Wutbürger" (enraged citizens), people who seek reassurance in archaic groups: his brother Uwe joins a fanatical religious group; and his old school friend Ingo Dresen leads MASCULO, an antifeminist gang of disgruntled and divorced men who argue that the rise of feminism has led to the downfall of the nation (205).

But the yearning for a simpler life competes with the realization that in an apocalyptic age all social norms and conventions can be broken. Sebastian's sadistic actions in the cellar are described in grim detail (233), reminding the reader of the perverted men who held Elisabeth Fritzl and

Natasha Kampusch captive for years: "Nie spürt man die eigene Macht so sehr wie in jenen Momenten, in denen man sie mißbraucht" (one never really feels one's own power so much as in those moments when one abuses it, 53), Sebastian muses. As the veneer of civilization peels away, he continues his internal monologue or rant, defending his actions with the excuse that with the world going to ruin, there is no need to pretend any more that men ever respected women as equals:

> It is a whim of our civilization that women were treated as equals in recent decades, just a fluke, not a given. Civilization is not based on amiability or a sense of right and wrong. A civilization will always support what makes it stronger, what it finds useful. To give women a voice in society only made sense as long as we held the hope that women, with their social competencies and their sense of responsibility and all that nonsense, would be able to save our skins one more time. Since climate change has taken its most devastating turn imaginable and we've come to realize that there is no way out, there is no longer any reason to allow women to share power. Justice? Justice is something that only the weak profit from.[20]

Macht was received with rather mixed reviews in the German press.[21] While Duve's description of Germany sliding into a dystopian future barely elicited a comment (presumably because, by 2016, literary critics had encountered too many dystopian or apocalyptic narratives), Duve's depiction of masculine lust and need for power divided critics between those who applauded her for speaking the truth so unreservedly and those who felt that her depiction of men was wide of the mark and unnecessarily provocative and polemical. For this study, it is of particular importance to consider why Duve chose the mode of SF for her novel. In an interview at the Frankfurt Book Fair in 2016, Duve revealed that she had initially intended to write her novel as a crime story but had reconsidered in favor of a SF setting:

> The only reason I switched to science fiction is because I realized this: if I want to construct the figure of a normal guy who may be extreme but not so much that he belongs in a psychiatric ward, someone who isn't a complete psychopath (which would make this really boring), then I needed a setting where it is believable that normal people suddenly do things that were completely outside their frame of reference before. In such a case the end of a world makes a great setting, so, in the year 2031 people just know that the world will end in five years, maybe seven or eight, but it is highly unlikely that anything can be discovered to avert this.[22]

Just as it did for Naomi Alderman in her novel *The Power* (also published in 2016), SF allows Duve (and authors like her) to make strong feminist statements in a way that reduces the need for realism and at the same time increases the opportunities for social satire. Susan Watkins has suggested that female writers are partly drawn to apocalyptic settings because they harbor "a suspicion of techno-science for its destructive complicity with patriarchal and colonial enterprises."[23] In Duve's case, this is certainly true, since she makes an explicit connection between male ambition for power and the dystopian world it has created, even though this insight is attributed to Sebastian:

> By now I understand a little more what must have going through the minds of the bosses of the agriculture and oil industries, why they were so dead set on pursuing their catastrophic course that was leading us all to ruin. They weren't interested in squeezing us for another dollar or two; nor was it stupidity or ignorance. It was the pleasure they got from exploiting weakness. They knew exactly what their CO_2 emissions and their effluents and the cutting down of the rain forest were doing. It must be an intoxicating feeling to do something so utterly evil, something that the world had not seen before. And no one stops you because they don't notice or because they don't believe the ones who do.[24]

♦ ♦ ♦

QualityLand (2017) is a novel-length satire by songwriter and political stand-up comedian Marc-Uwe Kling.[25] After another economic crisis, management consultants have relaunched the Germany of the near future as "QualityLand," ringing in the "QualityTime" (10) in which work, leisure, and relationships have been so completely optimized by algorithms that everything is simply "optimal." As in Burckhardt's *Score*, one's social status is determined by one's conformity to the system, and citizens are named after the occupation of their parents—for example, John Mechanic or Susan Librarian. The German language does not know the positive or the comparative anymore, only the superlative. Thus, every burger is the best burger; every majority is the greatest majority; and the government is formed by the greatest coalition in the QualityParlament (formed by the QualityAlliance and the ProgressParty). In school, children learn to be good consumers ("Neues kaufen, das ist recht. Reparieren, das ist schlecht." To buy new is cool; whoever repairs is a fool, 89), and they no longer study history but receive a "Zukunftsunterricht" (future lesson) that tells them that everything will be all right since every problem has a technological solution (22).

The protagonist Peter Arbeitsloser (Peter Unemployed) has a small business using a scrap press to recycle malfunctioning AI equipment, though he often keeps the AIs "alive" in a spare room. His collection includes a battle robot with posttraumatic stress disorder, a sex robot with erectile dysfunction, a drone with a fear of flying, and, most recently, the writing program *Kalliope 7.3*, which is designed to produce personalized "Bücher für dich" (books for you) but was thrown out when it refused to produce a Jane Austen porn novel (98). One day, Peter receives an unwanted delivery from TheShop™ via drone (the company sends its customers goods before they even know that they want them); he decides to return it. This leads him on an odyssey and a downward spiral as a return is simply not in the terms and conditions, and an algorithm cannot be wrong. His girlfriend Sandra, who works for WeltWeiteWerbung (Worldwide Advertising) and is responsible for product placement in news programs, leaves him and he becomes increasingly isolated until he meets a group named Vorderste Widerstandsfront gegen die Herrschaft der Maschinen (VWfgdHdM, first resistance front against the rule of machines) and manages to confront the CEO of TheShop™.

An astute observer of the absurdities of modern life, Kling ridicules the vacuous promises of the modern consumer society, the way it produces desires for products no one needs, and the well-honed marketing language that goes with it. But his satire goes deeper than a critique of consumerism. He looks at the lure of simple political messages that attack our political system. The ProgressParty fields an AI named "John ofUs" as their candidate for president as "die körpergewordene Stimme der reinen instrumentalen Vernunft" (the embodied voice of pure instrumental reason, 56) who declares that "Maschinen machen keine Fehler" (machines don't make mistakes, 79). John ofUs is defeated in the election because he is too rational and does not promise the impossible, in stark contrast to his opponent Conrad Koch, who is a caricature of Donald Trump.

Kling does not offer a solution to our increasing dependence on communication technology and the way it encourages simplification, political polarization, and dehumanization of meaningful relationships. He simply extrapolates its worst excesses and points out the absurdities it produces. As a statement of cultural pessimism, the novel is reminiscent of Friedrich Nietzsche and Oswald Spengler (which is deeply worrying considering his pedigree as a comedian).[26] As a work of SF, it is more akin to the animated television series *Futurama* than "serious" literature, but that, of course, is the whole point, as the mode itself becomes the message. This view was shared by the jury that awarded *QualityLand* the German SF Prize 2018 for its sheer inventiveness and black humor.[27]

♦ ♦ ♦

For my last exhibit I return to Juli Zeh, whose novel *Leere Herzen* (Empty Hearts, 2017) caused a considerable stir when she confronted her German readers with another dark vision of the future.[28] Her disdainful dedication at the beginning of the book throws down the gauntlet: *Da. So seid ihr.* (There. That's how you are, 5) In the year 2025, Britta Söldner (the last name means mercenary) and her business partner Babak Hamwi run a successful business called "Die Brücke" (The Bridge), which uses sophisticated algorithms to identify suicidal people and help them with their problems. They employ a twelve-stage process that tests their "clients'" resolve to the limit (for example by waterboarding them). The majority of these clients decide to live, and they often pay Britta and Babak handsomely for saving them. But the company has a much more lucrative income stream: it identifies those who are absolutely determined to blow themselves up for a "good" cause and it matches them with organizations that require suicide bombers. The "bridge" is thus revealed to be the link between the suicide bomber's convictions and an extremist organization that has compatible aims.

Britta is a perfectionist, has a lovely house, family and friends, and lives the wealthy lifestyle of Germany's affluent, trendy, and fashionable middle classes, but she has lost her moral compass. Zeh's near-future Germany is becoming increasingly nationalistic, inward looking and protofascist following the "democratic" takeover of the Besorgte Bürger Bewegung (concerned citizens movement, BBB). In government, the BBB introduces "Effizienz-Pakete" (efficiency packets) to roll back democratic rights and the system of democratic oversight. Britta doesn't vote and, as long as she is left alone, doesn't care if the world around her is falling apart:

> Even if she is obliged to follow politics in broad terms because of her job, she doesn't believe that one has to talk about it at home. It is clear that Knut hasn't figured out that politics is like the weather: it happens, whether you watch it or not, and only idiots complain about it. She dimly remembers a time when things were different. She sees herself standing in a voting booth and putting an x in the box, full of conviction. She knows that she had discussed the question who to vote for with others, and that the answer seemed important. She can't quite remember when that was, definitely before the refugee crisis, Brexit and Trump, long before the second financial crisis and the rapid rise of the Concerned Citizens Movement. It was in a completely different era.[29]

When it appears as though a competitor has entered the market, Britta and Babak begin to question their business model; however, Britta has long ago lost her idealism and belief in the possibility of a better world.

To her, seemingly disparate developments and events have taken a cumulative toll:

> Fear of the future. Burnout. Erosion of gender roles. Second financial crisis. Degeneration of the underclass. Increasing discrimination against marginalized groups. Bad diets. Loneliness. Lack of exercise. Decadence. Guilt complexes. The child-rearing failure of the 1990s parent generation. "I believe that deep within us there is a hole," says Britta.[30]

Politically, Germany has completed a program of "aufräumen" (cleaning house, 56), a euphemism for the policies of Regula Freyer, the successor of Chancellor Angela Merkel. What exactly happened is left to the reader's imagination, but, as we piece together the bits of information, it becomes clear that Germany has succumbed to populism, just like the rest of the world has. But this political situation is merely the background to and a manifestation of the pragmatism and lack of values of Germany's citizens that is exemplified in Britta's attitudes:

> Britta loves her work. She works with people, lives by her own rules and does a lot of good. Saving potential suicides represents the largest part of her work. When assassins are placed, *Die Brücke* follows a strict code—a limited number of casualties, careful avoidance of escalation, no collateral damage. . . . As the first and up to now only terror service agency in the Republic, *Die Brücke* has pacified and stabilized the industry. She ensures the right level of threat that every society requires.[31]

But then "Die Brücke" is involved in an attempted putsch against the BBB by former administrators and officials led by the mysterious Guido Hatz, who plans to bring back Merkel, stop the hollowing out of the Basic Law, and shut down the "Bundeszentrale für Leitkultur" (Federal Center for Dominant Culture, 310).[32] The company provides a whole army of "empty-hearted" terrorists for the planned coup. Unsurprisingly, Britta is of two minds about her involvement, as her cynicism trumps her reawakening idealism. She imagines that "der Aufstand der Gerechten" (the uprising of the righteous) would return Germany to its democratic principles, and that a moral renewal would silence

> those notorious grumblers that have been undermining the foundations of democracy with their envy and pettiness. . . . They get their greatest satisfaction through anonymous hatefulness. These ill-tempered postdemocratic bottom feeders who are well on the way to sacrificing the greatest achievement of civilization in human

history on the altar of their personal inferiority complexes. To hell with them![33]

But Britta decides to do the opposite and torpedoes the action so that it fails. She concludes that a moral renewal cannot be forced upon people, that they have to see the light themselves. Disillusioned by the false dawn of a new era at the beginning of the 1990s when the fall of communism had given people hope that the age of war and arms races was over, she cannot muster the courage to believe that people could be made to see reason. Instead, she decides that those who got Freyer and her ilk into office must also vote them out (325).

Leere Herzen was reviewed enthusiastically in the German press. Gustav Seibt argued that Juli Zeh had provided a mirror for the German public to see themselves in, and that what she was showing was the sad truth, even if it was exaggerated. She had merely extrapolated the rising disaffection of those East Germans who shout "Merkel muß weg" (Merkel must go), as well as the lack of engagement of the educated middle classes, who seemed to have abandoned the consensus of solidarity and shared responsibility for the democratic system.[34] Jaqueline Thör compared the novel to Michel Houellebecq's *Submission* (2015) but suggested that Britta's heart may not be completely empty as she does seem to discover her conscience at the end of the book.[35] Julia Enke observed that Juli Zeh, like so many SF writers before her, had used the novel for a "Versuchsanordnung" (experimental setup) to show what would happen not only to the country but also to individuals; this made the book a perfect "Psychothriller."[36] Stefan Jäger praised Zeh for showing her audience what consequences the current "Politikverdrossenheit" (disenchantment with politics) could have.[37]

Leere Herzen is the darkest of the social satires discussed in this chapter. The coinage of the term "Terrordienstleister" (terror service provider, 72) sets the scene, as does Britta's flippant observation: "Es gibt tatsächlich immer noch Menschen, die so tun, als könnte man dieser durchgedrehten Welt mit Haltung begegnen" (there are still some people who think they can face this crazy world with integrity, 68). Her protagonist's pragmatic worldview is best summed up in her observation that every industrialized society seems to need a certain amount of running amok, "während die Erscheinungsform nur eine Frage der jeweiligen Mode ist" (while its manifestation only depends on the fashion of the time, 185). Perhaps the most sardonic passages are those in which she pillories her fellow intellectuals for having retreated from the battle. While engaged writers and intellectuals waste their time in pointless debates, Juli Zeh bitterly observes, the democratic state is handed over to its enemies:

Nonvoters who are fed up with democracy win elections, while engaged democrats quit voting. Intellectual newspapers are busy overcoming humanism while the populist gutter press holds on to the ideals of the Enlightenment. In a world full of contradiction, it is hard to think and speak—after all, every thought negates itself and every word has the opposite meaning.[38]

Satire can and should cause laughter, and it can make us think about how close or how far we are from the exaggerated worlds we are presented with. In the case of SF, which thrives on estrangement, social satires seem to be doing the opposite by bringing the strange future worlds much closer to reality. In their earnest desire to confront what they see as dangerous social developments arising out of our technological capabilities, the authors discussed in this chapter have used the mode of SF, but they have stripped it of its optimism. Whether this is a distinctively German trait or whether mainstream authors simply find the mode particularly convenient will be discussed in my conclusion. Now, however, it is time to move from the near to the very far future, and to explore what may be when humans as we know them are no more.

17: Critical Posthumanism: Twilight of the Species or a New Dawn?

SCIENCE FICTION HAS long anticipated a future after the Anthropocene, whether that involves augmented humans, cyborgs, artificial intelligences, new species, or something else. In the anglophone world, we have key texts like H. G. Wells's *The Man of the Year Million* (1893), Olaf Stapledon's *Last and First Men* (1930), Dan Simmon's *The Hyperion Cantos* (1989–97), and Margaret Atwood's *Oryx and Crake* (2003). As Stefan Herbrechter has argued, SF often seems to suggest that a "posthuman era" is inevitable, since it assumes that by using technology (biotechnology and digitalization) humanity will somehow overcome its current state and become something radically different.[1] A "critical" posthuman approach acknowledges the challenges to what we consider human characteristics (e.g., consciousness, emotion, language, intelligence, morality, humor, and mortality). At the same time, it avoids naïve technophilia as well as apocalyptic gloom and it seeks to define what aspects of humanness need to be protected.[2]

Dietmar Dath is one of the most prolific writers of German SF with five novels in the last ten years: *Die Abschaffung der Arten* (2008, *The Abolition of Species*, 2018), *Pulsarnacht* (2012), *Venus Siegt* (2016), *Der Schnitt durch die Sonne* (2017), and *Neptunation* (2019). In spite of winning the Kurd Laßwitz prize twice, he is not a "typical" SF writer; nor, however, does he belong to the "mainstream." Best described as a nondogmatic Marxist cultural critic, Dath is well aware that his way of writing SF is not exactly crowd-pleasing:

> Science fiction is the genre in which the twentieth century has learned to treat the political and scientific questions of the age as aesthetic ones, in a popular form. I like that, and try to do the same, only in a less popular manner. Whether this is successful will be decided in the new century.[3]

Nevertheless, with *Die Abschaffung der Arten*, a fictional continuation of Charles Darwin's *On the Origin of Species* (1859), Dath has managed to garner both critical acclaim and produce a bestseller. The book starts with a quotation from Nietzsche:

Error has turned animals into humans; might truth be capable of turning the human being into an animal again?[4]

In the novel, the Anthropocene is over. Humans have been replaced by the Gente, highly intelligent animals who communicate by scent and control their own evolution. The leader of the three city-states Kapseits, Landers, and Borbruck in former Europe is the lion Cyrus Golden, who is advised by his daughter, the lynx Lasara, and her partner, the wolf Dmitri. The Gente can splice their genes and change their gender at will, thus producing an endless variety of new races. Dath clearly enjoys world-building, and he leisurely explores his creation, often through philosophical discussions and lengthy conversations between the various genetic manifestations. The action speeds up when the Gente are threatened by the Ceramics (a postbiological collective intelligence that has developed in the Amazonian jungle) and are forced to leave Earth. Five thousand years later, Feuer and Padmasambhava, descendents of the Gente who have developed different and new civilizations by accelerating their genetic evolution on Mars and Venus, return to Earth and explore the ruins of previous civilizations.

Right from the start, *Die Abschaffung der Arten* adopts a pragmatic and yet elegiac tone—for example, when the Gente reflect on the demise of humankind (from a mixture of pity and perverse fascination, they keep a small number of surviving humans in zoos):

> If it hadn't been love that caused humanity to fail, then why had its noisy, stinking, all-encompassing desire to rule the world ended so bloodily? Would it have been possible for them to continue to grow, like rattan that thrived without moisture, like a reed without water? For the time being, if one searched in the archives, it still stood in a kind of melancholic final flush, as memory in texts. But even before you could cut it and take it with you, it had already wilted. The hope of mankind, the greatest talent of the ingenious destroyers, was lost, their confidence gone, their ambition mere cobwebs on books that no one would ever open again.
>
> They had trusted their house, but it hadn't kept them safe. They had stood in sunshine, full of vim and vigor, and the offshoots of their plantations had overgrown their garden. Roots had wrapped around piles of rocks and clung to the boulders. Having been eradicated from their home, it now denounced them and did not know them.[5]

In this passage, Dath tells us that humans lost their right to rule the Earth when they lost love (solidarity) and treated their planet with disdain (pollution, exhaustion of resources, climate change). This led to hopelessness, which in turn killed their ingenuity, their confidence, and their ambition. With humanity responsible for its own demise, the question is whether intelligent animals who are not handicapped by human morality can do better. The Gente are not necessarily smarter than humans, as their endless political squabbling shows, but they reach a kind of happiness at the end of their evolutionary journey.

In a wide-ranging interview that was published in conjunction with the novel, Dath responded at length to the question whether he saw *Die Abschaffung der Arten* as a utopian or a dystopian novel.[6] He stressed that he preferred the term SF (even though the book was not labeled or marketed as such) because it was able to offer a concrete vision of the future, which the audience then had the opportunity to instinctively accept or reject, as well as to critically reflect on. While utopians were admittedly naïve, they were at least humane, while dystopians were too lazy in their comfortable "Meckern und Jammern" (complaining and moaning) attitude to actually engage with the challenges of the present and seek solutions for them. As he was presenting a world that had utopian and dystopian elements, the reader had to work harder and weigh up whether the disadvantages of the fictive future outweighed the disadvantages of the present—a properly dialectical approach.

Die Abschaffung der Arten was widely praised for its intelligent anticipation of the next technological revolution, the "Transformation der Biologie" reflecting the step-change in biological sciences with our newfound ability to control our own evolution.[7] What has been overlooked, as far as I can see, is the other allusion in the title to the Act for the Abolition of the Slave Trade (1807), which signified the beginning of a global awareness of the ethical wrongs involved in the human exploitation of "lesser races" and which is replicated in the novel through the relationships between the various species that follow humanity on the evolutionary ladder. As such, I would argue that Dath's protestations against a utopian worldview should be taken with a large pinch of salt. At heart, his project is a socialist one, and his dream is that of a pacified, if complex, utopian world.

♦ ♦ ♦

Reinhard Jirgl's novel *Nichts von Euch auf Erden* (2013) emphatically does not share Dath's (qualified) optimism.[8] Set five hundred years in the future, the book insists that nothing will ever change the old adage that man will be a wolf to his fellow man (*homo hominem lupus*). With resources depleted on Earth (hydropower from melting glaciers keeps the lights on) and humanity hiding under so-called "Imago-Sphären," which guarantee a sheltered existence, the "Tat=Menschen" (the doers, 26) have left Earth in the twenty-third century to live on Mars, leaving behind a human species that has been stripped of its aggressive nature due to an accidentally released "Detumeszenz-Gen" (detumescence gene, 19) and now leads a life of depressing monotony:

> By means of the *Imago Spheres* they had been able to create their own heaven, without God or other superior beings. The Earth became Terran; day and night, sun and moon are now merely the reflection of human souls. The power of action had shrunk, almost broken and neutralized. On the other hand, the powers of the soul had risen and become the only criterion of truth. In the process, however, humans had not only forgotten the real sun, the real sky with its weather, and the real night with its lethal darkness, but also lost the experience of joy found in work and achievement.[9]

When attempts to terraform Mars fail and life becomes unbearable on Mars, the "Tat=Menschen" return and brutally wrest power from the defenseless humans on Earth. All this the reader can glean from a forty-two-page introduction written in relatively straightforward German. What follows, though, is a tour de force: In two sections, the development from the twenty-third to the twenty-fifth century is recorded and commented on by a number of voices, including the half "Martian" BOSIXERKABEN and his parents who offer different perspectives and interpretations of humanity's future history. In a handbook that explains the Martians' strategy for the violent recolonization of Earth, the reader gets not only an insight into their unbridled brutality and aggression but also a sense that behind "Earth humans" and "Mars humans" sits an artificial intelligence ("die morphologischen Bücher," the morphological books, 401), which ultimately survives the showdown that leaves both planets destroyed.

Reinhard Jirgl isn't usually associated with SF, but he is perhaps one of the most respected German authors discussed in this book. He lived and worked in the GDR and only came to wider public notice after the fall of the Berlin Wall. As a recipient of the Georg Büchner prize in 2010, he belongs to Germany's literary elite. He is known for his radically uncompromising writing style that obeys its own aesthetic, comparable to that of Arno Schmidt. Because of his high profile in German literature, and because *Nichts von Euch auf Erden* appeared on the shortlist for the German Book Prize in 2013, professional critics were obliged to engage with his foray into "genre fiction." Their response was mixed: they applauded the author for his brave attempt to break the boundaries of language and taste, but they were also unsure about the work's ultimate message. Oliver Jungen acknowledged that Jirgl was challenging his readers to the utmost with extremes of brutality (to solve the problem of overpopulation and poverty, little children are served in restaurants on Mars) and pessimism ("Äußerste Liebe des Menschen ist Liebe zur Menschlosigkeit," the greatest philanthropy is the love for a world without humans, 322), but he argued that ultimately the novel was "eine der großartigsten Phantasmagorien der jüngeren deutschen Literatur" (one of the greatest phantasmagories of the newer German literature).[10] Hubert Winkels praised Jirgl's language as "a kind of hallucinogenic-holographic reality installation," yet he declared himself exhausted by "seitenlange florale Orgasmusmetaphernwucherungen" (lengthy floral metastases of orgasmic metaphors) and "futuristisch aufgepimpte geologische Fachsprachenstrapazen" (futuristically pimped-out geological exertions of jargon).[11] Hans-Jost Weyandt suggested that Jirgl's excursion into SF was a move worthy of a master storyteller who reasserted the avant-garde's claim to speak to the future.[12] Julian Werlitz provided a broader perspective, analyzing Jirgl's novel in the context of SF's penchant for using books as repositories of "future histories" and of the unreliability of memory given its subjective nature.[13]

Given the uncompromising pessimism with which Jirgl treats his readers to his vision of humanity's ultimate end, some doubt about the work's ultimate "usefulness" may be appropriate. As Elfried Müller rightly argues in her review, Jirgl's attempt to "estrange" his future world by torturing the German language is an aesthetic overkill given the message that we are all doomed anyway.[14] As a contribution to critical posthumanism, though, *Nichts von Euch auf Erden* needs to be taken literally. The genetically "neutered" humans on Earth have organized their lives in the protected zones of the "Imago Sphären" with strict laws to conserve the remaining resources. This in turn requires compliance and social cooperation, something that does not come naturally to the "Tat=Menschen."

While some of Jirgl's dark vision of humanity's future can be attributed to his experience of a totalitarian system in the GDR, his life after the fall of the Berlin Wall hasn't changed his skeptical view of our basic nature. In a lengthy discussion or interview with Alexander Kluge on occasion of the premiere of the dramatized version at the *Munich Kammerspiele* in 2015, Jirgl explained his long view of human history and his desire to create a "playing field" that was as far removed from the present as the Thirty Years' War was removed from us.[15] This suggests that humanity was incapable of learning from its mistakes and inexorably moving toward its own extinction. Whether his work serves as a call for reflection, a Cassandra warning, a call to action, or as a depressing confirmation that humanity is beyond hope ultimately depends on the disposition of the reader (who need not necessarily buy into Jirgl's vision). Yet therein lies the problem, not only with *Nichts von Euch auf Erden*, but more broadly with a critical posthumanism that cannot offer a positive perspective. The writer and critic Beatrix Langner put it succinctly when she asked:

So what is the point of a novel—no matter how brilliantly written—where human beings, ethically shaped by antiquity, humanism, and enlightenment simply do not feature anymore because they have been replaced by amorphous flesh, blood, and tissue samples or digital holograms of human beings, simply so that it can perform Jirgl's posthumanist private theater of cruelty?[16]

◆ ◆ ◆

If hope is in short supply in Reinhard Jirgl's posthuman future, Leif Randt's novel *Planet Magnon* (2017) appears to offer it in abundance.[17] Far in the future, humanity has settled a solar system with six habitable planets (Blink, Blossom, Cromit, Sega, Snoop, and Toadstool), each with distinctive characteristics and home to "collectives" that share certain ideals and characteristics. They are "governed" by an artificial intelligence that guarantees a classless society, peace, and a comfortable lifestyle for everyone. To ensure a fair distribution of labor and resources, the computer system ActualSanity runs a mixture of a planned economy (for transport, health, and so on) and a BonusEconomy that encourages individual entrepreneurship in trade and services, all based on statistical analysis of material as well as psychological data. The collectives are permeable, and individual members can switch allegiance and apply to become members of another collective if they wish. They all subscribe to a "postpragmatic" world view called "PostPragmaticJoy" (293) that favors self-fulfillment, tolerance, and an emotional equilibrium that eschews pity, excitement, or strong emotional attachments ("Wir sind füreinander da, aber nicht aneinander verloren," we look after each other, but we are not lost in each other, 42).[18] The pride of belonging to a particular collective (CX2, Dolfin, Fuel, Ideal, Kelly, Post-Volta, Purpur, Shift, Volta, Westphal and Zelda) is inculcated in school and college through "stilprägende Praktiken" like dress codes, sporting events, competitions, excursions, and festivals where recreational drug taking is widespread and encouraged.

Unsurprisingly, this world has its drawbacks and contradictions. For one, the original programmers of ActualSanity have mysteriously disappeared via "Diffusionierung" (diffusion, 278, 283). The computer system now self-selects the teams necessary for its maintenance. There is also the sense among some that the detached attitude that is encouraged to guarantee peaceful coexistence does not meet the human need for emotional closeness and even leads to the occasional heartbreak. ActualSanity has overcome warfare, inequality, and poverty, but it has done so at the price of much that characterized and contributed to a deeper, more typically "human" existence–whether uncontrollable emotions, memories of the past, or disastrous relationships, all of which are associated with the "Alte Zeit" (old days, 279). To break the culture of "cool," a resistance group has formed that describes itself as "the collective of the broken hearts." The "Hanks" disrupt the peaceful equilibrium of the collectives, initially with flyers, but also by releasing a substance called Ketasolfin that causes doubt and nostalgia in small doses but with greater exposure can lead to paralysis or panic.

Two well indoctrinated members of the Dolfin collective, Marten Eliot and Emma Glendale, are dispatched to find the dissenters, and their quest offers the author the opportunity to explore the six planets and two moons, as well as the other collectives. Marten and Emma eventually find the Hanks on the planet Toadstool, where rubbish and toxic waste from the other planets is collected and processed and where members of each collective serve a period of time supervising the workers. The implication is that exposure to the dystopian environment on Toadstool (with its allusion to the poisonous fungus) may remind the "postpragmatic" visitors of the wider range of emotions available.

Planet Magnon was enthusiastically reviewed.[19] Nils Markwardt interpreted the novel as an inspired critique of the "Zukunftsfanatismus" (fanaticism about the future) à la Silicon Valley, as it pointed to the emotional losses that come with the belief in, and the adoption of, an optimized existence.[20] Philipp Theisohn honed in on the significance and topicality of the "collective" as a posthuman alternative to the humanist concept of the individual,[21] but it was the Austrian writer Eva Menasse, giving the laudation on occasion of Leif Randt winning the Erich Fried prize in 2016, who cut through to the unsettling message of the book, asking whether we were not already well on the way to becoming posthuman.[22]

A posthuman condition, Menasse argues, will inevitably lead to major psychological alienation, a process that she feels is already visible today in the aggrieved "emotional losers" (Hillary Clinton's speaking about the so-called "deplorables," the Brexiteers, and the right-wing populists?) who vent their pain, fear, and frustration on social media and on the streets. In the meantime, the privileged citizens of the affluent parts of the world already have access to the life-extending medicines and cosmetic surgeries, mood-enhancing drugs, gated communities, private education, and global networks that ensure they are never exposed to the indignities of a fight for survival.

Much of what Leif Randt describes in *Planet Magnon* will feel familiar to Germans who lived through the twentieth century. Again and again, the utopian concept of a "New Man" was propagated: by the Nazis through an ideology that sought to replace an individual's exposure to the "bourgeois" (but also moral) family unit with indoctrination in the Hitlerjugend, the Deutsche Arbeitsfront, Lebensborn, and so on; by the GDR, through its initiation of individuals into socialist organizations like the Freie Deutsche Jugend and the Gesellschaft für Sport und

Technik with the ultimate aim of turning them into the Communist New Man; and by the "68ers" (the Sozialistischer Deutscher Studentenbund, Kommune I), through their denunciation of the nuclear family as the breeding ground for the authoritarian character.

In fact, all three texts discussed in this chapter allude to the attempts to create a "posthuman" on German soil. They do not seek to relive the past but rather to learn from it. It is in the recognition of, and through the confrontation with, the possible downsides of a posthuman condition that Dietmar Dath, Reinhard Jirgl, and Leif Randt, to varying degrees, challenge the utopian and especially the technological and (bio-)evolutionary narrative of progress: they seriously engage with the discourse of the posthuman but emphasize that a posthuman life may well feel meaningless to humans. In this respect, they illustrate the psychological impact of the technological future described in Yuval Harari's *Homo Deus* (2016), thus enabling readers to anticipate, and, if they so choose, to actively and consciously direct their path to the future.

18: High Concept: Time, the Universe, and Everything

THIS FINAL CHAPTER is not intended as a "mop-up operation" for German SF narratives that do not fit into the thematic strands explored thus far. In fact, each of the following examples could have easily found a home in one or more of the strands discussed before. But what sets them apart is an elusive quality of transcendence, a search for epiphanic moments, a desire not to be too specific in their anticipation of the future but rather to act as artistic statements—about concepts like time, love, or the meaning of life—that the readers or viewers will have to come to terms with for themselves.

Marlen Haushofer's novel *Die Wand* (1963) is a perfect example of this type of text: an unnamed forty-year-old woman spends her vacation in a hunting lodge in the Austrian Alps.[1] Overnight, a transparent wall appears that separates the woman and the mountain region around her from the outside world. There is no sign of life outside the wall; in fact, beyond the wall animals (and a single person visible in the distance) seem to be immobile while plants continue to grow. The woman is left not simply to survive on her own but also to develop the resilience to cope with her loneliness. She quickly rules out ending her life:

> I lay in bed shivering, wondering what to do. I could commit suicide or try to dig under the wall, something that would most likely turn out to be a more laborious way of killing myself. Of course, I could simply stay and try to remain alive. I wasn't young enough to seriously contemplate suicide. What really prevented me from going through with that was the thought of Luchs and Bella [the dog and the cow], and a certain curiosity. The wall was an enigma, and I would have never been able to steal away while there was a riddle to be solved.[2]

With hard work, she manages to eke out a life, having only a dog, a cat, and a pregnant cow as her companions. She learns to look after the animals and secure food, and she spends the summer months further up the mountains in a hut on the alpine pastures, experiencing moments of inner peace and acceptance of her situation. After two years, a stranger appears and, for no apparent reason, kills her calf and dog before she can shoot him (killing the stranger proves less traumatic to her than the loss of her animals). The narrative is her account that she writes in order to help her come to terms with the situation.

Lisa Cornick has described *Die Wand* as "premise fiction,"[3] which is arguably a key element of all SF. This particular "what if?" narrative in its purest form does not rely on space travel, future technology, or robots, but it nevertheless introduces what, at the time, is an inexplicable element. It also challenges our sense of reality, thus linking us to the psychological "inner spaces" of awareness and perception that currently go beyond what can be measured with scientific instruments.

The experience and description of the woman's isolation allow for a broad range of interpretations.[4] We can read them as an exploration of the essential loneliness of the modern individual, a Robinsonade, a *Zivilisationskritik*, a blueprint for radical female emancipation, or a postnuclear apocalypse scenario. They expand on the experience of a survivor coming to terms with a world that has simply "stopped." In 2009, the French blogger Diglee discovered the book and posted her impressions on Instagram, which led to a hasty reprint of *Le Mur Invisible* by the Actes Sud publishing house.[5] The novel was then made into a film in 2012 by director Julian Pölsler with one of Germany's best-known actors, Martina Gdeck.[6] It was also put on stage at the Burgtheater in Vienna by Christian Nickel in the same year.[7]

We may well wonder why a simple, if mesmerizingly told, story of a woman who finds herself not only isolated from the world but also quite likely one of the few surviving human beings on the planet has struck a nerve fifty years after it first appeared. This may have to do with the similarities between the Cold War uncertainties and our postmillennial sense of insecurity about the future that has made strange bedfellows of the back-to-nature and the survivalist or prepper movements. In SF, we have seen a large number of postapocalyptic and dystopian narratives in the last two decades—from "last human" narratives (discussed in chapter 10) to popular television shows like *Lost* (2004–10) and films like *Arrival* (directed by Dennis Villeneuve, 2016) or *Annihilation* (directed by Alex Garland, 2018) that play with, and feed on, the inexplicability of the liminality their protagonists experience. These all delay or completely deny their audiences a rational, scientific explanation, thus testing the traditional pact between science and SF, even though they still hold open the door to the possibility that superior intelligences or phenomena yet to be understood are the cause.

The impenetrable barrier itself is, of course, both an enigma and a symbol that can signify both the inability to communicate with a partner, colleagues, or the world, and the physical walls that have come down (in the case of the Berlin Wall and the border between the two Germanies) or have gone up between Israel and Palestine and between the United States and Mexico. We have seen a wall "protect" affluent northern Europe from migrants in Lars Kraume's *Die kommenden Tage*. The fact that the wall is transparent in Haushofer's *Die Wand* and that we do not know who or what erected it is particularly disquieting: The outside world remains tantalizingly visible yet out of reach while living on the "inside" can appear like living in a goldfish bowl under scrutiny by unseen forces.

♦ ♦ ♦

Andreas Eschbach's novels *Die Haarteppichknüpfer* (1995) and *Quest* (2001) also fall into the "high concept" category. They depict a galactic empire that, with its unfathomable history, mythology, and religion, has Kafkaesque features, and in which people, as in our world, are confronted with existential questions such as power, oppression, freedom, and the search for meaning. *Die Haarteppichknüpfer* was awarded the German SF Prize in 1996, and it appeared in English in 2005 as *The Carpet Makers* with a foreword by Orson Scott Card.

The novel describes the galaxy Gheera, in which the "Sternenkaiser" (star emperor) is worshiped on thousands of planets like a god. Each planet has to produce an annual tribute, in the form of thousands of carpets woven from human hair. This cult dominates economies and societies, superstructure and base. The carpet makers, who devote a lifetime's work to weaving these delicate carpets from the hair of their wives and daughters, may each have only one son; he will one day take over their task. If a second son is born, the father must kill one of the two sons. The rugs are ceremoniously handed over to the imperial traders, who move them to collection points, from where they are transported to the central planet, allegedly to decorate the palace of the "immortal" emperor. Step by step, Eschbach allows the reader deeper insights into the strictly ordered culture on one of these planets, but he prevents any deeper identification with the protagonists by constantly changing the scene and perspective from chapter to chapter.

The rumors circulating for years (and suppressed as heresy)—that the God emperor has been overthrown by a revolutionary movement—prove to be true. In fact, emissaries of the revolutionary government are trying to figure out what to do with these remote planets and the carpet cult. It turns out that the once-thriving planets were bombed back to a lower level of civilization thousands of years ago, and that the imperial cult was enforced through indoctrination and the brutal exercise of power. This immense logistical and ideological effort, however, springs from nothing more than an insult and the resulting revenge has gone on for thousands of years, so that only the emperor's archivist still knows its origin. The sheer scale of the tragedy carried out in dumb obedience takes the reader's breath away.

The novel is poetically formulated, psychologically empathetic, and meticulously conceived. In an extending spiral, Eschbach widens the focus and thus allows the reader to gain an ever-increasing understanding of the context. The reader's task (as is typical for SF) thereby lies in combining the information into a meaningful whole by means of various hypotheses that have to be corrected time and again. It is this constant reorientation that prevents identification with the protagonists and thus opens the readers' eyes to questions about how people are trapped in traditions determined by others, the motives of the revolutionaries (which are also determined by others), and the profound irony involved in the fact that the revolution also relativizes itself and abandons the "liberated" carpet makers to a meaningless future.

This is the point: although the novel seems to be set in the Middle Ages (in relation to the history of our own world), Eschbach is concerned about the future. The confrontation with the revolutionaries, who travel in spaceships between planets, as well as the highly developed technology of the empire, cause uncertainty for the reader. If the future is only a repetition of the past, if the spaceships we associate with the concept "future" do nothing other than the merchant caravans of the Middle Ages, what is the meaning of revolutions and progress? Eschbach may sound like an anti-Marxist, but behind his apparent fatalism hides a spark of utopian anticipation that humanity will escape the historical cycle.

Eschbach combines his anthropological and ethnological interests in a seemingly primitive culture with an optic that challenges the reader to ask uncomfortable but fundamental questions: who determines our lives ("It has always been like this, and always will be," 11)? How do we ensure that our values and standards of behavior are adequate? How reliable is our frame of reference? The hair carpet trader can fool the simple villagers ("Is it possible for the emperor to abdicate? Can the sun shine without him? Would the stars in the night sky not be extinguished without him?" 18), but his daughter is already full of doubt, as the narrator reveals: "If it were the nature of the world that such certainty as she had felt could be an illusion, then she didn't want to live in this world anymore" (26).

After the revolution, these questions can only be answered in the imperial archives, and yet the accumulated knowledge is forgotten again and again or requires reinterpretation through intense research. Here, Eschbach references SF classics such as Jorge Luis Borges's *La biblioteca de Babel* (The Library of Babel, 1941) and Isaac Asimov's *Foundation Trilogy* (1951–53), but he also integrates the experience of our modern information society, in which knowledge and values are increasingly subject to spin and manipulation.

For the SF critic John Clute, the novel initially felt "a bit archaic, a bit European, a bit choked with extraneous meaning, a bit *metaphorical*;"[8] but he soon realized that this book was extraordinary. Eschbach's novel, Clute argues, represents a significant advance in the history of SF through its open structure, in which the individual chapters can never stand alone and never really come to an end. As a consequence, the reader waits for an end that never comes. "Eschbach's novel . . . is therefore not about Time, but Death: stories that do not conclude being death to time" (163). Central to Clute's reading is the image of the millions of hair carpets that are laboriously made on thousands of planets, but that can never really be fully comprehended: "The *Carpet Makers* is—like the carpets it does not describe—woven into the shape of a carpet it does not describe" (164).

It is tempting to read the world of *Die Haarteppichknüpfer* as an allegory—for example, of the former communist states, shaken to their ideological foundations, or of Iraq before the two Gulf wars. However, the text resists such simple interpretations. The revolutionaries, who could win only because the emperor had grown tired of his power, find no substitute for the imperial cult—the promise of "freedom" turns out to be hollow. Only the young generation that has not been indoctrinated is able to imagine another life at all.

Eschbach's achievement lies in the powerful description of a coherent, seemingly familiar, and, at the same time, completely alien culture, which is characterized by emotional coldness and fatalism. Only at the end of the novel—when Ostvan, the grown-up son of the carpet maker who has killed his older brother Abron in the first chapter, finally realizes that the supposedly unchangeable world no longer exists—does Eschbach allow a cathartic moment.

Eschbach returned to the universe he first explored in *Die Haarteppichknüpfer* with the novel *Quest* in 2001.[9] While the former was mainly focused on a single planet, the latter explores the vastness of space and the outer reaches of the galaxy Gheera. The title "Quest" refers both to the main protagonist, but also to his final task, which is to find the origin of life, and God himself. Set one hundred thousand years before the events narrated in *Die Haarteppichküpfer*, the tenth *Sternenkaiser* is about to invade the galaxy Gheera. Eftalan Quest, a high-ranking officer and a commander of the spaceship Megatao, sets out to find the mythical "planet of origin', from which all life is supposed to have sprung.

Quest is deeply troubled as he hasn't been able to stop the invasion of his home planet Toyokan, where all living beings were wiped out. In addition to this psychological trauma, he is also terminally ill; however, he hides this from the crew and his superiors so that he can continue the mission. His second-in-command, Dawill, sits too low in the strict caste system to have access to the mission details, which contain only routine orders to patrol a region of space. At the beginning of the mission, Quest orders the raid of the "Pashkanarium," an archive belonging to the brotherhood of Pashkan, which, in theory, enjoys autonomy. In the archives, Quest's experts find information about nonhuman races and the location of their planets. They learn about the existence of the "Yorsen," and they head for their home planet.

On the way, they encounter an ancient spaceship that has lost its FTL (faster-than-light) drive. Only ten members of the crew, including the ship's captain, Smeeth, have survived the cold sleep. It turns out that Smeeth is one of the twelve immortals of Gheeran mythology, and that he had already visited Yorsa and tried to establish contact with its inhabitants. When the Megatao finally encounters the Yorsen (who are busy using their advanced technology to move whole solar systems with their nonhuman populations out of the galaxy to protect them from the reach of the Sternenkaiser), Quest learns that the Yorsen do not know the location of the "planet of origin" either, and that there is an even older species called Mem'taihi that does have the information he is seeking. Unfortunately, the location of their planet is in another galaxy and Quest collapses during the transition through hyperspace. Smeeth takes over as captain and they find the planet, but they are once again too late: the planet of the Mem'taihi is abandoned and its buildings disintegrate when the crew of the Megatao enter them. Smeeth now admits that he knows the location of the "planet of origin" and Quest, who is close to death, lands there on his own to demand an explanation for his mysterious illness and for why he alone has survived the battle for his home planet. Quests returns from the planet's surface a changed man. He believes that he has actually met God, and he dies in peace. Smeeth departs on his own in his repaired ship, but he counsels the crew of the Megatao to abolish its antiquated caste system and to not return home, since the Sternenkaiser's army will by that point have overrun Gheera. In the end, it turns out that Smeeth has not told the truth: the planet that Eftalan Quest landed on is not the "planet of origin," and his epiphany is an illusion.

This summary still gives only a taste of Eschbach's vivid imagination and skill in creating entire worlds and mythologies. To call *Quest* a "space opera" (implying space battles, a melodramatic plot, and two-dimensional characters) would be a mistake, though, as the sheer scale of the stage merely serves to illustrate what the author states in the first sentence:

> The most surprising discovery made by humans when they started to explore space was this: all life in the universe is connected in one form or another.[10]

Both *Die Haarteppichknüpfer* and *Quest* ask complex ethical and uncomfortable moral questions. The ruthless raid against the extraterritorial archives on Pashkan is just the start of a literally endless quest for information and understanding, driven in this case by Eftalan Quest's traumatic experience of the destruction of all life on his home planet that he had been powerless to prevent. The ultimately fruitless search for the origin of all life and the relentless threat of the armies of the Sternenkaiser seem to leave no room for hope. As Smeeth tells the new captain, Dawill, before his departure:

> The star emperor's realm encompassed several galaxies and is one enormous military machine. There is no art, no song, nothing beautiful that would make life worth living. There are just weapons and military equipment, all serving one single purpose—conquest.[11]

The only hope to break the cycle of violence, Smeeth continues, is to refuse to participate; to end the artificial social divisions of the caste system, and start again:

> Don't fly back. You are in the fortunate situation that the MEGATAO has disappeared without trace, and that nobody in the Empire knows where it went. No-one will ever find you. Look for a pleasant, livable planet somewhere in this galaxy and settle down. You have all the equipment you need to create a wonderful new world.[12]

As in *Die Haarteppichknüpfer*, there is an all-pervasive sense of loss in *Quest*—the meaning of "life, the universe and everything" has been erased. Hence the "quest" to discover the origins of life, and the creator, and to remonstrate with whomever engineered humanity to be so violent. But the message, and the context, of both books may not be all that abstract. With reference to *Die Haarteppichknüpfer*, Germanist Vibeke Rützou Petersen argues:

> In Eschbach's novel, the strict hierarchical family set-up adheres to the oppressive laws of the God emperor at terrible psychological and physical cost. . . . Women are chosen as mates—and men can take multiple mates/wives—solely for the strength and color of their hair. Here, too, the novel enters an area where Nazi ideology has made itself felt. Although there certainly was a greater complexity to the Aryan notion of the perfect woman/mother other than hair and eye color, this is another case where there is no escape from the long shadow cast by the Nazi decrees of Aryanization.[13]

She continues:

> While the use of the human female hair can function as a "more general sign of brutal dehumanization, violence, and violation" (von der Osten), its deployment in a work of German SF brings the specific Nazi horror to the fore. In my reading, by bringing this trope into the light as a myth about carpet makers in an empire far, far away,

the narrative aids in robbing the images of their context while also weakening their link to history or historical referent.[14]

Petersen has argued elsewhere that German SF has long mined Germany's "fertile historical ground" while engaging with present cultural concerns.[15] In particular, she claims that the Nazi period and the Holocaust manifest themselves in a number of its narratives. This, she believes, makes German SF different, "because German history made dystopias of the most radical kind a reality" (34). Recalling its own history, with its burden of Fascist horror and genocide "is a most bold gesture" (35), as the SF writers' "enlightenment-like faith" (36) in progress runs the risk of trivializing the experiences of the victims:

> An apocalypse *did* take place during the Third Reich and it constitutes *the* abyss in modern Western civilization and history. We are all touched by it to varying degrees, but it occurred on German and German-occupied soil. This fact structures a difference between German and other Western Science Fiction.[16]

While Petersen is entirely persuasive in her analysis ("German SF, therefore, is an aporia, a site of inextricable contradictions," 40–41), I would suggest that she arrives at her conclusion on the basis of a limited and highly selective sample. As we have seen in the various thematic strands in this study, German SF, especially since the new millennium, has cut some of its ties with its national trauma and has engaged with a broader range of issues, some domestic and some global. At the same time, it tries to overcome a mentality that seeks to permanently reconstruct the past in the name of exorcizing the past (*Vergangenheitsbewältigung*) without a perspective to prevent its repetition or a positive way out—for example, by pointing to strategies that could lead to a mindset that is better equipped to face the moral, ethical, and ideological challenges we will be facing or what I call coping with the future (*Zukunftsbewältigung*). If, as Petersen avers, "Science Fiction as a genre has . . . claimed the right to reconstruct, reimagine, and re-present the twentieth-century German past" (45), then it strikes me that to hold German writers to a higher standard than anglophone writers is not just unfair but counterproductive.

If we look at *Die Haarteppichknüpfer* again in this light, we find that Eschbach *does* point to a solution, even if it is not without its own contradictions. The revolutionaries who have finally overthrown the Sternenkaiser and set about to undo thousands of years of indoctrination and oppression do not have all the answers; but they certainly allow the locals to make their own decisions about their future. Petersen would no doubt interpret these as the equivalent of the acts of the victorious Allied forces and their reeducation program in Germany, except that Eschbach might also be talking about the Cold War and the confrontation of the superpowers in which both German states were merely pawns. As to *Quest*, we could add the context supplied by the first Gulf War (1990–91), the Bosnian War (1992–95), the Rwandan genocide (1994), the Kosovo War (1998–99), in which the Federal Republic, for the first time, involved itself militarily, as well as that of Francis Fukuyama's *The End of History and the Last Man* (1992), all of which could arguably be the subject of Eschbach's analysis of humanity's predilection for violence and selfishness. Indeed, it could be said that Germany's long struggle to come to terms with, and learn from, its past might ideally qualify its writers to help others to become empathetic and to break the cycle of violence.[17] Seen in this light, *Quest*, as the name suggests, may well be determined by a much older German cultural tradition—namely, the medieval search for the Holy Grail as a means of salvation, and, as such, by humanity's eternal search for the meaning of life.

◆ ◆ ◆

In his 2005 novel *42*, Thomas Lehr devotes himself to another "high concept": the subject of time.[18] At CERN (Conseil Européen pour la Recherche Nucléaire [European Organization for Nuclear Research]), near Geneva, a serious accident happens when, on August 14, 2000, a group of seventy science journalists, politicians, and tourists visit the underground particle accelerator DELPHI (Detector for Lepton, Photon and Hadron Identification). When they return to the daylight on this sunny day, they realize that time is "frozen" at exactly 12:47 and forty-two seconds p.m. (hence the title, *42*). Birds and airplanes hang motionless in the air; people sit or stand, frozen in motion like statues; even the sun appears nailed to the zenith. The first-person narrator Adrian Haffner, a science journalist from Munich, reports in flashbacks over the next five years during which the scientists (the "Cernies") try to get to the bottom of the cause of the catastrophe, while others start a religious sect or go exploring across Europe.

Initially, the group of the "chronified" acts in solidarity. They investigate the circumstances of the stopped time and share information at their annual conferences about the "new physics" (51). But, as it becomes clear that time will not "start" again, the psychological pressure becomes too much for some, leading to suicides, mistrust, crime, perverse acts with fellow human beings frozen in time, and increasing despair. One of the "survivors" attempts to strengthen the group's sense of belonging. He produces a monthly bulletin with the "Complete List of Humanity in Geneva" and "Rules of Survival" to cope with this physically alien world (vehicles do not work; a door can only be opened by strenuous effort; the survivors can only hear each other from close range). In addition, he names the typical phases of the psychological response to the disaster: shock, orientation, abuse, depression, and fanaticism. In chapters bearing the same names, Lehr illustrates these levels of moral degeneration so clearly that the claustrophobic sense of isolation is transferred directly to the reader.

Haffner is initially determined to wait stoically and make the best of the situation: "You have survived. Point one. You are not completely alone. Point two. Once again, it hit others" (34). However, as his isolation increases, he loses his certainties. His wife Karin, who he imagined had been on vacation by the Baltic Sea, where he arrives after months of walking, had actually been in Florence at the time of the disaster with her lover. A year later he has found her, and he is tempted to throw the statue of the lover out of the window. Not that Haffner is too worried about marital fidelity himself—like most of the males who have been "chronified," he gets used to increasingly ruthless sexual intercourse with the helpless statues he calls "Fuzzis."

In lengthy passages, Haffner philosophizes about the "flatus temporalis" (fleeting fart):

> Time, we thought back then, when the apple still happily fell from the tree, . . . is the great river that flows through the endless glass shaft of the room, which captures everything, overflows, and carries along on its irreversible run to the future.[19]

The survivors find themselves under a spell ("Verwunschenheit," enchantment, 114), a world of magical sleep ("Dornröschenschlaf," Sleeping Beauty's sleep, 112), hopelessly floating on the rapids like a cork ("Schwimmkorken auf den Stromschnellen der Zeit," 127). They call themselves "zombies" (98), who—full of self-disgust and despair—fathom the abysses of their own soul:

> You are the ignoble savage chosen by DELPHI to play with the glass beads of the world. You are free, so terribly free, that suddenly the forgotten philosophy comes true, according to which your fear should be nothing more than the frightening discovery of your own possibilities.[20]

In this passage Lehr employs well-known motifs and symbols of world literature—from William Golding's *The Lord of the Flies* ("We are the savages of the time, the relativistic barbarians." 263) or from the theme of the "last human" who is confronted with himself.

After five years, the world experiences the "great lurch" (der große Ruck); time actually moves forward for three seconds, but then stops again. Adrian experiences this moment in Munich, and instinctively all the "chronified" return to Geneva, full of hope for a normalization of conditions. Although the scientists succeed in restarting time, Haffner's link to his former life remains blocked. Full of self-loathing, he reflects on his personal failure:

> I do not want to think about time anymore. Either everything is fire, freedom and movement and nothing will return. Or everything that happens, has happened, can happen, is already there, immovable, enormous, in a monstrous, madly branched, iron tree of the world, on which no leaf stirs.[21]

The reviewers were generally enthusiastic, and they extolled Lehr's linguistic virtuosity. Beatrix Langner praised the "expressionistic power of his style," which she characterized as "poetic surrealism."[22] Moreover, with his fourth novel (which made it to the shortlist for the German Book Prize in 2005), Lehr had proved that it was possible to write literature at the level of modern scientific knowledge. All this appreciation, however, also contained a snide remark directed at readers of SF, who, according to Helmut Böttiger, were facing a "specific challenge" in this novel because the book did not offer run-of-the-mill prose but a literary experimental arrangement in which the old world and the new were ingeniously rendered by connecting the physical and the poetic in a previously unknown manner.[23]

What critics like Böttiger overlook is the fact that SF does not hold any fear of contamination by "high culture"; rather, SF assimilates and utilizes it for its own purposes. Thus, *42* is the infernal vision of a never-ending present, crystallized in a moment, which, of course, is a modern interpretation of Faust's exclamations—"If ever I should tell the moment: O stay, you are so beautiful!" (Goethe, *Faust* I, 4.1699–700) and "the clock may stop, the hand be broken, then time be finished unto me!" (4.1705–6). These lines provide the literary foundation for Lehr's vision of a disaster caused by human arrogance, from which Haffner, unlike Faust, cannot be liberated by a miraculous intervention.

Read this way, the work of scientists at CERN, driven by curiosity and (literally) boundless energy, becomes a challenge to the "natural order." In their hubris they strive for knowledge of "what the world contains in its innermost heart and finer veins" (*Faust* I, 1.383–84), but they are unable to reverse the consequences of their actions. In contrast to Faust's utopian dream of the "bold and industrious people" (*Faust* II, 5. 6.11928) Lehr presents the sober observation that man, set free from moral and social ties, becomes an animal again. Lehr's uprooted souls accordingly develop an amazing criminal energy. Living outside of time (Mephistopheles's "everlasting void"), they lose every concept of personal integrity and morality. They literally have gone to hell.

♦ ♦ ♦

Like Thomas Lehr's novel *42*, Sebastian Hilger's film *Wir sind die Flut* (We Are the Flood, 2016) starts with a physical anomaly but turns it into an inquiry into the human condition (childhood, parenting, ambition, rivalry, love, betrayal, death, grief, hope, and despair). In a physics lecture at the Humboldt University in Berlin, PhD student Michael Wiedmer (Micha) explains to new students how fifteen years earlier, on April 5, 1994, the ocean along a ten-mile stretch of the North Sea coastline near the north Friesian village of Windholm simply disappeared, leaving the mudflats empty in a semicircular area with an eight-mile radius. Since the tides depend on the gravitational pull, their disappearance clearly defies the laws of physics. Scientists are completely baffled. But there is another aspect to the phenomenon: at the same time as the tides stopped, all the children in the village vanished without a trace.

When Micha comes up with a new theory that the gravitational constant might not be universal and wants to test it, his department refuses to fund him, so he sets off with his ex-girlfriend Jana and enters through the security cordon pretending that he has official permission. The traumatized villagers are deeply anxious about the fate of their children and are initially unwilling to speak to them—that is, all except Hanna, who, now nineteen years old, is the only child that did not disappear. Hanna tries to rebuild an abandoned swimming pool in the crumbling village, and she guides gawking tourists to the eerily silent coast. While Micha's experiments on the mudflats do not produce any reliable data, he and Jana discover a connection between the diary of one of the vanished children, Matti, and the unexplained phenomena. Matti had dreamed of becoming an astronaut before becoming terminally ill. Micha and Jana, who are coming to terms with their own failed relationship and Jana's decision to abort their unborn child, surmise that the boy had tried to stop time and died on the same day as the tide stopped coming in. In a mysterious encounter out on the mudflats, Micha thinks he is seeing the boy appear out of the mist, but ultimately the search is for naught and he and Jana are expelled from the village by the security personnel.

With such a mysterious plot that combines the laws of physics, the deep emotions of love and regret, the local people with their intense grief and, most importantly, the vista of the vast expanse of the mudflats that never see the tide come in, the film offers multiple lines of interpretation and comparisons with other high-concept SF works—most obviously with Christopher Nolan's film *Interstellar* (2014). Nadja Weber points out that, with the disappearance of the children, the village has lost its vitality and future as time seems to stand still.[24] Weber also calls attention to the transition from a "hard science" to a more intuitive approach when Micha begins to realize that his theories are inadequate to explain the phenomena that seem to be connected to his own childhood (he tells Matti's father that he recognizes the boy's drawings and that he had also dreamt of becoming an astronaut as a child). The mystery of what happened is never solved, and, as Hanna tells a group of tourists, what they see out in the mudflats may well be a mirror of what is in them:

> There are people who are afraid of the void. . . . When they look at the emptiness, they don't feel they are looking out, but rather into themselves.

Gabriele Mueller sees the film as in keeping with other recent European films that are increasingly visualizing fears about the future and "imagining dystopian scenarios that stand against the idea of a peaceful and united Europe."[25] She criticizes what she sees as Hilger's "mangelnde Zukunftsvisionen" (defective visions of the future, 141) and overly explicit depiction of the "Misere, Enttäuschung und Perspektivlosigkeit der jungen Generation" (misery, disappointment, and loss of perspective of the young generations, 145). At the same time, she concedes that the positive ending of the film does offer some hope (152).

I agree with Mueller that *Wir sind die Flut* addresses both the demographic trends in Germany and the deep unease with which the current young generation views the future (Micha's precarious position in the university and the fact that he has to work other jobs to make ends meet is a prime example of this), but I would argue that the film, just like the other texts discussed in this chapter, raises broader issues as well. As Micha says at the beginning of his lecture: "Man sagt, daß es keine Geheimnisse mehr gibt. Das stimmt so nicht" (People say that there are no more secrets. That's not really true). His questioning of the gravitational constant marks him out as a lateral thinker, who, though committed to the scientific method, at least allows for the possibility that there are aspects of life that require a conceptual breakthrough.[26] This is of course the moment in which Romantic thought (defined by the German poet Novalis as "das Ungenügen an der Normalität" [the insufficiency of normalcy]), utopian thought (Ernst Bloch's "noch-nicht" [not-yet]) and the premises of SF (Kurd Laßwitz's *Über Zukunftsträume*) intersect. At the end of the film, a cassette tape is found and we hear the dying Matti comforting his father and reminding him "daß unsere Träume wahr werden, wenn wir nur fest genug daran glauben" (our dreams come true only if we really believe in them). This is a childlike anticipation of the utopian aspiration of the young adults who have been able to "think outside the box" and ask radical questions. The tide, as Hanna tells us at the close, has turned:

> When we were children we used to dream of a better world. We wanted to be a movement, to be many, just like the tide. Now that we are older, the low tide has caught up with us. It won't let us go.

But we are not afraid of it anymore. It is a part of us. It will not get us down. We are setting out, we are getting ready and making plans, even if you can't see it yet. One person has gone out and returned the tide.

◆ ◆ ◆

SF has never been afraid to ask the "big questions," to speculate about "the meaning of life, the universe, and everything."[27] The examples discussed in this chapter are neither better nor worse than their anglophone cousins, though they reflect a specific mentality and a cultural specificity that enable them to connect with local audiences. Confronted with the inexplicable (the transparent wall in Haushofer's *Die Wand*, the reason for the hair carpet cult in Eschbach's *Die Haarteppichknüpfer*, time coming to a stop in Lehr's *42*, and the disappearance of the tides and the children in Hilger's *Wir sind die Flut*), our desire to find answers is challenged to the utmost, at times frustratingly teased by these master storytellers, but ultimately rewarded as they not only enlighten us about ourselves, but return back to us some of the awe and wonder with which we used see the world around us.

Conclusion

SCIENCE FICTION ENGAGES with scientific progress and social change by imagining alternatives to the present status quo—often, but not exclusively, in future scenarios. It is a literary form that mirrors the changing human condition while at the same time it is capable of accommodating "the spatial scale and cultural heterogeneity of an entire planet."[1] Grounded in, and often explicitly critiquing, perceived political, social, economic, and cultural shortcomings, it confronts them with the impact of scientific and technological innovations. Freed from the shackles of realism but still working within the (remotely) possible, if not the plausible, science fiction writers and filmmakers set up thought experiments that allow their audiences glimpses of possible futures and the consequences of specific choices.

German SF builds on a broad tradition of utopian thought and the nation's calamitous history in the twentieth century. The alternative history approach has a particular appeal to German audiences because of the disastrous choices the country made in the past: the experience of hubris and the subsequent fall echo through a number of the works explored here. But Germany's experience of a totalitarian past does not have to be a permanent burden—rather, it has inoculated German SF writers who warn against the risks of ubiquitous surveillance, an uncritical adherence to the mantra of growth and progress, and the siren calls of demagogues.

German SF is distinctive because it tends to ask complex questions. Fritz Lang and Thea von Harbou's *Metropolis*, Carl Amery's *Der Untergang der Stadt Passau*, and Andreas Eschbach's *Die Haarteppichknüpfer* explore the mentality of tyranny and subservience, while Arno Schmidt's *Die Gelehrtenrepublik* sarcastically reflects the madness in the strategy of "mutually assured destruction." There is an elegiac and melancholy tone in some of the works discussed here—for example, Marlen Haushofer's *Die Wand*, Valerie Fritsch's *Winters Garten*, and Thomas von Steinaecker's *Die Verteidigung des Paradieses*. At the same time, German SF often assumes a more defiant, political stance, especially in critiquing capitalism. Rainer Werner Fassbinder's *Welt am Draht* and Leif Randt's *Planet Magnon* offer explicit deconstructions of capitalist excesses, while social satires like Martin Burckhardt's *Score* and Marc-Uwe Kling's *QualityLand* effectively ridicule the promises of Silicon Valley.

German SF is highly idealistic: even in dystopian guise, it urges its audiences to adapt to the challenges of the future, to learn from mistakes, to protest against injustices and inequalities, to empathize with victims, to mobilize for just causes, and to not lose hope while doing so. Obviously, there has been a major shift in tone and spirit from the high idealism of Kurd Laßwitz's *Auf zwei Planeten* and *Sternentau* to the more skeptical prose of Frank Schätzing and Andreas Eschbach, and from the optimism of *Raumpatrouille* to the more disturbing messages of *Die kommenden Tage*. But the sense that humanity is capable of creating a better world permeates many works—most obviously in the Perry Rhodan series—and can be felt even in Dietmar Dath's posthumanist *Die Abschaffung der Arten*.

What unites the utopians and futurists, as well as the writers and directors of this diverse collection of texts and films from the last 125 years, is their willingness and courage to think beyond the here and now. SF cannot forecast the future, but it can imagine some of the challenges that we may encounter, making us cocreating participants in an act of *Zukunftsbewältigung* that is as vital for the body politic as it is for our mental balance and emotional well-being. This may sound counterintuitive, since so many of the examples explored in this book paint a dystopian picture of the future. The point is, though, that the dystopian worlds depicted in these imaginaries need not become reality if we do not want them to.

Of course, there is a sizeable gap between what the authors and filmmakers claim as their objective (to warn their audiences) and the reality of the market (to entertain audiences ever eager for new thrills). The sheer cumulative weight of the relentless misery and pessimism conveyed in their works puts a question mark over their function as "critical dystopia," as well as over the role of poets as "unacknowledged legislators of the world" when some writers and directors could well be accused of a dereliction of duty.[2]

What comes through strongly in all the works discussed here is a spirited response to utopian thought, the wellspring of joyous world-building and world-destruction, where the exercise of the untrammeled imagination develops our sense of possibility (*Möglichkeitssinn*), which can have an energizing effect that then leads to action (or at least a greater openness to change). To quote William Blake (who was of the utopians' party without knowing it): "Every thing possible to be believ'd is an image of truth."[3] It is certainly no surprise to read how many scientists have been inspired by SF (and vice versa).[4]

The reference to William Blake is no glib comment. Both anglophone and German SF operate within a shared cultural and literary tradition, from Greek mythology (Prometheus) to Shakespeare's and Goethe's plays.[5] Of course, meanings can and will change: after Aldous Huxley, we no longer associate the phrase "brave new worlds" with something altogether desirable, nor do we place as much credence in Faust's achievements after the unleashing of the power "that binds the world's innermost core together" (*Faust* I, 1.383). Moreover, anglophone and German SF live in a symbiosis, not just through the adoption of many English scientific and technological terms (which East German SF studiously avoided) but also through translations, shared cultures (fanzines, conventions), and, most importantly, a shared utopian world view. While German SF may be more skeptical owing to the country's historical experience with having too much power, for many years it also looked (with slightly rose-tinted glasses) to America, the "land of endless opportunity" and its ebullient self-confidence.

When it comes to cultural differences between the "two cultures," they appear to dissolve in a number of areas. German writers and filmmakers genuinely try to understand and faithfully depict the mindset of scientists and engineers—and to portray the significance and likely social impact of their work in the areas of computing, bioengineering, and climate research—while the large tech corporations in turn eagerly mine SF for new ideas. Similarly, the barrier between "mainstream" and niche "genre" is dissolving,[6] as SF writers and filmmakers are becoming more ambitious in language, style, and presentation while "mainstream" writers and film directors adopt the instruments of SF to extend their possibilities and reach.[7] In this respect, the practitioners (and the publishers and studios) seem ahead of the critics and those academics who do not consider SF worthy of their attention (the absence of reviews of Andreas Eschbach's *Nationales Sicherheitsamt* in the national press being just the most recent example). As long as German literary histories cut out a significant chunk of cultural production, and as long as literary scholars continue with their singular focus on the past and the present while closing their eyes to what Caroline Edwards has termed the "fictions of the not-yet,"[8] German studies will miss out on some of the brightest talents and will lose its relevance in the twenty-first century.

Admittedly, there is a *Berührungsangst* (fear of proximity) on both sides of the divide. Hannes Riffel, the guest editor of a special issue on fantastic literature in one of the bulwarks of Germany's mainstream literary tradition, the venerable *Neue Rundschau*, has no illusion that the barriers will fall soon:

> It would be fair to say that, in this issue, two (or more) worlds collide. Literature—with a capital L—tends to look down on the fantastic. . . . The readers of Sf and fantasy, on the other hand, tend to idealize the ghetto they are being put into, or into which they themselves have chosen to go.[9]

Riffel's qualification "or more" is highly perceptive. In German literary circles, we can still observe deep suspicions about the literary worthiness of SF that have little to do with the "two cultures" divide between the sciences and the humanities but a lot to do with deeply ingrained attitudes. Furthermore, as we have seen repeatedly in my case study of German SF, there exist significant differences between the dominant anglophone way of looking at SF and the way others may perceive and practice it. While some valiant attempts have been made to increase diversity in the United States (e.g., *The Big Book of Science Fiction* edited by Ann and Jeff VanderMeer and the crowdfunded translations in *Clarkesworld* magazine),[10] the fact remains that SF is seen by many scholars as an anglophone invention and it is treated both as a means of cultural hegemony and an economic export asset. German-language authors and filmmakers are acutely aware of this tilted playing field. While they are all well-read in the anglophone tradition and can locate precisely the pressure points where SF has succumbed to the mechanisms of the culture industry, they have to be careful in their "nonanglophoneness" not to come across as "anti-American," as that would lose their chances to reach a broader audience. On the other hand, we should acknowledge that those German utopians, futurists, and utopian storytellers who succeeded in the United States (Wernher von Braun, Herbert Marcuse, Roland Emmerich, Werner Herzog) did so emphatically by sticking to their unique visions.

Much depends on what gets translated into English. There are positive signs: more texts, for instance, are being translated, often for independent publishers, and the more recent books, in particular, stand a good chance as the global public is sensitized to the challenges of the future (think Green New Deal and Fridays for Future), Publishing costs go down and production companies compete for new ideas and content. But even a one-in-five chance leaves four-fifths untranslated. And it would be a huge loss if the English-speaking world missed out on another genuine classic like Kurd Laßwitz's *Auf zwei Planeten* (1897), which only appeared in English seventy-five years after it was published in Germany, and even then only in a cruelly abridged version.

Looking back over 125 years of German SF, one cannot help but marvel at the distance traveled, but also at the longevity of its utopian dreams. Robert Brenner's *Signale vom Jupitermond* (1968),[11] published more than fifty years ago, still amazes through its accurate predictions but also its wide-eyed innocence.[12] To be fair, while the author imagines a perfect world (with a global government headed by a black world president, free public transport, videoconferencing, genetic engineering, distance learning, electronic payments made possible by international electronic data transfer, interracial marriages, global job mobility, direct democracy, and collective responsibility), the interspersed interviews with real-life "experts" were rather more realistic (and accurate) in terms of the challenges to be faced. One of these, the futurist Ossip Flechtheim, predicted that the arms race between the superpowers would continue, and he foresaw civil wars and the persistence of hunger and poverty in the "Third World." At the same time, he struck an optimistic note, echoing humanity's utopian dream:

> As desperate as the outlook for the year 2000 may seem, a desperate effort remains the only chance for a turn for the better. Only in this way will we ensure that humanity will at least see in the year 2000 and survive the catastrophes. In that case it will be in a better position than today and get significantly closer to its old dreams of freedom and peace, equality and brotherhood.[13]

Reading such long-forgotten visions of the future can fill one with nostalgia for a seemingly simpler world; but it can also instill pride in what has been achieved, as well as relief that the worst predictions have not (yet) come true. In particular, what Robert Jungk calls the "Ingenieurkunst auf molekularer Ebene" (the art of engineering on a molecular level, 116) in the form of bioengineering has given us access to much that would have been regarded as pure "science fiction" fifty years ago. It is not inconceivable that in another fifty years we will have taken steps to slow down climate change, have moved toward sustainable economies, have found a cure for cancer, and have significantly reduced the number of people living in poverty.

What comes next? I hope to have provided sufficient information for readers to follow their own interests in specific writers, themes, or periods. As this study has shown, other language cultures have equally significant traditions and culturally distinctive approaches to speculative fiction; hence, one goal of future research should be to focus on what might be called the "transcultural fantastic": the production of SF locally and globally across languages, helping to build the global consciousness and planetary culture so often evoked in utopian writing. While I have positioned German SF almost exclusively in relation to anglophone SF, we should not ignore the fact that the former is routinely translated, not necessarily into English but into French, Spanish, Italian, and Russian, just as many Russian, Chinese, French, and Polish SF texts have influenced German SF. A study of the flow and the trajectories of global SF, in the context of recent advances in our understanding of "world literatures" (a discourse that has also hitherto ignored SF), would certainly help us to understand it as a truly transcultural mode, an essential part of "global writing" in the twenty-first century.[14]

Another area worthy of attention is the large number of dramatizations of German SF. A sampling from the last ten years alone could include Christian Kracht's *Ich werde hier sein im Sonnenschein und im Regen*, directed by Armin Petras at the Stuttgarter Staatstheater in 2010; Juli Zeh's *Corpus Delicti*, which has involved several productions, most recently by Marie Schwesinger at the Schauspiel Frankfurt in 2019; Dietmar Dath's *Die Abschaffung der Arten*, directed by Kevin Rittberger at the Deutsches Theater Berlin in 2009; Marlen Haushofer's *Die Wand*, directed by Christian Nickel at the Burgtheater Wien in 2012; Reinhard Jirgl's *Nichts von Euch auf Erden*, directed by Felix Rothenhäusler at the Münchner Kammerspiele in 2015; and Leif Randt's *Planet Magnon*, directed by Alexander Eisenach at the Düsseldorfer Schauspielhaus in 2016. While the venerable radio play has seen a decline in popularity in Germany in recent decades, audience numbers for SF on stage have steadily grown; this suggests an appetite by directors and audiences for engaging with the future in a more immediate art form.

SF can have great relevance for our lives. It can raise consciousness and make us think; it can perhaps even motivate us to act. It has grown into a mode of thinking that reflects the past and the present yet projects both into the future. It raises vital ethical and moral questions, which is why it is so popular especially with young audiences. But learning about responsibility is a lifelong task: SF teaches us to manage hope and despair, to cope with our increasingly complex societies and the advances in science and technology, to test the validity of our concepts, and tackle them with confidence.

◆ ◆ ◆

I started this project with the assumption that if literary efforts have a positive impact on *Vergangenheitsbewältigung* in Germany (as evidenced for instance in the works of Günter Grass, Uwe Timm, or W. G. Sebald), then SF may render a similar service to *Zukunftsbewältigung*. After all, they present us with scenarios born out of a utopian impulse to empower us to imagine likely futures and make informed moral and ethical choices in and for our lives. But I must also admit that, having worked through such a large corpus of narratives, so many of them dystopian, I am no longer so sure.

Dystopian narratives are decidedly political since they warn us against sleepwalking into a future nobody wants, and in which only the elites are able to reap the benefits of scientific and technological progress. But does this interpretation still ring true when the market is flooded with novels imagining every possible horror scenario, perhaps deadening our sensitivity and luring us into a state of apathy while creating a climate of fear that in turn breeds either a desire to escape a seemingly hopeless future or a yearning for populist strongmen to "sort it all out"? The utopian critique of a reality found wanting risks being replaced by a dystopian mirror of a reality found overwhelming. At their best, German dystopian narratives engage with scientific and technological developments and work through their implications for our lives, in order for us to anticipate and adapt to, albeit rarely to control, the forces unleashed. Perhaps even this is expecting too much of a literary and cinematic form that seeks to entertain at the same time as it reflects our post-postmodern sense of unreliable realities.

On the other hand, we can take heart from the fact that we can, collectively, meet the challenges of the future by taking note of the strategies dystopian narratives mark out as important: to mistrust power; to think for ourselves; to stand up for equality; to resist nationalism, racism, jingoism, bigotry, escapism, gender bias, collectivism, and surveillance in the name of security; to fight ignorance; to respond creatively. They teach us to accept change as part of being human; to think about how we can manage our new powers and share their benefits; and to understand that the future may be scary and messy but that it is also, as yet, unwritten.

Appendix 1: Chronological List of German SF Novels—A Selection

Laßwitz, Kurd. *Auf zwei Planeten*, 1897. (In English: *Two Planets*, 1971).
Scheerbart, Paul. *Die große Revolution: Ein Mondroman*, 1902.
Laßwitz, Kurd. *Sternentau: Die Pflanze vom Jupitermond*, 1909.
Kellermann, Bernhard. *Der Tunnel*, 1913 (In English: *The Tunnel*, 1915).
Scheerbart, Paul. *Lesabéndio: Ein Asteroiden-Roman*, 1913 (In English: *Lesabéndio*, 2012).
Dominik, Hans. *Die Macht der Drei: Ein Roman aus dem Jahre 1955*, 1922.
Döblin, Alfred. *Berge, Meere und Giganten*, 1924.
Dexheimer, Ludwig (pseudonym Ri Tokko). *Das Automatenzeitalter: Ein prognostischer Roman*,1930.
Illing, Werner. *Utopolis*, 1930.
Dominik, Hans. *Der Wettflug der Nationen*,1932.
Hesse, Hermann. *Das Glasperlenspiel*, 1943 (In English: *The Glass Bead Game*, 1949).
Werfel, Franz. *Stern der Ungeborenen: Ein Reiseroman*, 1946.
Jünger, Ernst. *Heliopolis*, 1949.
Schmidt, Arno. *Die Gelehrtenrepublik*, 1957 (In English: *The Egghead Republic*, 1979).
Franke, Herbert. *Der grüne Komet*, 1960.
Haushofer, Marlen. *Die Wand*, 1963 (In English: *The Wall*, 1990).
Brenner, Robert. *Signale vom Jupitermond: Ein Bericht aus dem Jahre 2028*, 1968.
Franke, Herbert. *Zone Null*, 1970 (In English: *Zone Null*, 1974).
Amery, Carl. *Der Untergang der Stadt Passau*, 1975.
Steinhäuser, Gerhard. *Unternehmen Stunde Null: Leben nach dem jüngsten Tag*, 1975.
Erlenberger, Maria. *Singende Erde: Ein utopischer Roman*, 1980.
Jeschke, Wolfgang. *Der letzte Tag der Schöpfung*, 1981.
Steinmüller, Angela, and Karlheinz Steinmüller. *Andymon: Eine Weltraum-Utopie*, 1982.
Ziegler, Thomas. *Alles ist Gut*, 1983.
Pausewang, Gudrun. *Die Wolke*, 1987.
Fleck, Dirk C. *Go! Die Ökodiktatur*, 1993.
Ziegler, Thomas. *Stimmen der Nacht*, 1993.
Ransmayr, Christoph. *Morbus Kitahara*, 1995 (In English: *The Dog King*, 1997).

Eschbach, Andreas. *Die Haarteppichknüpfer*, 1995 (In English: *The Carpet Makers*, 2005).
Rabisch, Birgit. *Duplik Jonas 7*, 1997.
Eschbach, Andreas. *Das Jesus-Video*, 1998.
Kerner, Charlotte. *Blueprint Blaupause*, 1999.
Kirchner, Barbara. *Die verbesserte Frau*, 2001.
Eschbach, Andreas. *Quest*, 2001.
Schätzing, Frank. *Der Schwarm*, 2004 (In English: *The Swarm*, 2006).
Jeschke, Wolfgang. *Das Cusanus-Spiel*, 2005.
Lehr, Thomas. *42*, 2005.
Weiner, Richard M. *Das Miniatom-Projekt*, 2006.
Zelter, Joachim. *Schule der Arbeitslosen*, 2006.
Dath, Dietmar. *Die Abschaffung der Arten*, 2008 (In English: *The Abolition of Species*, 2018).
Kracht, Christian. *Ich werde hier sein im Sonnenschein und im Schatten*, 2008.
Schätzing, Frank. *Limit*, 2009.
Zeh, Juli. *Corpus Delicti: Ein Prozess*, 2010 (In English: *The Method*, 2012).
Trojanow, Iliya. *EisTau*, 2011.
Eschbach, Andreas. *Herr aller Dinge*, 2011 (In English: *Lord of All Things*, 2014).
Stein, Benjamin. *Replay*, 2012.
Whey, Florian Felix. *Toggle*, 2012.
Jeschke, Wolfgang. *Dschiheads*, 2013.
Jirgl, Reinhard. *Nichts von euch auf Erden*, 2013.
Hillenbrand, Tom. *Drohnenland*, 2014 (In English: *Drone State*, 2019).
Weiner, Richard M. *Aufstand der Denkcomputer*, 2014 (In English: *Rise of the Thinking Machines*, 2016).
Uhrmann, Erwin. *Ich bin die Zukunft*, 2014.
Burckhardt, Martin. *Score*, 2015.
Fritsch, Valerie. *Winters Garten*, 2015.
Duve, Karen. *Macht*, 2016 (In English: *The Prepper Room*, 2018).
von Steinaecker, Thomas. *Die Verteidigung des Paradieses*, 2016.
Kyr, Oliver. *Ascheland*, 2016.
Brandhorst, Andreas. *Das Erwachen*, 2017.
Kling, Marc-Uwe. *QualityLand*, 2017 (In English: *QualityLand*, 2020).
Randt, Leif. *Planet Magnon*, 2017.
Timm, Uwe. *Ikarien*, 2017.
Hannig, Theresa. *Die Optimierer*, 2017.
Zeh, Juli. *Leere Herzen*, 2017.
Brandhorst, Andreas. *Ewiges Leben* 2018.
Eschbach, Andreas. *NSA—Nationales Sicherheits-Amt*, 2018.
Schätzing, Frank. *Die Tyrannei der Schmetterlinge*, 2018.
Moini, Bijan. *Der Würfel*, 2018.
Hillenbrand, Tom. *Hologrammatica*, 2018.
Eschbach, Andreas. *Perry Rhodan—Das größte Abenteuer*, 2019.
Hannig, Theresa. *Die Unvollkommenen* 2019.

Appendix 2: Chronological List of German SF Films—A Selection

Lang, Fritz, dir. *Metropolis*, 1927.
Lang, Fritz, dir. *Frau im Mond*, 1929.
Hartl, Karl, dir. *F.P.1 antwortet nicht*, 1932.
Bernhardt, Kurt, dir. *Der Tunnel*, 1933.
Kutter, Anton, dir. *Weltraumschiff I startet*, 1937.
Hilpert, Heinz, dir. *Der Herr vom andern Stern*, 1948.
Maetzig, Kurt, dir. *Der schweigende Stern*, 1960.
Braun, Michael, dir. *Raumpatrouille Orion*, 1966.
Zschoche, Hermann, dir. *Eolomea*, 1972.
Fassbinder, Rainer Werner, dir. *Welt am Draht*, 1973.
Erler, Rainer, dir. *Operation Ganymed*, 1977.
Emmerich, Roland, dir. *Das Arche Noah Prinzip*, 1984.
Fleischmann, Peter, dir. *Es ist nicht leicht, ein Gott zu sein*, 1990.
Schübel, Rolf, dir. *Blueprint*, 2003.
Herwig, Michael Bully, dir. *Traumschiff Surprise. Periode 1*, 2004.
Herzog, Werner, dir. *The Wild Blue Yonder*, 2005.
Alvart, Christian, dir. *Pandorum*, 2009.
Lucacevic, Damir, dir. *Transfer. Der Traum vom ewigen Leben*, 2010.
Fehlbaum, Tim, dir. *Hell*, 2011.
Kraume, Lars, dir. *Die kommenden Tage*, 2011.
Tykwer, Tom, Lana and Lilly Wachowski, dirs. *Der Wolkenatlas*, 2012.
Pölsler, Julian, dir. *Die Wand*, 2012.
Hilger, Sebastian, dir. *Wir sind die Flut*, 2016.
Ruzowitzky, Stefan, dir. *Acht Tage*, 2019.
Koch, Philip, dir. *Tribes of Europa*, 2020.

Notes

Introduction

[1] Briegleb and Weigel, eds., *Gegenwartsliteratur seit 1968* (1992); Schnell, *Geschichte der deutschsprachigen Litearatur seit 1945* (1993); Weidermann, *Lichtjahre: Eine kurze Geschichte der deutschen Literatur von 1945 bis heute* (2006); Brockmann, *A Critical History of German Film* (2020); Minden, *Modern German Literature* (2011).

[2] See Deutscher Buchpreis Archiv, accessed February 28, 2020, https://www.deutscher-buchpreis.de/archiv/.

[3] See New Books in German: The Essential Resource for Publishers, Translators, Boooksellers, and Readers, accessed February 28, 2020, http://www.new-books-in-german.com/index.php/.

[4] For example, Stuart Taberner, ed., *Contemporary German Fiction: Writing in the Berlin Republic* (2007); Lyn Marven and Stuart Taberner, eds., *Emerging German-Language Novelists of the 21st Century* (2011); Valerie Heffernan and Gillian Pye, eds., *Transitions: Emerging Women Writers in German-Language Literature* (2013); see also Necia Chronister, "Narrating the Fault Lines: German Literature since the Fall of the Wall" (2014).

[5] Cf. Stuart Taberner and Paul Cooke, eds., *German Culture, Politics, and Literature into the Twenty-First Century: Beyond Normalization* (2006).

[6] Cf. Thomas Assheuer, "NS Vergangenheit: Hauptsache, starke Bilder" (2019).

[7] Rosi Braidotti, *The Posthuman* (2013), 59.

[8] Cf. Donald Rumsfeld, "Defence Secy Comments on Europe, France, Germany," AP Archive, streamed live on January 23, 2003, YouTube video, https://www.youtube.com/watch?v=E0GnRJEPXn4.

[9] See Deutscher Germanistenverband, accessed February 28, 2020, http://www.germanistentag2019.de/; Gesellschaft für Fantastikforschung, accessed February 28, 2020, http://www.fantastikforschung.de/

[10] A laudable exception is Sonja Fritzsche's landmark study on East German SF: *Science Fiction Literature in East Germany* (2006).

[11] I do not claim to have invented the term *Zukunftsbewältigung*. Several attempts have been made over the years to introduce the concept into academic discourse: Dieter Wessels used it back in 1974 (Dieter Wessels, *Welt im Chaos. Struktur und Funktion des Weltkatastrophenmotives in der neueren Science Fiction*, 104), and it has been used in a number of different contexts since then—for example, in the German translation of Gordon Rattray Taylor's 1975 book *How to Avoid the*

Future. The Germanist Frederick Lubich used it in 1985 in an article on Günter Grass ("Günter Grass' Kopfgeburten: Deutsche Zukunftsbewältigung"); the computer scientist Karl Steinbuch used it in 1995 in the title of his last book, *Zukunftsbewältigung: Deutschland auf der Suche nach seiner Identität*.") The Assyriologist Stefan Maul used it in 1999 to explain how Mesopotamians sought to avert future catastrophes by engaging in appropriate rituals ("Zukunftsbewältigung: Eine Untersuchung altorientalischen Denkens anhand der babylonisch-assyrischen Löserituale (Namburbi).") The term has also entered legal German (see, for example, a 1993 inaugural lecture by the environmental lawyer Michael Kloepfer, "Verfassungsgebung als Zukunftsbewältigung aus Vergangenheitserfahrung. Zur Verfassungsgebung im vereinten Deutschland"), and the press via journalists like Ina Beyer in her 2006 article "Zukunftsbewältigung in Anklam." However, while both terms—*Vergangenheitsbewältigung* and *Zukunftsbewältigung*—have seen a significant increase in use, the former is vastly more common.

[12] Franz Rottensteiner, ed., *The Black Mirror and Other Stories* (2008).

[13] There are laudable exceptions: In the introduction to their 2016 anthology *The Big Book of Science Fiction*, Ann and Jeff VanderMeer acknowledge "the important role of international fiction" (25–26). See also James and Kathryn Morrow, eds., *The SFWA European Hall of Fame* (2008).

[14] See Unsettling Scientific Theories: Expertise, Narratives, and Future Histories, accessed February 28, 2020, http://unsettlingscientificstories.co.uk/.

[15] Cf. Bernhard Malkmus, "Maikäfer, flieg! Das Sterben der Arten und das Schweigen der Literaten" (2018).

[16] Mary Shelley's *Frankenstein, or The Modern Prometheus* (1818) is widely regarded as the first SF novel. See also Thomas Moynihan's 2019 article "The End of the World: A History of How a Silent Cosmos Led Humans to Fear the Worst."

[17] Elinor Shaffer, ed., *The Third Culture: Literature and Science* (1998), 11–12.

[18] See, for example, the following list of SF literary series: Studies in Global Science Fiction (available at https://www.palgrave.com/gp/series/15335); World Science Fiction (available at https://www.peterlang.com/view/serial/WSFS); New Dimensions in Science Fiction (available at https://www.uwp.co.uk/series/new-dimensions-in-science-fiction/); and Liverpool Science Fiction Texts and Studies (available at https://www.liverpooluniversitypress.co.uk/series/series-12324/).

[19] See European Science Fiction Society, accessed February 28, 2020, https://esfs.info/.

[20] Sonja Fritzsche, ed., *The Liverpool Companion to World Science Fiction* (2014).

[21] See "Hoffnungen zum Jahreswechsel," Institut für Demoskopie Allensbach, accessed February 28, 2020, https://www.ifd-allensbach.de/fileadmin/_migrated/pics/Seit_1949_Stimmungsbild_2018.gif.

[22] Germany's chief polemicist Thilo Sarrazin argues in his recent book *Wunschdenken* (2016) that the German government under chancellor Angela Merkel allowed itself to be guided by "utopisches Denken" (i.e., utopian thinking in the sense of wishful, magical thinking), which was increasingly replacing technocratically-led

problem solving. See also Stefan Wagstyl's review of the book in the *Financial Times*, July 4, 2016.

[23] Yuval Noah Harari, "Life 3.0 by Max Tegmark—We Are Ignoring the AI Apocalypse" (2017).

[24] Anthony Andrew, "The Idea of Free Information is Extremely Dangerous" (2018).

[25] Dave Lee, "Amazon's Next Big Thing May Redefine Big" (2019).

Chapter 1

[1] Frank E. Manuel, ed., *Utopias and Utopian Thought* (1973); Frank E. and Fritzie P. Manuel, *Utopian Thought in the Western World* (1979).

[2] Dan Chodorkoff, "The Utopian Impulse: Reflections on a Tradition" (1983).

[3] Chodorkoff, "The Utopian Impulse," .

[4] The Society for Utopian Studies, accessed February 28, 2019, https://utopian-studies.org/. See also "21st Conference of the Utopian Studies Society Europe," Utopian Studies Society, accessed February 28, 2019, http://utopian-studies-europe.org/conference/.

[5] See the definition of utopianism offered in Gregory Claeys and Lyman Tower Sargent, eds., *The Utopia Reader* (1999), 1: "Utopianism generally is the imaginative projection, positive or negative, of a society that is substantially different from the one in which the author lives." See also the definition given there of the utopian impulse: "that need to dream of a better life, even when we are reasonably content" (2). Cf. Lewis Mumford, *The Story of Utopias: Ideal Commonwealths and Social Myths* (1922). Claeys and Sargent speak of "utopias of sensual gratification" and "utopias of human contrivance" (2).

[6] Frederic Jameson, *Archaeologies of the Future* (2005), xii.

[7] Cf. Andrew Milner, "Archaeologies of the Future: Jameson's Utopia or Orwell's Dystopia?" (2009), 101–19.

[8] Lyman Tower Sargent, *Utopianism* (2010), 5.

[9] Gregory Claeys, ed., *Searching for Utopia* (2011), 7.

[10] Ruth Levitas, *Utopia as Method* (2013), xi.

[11] James R. Simmons, "Utopian Cycles: Trends in American Visions of the Alternative Society" (1998), 199. See also Enzo Traverso, *Left-Wing Melancholia* (2017).

[12] In *The Soul of Man under Socialism* (1891) Oscar Wilde famously observed (40):

"A map of the world that does not include Utopia is not worth even glancing at, for it leaves out the one country at which Humanity is always landing. And when Humanity lands there, it looks out, and, seeing a better country, sets sail. Progress is the realisation of Utopias."

[13] Eric Olin Wright, *Envisioning Real Utopias* (2010).

14 Mark Featherstone, "The Kinetic Utopia" (2010).

15 Rutger Bregman, *Utopia for Realists* (2017). At the 2019 World Economic Forum in Davos, Bregman confronted the assembled billionaires for not paying their fair share. See Martin Farrer, "Historian Berates Billionaires at Davos over Tax Avoidance," *Guardian*, January 30, 2019, https://www.theguardian.com/business/2019/jan/30/historian-berates-billionaires-at-davos-over-tax-avoidance.

16 Bregman, 20.

17 Paul Mason, *PostCapitalism: A Guide to our Future* (2015).

18 George Monbiot, *Out of the Wreckage: A New Politics for an Age of Crisis* (2017).

19 Monbiot, 10.

20 "What's Gone Wrong with the World?" The Good Country, accessed February 28, 2020, https://www.goodcountry.org/good-country/the-idea.

21 Zygmunt Bauman, *Retrotopia* (2017).

22 Aaron Bastani, *Fully Automated Luxury Communism* (2019).

23 Andy Beckett, "Fully Automated Luxury Communism by Aaron Bastani—A Manifesto for the Future" (2019).

24 Immanuel Kant, "Idee zu einer allgemeinen Geschichte in weltbürgerlicher Absicht" (1784), 385–411.

25 Immanuel Kant, *Zum ewigen Frieden* (1795).

26 Walter Ulbricht declared that the GDR was a Faust Part III, with "free people on acres free," and where scientific socialism had made Goethe's vision a reality, thus obviating the need for any utopian dreams. Cf. Inez Hedges, "Faust and Utopia: Socialist Visions" (1999), 49.

27 Karl Marx and Friedrich Engels, *Die deutsche Ideologie* (1846). In the struggles for supremacy in the socialist movement, Friedrich Engels would later denounce its utopian tradition as a project of the bourgeoisie. Cf. Friedrich Engels, *Die Entwicklung des Sozialismus von der Utopie zur Wissenschaft* (1882).

28 August Bebel, *Die Frau und der Sozialismus* (1879).

29 Ernst Bloch, *Geist der Utopie* (1918).

30 Bloch, 13. Italics in the original. The Latin phrase, which is frome Dante's *La Vita Nuova*, means "here begins a new life."

31 Ernst Bloch, *Das Prinzip Hoffnung* (1959).

32 Cf. Ernst Bloch, *The Utopian Function of Art and Literature* (1988).

33 Martin Buber, *Pfade in Utopia* (1950).

34 Tillich, Paul, *Politische Bedeutung der Utopie im Leben der Völker* (1951), 14.

35 Cf. Ronald H. Stone, "On the Boundary of Utopia and Politics" (2009), 208–20.

36 Herbert Marcuse, *Das Ende der Utopie* (1967), 9–43.

37 Christian Fuchs points out that Marcuse had not developed a theory of utopia at that point; nor, Fuchs argues, did he use the term consistently. Fuchs, "Fortschritt und Utopie" (2003), 41–63.

38 Jost Hermand, "Von der Notwendigkeit utopischen Denkens" (1974), 10.

39 Hermand, 12.

40 See my discussion of Andreas Eschbach's novel *Nationales Sicherheitsamt* in chapter 12.

41 Carl Friedrich von Weizsäcker, *Bewußtseinswandel* (1988).

42 von Weizsäcker, 21.

43 Karl Mannheim, *Ideologie und Utopie* (1929).

44 Cf. Arnhelm Neusüss, ed., *Utopie. Begriff und Phänomen des Utopischen* (1972), 265.

45 Popper, Karl, "Utopie und Gewalt," in Neusüss, *Utopie*, 314.

46 Fest, Joachim, *Der zerstörte Traum* (1991).

47 Fest, 57.

48 Jürgen Habermas, *Der philosophische Diskurs der Moderne* (1985), 161.

49 Fest, 100.

50 Jürgen Habermas, "The Concept of Human Dignity and the Realistic Utopia of Human Rights" (2010).

51 Richard David Precht, *Jäger, Hirten, Kritiker: Eine Utopie für die digitale Gesellschaft* (2018).

52 Harald Welzer, *Alles könnte anders sein: Eine Gesellschaftsutopie für freie Menschen* (2019).

53 "Just as the light pollution in our cities eclipses the stars, so does the present blind us to the future." (45); "Every culture needs to answer the question whether it makes people happier, perhaps even brighter, friendlier, and more cultivated" (54).

54 Precht, 124.

55 Precht, 172.

56 Futurzwei, accessed February 28, 2019, https://futurzwei.org/.

57 Bernd Sommer and Harald Welzer, *Transformationsdesign* (2017).

58 Welzer, 43.

59 Wilhelm Vosskamp, ed., *Utopieforschung* (1982).

60 Wilhelm Vosskamp, Günter Blamberger, and Martin Roussel, eds., *Möglichkeitsdenken* (2013).

61 Martin Seel, "Drei Regeln für Utopisten" (2001), 747.

62 Thomas Schölderle, *Geschichte der Utopie* (2017), 7.

63 The problem with this terminological chaos, as we shall see in the following chapters, is that it leads to all kinds of contortions in defining utopian literature. For example, is utopian writing an aspect of SF (Darko Suvin) or is SF a subgenre of the utopian (Gregory Claeys)? Does utopian always mean the ideal or is utopia,

literally no place, the greater category that contains both the positive (eutopia) and the negative (dystopia)? Ironically, Schölderle ends his defense of the utopian by further adding to the "Sammelsurium von Begriffsmustern" (hodgepodge of concept patterns) by elevating it to the level of "Medium" (163).

[64] Michel Foucault, "Of other Spaces: Utopias and Heterotopias" (1967), available at http://web.mit.edu/allanmc/www/foucault1.pdf.

[65] Elke Schmitter, "Utopien—was von den Träumen übrig blieb" (2017).

[66] For Britain this means "Brexit." Citizens of the world, according to Prime Minister Theresa May at the Conservative Party conference in 2016, are "citizens of nowhere." See Max Bearak, "Theresa May Criticized the Term 'Citizen of the World.' But Half the World Identifies That Way." *Washington Post*, October 5, 2016, https://www.washingtonpost.com/news/worldviews/wp/2016/10/05/theresa-may-criticized-the-term-citizen-of-the-world-but-half-the-world-identifies-that-way/?noredirect=on&utm_term=.186313205c5e.

[67] Ulrike Guérot, *Warum Europa eine Republik werden muss!* (2016).

[68] Andrian Kreye, "Wie aus Hippie-Utopien Monopolkapitalismus wurde" (2018).

[69] See "Inventor of Internet: Regulate Social Media Companies," Deutsche Welle, March 13, 2018, https://www.dw.com/en/inventor-of-internet-regulate-social-media-companies/a-42951226.

[70] Cf. Andrei S. Markovits and Philip S. Gorski, *The German Left: Red, Green, and Beyond* (1993), 119–23.

[71] Michael Bohmeyer and Claudia Cornelsen, *Was würdest du tun?* (2019).

[72] Stefan Schultz, "Was nach der Leistungsgesellschaft kommt" (2019).

[73] Ilija Trojanow, "Nie gut, aber besser" (2019).

[74] Cf. Herbert Marcuse, *Essay on Liberation* (1969), 14: "The notion that happiness is an objective condition which demands more than subjective feelings has been effectively obscured; its validity depends on the real solidarity of the species "man," which a society divided into antagonistic classes and nations cannot achieve. As long as this is the history of humanity, the "state of nature," no matter how refined, prevails: a civilized *bellum omnium contra omnes*, in which the happiness of the ones must coexist with the suffering of the others."

Chapter 2

[1] See Kim Parker, Rich Morin, and Juliana Menasce Horowitz, "Looking to the Future, Public Sees an America in Decline on Many Fronts," Pew Research Center, March 21, 2019, https://www.pewsocialtrends.org/2019/03/21/public-sees-an-america-in-decline-on-many-fronts/.

[2] See Institut für Demoskopie Allensbach, accessed February 28, 2010, www.ifd-allensbach.de.

[3] Not to be confused with the Italian artistic *Futurismo* movement in the early twentieth century.

⁴ See, for example, the predictions of the American physicist and popularizer of science Michio Kaku: *Physics of the Future* (2011); *The Future of Humanity* (2018).

⁵ Jennifer M. Gidley, *The Future* (2017), 1.

⁶ Cf. Pewter J. Bowler, *A History of the Future* (2017).

⁷ Gidley, 46.

⁸ See *Global Trends Paradox of Progress* (2017), available at https://www.dni.gov/files/documents/nic/GT-Full-Report.pdf.

⁹ Josef Weizenbaum, *Computer Power and Human Reason* (1976), 1. See also the documentary films *Weizenbaum: Rebel at Work* (2006) and *Plug and Pray* (2010).

¹⁰ For example, Harvard's Science and Technology Studies (STS) postgraduate program explicitly offers a "particular focus on the risks that S&T may pose to peace, security, community, democracy, environmental sustainability, and human values. Driving this body of research are questions like the following: how should states set priorities for research funding; who should participate, and how, in technological decisionmaking; should life forms be patented; how should societies measure risks and set safety standards; and how should experts communicate the reasons for their judgments to the public?" See Program on Science, Technology & Society, accessed February 28, 2020, http://sts.hks.harvard.edu/.

¹¹ Cf. Jamie Morgan, "The Fourth Industrial Revolution Could Lead to a Dark Future" (2020).

¹² Shoshana Zuboff, *The Age of Surveillance Capitalism* (2018).

¹³ See also Shoshana Zuboff, "Wie wir Googles Sklaven wurden," *Frankfurter Allgemeine*, March 5, 2016, https://www.faz.net/aktuell/feuilleton/debatten/die-digital-debatte/shoshana-zuboff-googles-ueberwachungskapitalismus-14101816.html.

¹⁴ Rory Cellan-Jones, "Stephen Hawking Warns Artificial Intelligence Could End Mankind," BBC News Online, December 2, 2014, https://www.bbc.co.uk/news/technology-30290540.

¹⁵ Toby Walsh, *Android Dreams* (2017), 221–22.

¹⁶ "Asilomar AI Principles," Future of Life Institute, accessed February 28, 2020, https://futureoflife.org/ai-principles/.

¹⁷ Max Tegmark, *Life 3.0* (2017), 169.

¹⁸ Tegmark, 203.

¹⁹ Yuval Noah Harari, *Sapiens* (2011), 294–301.

²⁰ Harari, 207. See also "Yuval Noah Harari: Homo Sapiens as We Know Them Will Disappear in a Century or so" (*Guardian*, March 19, 2017).

²¹ "Overwhelming evidence now confirms that humans are changing Earth in unprecedented ways. Global climate change, acidifying oceans, shifting global cycles of carbon, nitrogen and other elements, forests and other natural habitats transformed into farms and cities, widespread pollution, radioactive fallout, plastic accumulation, the course of rivers altered, mass extinction of species, human transport and introduction of species around the world. These are just some of

the many different human-induced global environmental changes that will most likely leave a lasting record in rock: the basis for marking new intervals of geologic time." Erle C. Ellis, *Anthropocene* (2018, 3). See also Jürgen Renn and Bernd Scherer, eds., *Das Anthropozän* (2015). Cf. Joseph Romm, *Climate Change* (2018); David Wallace-Wells, *The Uninhabitable Earth* (2019).

22 Cf. Rosi Braidotti, *The Posthuman* (2013); Donna J. Haraway, *Staying with the Trouble* (2016).

23 Jaron Lanier, *Dawn of the New Everything* (2017), 2–3.

24 "The power of CRISPR truly is the power of a god, in that manipulating the germline of an organism could forever change its evolution." Doug Dluzen, "How and Why CRISPR will change the World" (2018). Cf. N. Katherine Hayles, *How We Became Posthuman* (1999); and Stefan Herbrechter on the use of the term "posthuman" in Stefan Herbrechter, "Stefan Herbrechter Interview," interview by Jerome Garbrah, Critical Posthumanism: Genealogy of the Posthuman, November 2013, http://criticalposthumanism.net/the-posthuman-review/stefan-herbrechter-interview/.

25 Unless, of course, they are published in English in the first place, e.g., Roman Peperhove, Karlheinz Steinmüller, and Hans Liudger Dienel, eds., *Envisioning Uncertain Futures* (2018).

26 See "Germany Reloaded," Die Arbeitgeber, accessed February 28, 2020, https://www.futurework.online/germany-reloaded.html; Siemens: Ingenuity for Life, accessed February 28, 2020, https://new.siemens.com/de/de.html.

27 For example, the Fraunhofer Institute for Technological Trends Analysis in Euskirchen, available at https://www.int.fraunhofer.de/; the Institute for Futures Studies and Technology Assessment) in Berlin, available at https://www.izt.de/; or the Foresight Company Z_punkt in Cologne (with SF writer Karlheinz Steinmüller as its scientific director), available at https://www.z-punkt.de//.

28 "Future Work—The Transition to the 22nd Century," FutureWork, accessed February 28, 2020, https://arbeit2100.de/the-project/.

29 Cf. Oliver Sukrow, *Arbeit. Wohnen. Computer* (2018).

30 Cf. Robert Weninger, *Sublime Conclusions* (2017), 381–99.

31 See "Futurologie: Die Zukunft des Menschen wird geplant," *Der Spiegel*, December 26, 1966, https://www.spiegel.de/spiegel/print/index-1966-53.html.

32 Cf. Kursbuch 14, 1968, *Kritik der Zukunft*, esp. Hans Magnus Enzensberger's interview "Ein Gespräch über die Zukunft mit Rudi Dutschke, Bernd Rabehl and Christian Semler," 110–45.

33 Cf. Sven Reichardt, *Authentizität und Gemeinschaft* (2014).

34 Ulrich Beck, *Risikogesellschaft* (1986) and *Weltrisikogesellschaft* (2007); Frank Biess, *Republik der Angst* (2019).

35 Christa Langheiter, *Mut zur Auszeit* (2012).

36 Harald Lesch and Klaus Kamphausen, *Die Menschheit schafft sich ab* (2018).

37 Cf. Lucian Hölscher, *Die Entdeckung der Zukunft* (2016); See also Lucian Hölscher, ed., *Die Zukunft des 20. Jahrhunderts* (2017).

38 Arthur Brehmer, ed., *Die Welt in 100 Jahren* (2012).

39 Ernst A. Grandits, ed., *2112. Die Welt in 100 Jahren* (2012).

40 Grandits, 26.

41 See Bernard Marr, "Chinese Social Credit Score: Utopian Big Data Bliss or Black Mirror on Steroids," *Forbes*, January 21, 2019, https://www.forbes.com/sites/bernardmarr/2019/01/21/chinese-social-credit-score-utopian-big-data-bliss-or-black-mirror-on-steroids/#4731d27048b8.

42 Angela and Karlheinz Steinmüller, *Visionen 1900, 2000, 2100* (1999). See also Joachim Radkau, *Geschichte der Zukunft* (2017).

43 See "2057—Unser Leben in der Zukunft," ZDF, accessed February 28, 2020, https://zdf-enterprises.de/programmkatalog/international/zdfeunscripted/science-knowledge/2057-unser-leben-in-der-zukunft.

44 Karl Olsberg, Claudia Ruby, and Ulf Marquardt, *2057. Unser Leben in der Zukunft* (2007), 8.

45 Olsberg, Ruby, and Marquardt, 185–86.

46 Ulrich Eberl, *Zukunft 2050* (2011), 5.

47 See my discussion of Rainer Werner Fassbinder's *Welt am Draht* (1973) in Chapter 11.

48 Henning Jauernig and Isabella Reichert, "Wie wir 2037 leben werden" (2018).

49 Karl-Heinz Land, *Erde 5.0—Die Zukunft provozieren* (2018).

50 Thomas Straubhaar, *Die Stunde der Optimisten* (2019).

51 See Vera Kämper, "Die Kanzlerin entdeckt #Neuland," *Der Spiegel*, June 19, 2013, https://www.spiegel.de/netzwelt/netzpolitik/kanzlerin-merkel-nennt-bei-obama-besuch-das-internet-neuland-a-906673.html.

52 See "The German Energy System: Transforming Germany's Energy System," accessed February 28, 2020, http://www.energiewende-global.com/en/.

53 See "Committee on the Digital Agenda," Deutscher Bundestag, accessed February 28, 2020, www.bundestag.de/en/committees/a23; "Enquete-Kommission 'Künstliche Intelligenz-Gesellschaftliche Verantwortung und wirtschaftliche, soziale und ökologische Potenziale," Deutscher Bundestag, accessed February 28, 2020,https://www.bundestag.de/ausschuesse/weitere_gremien/enquete_ki.

54 See "Enquete-Kommission 'Künstliche Intelligenz' hat sich konstituiert," Deutscher Bundestag, accessed February 29, 2020, https://www.bundestag.de/dokumente/textarchiv/2018/kw39-pa-enquete-kuenstliche-intelligenz-567956.

55 See "Strategie Künstliche Intelligenz der Bundesregierung," Bundesministerium für Wirtschaft und Energie, accessed February 28, 2020, https://www.bmwi.de/Redaktion/DE/Publikationen/Technologie/strategie-kuenstliche-intelligenz-der-bundesregierung.html.

56 See Deutsches Forschungszentrum für Künstliche Intelligenz, accessed February 28, 2020, https://www.dfki.de/web/.

57 See Mirjam Hecking, "'Dass die Chinesen uns überholt haben, ist reine Folklore,'"

Manager Magazin, January 7, 2019, https://www.manager-magazin.de/unternehmen/industrie/kuenstliche-intelligenz-deutschand-ist-bei-ki-nicht-von-china-abgehaengt-a-1244761.html.

58 See "Künstliche Intelligenz birgt Chancen und Herausforderungen gleichermaßen," Deutscher Bundestag, streamed live on March 12, 2019, YouTube video, https://www.youtube.com/watch?v=eHOcgdFgl3A.

59 See Future Affairs Berlin 2019, accessed February 28, 2020, https://futureaffairs19.re-publica.com/en.

60 See "Rede von Außenminister Heiko Maas zur Eröffnung der Konferenz FUTURE AFFAIRS—'Digital Revolution: Resetting global power politics?'" Auswärtiges Amt, accessed February 28, 2020, https:/auswaertiges-amt.de/en/newsroom/news/maas-future-affairs/2222698.

61 See Futurium, accessed February 28, 2020, https://www.futurium.de/en/.

62 See "Tomorrow Begins Today: Futurium Has Opened," Futurium, September 5, 2019, https://futurium.de/en/press/tomorrow-begins-today-futurium-has-opened.

63 Anthony Giddens and Christopher Pierson, *Making Sense of Modernity* (1998), 94.

64 See the cover of *Der Spiegel* from April 1, 2017, available here: https://www.spiegel.de/spiegel/print/index-2017-14.html.

Chapter 3

1 Cf. Umberto Eco, *The Book of Legendary Lands* (2013).

2 John Carey, ed., *The Faber Book of Utopias* (1999).

3 Ian Sansom, "A Place for Tougher People" (1999).

4 "The philosophers have only interpreted the world in various ways; the point is to change it." Karl Marx, *Eleven Theses on Feuerbach* (1845).

5 Fatima Vieira, "The concept of Utopia," in *The Cambridge Companion to Utopian Literature*, ed. Gregory Claeys (2010), 15.

6 M. Keith Booker, *Dystopian Literature* (1994), 3.

7 Cf. M. Keith Booker, *The Dystopian Impulse in Modern Literature* (1994).

8 Tom Moylan, *Demand the Impossible* (1986), 9.

9 Moylan, 42.

10 Tom Moylan, *Scraps of the Untainted Sky* (2000), 147.

11 Raffaella Baccolini and Tom Moylan, *Dark Horizons* (2003), 7. I would interpret this as wishful thinking and will argue later that with the sheer number of dystopian texts we have an aestheticization of evil and an anaesthetization of the audience.

12 Russell Jacoby, *Picture Imperfect* (2005), 149.

13 Alexander Charles Oliver Hall, "I am trying to believe" (2009), 69–82. See also Alex Hall, "A Way of Revealing" (2009), 58–66.

[14] Fatima Vieira, "The concept of Utopia," in *The Cambridge Companion to Utopian Literature*, ed. Gregory Claeys (2010), 17.

[15] Sean Seeger and Daniel Davison-Vecchione, "Dystopian literature and the sociological imagination" (2019).

[16] Peter Marks, *Imagining Surveillance* (2015), 5.

[17] Gregory Claeys, *Dystopia* (2017), 4.

[18] Claeys, 501.

[19] John Lanchester, *The Wall* (2019).

[20] Cf. Burkhard Müller, "Eine Mauer um die ganze Insel" (2019).

[21] Lionel Shriver, "Lionel Shriver's Guide to Dystopia" (2016).

[22] Birgit Affeldt-Schmidt, *Fortschrittsutopien* (1991), 55.

[23] Gert Ueding, "Literatur ist Utopie," in *Literatur ist Utopie*, ed. Gert Ueding (1978), 7.

[24] Burghart Schmidt, "Utopie ist keine Literaturgattung," in *Literatur ist Utopie*, ed. Gert Ueding (1978), 17–44.

[25] Wolfgang Biesterfeld, *Die literarische Utopie* (1982).

[26] Hiltrud Gnüg, *Literarische Utopie-Entwürfe* (1982).

[27] Götz Müller, *Gegenwelten* (1989).

[28] Rolf Schwendter, *Utopie* (1994).

[29] Jan Robert Bloch, *Utopie: Ortsbestimmung im Nirgendwo* (1997), 13–14.

[30] Hiltrud Gnüg, *Utopie und utopischer Roman* (1999), 17.

[31] Marvin Chlada, *Der Wille zur Utopie* (2004).

[32] Rudolf Maresch and Florian Rötzer, eds., *Renaissance der Utopie* (2004), 8–9.

[33] Maresch and Rötzer, 13.

[34] Elena Zeißler, *Dunkle Welten* (2008).

[35] Zeißler, 31.

[36] Rolf Steltemeier, Sascha Dickel, Sandro Gaycken, and Tobias Knobloch, eds., *Neue Utopien* (2009), 8.

[37] Steltemeier et al., 13 (italics in the original).

[38] Peter McIsaac, Gabriele Mueller, and Diana Spokiene, eds., *Visions of Tomorrow* (2012), 2–3.

[39] Viviana Chilese and Heinz-Peter Preusser, eds., *Technik in Dystopien* (2013), 8.

[40] Brian Stapleford, "Ecology and Dystopia," in *The Cambridge Companion to Utopian Literature*, ed. Gregory Claeys (2010), 279.

[41] Cf. Paul Feyerabend, *The Tyranny of Science* (2011).

[42] Cf. E. Ann Kaplan, *Climate Trauma* (2016).

[43] Jill Lepore, "A Golden Age for Dystopian Fiction" (2017).

[44] Cf. Axel Goodbody, "Melting Ice and the Paradoxes of Zeno" (2013), 92–102.

[45] Cf. Gerhard Kaiser, ed., *Poesie der Apokalypse* (1991), 9.

[46] See Amy Stapleton, *Utopias for a Dying World* (1993), 7. Cf. Wendy Everett and Axel Goodbody, eds., *Revisiting Space* (2005) 79.

[47] Christine Haase, *When Heimat meets Hollywood* (2007), 103.

[48] Reto Sorg and Stefan Bodo Würffel, eds., *Utopie und Apokalypse in der Moderne* (2010).

[49] Franz Wuketits, "Apokalyptische Rhetorik als politisches Druckmittel" (2012).

[50] Cf. Judith Schossböck, Letzte Menschen (2012).

[51] Eva Horn, *Zukunft als Katastrophe* (2014).

[52] Horn, 11.

[53] Walter Benjamin, "Zentralpark," in *Gesammelte Schriften*, ed. Hermann Schweppenhäuser and Rolf Tiedemann (1991), 683.

[54] Horn, 23.

[55] Eckart Voigts and Alessandra Boller, eds., *Dystopia, Science Fiction, Post-Apocalypse* (2015).

[56] Voigts and Boller, 2.

[57] Lars Schmeink (2016), 14.

[58] Robert K Weninger, *Sublime Conclusions* (2017).

[59] Weninger, 508.

[60] Johan Norberg, *Progress* (2016).

[61] See also Oliver Burkeman, "Is the world really better than ever?" (2017); see also Henrik Müller, "Stell dir vor, alles wird gut" (2018).

[62] Frederic C. Beiser, *Weltschmerz* (2016).

Chapter 4

[1] John Rieder, "On Defining SF, or Not" (2010).

[2] In an interview with *The Guardian* in 2016, SF writer Ursula LeGuin observed: "Realism is a genre—a very rich one, that gave us and continues to give us lots of great fiction. But by making that one genre the standard of quality, by limiting literature to it, we were leaving too much serious writing out of serious consideration. Too many imaginative babies were going out with the bathwater. Too many critics and teachers ignored—were ignorant of—any kind of fiction but realism." See Ursula Le Guin, "I Wish We Could All Live in a Big House with Unlocked Doors," interview by Bryan Hood, *Guardian*, October 18, 2016, https://www.theguardian.com/books/2016/oct/18/ursula-k-le-guin-interview-complete-orsinia.

[3] Tom Moylan, *Scraps of the Untainted Sky* (2000), xvii.

[4] Cf. John Crowley, *Totalitopia* (2017), 29.

[5] The standard excuse is that SF written in other languages is "beyond the expertise" of the scholar concerned, though I would argue that aspects like cultural hegemony, commercial interests, and fear of ideological "contamination" have a major role to play here.

[6] See Edward James, *Science Fiction in the 20th Century* (1994).

[7] James Gunn, "Science Fiction around the World" (2010), 27–29. Gunn is referring to the first publication of *Amazing Stories*, the American SF magazine.

[8] Gary Wolfe, *The Known and the Unknown* (1979); Mark Rose, *Alien Encounters* (1981).

[9] Wolfe, 225.

[10] Rose, 33.

[11] Tom Shippey, "Introduction," in *Magill's Guide to Science Fiction and Fantasy Literature* (1996).

[12] Darko Suvin, *Poetik der Science Fiction* (1979).

[13] Carl Freedman, "Science Fiction and Utopia" in *Learning from other Worlds*, ed. Patrick Parrinder (2000), 73.

[14] Edward James and Farah Mendlesohn, eds., *The Cambridge Companion to Science Fiction* (2003), 9.

[15] Gregory Claeys, ed., *Searching for Utopia* (2011), 163. This argument has been supported by Andrew Milner and Sean Redmond. They argue:

Utopia is a far older genre than SF. It is one of the defining features, however, of Suvinian sociocriticism, which clearly influences Moylan, Freedman and Jameson, that SF be understood as retrospectively "englobing" utopia, thereby in effect transforming the latter into "the socio-political subgenre of Science Fiction."

See Andrew Milner and Sean Redmond, "Introduction to the Special Edition on Science Fiction" (2015), 5.

[16] Peter Fitting, "Utopia, Dystopia and Science Fiction," in *The Cambridge Companion to Utopian Literature*, ed. Gregory Claeys (2010), 135.

[17] Istvan Csicsery-Ronay, *The Seven Beauties of Science Fiction* (2008), 1. This observation is increasingly valid. At the time of writing, news about scientists in Cambridge setting up a research center to develop new ways to repair and geoengineer the Earth's climate (and the German ethics council arguing for a delay before scientists engage in genome editing of embryos outstrips some of the technofantasies offered by SF writers like Cixin Liu or Daniel Suarez. See Pallab Ghosh, "Climate Change: Scientists Test Radical Ways To Fix Earth's Climate," BBC News, May 10, 2019, https://www.bbc.co.uk/news/science-environment-48069663; "Eingriff ins Erbgut noch 'unverantwortlich,'" Tagesschau, May 9, 2019, https://www.tagesschau.de/inland/genveraenderung-ethikrat-101.html.

[18] Mike Ashley, *Out of this World* (2011), 6.

[19] Veronica Hollinger, "Genre vs. Mode," in *The Oxford Handbook of Science Fiction*, ed. Rob Latham (2014), 139–54.

[20] Sherryl Vint, *Science Fiction. A Guide for the Perplexed* (2014), 4.

[21] Vint, 135.

[22] Tom Shippey, *Hard Reading* (2016), xi.

23 See Ann and Jeff Vandermeer, "Building a Better Definition of Science Fiction," Literary Hub, July 14, 2016, https://lithub.com/building-a-better-definition-of-science-fiction/.

24 Ann and Jeff Vandermeer, *The Big Book of Science Fiction* (2016), 29.

25 Paul Kincaid, "This is Science Fiction?" (2016).

26 See Clarkesworld, accessed February 28, 2020, www.clarkesworldmagazine.com.

27 Russell Blackford, *Science Fiction and the Moral Imagination* (2017).

28 Blackford, 14.

29 Blackford, 43. Cf. Damien Broderick, "Reading SF as a Mega-Text" (1992).

30 Blackford, 179.

31 Dina Brandt, *Der deutsche Zukunftsroman 1918–1945* (2007); see also my review in *Modern Language Review*, 104, no.1 (2009): 260–61.

32 See Elizabeth Garbee, "Pulp Sci-Fi's Legacy to Women in Science," *Slate*, November 16, 2015, https://slate.com/technology/2015/11/pulp-science-fictions-legacy-to-women-in-science.html.

33 Cf. Gotthard Günther, *Science Fiction als neue Metaphysik?* (2015).

34 Martin Schwonke, *Vom Staatsroman zur Science Fiction* (1957), preface.

35 Manfred Nagl, "National Peculiarities in German SF" (1981), 29–34.

36 Peter Nicholls, ed., *Encyclopedia of Science Fiction* (1981), s.v. "German Science Fiction," 252.

37 Karl Guthke, *Der Mythos der Neuzeit* (1983), 31.

38 William B. Fischer, "German Theories of Science Fiction" (1976).

39 William B. Fischer, *The Empire Strikes Out* (1984), 12–13.

40 Gerd Hallenberger, *Macht und Herrschaft in den Welten der Science Fiction* (1986), 11–12.

41 Jost Hermand, *Old Dreams of a New Reich* (1992).

42 Hans-Edwin Friedrich, *Science Fiction in der deutschsprachigen Literatur* (1995).

43 Torben Schröder, *Science-fiction als social fiction* (1998), 37.

44 Hans Richard Brittnacher and Markus May, ed., *Phantastik* (2013), 319.

45 In a passage in the essay "Was ist Science Fiction, was ist Fantasy?" (2016), Franz Rottensteiner beautifully illustrates science fiction's knack for experimentation:

> People have called science fiction the "American fairy tale" or even a "modern myth." But this sells it short. Science fiction isn't a myth, but it can contain mythical qualities or expand mythical themes: Prometheus, Faust, or Sisyphus. However, it can also offer philosophical parables, scientific and theoretical reflections, or theological speculation. It can search for an answer to the question of what makes man and his identity, or how the clash of cultures that are completely alien to each other will turn out. It is an expression of fears and hopes; it can provide blueprints

for the future or self-destructive prophecies. It can talk about the future but mean the present; most importantly, though, it is this: an exercise for our sense of possibilities.

[46] Bruce Campbell, Alison Guenther-Pal, and Vibeke Rützou Petersen, eds., *Detectives, Dystopias and Poplit* (2014).

[47] Campbell, Guenther-Pal, and Petersen, 7.

[48] See Gesellschaft für Fantastikforschung, accessed February 28, 2020, http://www.fantastikforschung.de/; "Über die ZFF," Gesellschaft für Fantastikforschung, accessed February 28, 2020, http://www.fantastikforschung.de/index.php/ueber-die-zff; ZFF News, accessed February 28, 2020, https://zff.openlibhums.org/.

[49] Hans Esselborn, "Der Wandel der deutschen Science Fiction" (2012), 443.

[50] Kurd Laßwitz Preis, accessed February 28, 2020, http://www.kurd-lasswitz-preis.de/; Der Deutsche Science-Fiction-Preis, accessed February 28, 2020, https://www.dsfp.de/. See also Hans Esselborn, "Möglichkeiten der (westdeutschen) Science Fiction" (2013).

[51] Hans Esselborn, ed., *Die Erfindung der Zukunft in der Literatur* (2019).

[52] Esselborn, 11.

[53] Laurence A. Rickels, *Germany. A Science Fiction* (2014).

[54] Cf. Peter Dickens, "Alternative Worlds in the Cosmos," in *Alternative Worlds. Blue-Sky Thinking since 1900*, ed. Ricarda Vidal and Ingo Cornils (2015), 255–81.

[55] Truffaut's film is based on Ray Bradbury's novel *Fahrenheit 451*, first published in 1953.

[56] Max Horkheimer and Theodor Adorno, *Dialektik der Aufklärung* (1944). See also Leslie A. Adelson, "The Future of Futurity" (2011).

Chapter 5

[1] Vibeke Rützou Petersen, "Freud in the Future" (2006), 78.

[2] Petersen, 79.

[3] Vibeke Rützou Petersen, "What is the Holocaust doing in German SF?" (2014), 221–43.

[4] Petersen, 236.

[5] Petersen, 238.

[6] Horst Heidtmann, *Utopisch-phantastische Literatur in der DDR* (1982).

[7] Karlheinz Steinmüller, "Das Ende der Utopischen Literatur" (1992). See also Eric Simon, "Die Science Fiction Literatur der DDR" (2019).

[8] This (West German) author has fond memories of watching East German children's television programs on Saturday and Sunday afternoons during the 1960s. Soviet SF films with heroic cosmonauts engaged in peaceful exploration and scientific endeavor featured regularly.

[9] Sonja Fritzsche, "East Germany's 'Werkstatt Zukunft'" (2006), 367.

[10] Sonja Fritzsche, *Science Fiction Literature in East Germany* (2006).

11 Cf. Rainer Rother and Annika Schaefer, eds., *Future Imperfect* (2017).
12 Thomas Elsaesser, *Metropolis* (2000), 17.
13 Stephen Brockmann, *A Critical History of German Film* (2010).
14 Brockmann, 81.
15 Cf. Dominic Topp, "Retrospective 2017: Future Imperfect" (2017).
16 Tobias Haupts, "The Empty Sky" (2017), 68.
17 Julia Thurnau, "German Science-Fiction: Iron and Pencil Sharpener" (2017).
18 Wikipedia, s.v., "Operation Ganymed," last modified August 19, 2019, 15:34, https://de.wikipedia.org/wiki/Operation_Ganymed; https://www.imdb.com/title/tt0076502/.
19 See Wikipedia, s.v., "Das Arche Noah Prinzip," last modified April 28, 2018, 09:17, https://de.wikipedia.org/wiki/Das_Arche_Noah_Prinzip; *Das Arche Noah Prinzip* (dir. Roland Emmerich, 1984), IMDb.com, accessed February 28, 2020, https://www.imdb.com/title/tt0086911/.
20 Thurnau, "German Science-Fiction" (2017). Cf. Lutz Koepnick, "The Limits of Futurity" (2013, 81–84, 88).
21 Cf. Tom Shippey, *Hard Reading* (2016, 14).
22 Cf. Heribert Münkler, *Die Deutschen und ihre Mythen* (2009); Gert Mattenklott, "Faust," in *Deutsche Erinnerungsorte*, ed. Etienne Francois and Hagen Schulze (2001), 603–19.
23 Roland Borgards, "Posthumanismus und Anthropozän" (2018), 568.

Chapter 6

1 Cf. Wernher von Braun, "Crossing the Last Frontier" (1952). See also his "epigraph" in Kurd Laßwitz, *Two Planets*, trans. Hans H. Rudnick (1971), vii; and Matthias Schulz, "Himmelfahrt auf Usedom" (2001).
2 NASA's German-born conceptional artist Harry Lange worked on Stanley Kubrick's SF film *2001: A Space Odyssey*. His images are both modern interpretations and faithful copies of Laßwitz's original ideas (for images of the resulting artwork see 2001 Archive, accessed February 28, 2020, https://2001archive.org/).
3 Cf. Rudi Schweikert, "Von Martiern und Menschen," in Kurd Laßwitz, *Auf zwei Planeten* (1897), 887–88.
4 Kurd Laßwitz, *Auf zwei Planeten*, 264.
5 Cf. Götz Müller, *Gegenwelten* (1989), 160.
6 Laßwitz, 606.
7 Rudi Schweikert, "Von Martiern und Menschen" (1998), 849–50.
8 William Fischer, *The Empire Strikes Out* (1984), 57–58.
9 Wilhelm Bölsche, Vom Bazillus zum Affenmenschen (1900), 337.

[10] Bertha von Suttner was a famous advocate for peace at the time. Her novel *Die Waffen nieder!* first appeared in Dresden in 1889, and it was widely read. Although she was ultimately derided and was certainly ineffective against the military elites—both in her native Austria and in Germany—she was successful in organizing peace societies and in convincing Alfred Nobel to institute the Nobel Peace Prize, which she herself was awarded in 1905.

[11] Bertha von Suttner, "Die Numenheit" (1898), 116.

[12] This quotation is taken from the English translation of *Auf Zwei Planeten*. See Laßwitz, *Two Planets* (1971), 181.

[13] Laßwitz, 92.

[14] Laßwitz, 100.

[15] Fischer, *The Empire Strikes Out*, 139–40.

[16] Laßwitz, 98.

[17] Laßwitz, *Auf zwei Planeten*, 457.

[18] A recent reissue was initially only available directly from the publisher: Kurd Laßwitz, *Sternentau* (2008).

[19] Laßwitz, "Einführung" (1903), ix–x.

[20] Laßwitz, *Sternentau*, 19.

[21] Passages like these remind the reader of Goethe's *Die Metamorphose der Pflanzen* (1798), and they suggest a connection between his poem *Weltseele* and the Erdgeist in his *Urfaust*.

[22] Laßwitz, 121–22.

[23] Laßwitz, 125.

[24] Cf. Dieter von Reeken, ed., *Über Kurd Laßwitz* (2014).

[25] Laßwitz, 175.

[26] Laßwitz, 195.

[27] Laßwitz, 233.

[28] For a summary of "the biggest botanical bunfight since the Romantic era," see Ian Sample, "Group of Biologists Tries to Bury the Idea that Plants are Conscious" (2019).

[29] Laßwitz, "Pflanzenseele" (1919): 195–96.

[30] See "I Am Not Convinced, Fischer Tells Rumsfeld," *Telegraph*, February 10, 2002, https://www.telegraph.co.uk/news/worldnews/europe/germany/1421634/I-am-not-convinced-Fischer-tells-Rumsfeld.html; "German FM Makes Impassioned Plea for Peace," AP Archive, July 21, 2015, YouTube video, https://www.youtube.com/watch?v=CpuN-yM1sZU.

[31] Schätzing, 885

[32] Schätzing, 782.

[33] Irene Jung, Wie der 'Schwarm' weiterzog" (2005).

[34] Robin Detje, "Die Rache des Killerschleims" (2004).

[35] Cf. Andrew Milner and J. R. Burgmann, "Ice, Fire and Flood" (2015).

[36] Gabriele Dürbeck, Urte Stobbe, Hubert Zapf, and Evi Zemanek, eds., *Ecological Thought in German Literature and Culture* (2017), 341.

Chapter 7

[1] Cf. Cornelius Partsch, "Paul Scheerbart and the Art of Science Fiction" (2002); Adam Kirsch, "The Strange Paradise of Paul Scheerbart" (2015); Susana Oliveira, "Paul Scheerbart's Kaleidoscopic Fantasies" (2017).

[2] See the discussion published online by Robert Leucht, "CFP: GSA Panel Series 'Incipit Scheerbart,' Pittsburgh, PA," H-Germanistik, January 19, 2018, https://networks.h-net.org/node/79435/discussions/1271418/cfp-gsa-panel-series-incipit-scheerbart-pittsburgh-pa-10022018.

[3] Cf. Lutz Koepnick, *The Dark Mirror* (2002).

[4] Cp Vanessa Cirkel-Bartelt, "Beautiful Destruction" (2017).

[5] Alfred Döblin, *Berge Meere und Giganten* (1924). An English translation by C. D. Godwin is available online at "Mountains Oceans Giants—Fully Revised and Complete," Beyond Alexanderplatz, accessed February 28, 2020, https://beyond-alexanderplatz.com/mountains-oceans-giants-complete/.

[6] Evan Torner, "A Future-History out of Time" (2014), 50; see also Carl Gelderloos, "Jetzt kommt das Leben" (2015).

[7] Günter Grass, "Im Wettlauf mit den Utopien" (1978).

[8] Cf. Thea von Harbou, *Metropolis* (1984), 47, 94.

[9] Arthur C. Clarke, *Profiles of the Future* (1973), 14, 21, 36.

[10] Cf. Michael Minden and Holger Bachmann, eds., *Fritz Lang's Metropolis* (2000).

[11] Rainer Eisfeld, "Frau im Mond" (1989), 207.

[12] Michael Stürzer, "Als Hitlers Raketen ins Weltall flogen" (2017).

[13] Erica Quinn, "At War: Thea von Harbou, Women, and the Nation" (2017); see also Iris Luppa, "Madonna in Moon Rocket with Breeches" (2009).

[14] Stefanie Harris, "Calling the Nation" (2012), 21.

[15] Cf. Joerg Hartmann, "An Absolutely Fascinating Period Piece" (2016).

Chapter 8

[1] Johann Gottfried Schnabel, *Insel Felsenburg. Wunderliche Fata einiger Seefahrer (1731, 1732, 1736, 1743)* (1997).

[2] Cf. Jan Roidner, "Vom Verschwinden der Utopie in Johann Gottfried Schnabels Insel Felsenburg" (2007).

[3] Thomas Schölderle, *Geschichte der Utopie* (2017), 100.

[4] Schnabel, Insel Felsenburg, Vol. 2, 195.

[5] Schnabel, *Insel Felsenburg*, Vol.4, 103.

[6] Werner Illing, *Utopolis* (1930).

[7] Illing, 23.

[8] *Der Herr vom anderen Stern*, directed by Heinz Hilpert (1948). The film is available at https://archive.org/details/1948DerHerrVomAnderenStern#.

[9] Cf. Hans-Ulrich Pönack, "Der Herr vom anderen Stern," Pönis Kinowoche, October 29, 2018, https://poenack.de/der-herr-vom-anderen-stern/.

[10] Ludwig Dexheimer (pseudonym Ri Tokko), *Das Automatenzeitalter* (1930).

[11] Hermann Hesse, *Das Glasperlenspiel* (2001).

[12] "Master of the Game", review of Magister Ludi by Hermann Hesse, *Time*, October 17, 1949.

[13] Hesse, 11.

[14] Hesse, *Ausgewählte Briefe* (1974), 438.

[15] Hesse, *Magister Ludi* (1969).

[16] J. P. Stern, "A Game of Utopia" (1980), 94–107.

[17] Adolf Muschg, "Hesses Glasperlenspiel" (2002), 132.

[18] Ernst Bloch, Das Prinzip Hoffnung (1985), 6–7.

[19] Béatrice Poulain, "Das Glasperlenspiel: Mythos oder Utopie?" (2003), 67–82.

[20] Poulain, 68–69.

[21] Cf. Ingo Cornils, "Ein Glasperlenspiel im Internet. Hesse lesen im globalen Zeitalter" (2004), 399–413.

[22] Elena Seredkina, "Drei Modelle der Planetarkultur im Kontext des Romans von Hermann Hesse Das Glasperlenspiel," Hermann Hesse Page, University of California, Santa Barbara, accessed February 28, 2020, http://www.gss.ucsb.edu/projects/hesse/papers/modelle.pdf, 5.

[23] Michael Kleeberg, "70 Jahre Glasperlenspiel. Warum nicht alles auserzählen?" (2013).

[24] Franz Werfel, *Stern der Ungeborenen* (1946).

[25] Cf. Christian Zemsauer, "Wortschöpfungen für Zukünftiges in Franz Werfels Stern der Ungeborenen" (2013), available at http://othes.univie.ac.at/26603/1/2013-02-14_9217490.pdf; Caspar Battegay, "Gleichzeitigkeit. Utopie und Exil in Franz Werfels Stern der Ungeborenen" (2017).

[26] Cf. Paul Hühnerfeld, "Heliopolis oder die Stadt ohne Liebe" (1950); Hans Krah: Die Apokalypse als literarische Technik (2004); Alan Corkhill, *Spaces for Happiness in the Twentieth-Century German Novel* (2012), 119–46.

[27] See Mapping the Republic of Letters, Stanford University, accessed February 28, 2020, http://republicofletters.stanford.edu/.

[28] For example, Robert M. Adams, "Devil's Brew" (1981); Boy Hinrichs, *Utopische Prosa als längeres Gedankenspiel* (1986).

[29] Angela and Karlheinz Steinmüller, *Andymon: eine Weltraum-Utopie* (2018).

[30] David Draut, *Zwiespältige Zukunftsversionen* (2014), 145.

[31] Cf. Carl Gelderloos, "Breaking Open Utopia" (2015).

32 Steinmüller, 351.

33 Steinmüller, 351.

34 Uwe Timm, *Ikarien* (2017).

35 Timm spent a number of years as a member of the German Communist Party agitating for a socialist revolution until he became disillusioned with the party's doctrines. Cf. Ingo Cornils, *Writing the Revolution* (2016), 113.

36 Timm quotes Darwin at the outset: "A man of science ought to have no wishes, no affections,—a mere heart of stone."

37 Cf. John Maynard Smith, "Eugenics and Utopia," in Frank E. Manuel, ed., *Utopias and Utopian Thought* (1973), 150–68.

38 See Rachel Gur-Arie, "American Eugenics Society (1926–1972)," The Embryo Project Encyclopedia, November 11, 2014, https://embryo.asu.edu/pages/american-eugenics-society-1926-1972.

39 Timm, 242.

40 Christian Buß, "Stunde Null Roman von Uwe Timm: Sex in den Trümmern des Übermenschen" (2017); Michaela Schmitz, "Die Geburt der Rassenhygiene aus dem Geist der Utopie" (2017).

Chapter 9

1 Cf. Evan Torner, "Casting for a Socialist Earth" (2014).

2 The first five issues of *Perry Rhodan* ("Unternehmen Stardust," "Die Dritte Macht," "Die strahlende Kuppel," "Götterdämmerung," and "Atom-Alarm") are available, in slightly edited versions, in William Voltz, ed., *Perry Rhodan. Die Dritte Macht* (1978).

3 See "Perry Rhodan—Unser Mann im All," Perrypedia, last modified March 2, 2020, https://www.perrypedia.proc.org/wiki/Perry_Rhodan_-_Unser_Mann_im_All.

4 Manfred Nagl, "National Peculiarities in German SF" (1981), 32.

5 Wolfgang Biesterfeld, *Die literarische Utopie* (1982), 111.

6 Biesterfeld, 111.

7 Hans Esselborn, *Die Erfinding der Zukunft in der Literatur* (2019), 318.

8 Cf. the documentary for the fiftieth anniverary, *Perry Rhodan—Unser Mann im All* (dir. Andre Schäfer, 2011), accessed February 28, 2020, https://www.imdb.com/title/tt2009550/.

9 Cf. "Perry Rhodan," Project Gutenberg Self-Publishing Press, accessed February 28, 2020, http://www.self.gutenberg.org/articles/Perry_Rhodan.

10 Robert Reginald, *Xenograffiti* (2005), 257–58.

11 See "Retro-Futurismus.de: Ein Rückblick auf die Zukunft von gestern," Retro-Futurismus, accessed February 28, 2020, http://klausbuergle.de/.

12 Andreas Eschbach, *Perry Rhodan. Das größte Abenteuer* (2019).

[13] For a summary of the issues see Thomas W. Kniesche, "Germans to the Final Frontier" (2007), 157–85.

[14] The 1960s saw a series of experiments to discover whether humanity could live under water: Jacques Cousteau established an underwater house in 1962, and the US Navy's underwater habitats SEALAB I (1964), II (1965), and III (1968–69) established the viability of the concept. See Angela and Karlheinz Steinmüller, *Visionen 1900–2000–2100* (1999), 198–200.

[15] The 1960s are regarded as the key decade for the advancement of human knowledge in spaceflight—from Yuri Gagarin's first orbit around the Earth in 1961 to the landing on the moon in 1969.

[16] My translation. The German original has considerable poetic rhythm and flow. For the original video, see *Raumpatrouille*, Episode 2 "Planet außer Kurs" (English subtitles), uploaded by Raumpilot Ruby, June 10, 2014, YouTube video, https://www.youtube.com/watch?v=52mGF5FDUGE.

[17] Cf. Josef Hilger, *Raumpatrouille* (2000), 121–23.

[18] Hilger, 137–43.

[19] See "Die Tanzszenen—Best of 'Raumpatrouille,'" uploaded by BiggerFish, May 10, 2011, YouTube video, 4:44, https://www.youtube.com/watch?v=EW2tGDjyEAw.

[20] Cf. Ingo Cornils, "Problems of Visualisation" (1997), 293.

[21] Wolfgang Ruppert, ed., *Um 1968—Die Repräsentation der Dinge* (1998), 8.

Chapter 10

[1] Cf. John Clute and Peter Nicholls, *Encyclopedia of Science Fiction* (1993), s.v. "Apocalyptic and Post-Apocalyptic SF," 581.

[2] Carl Amery, *Der Untergang der Stadt Passau*, 5.

[3] Darko Suvin, *Metamorphoses of Science Fiction.* (1979), 137.

[4] Susan Sontag, "The Imagination of Disaster," in *Science Fiction. A Collection of Critical Essays*, ed. Mark Rose (1976), 130.

[5] Peter Nicholls, ed., *Encyclopedia of Science Fiction* (1979), s.v. "Post-Holocaust," 292; see also Ulrich Suerbaum, Ulrich Broich, and Raimund Borgmeier, *Science Fiction* (1981), 108.

[6] Gertrud Lehnert, "Endzeitvisionen in der Science Fiction" (1991), 303.

[7] Lehnert, 312.

[8] Cf. Ulrike Gottwald, *Science Fiction (SF) als Literatur in der Bundesrepublik der siebziger und achtziger Jahre* (1990); and Hans-Edwin Friedrich, *Science Fiction in der deutschsprachigen Literatur* (1995), 50–51.

[9] William B. Fischer, *The Empire Strikes Out* (1984), 13.

[10] Axel Goodbody, "Catastrophism in Post-war German Literature" (1997), 159.

[11] Goodbody, 164.

12 Cf. Andrei Markovits and Philip Gorski, *The German Left: Red, Green and Beyond* (1993).

13 Amy Stapleton, *Utopias for a Dying World* (1993), 147.

14 Fischer, 274.

15 *Zone Null* was published by the Seabury Press in 1974. Franke's previous novels *Das Gedankennetz* and *Der Orchideenkäfig* were published in English by DAW Books.

16 Herbert Franke, *Zone Null*, 23. English readers will be familiar with this litany of objectivity from C. S. Lewis's *That Hideous Strength* (1945).

17 At the end of the novel, a press statement announces that the last survivor of the expedition has died from "a virus." Efforts to make the zone viable are proudly announced but the zone continues to be off limits.

18 Cf. Fischer, 271.

19 Cf. Paul Brians, *Nuclear Holocausts* (1987).

20 This predates "the Core" in Dan Simmons's *Hyperion Cantos* (1989–97) by two decades.

21 Franke, 69–70.

22 Carl Amery, *Der Untergang der Stadt Passau* (1975).

23 Amery, 29. Chaplain Egid's vulgar Latin chronicle is "reproduced" in an equally antiquated baroque translation—and printed in old style German Fraktur type.

24 Cf. Friedrich Leiner, "Carl Amery: Der Untergang der Stadt Passau. Science-Fiction-Roman" (1982).

25 Cf. Walter Bühler, "Positive ökologische Utopie und politische Science Fiction" (1982).

26 For an overview in English see Axel Goodbody, ed., *The Culture of German Environmentalism* (2020).

27 Cf. Amy Stapleton, *Utopias for a Dying World* (1993), 16.

28 Cf. Karlheinz Steinmüller, "Laudatio auf Carl Amery anläßlich der Verleihung des Deutschen Fantasy Preises 1996" (1996), 16.

29 Examples of this would be Gudrun Pausewang's *Die letzten Kinder von Schewenborn* (1983), Peter Schmidt's *Das Prinzip von Hell und Dunkel* (1986), and Reinmar Cunis's *Wenn der Krebsbaum blüht* (1987).

30 Thomas Ziegler, *Alles ist gut*, 40.

31 Ziegler, 97–98. In the German original, the mantra is typographically arranged like a cross.

32 Ziegler, 131.

33 Cf. Patrick Parrinder, *Science Fiction: Its Criticism and Teaching* (1980), 43.

34 Dieter Wessels, *Welt im Chaos* (1974), 104.

35 Fischer, 304.

36 Rüdiger Suchsland, "Lars Kraumes düstere Vision von Deutschland" (2010).

37 Thomas von Steinaecker, *Die Verteidigung des Paradieses* (2016).

38 Valerie Fritsch, *Winters Garten* (2015); Oliver Kyr, *Ascheland* (2016). See also "All Life on This Planet Is Our Family," One Planet. One Family, accessed February 28, 2020, https://oneplanetonefamily.is/.

39 Christoph Schröder, "Deutschland ist zerstört" (2016).

40 Schröder (2016).

41 Oliver Jungen, "Und hätte die Liebe nicht" (2016).

42 E.g., Carolin Ströbele, "Acht Tage: In Zweierreihen zur Apokalypse" (2019); Benedict Frank, "Serie 8 Tage—Apokalypse light" (2019).

43 See Rafael Parente and Stefan Ruzowitzky, "Final Countdown," interview by Michael Pickard, Tag Archives: Acht Tage (Eight Days), March 1, 2019, https://dramaquarterly.com/tag/acht-tage-eight-days/.

44 John Higgs, *The Future Starts Here.* (2019), 15.

Chapter 11

1 The SF author Charles Platt has commented on Philip Dick's work as follows: "All of his work starts with the basic assumption that there cannot be one, single, objective reality. Everything is a matter of perception. The ground is liable to shift under your feet. A protagonist may find himself living out another person's dream, or he may enter a drug-induced state that actually makes better sense than the real world, or he may cross into a different universe completely." Charles Platt, *Dream Makers* 1980, 145.

2 Cf. Herbert Marcuse, *Repressive Tolerance* (1965), accessed February 28, 2020, https://www.marcuse.org/herbert/pubs/60spubs/65repressivetolerance.htm.

3 Various forms of "flickering" are used as a visual signal for the existence of the different levels of reality.

4 Cf. Karl S.Guthke, *Der Mythos der Neuzeit* (1983).

5 Rainer Werner Fassbinder, "Einige allgemeine Überlegungen" (2010), 179–84.

6 Cf. Wolf Donner, "EDV-Elegie" (1973).

7 Tim Schleider, "Voller Kraft, Verzweiflung, Gewalt und Anarchie" (2007).

8 Dörting, Torsten, "Besser paranoid als tot" (2010).

9 Cf. Ralf Schenk, "Bin ich? Oder bin ich nicht?" (2010).

10 Anthony Scott, "Fassbinder's Vibrating Sci-Fi Questions About Reality" (2010).

11 Cf. Szilvia Gellai, "Welten am Draht bei Daniel F. Galouye und Rainer Werner Fassbinder" (2016).

12 Benjamin Stein, *Replay* (2012). The book is one of the few SF novels recommended by "New Books in German," an initiative by the German book trade and the Goethe Institute to encourage the translation of German books into other languages (see http://www.new-books-in-german.com/index.php/replay). Tellingly, it is described as a "dystopian novel," but not as SF.

13 Stein, 49.

14 Cf. Catharina Koller, "Das Implantat" (2013).
15 Tom Hillenbrand, *Drohnenland* (2014).
16 Hannes Hintermeier, "Krimi im Überwachungsstaat" (2014).
17 Tom Hillenbrand, "Eine verführerische Logik" (2016).
18 Tom Hillenbrand, *Hologrammatica* (2018). Like *Drohnenland*, the book is not marketed as SF, even though the action is set relatively far in the future.
19 Hillenbrand, 119.
20 Hillenbrand, 282.
21 Sonja Stöhr, "Das Ein-Körper-Problem" (2018).
22 Cf. Jaron Lanier, *Dawn of the New Everything: A Journey through Virtual Reality* (2017).

Chapter 12

1 For an overview see Andy Duncan, "Alternate History" (2003).
2 Cf. Hans-Edwin Friedrich, "Das deutsche Volk schlief schlecht seit dem größten Sieg seiner Geschichte" (2006).
3 Cf. Heinrich Böll, "Galopp mit der Raum-Zeit-Maschine" (1974).
4 Christian Kracht, *Ich werde hier sein im Sonnenschein und im Schatten* (2008).
5 While normally restricting myself to German writers in this study, I make an exception in this case because Kracht's narrative has been extensively reviewed in Germany, and it has been staged at the *Schauspiel Stuttgart* and the *Maxim Gorki Theater* in Berlin.
6 Kracht, 128.
7 Kracht, 132.
8 Kracht, 138.
9 Dietmar Dath, "Ein schöner Albtraum ist sich selbst genug" (2008).
10 Cf. Claude D. Conter and Johannes Birgfeld, eds., *Christian Kracht: Zu Leben und Werk* (2009); see also Frank Finlay, "Surface is an Illusion but so is Depth" (2013).
11 *Druckfrisch* (2009).
12 Alexandra Kedves and Edgar Schuler, "Christian Kracht: Ich meine es todernst" (2010).
13 Wolfgang Jeschke, *Das Cusanus-Spiel* (2005).
14 Jeschke, 440.
15 Jeschke, 626.
16 Jeschke, 282.
17 Jeschke, 329.

[18] See Marshall Honorof, "Multiverse or Universe? Physicists Debate," Space.com June 4, 2013, https://www.space.com/21421-universe-multiverse-inflation-theory.html.

[19] Jeschke, 622.

[20] Andreas Eschbach, *NSA—Nationales Sicherheits-Amt* (2018).

[21] This forum is colloquially known as the "elektronische Klowand" (electronic toilet wall), since users can anonymously—so they think—smear their invective-laden hate speech and sexually perverted fantasies on it.

[22] Weimar is a small city redolent of associations with Goethe, German classicism, and the first attempt to create a democratic German republic; however, the acronym here also points to the National Security Agency (NSA) in the United States.

[23] Eschbach, 42.

[24] Possibly also a reference to the East-German Stasi (Staatssicherheitsdienst [state security service]), which described itself as "Schwert und Schild der Partei" (sword and shield of the party).

[25] The bugging of Chancellor Angela Merkel's phone by the NSA led to a parliamentary inquiry in 2014. See "Auschüsse der 18. Wahlperiode: Untersuchungsauschuss ('NSA')," Deutscher Bundestag, accessed February 28, 2020, https://www.bundestag.de/ausschuesse/ausschuesse18/ua/1untersuchungsausschuss.

[26] He did win the 2019 Kurd Laßwitz Preis for best German SF novel, though.

[27] Katharina Nocun, *Die Daten, die ich rief* (2018).

[28] Katharina Nocun, "Populisten im schlüsselfertigen Überwachungsstaat" (2018).

[29] Anne Haeming, "Politik und Science Fiction sind nicht fern voneinander" (2018).

Chapter 13

[1] See Verordnung (EU) 2016/679 des Europäischen Parlaments und des Rates, *Amtsblatt der Europäischen Union*, April 27, 2016, https://eur-lex.europa.eu/legal-content/DE/TXT/PDF/?uri=CELEX:32016R0679&rid=1.

[2] See "The Smart Living Market in Germany," Federal Ministry for Economic Affairs and Energy, accessed February 28, 2020, https://www.smart-living-germany.de/SL/Navigation/EN/About-Smart-Living/about-smart-living.html.

[3] See, for example, Richard David Precht and Juli Zeh, "Der getunte Mensch: Wie perfekt wollen wir sein?," ZDF, June 26, 2013, YouTube video, 45:23, .https://www.youtube.com/watch?v=pknMhHtoub0

[4] Juli Zeh, *Corpus Delicti. Ein Prozess* (2010).

[5] Zeh, 88–89.

[6] Zeh, 186.

[7] Sabine Mayr, *Juli Zeh: Corpus Delicti. Ein Prozess* (2013).

[8] Heinz-Peter Preußer, "Dystopia and Escapism" (2010); Carrie Smith-Prei, "Relevant Utopian Realism" (2012); Virginia McCalmont, "Juli Zeh's Corpus Delicti" (2012); Sarah Koellner, "Data, Love, and Bodies" (2016); Sabine Schönfellner, "Erzählerische Distanzierung und scheinbare Zukünftigkeit (2018).

[9] Henk de Berg, "Mia gegen den Rest der Welt" (2013).

[10] Cf. Henk de Berg, "Warum wir keine Utopien brauchen" (2012).

[11] Simon Ings, "The Method by Juli Zeh" (2012).

[12] Iain Bamforth, "The Method" (2012).

[13] Zeh, 9.

[14] Patricia Herminghouse, "The Young Author as Public Intellectual" (2008).

[15] Stephen Brockmann, "Review" (2009), 613.

[16] See Uwe Post, "Juli Zeh lehnt Nominierung für Kurd-Laßwitz-Preis ab," SF-Netzwerk.de, May 8, 2010, http://www.scifinet.org/scifinetboard/index.php/topic/10614-juli-zeh-lehnt-nominierung-f%C3%BCr-kurd-la%C3%9Fwitz-preis-ab/.

[17] "This isn't science fiction. We repeat: NO science fiction. This isn't 1984 in Oceania, but the present situation in the Federal Republic. In case you still do not feel under suspicion—congratulations. You are an indomitable optimist." Ilija Trojanow and Juli Zeh, *Angriff auf die Freiheit* (2010), 10.

[18] Florian Felix Weyh, *Toggle* (2012).

[19] Theresa Hannig, *Die Optimierer* (2017).

[20] Hannig, 7.

[21] This is an allusion to the "Neuererbewegung" introduced in the GDR to increase production and efficiency, but it is also a none-too-subtle dig at the trend for "administrative and management process optimization."

[22] Ominously, the software for this total surveillance is called "Blockwart," a title that used to be given in the Third Reich and the GDR to party members who informed on dissident behavior of residents in their "block."

[23] Hannig, 27

[24] Freitag is haunted by one wrong decision in his early career when he assigned a young Ercan Böser (now leader of the Optimierer Partei) the role of politician instead of that of an actor. Later, it turns out that Böser had used phrases from Georg Büchner's 1835 play *Dantons Tod* to trick Freitag into steering his client toward becoming a politician. This "mistake" was actually caused by the emerging artificial intelligence in order to have pliable people coming into power with their new party.

[25] "No matter how the general election tomorrow turns out: Blockwart will continue to record every possible information about every single citizen. No government will ever give up this golden key to general surveillance. Quite the opposite, in fact. They will keep and expand the software. Thus they continue to control our every step, every breath we take" (233).

[26] Goethe, *Faust* I, chapter 6: ". . . part of that power that eternally wills evil and eternally works good."

27 Judith Madera, "Interview mit Theresa Hannig" (2017).

28 Theresa Hannig, *Die Unvollkommenen* (2019).

29 It should be noted that Theresa Hannig, an outspoken feminist, started a controversy in March 2019 when she uploaded a list of more than one hundred female German-language SF writers to counteract the impression that only men write SF: Wikipedia, s.v., "Liste deutschsprachiger Science-Fiction-Autorinnen," last modified February 15, 2020, 12:42, https://de.wikipedia.org/wiki/Liste_deutschsprachiger_Science-Fiction-Autorinnen; see also Julian Dörr, "Frauen im Netz: Ferne Welten" (2019).

30 Bijan Moini, *Der Würfel* (2018).

31 Moini, 9.

32 See Geoffrey A. Fowler, "Alexa Has Been Eavesdropping on You This Whole Time," *Washington Post*, May 6, 2019, https://www.washingtonpost.com/technology/2019/05/06/alexa-has-been-eavesdropping-you-this-whole-time.

Chapter 14

1 Markus Giesler has identified four related fears associated with artificial intelligence: the fear of surveillance; the fear of enslavement by intelligent machines; the fear of the end of free will; the fear of losing what makes humans human. See Giesler, "Die Furcht vor KI wird immer größer" (2019).

2 Cf. Ray Kurzweil, *The Age of Intelligent Machines* (1990).

3 Cf. Sophie Wennerscheid, *Sex machina. Zur Zukunft des Begehrens* (2019).

4 Cf. Yuval Noah Harari, *Homo Deus* (2015).

5 Richard M. Weiner, *Das Miniatom-Projekt* (2006); see also Gesa Coordes, "Ein Physik-Roman zwischen Realität und Fiktion" (2008).

6 Richard M. Weiner, *Aufstand der Denkcomputer* (2016).

7 Weiner, 176–77.

8 Cf. Max Adams, *The Firebringers* (2009).

9 Weiner, 67.

10 Weiner is poking fun at Microsoft's ubiquitous operating system Windows™, with the names "Doors™" and "Roof™," indicating that the house has been completed though the software is leaky.

11 See Andreas Brandhorst Schriftsteller, accessed February 28, 2020, https://andreasbrandhorst.de/.

12 Andreas Brandhorst, *Das Erwachen* (2017).

13 See Rory Cellan-Jones, "Stephen Hawking Warns Artificial Intelligence Could End Mankind," BBC News, December 2, 2014, https://www.bbc.co.uk/news/technology-30290540. See also An Open Letter: Research Priorities for Robust and Beneficial Artificial Intelligence," Future of Life Institute, accessed February 28, 2020, https://futureoflife.org/ai-open-letter.

14 Brandhorst, 5.

15 The software intended to cause the social and economic paralysis of an enemy has been created by the American National Security Agency (NSA) and has the appropriately chosen name "Mephisto" (77).

16 See "What is Stuxnet?" McAfee, accessed February 28, 2020, https://www.mcafee.com/enterprise/en-gb/security-awareness/ransomware/what-is-stuxnet.html.

17 Cf. Frank Biess, *Republik der Angst* (2019).

18 Brandhorst, 169–70, italics in the original.

19 Brandhorst, 726.

20 Brandhorst, 727.

21 Cf. Elena Bernard, "Überlegene Maschinen" (2017).

22 Frank Schätzing, *Die Tyrannei des Schmetterlings* (2018).

23 Peter Körte, "Das Gespenst in der Maschine" (2018); Gerrit Bartels, "Und raus bist du" (2018); Gerhard Matzig, "Tief im Westen schmilzt der Streifen Abendrot" (2018); Anne Amend-Söchting, "Doppelte Inversion der Schöpfung" (2018).

24 Alard von Kittlitz, "Besser als ein zähes Entrecote" (2018).

25 Daniel-Dylan Böhmer and Martin Scholz, "Auch Deutsche dürfen unterhalten" (2014).

26 Schätzing, 626.

27 Schätzing, 70.

28 Schätzing, 142.

29 Schätzing, 147.

30 Schätzing, 357. The author is referring here to German philosopher Rüdiger Safranski's book *Romantik: Eine deutsche Affäre* (2007), 393.

31 Schätzing, 408.

Chapter 15

1 Of course, literature—, ranging from Wolfram von Eschenbach's thirteenth century poem *Parzival* to its musical adaptation by Richard Wagner in *Parcival* (1882) and from Percy Shelley's poem *Ozymandias* (1818) to Dara Horn's recent novel *Eternal Life* (2018)—is also full of warnings that eternal life is not meant for humans.

2 *Encyclopedia of Science Fiction*, s.v., "Immortality," last modified February 19, 2020, http://www.sf-encyclopedia.com/entry/immortality.

3 See "Zellaktivator," Perrypedia, last modified March 13, 2020, https://www.perrypedia.proc.org/wiki/Zellaktivator.

4 Cf. Maya Oppenheimer, "Designed Surfaces and the Utopics of Rejuvenation" (2015).

5 See 2045: Strategic Global Initiative, accessed February 28, 2020, http://2045.com/; Alex Moshalis, "How to Live Forever" (2019); "What is Cryonics?"

ALCOR Life Extension Foundation, accessed February 28, 2020, https://alcor.org/AboutCryonics/; Hendrik Otembra, *Kachelbads Erbe* (2019).

[6] Article 11 of UNESCO's Universal Declaration on the Human Genome and Human Rights from 1997 asserts that the reproductive cloning of human beings is contrary to human dignity.

[7] Cf. Jürgen Habermas, *The Future of Human Nature* (2003).

[8] Elizabeth Bridges, "Nasty Nazis and Extreme Americans" (2014).

[9] The book was enthusiastically reviewed—for example, by Iris Mainka, "Ein Volltreffer" (1999)—and it continues to be popular as a set text in German schools.

[10] For a review of the film see Oliver Hüttmann, "Der traurige Klon" (2004).

[11] For example, Jan Freitag, "Transfer im ZDF: Der Traum vom ewigen Leben" (2013); Heike Hupertz, "Ihr neuer Körper sitzt wie ein Maßanzug" (2013).

[12] Cf. Stuart Taberner, *Aging and Old-Age Style in Günter Grass, Ruth Klüger, Christa Wolf, and Martin Walser* (2013).

[13] Priscilla Layne, "The Darkening of Europe" (2010).

[14] See Andreas Brandhorst, "Wollen wir wirklich unsterblich sein?" interview with Piper Verlag, accessed February 28, 2020, https://www.piper.de/ewiges-leben.

[15] Brandhorst, *Ewiges Leben*, 637.

Chapter 16

[1] Joachim Zelter, *Schule der Arbeitslosen* (2006).

[2] Zelter, 16.

[3] Note that in Germany an application is usually accompanied by a recent photograph of the applicant.

[4] See "Mehr Jobs, aber schlechtere," Hans Böckler Stiftung, accessed February 28, 2020, https://www.boeckler.de/de/europaische-union-18295-mehr-jobs-aber-schlechtere-4535.htm.

[5] Cf. Jennifer Karns Alexander, *The Mantra of Efficiency* (2008).

[6] Zelter, 181.

[7] Sigrid Lehmann-Wacker, "Die völlige Irrationalität der Bundesagentur darstellen" (2007), 13.

[8] Susanne Hahn, "'Das Vernichtungslager für Arbeitslose'" (2018).

[9] Martin Burckhardt, *Score: Wir schaffen das Paradies auf Erden* (2015).

[10] Burckhardt, 27.

[11] Burckhardt, 30.

[12] Once a futuristic device in SF narratives, these sensors and practices are becoming a reality: Google started selling its Google Glass in 2013. See Google Glass, accessed February 28, 2020, https://www.google.com/glass/start/. Google began tracking its users universally across all its services in 2012. Cf. Claire Cain Miller, "The Plus in Google Plus? It's mostly for Google" (2014).

13 Burckhardt, 37.

14 Burckhardt, 225, italics in original.

15 Thomas Wörtche, "Ein futuristischer Hightech-Politthriller" (2015).

16 This was replaced by Google's new parent company *Alphabet* in 2015 with the motto "Do the right thing."

17 Karen Duve, *Macht* (2016).

18 A country once notorious for granting fleeing Nazis protection from prosecution, including "Jose" Mengele. See Alan Riding, "Where Nazi Refugees Found the Climate to Their Liking," *New York Times*, June 16, 1985, https://www.nytimes.com/1985/06/16/weekinreview/where-nazi-refugees-found-the-climate-to-their-liking.html.

19 Duve, 38.

20 Duve, 170–71.

21 For example, Gunda Bartels, "Männer sind Knalltüten" (2016); Julia Enke, "Hauptsache, gebrüllt" (2016); Christoph Schröder, "Männer sind der Welt Untergang" (2016).

22 See "taz Studio Buchmesse: Karen Duve Macht," taz, May 24, 2018, YouTube video, 30:47, https://www.youtube.com/watch?v=036xWO6_wlE.

23 Susan Watkins, "Future Shock" (2012), 119.

24 Duve, 52.

25 Marc-Uwe Kling, *QualityLand* (2017).

26 Eva Thöne, "Im Schatten des Kängurus" (2017).

27 See Ralph Bodemann, "Laudatio 2018 Bester deutschsprachiger Roman," Science Fiction Club Deutschland, e.V., September 2018, https://www.dsfp.de/preistraeger/2018-2/laudatio-2018-bester-deutschsprachiger-roman.

28 Juli Zeh, *Leere Herzen* (2017).

29 Zeh, 19.

30 Zeh, 47.

31 Zeh, 72.

32 According to Wikipedia, *Leitkultur* is "a German concept, which can be translated as 'guiding culture' or 'leading culture', less literally as 'common culture', 'core culture' or 'basic culture'. . . . From 2000 onward the term figured prominently in the national political debate in Germany about national identity and immigration." See Wikipedia, s.v. "Leitkultur," last modified October 5, 2019, 21:35, https://en.wikipedia.org/wiki/Leitkultur. I have chosen to translate it as "dominant culture" as that is what its proponents actually mean and argue for.

33 Zeh, 313.

34 Gustav Seibt, "Selbstsicher" (2017).

35 Jacqueline Thör, "Gibt es noch Hoffnung in Dunkeldeutschland?" (2017).

36 Julia Encke, "Wo geht's zum Abgrund?" (2017).

37 Stefan Jäger, "Mit dem Grüntee-to-go zum Waterboarding" (2017).

[38] Zeh, 276.

Chapter 17

I am indebted to Dr. Hanna Schumacher, whose PhD dissertation *Zur Verhandlung der Conditio Posthumana in der zeitgenössischen deutschsprachigen Gegenwartsliteratur—Gesellschaftskonstitution, Subjektivitätsentwicklung und Kunst* (University of Warwick, 2018) has helped me appreciate these texts.

[1] See Stefan Hertbrecher, "Stefan Herbrechter Interview," interview by Jerome Garbrah, *Critical Posthumanism: Genealogy of the Posthuman*, November 2013, http://criticalposthumanism.net/the-posthuman-review/stefan-herbrechter-interview/.

[2] Cf. Stefan Herbrechter, *Posthumanism: A Critical Analysis* (2013).

[3] Ulf Poschardt, "In Lenins Schriften ist viel Nützliches" (2008).

[4] Friedrich Nietzsche, *Human, All Too Human*, aphorism 519 (1886).

[5] Rath, 15.

[6] See the website for Dietmar Rath, accessed February 28, 2020, http://www.cyrusgolden.de/index_js.html.

[7] Daniel Schneider, "Evolution und Beziehungen bei Monika Maron und Dietmar Dath (2012) 114. See also Lars Schmeink, *Biopunk Dystopias* (2016) and Michael Morrison's review (2018).

[8] Reinhard Jirgl, *Nichts von euch auf Erden* (2013).

[9] Jirgl, 34.

[10] Oliver Jungen, "Ich bin die Lüge in euren Ängsten" (2013).

[11] Hubert Winkels, "Außerirdisch ambitioniert" (2013).

[12] Hans-Jost Weyandt, "Furor im Weltall" (2013); see also Sven-Eric Wehmeyer, "Diktatur der Sanftheit" (2013); Jutta von Sternburg, "Die letzten Jahre der Menschheit" (2013).

[13] Julian Werlitz, "Was wir gewesen sein werden" (2014), 247.

[14] See Elfriede Mueller, "Die langweilige Apokalypse," Culturmag, April 24, 2013, http://culturmag.de/rubriken/buecher/reinhard-jirgl-nichts-von-euch-auf-erden/69831.

[15] See Alexander Kluge, "Alexander Kluge und Reinhard Jirgl über *Nichts von euch auf Erden*, Teil I—Das Drama vom Ende der Welt," Münchner Kammerspiele, Vimeo video, 45:00, accessed February 28, 2020, https://vimeo.com/145543892.

[16] Beatrix Langner, "Der Mensch schafft sich ab" (2013).

[17] Leif Randt, *Planet Magnon* (2017).

[18] Cf. Anja Kümmel, "Postpragmatischer Genuß" (2015).

[19] E.g., Sebastian Hammelehle, "Wohlstandsmüde im Weltraum" (2015); Richard Kämmerlings, "Weltuntergang? Aber selbstverständlich!" (2015); Lena Bopp,

"Eine Welt ohne Liebesschmerz, wie wäre die?" (2015); Judith von Sternburg, "Cooler ambivalent sein" (2015).

[20] Nils Markwardt, "Im All liegt das Paradies" (2015).

[21] Philipp Theisohn, "Literarische Droge" (2015).

[22] Eva Menasse, "Das Kollektiv der gebrochenen Herzen" (2016).

Chapter 18

[1] Marlen Haushofer, *Die Wand* (1963).

[2] Haushofer, 40.

[3] Lisa Cornick, "Identity in Women's Writings" (1992).

[4] Cf. Sabine Frost, "Looking Behind Walls" (2017).

[5] See Maria Jaso, "Instagram fait remonter le livre 'Le Mur Invisible' en tête des ventes Amazon," Le Huffington Post, February 1, 2019, https://www.huffingtonpost.fr/2019/02/01/instagram-fait-remonter-le-livre-le-mur-invisible-en-tete-des-ventes-amazon_a_23658570/.

[6] See "*The Wall* Official UK Trailer," New Wave Films, June 26, 2013, YouTube video, 1:58, https://youtu.be/fPtk3XDFY48; Cf. Martin Schwickert, "Gefangen in sich selbst" (2012). *Time Out* described the film as "Sylvia Plath meets The Twilight Zone." See "The Wall," *Time Out*, July 2, 2013, https://www.timeout.com/london/film/the-wall-2012.

[7] See "Die Wand," Burgtheater, accessed February 28, 2020, https://www.burgtheater.at/en/event/200.

[8] John Clute, *Canary Fever: Reviews* (2009), 161 (italics in original).

[9] Andreas Eschbach, *Quest* (2001).

[10] Eschbach, 11.

[11] Eschbach, 518.

[12] Eschbach, 519.

[13] Vibeke Rützou Petersen, "What is the Holocaust doing in German SF?" (2014), 229.

[14] Petersen, 231.

[15] Vibeke Rützou Petersen, "German SF: Its Formative Works and its Postwar Uses of the Holocaust" (2014), 31.

[16] Petersen, 40.

[17] Cf. Stuart Taberner and Paul Cooke's forward-looking research projects: "Transnational Holocaust Memory," University of Leeds School of English Website, accessed February 28, 2020, https://ahc.leeds.ac.uk/english/dir-record/research-projects/597/transnational-holocaust-memory; "Changing the Story," University of Leeds Website, accessed February 28, 2020, https://changingthestory.leeds.ac.uk/.

[18] Thomas Lehr, *42* (2005).

[19] Lehr, 221.

[20] Lehr, 200.

[21] Lehr, 367.

[22] Beatrix Langner, "Odyssee durch die Gegenwart," *Neue Zürcher Zeitung*, October 18, 2005.

[23] Helmut Böttiger, "Wenn plötzlich die Zeit stillsteht" (2005).

[24] Nadja Weber, "Science Fiction, Mystery, Drama" (2016). See also Lukas Stern, "Ebbedrama 'Wir sind die Flut'" (2016).

[25] Gabriele Mueller, "'Rattenfänger' von Europa" (2018), 138.

[26] See *Encyclopedia of Science Fiction*, s.v. "Conceptual Breakthrough," last modified March 22, 2016, http://www.sf-encyclopedia.com/entry/conceptual_breakthrough.

[27] This is also the question of Douglas Adams's *The Hitchhiker's Guide to the Galaxy* (1978), to which the answer is 42. For a physics perspective, see Natalie Wolchover, "A Different Kind of Theory of Everything" (2019).

Conclusion

[1] Ursula K. Heise, "Science Fiction and the Time Scale of the Anthropocene" (2019), 276.

[2] Cf. Johannes Schneider, "Die Apokalypse ist leider auserzählt" (2019).

[3] William Blake, *The Marriage of Heaven and Hell* (1794), plate 8.

[4] Cf. Anon., "When Science Fiction Inspires Real Technology" (2018); Judith Blage, "Wissenschaft, inspiriert durch Science Fiction" (2019).

[5] In *The Tempest*, 5.1.184–87, Miranda exclaims: "O, wonder! / How many goodly creatures are there here! / How beauteous mankind is! O brave new world / That has such people in it!" In *Faust* II, 5.3.11245–48, Faust brags about his achievements: "My eyes revealing, under the sun / a view of everything I have done / surveying, as the eyes fall on it / a masterpiece of the human spirit."

[6] Cf. Robert T. Tally, "In the File Drawer labelled 'Science Fiction'" (2017).

[7] David Mitchell's novel *The Cloud Atlas* (2004) is a case in point here. With its message that "Everything is connected" it inspired an Anglo-German film directed by Tom Tykwer and the Wachowski sisters (2012) that comfortably switches between traditional styles and genres as it does between the past and the future. See also James Dorson, "Cormac McCarthy and the Genre Turn in Contemporary Literary Fiction" (2017).

[8] Cf. Caroline Edwards, *Utopia and the Contemporary British Novel* (2019).

[9] Hannes Riffel, ed., *Jenseits von Raum und Zeit*, 5.

[10] See Clarkesworld, accessed February 28, 2020, http://clarkesworldmagazine.com/.

[11] Robert Brenner, *Signale vom Jupitermond* (1968).

[12] It sees Earth's population peaking at 7.2 billion people in 2021 when birth control is introduced worldwide. Of this population 2.7 billion are children and

adolescents who are not yet working, along with 600 million students. There are 2.2 billion people who are no longer working (the over fifty-five-year-olds!), and there are 1.5 billion people working in education, in entertainment, as care workers, in medicine, tending machines, overseeing automated food production, in research, in transport, and in energy.

[13] Robert Brenner, *Signale vom Jupitermond* (1968), 101.

[14] Cf. Adam Kirsch, *The Global Novel* (2017).

Bibliography

Primary Works

Literature

Akkad, Omar El. *American War*. New York: Picador, 2017.
Alderman, Naomi. *The Power*. London: Viking, 2017.
Alef, Rob. *Das magische Jahr*. Berlin: Rotbuch, 2008.
Amery, Carl. *Das Geheimnis der Krypta*. Munich: List, 1990.
———. *Das Königsprojekt*. Munich: Süddeutscher Verlag, 1987.
———. *Der Untergang der Stadt Passau*. Munich: Heyne, 1975.
———. *Die Wallfahrer*. Munich: Süddeutscher Verlag, 1986.
Atwood, Margaret. *The Handmaid's Tale*. Toronto: McClelland and Stewart, 1985.
Bachschneider, Wolfgang. "Das digitale Dachau." In *Das Digitale Dachau: Internationale Science Fiction Stories*, edited by Wolfgang Jeschke, 370–84. Munich: Heyne, 1985.
Barker, Nicola. *H(a)ppy*. London: Heinemann, 2017.
Berg, Sibylle. *GRM—Brainfuck*. Cologne: Kiepenheuer & Witsch, 2019.
Beyse, Jochen. *Fremd wie das Licht in den Träumen der Menschen*. Zurich: Diaphanes, 2017.
Brandhorst, Andreas. *Das Erwachen*. Munich: Piper, 2017.
———. *Ewiges Leben*. Munich: Piper, 2018.
Brenner, Robert. *Signale vom Jupitermond. Ein Bericht aus dem Jahre 2028*. Stuttgart: Ehapa, 1968.
Burckhardt, Martin. *Score*. Munich: Knaus, 2015.
Callenbach, Ernest. *Ökotopia. Notizen und Reportagen von William Weston aus dem Jahre 1999*. Berlin: Rotbuch, 1978.
Dath, Dietmar. *Die Abschaffung der Arten*. Frankfurt: Suhrkamp, 2008.
———. *Neptunation*. Frankfurt: Fischer, 2019.
———. *Pulsarnacht*. Munich: Heyne, 2012.
———. *Der Schnitt durch die Sonne*. Frankfurt: Fischer, 2017.
———. *Venus Siegt*. Frankfurt: Fischer, 2016.
DeLillo, Don. *Zero K*. London: Picador, 2016.
Dexheimer, Ludwig. *Das Automatenzeitalter. Ein prognostischer Roman*. Berlin: Shayol, 2004. First published 1930.
Dick, Philip K. *The Man in the High Castle*. New York: Putnam's, 1962.

Döblin, Alfred. *Berge Meere und Giganten.* Frankfurt: Fischer, 2013. First published 1924.
Dominik, Hans. *Atlantis.* Munich: Heyne, 1998. First published 1924.
———. *Die Macht der Drei. Ein Roman aus dem Jahre 1955.* Munich: Heyne, 1997. First published 1922.
———. *Der Wettflug der Nationen.* Munich: Heyne, 1990. First published 1932.
Duve, Karen. *Macht.* Berlin: Galiani, 2016.
Eggers, Dave. *The Circle.* New York: Alfred Knopf, 2013.
Erlenberger, Maria. *Singende Erde. Ein utopischer Roman.* Reinbek: Rowohlt, 1980.
Eschbach, Andreas. *Ausgebrannt.* Bergisch Gladbach: Lübbe, 2007.
———. *Eine Billion Dollar.* Bergisch Gladbach: Lübbe, 2001.
———. *Die Haarteppichknüpfer.* Munich: Heyne, 1998.
———. *Herr aller Dinge.* Cologne: Lübbe, 2011.
———. *Das Jesus-Video.* Munich: Heyne, 1998.
———. *Ein König für Deutschland.* Bergisch Gladbach: Lübbe, 2009.
———. *NSA—Nationales Sicherheits-Amt.* Cologne: Lübbe, 2018.
———. *Perfect Copy: Die zweite Schöpfung.* Würzburg: Bastei Lübbe, 2005.
———. *Perry Rhodan—Das größte Abenteuer.* Berlin: Fischer TOR, 2019.
———. *Quest.* Munich: Heyne, 2001.
Faber, Michael. *The Book of Strange New Things.* Edinburgh: Canongate Books, 2014.
Fleck, Dirk C. *Go! Die Ökodiktatur.* Hamburg: Rasch & Röhring, 1993.
———. *Maeva!* Rudolstadt: Greifenverlag, 2011.
Franke, Herbert. *Der grüne Komet.* Murnau: p.machinery, 2014. First published 1960.
———. *Zone Null.* Frankfurt: Suhrkamp, 1980.
Fritsch, Valerie. *Winters Garten.* Berlin: Suhrkamp, 2015.
Galouye, Daniel F. *Simulacron Drei.* Munich: Goldmann, 1983. First published 1964.
Gilman, Charlotte Perkins. *Herland.* London: Pantheon, 1979. First published 1915.
Händler, Ernst-Wilhelm. *Der Überlebende.* Frankfurt: Fischer, 2014.
Hannig, Theresa. *Die Optimierer.* Cologne: Bastei Lübbe, 2017.
———. *Die Unvollkommenen.* Cologne: Bastei Lübbe, 2019.
Hall, Sarah. *The Carhullan Army.* London: Faber & Faber, 2007.
Haushofer, Marlen *Die Wand.* Stuttgart: Klett, 2008. First published 1963.
Helle, Heinz. *Eigentlich müßten wir tanzen.* Berlin: Suhrkamp, 2015.
Henry, A. *Das Ende der Klassik.* Berlin: Galabuch, 2018.
Herzl, Theodor. *Altneuland.* Leipzig: Seemann Nachf., 1902.
Hillenbrand, Tom. *Drohnenland.* Cologne: Kiepenheur & Witsch, 2014.
———. *Hologrammatica.* Cologne: Kiepenheur & Witsch, 2018.
Houellebecq, Michel. *La Possibilité d'une île.* Paris: Knopf, 2005.
Hoyle, Fred. *The Black Cloud.* London: Heinemann, 1957.

Illing, Werner. *Utopolis*. Berlin: Shayol, 2005. First published 1930.
Jeschke, Wolfgang. *Das Cusanus-Spiel*. Munich: Droemer, 2005.
———. *Dschiheads*. Munich: Heyne, 2013.
———. *Der letzte Tag der Schöpfung*. Munich: Nymphenburger, 1981.
Jirgl, Reinhard. *Nichts von euch auf Erden*. Munich: Hanser, 2013.
Jünger, Ernst. *Heliopolis*. Stuttgart: Klett-Cotta, 1980. First published 1949.
Kellermann, Bernhard. *Der Tunnel*. Berlin: Fischer, 1913.
Kerner, Charlotte. *Blueprint Blaupause*. Weinheim: Beltz Verlag, 1999.
Khaled Towfik, Ahmed. *Utopia*. London: Bloomsbury, 2011.
Kirchner, Barbara. *Die verbesserte Frau*. Berlin: Verbrecher Verlag, 2001.
Kling, Marc-Uwe. *QualityLand*. Berlin: Ullstein, 2017.
Kracht, Christian. *Ich werde hier sein im Sonnenschein und im Schatten*. Cologne: Kiepenheuer & Witsch, 2008.
Kyr, Oliver. *Ascheland*. Hamburg: Abacus, 2016.
Lanchester, John. *The Wall*. London: Faber & Faber, 2019.
Laßwitz, Kurd. *Auf zwei Planeten*. Munich: Heyne, 1998. First published 1897.
———. "Einführung." In *Nanna, oder Über das Seelenleben der Pflanzen*, by Gustav Theodor Fechner. 3rd ed. Hamburg: Leopold Voß, 1903.
———. *Homchen, und andere Erzählungen*. Munich: Heyne, 1986.
———. "Pflanzenseele." In *Empfundenes und Erkanntes: Aus dem Nachlasse*, 186–96. Leipzig: Verlag von B. Elischer Nachfolger, 1919.
———. *Sternentau: Die Pflanze vom Jupitermond*. Lüneburg: Dieter von Reeken, 2008. First published 1909.
———. *Two Planets*. Carbondale: Southern Illinois University Press, 1971.
———. "Über Zukunftsträume." In *Homchen, und andere Erzählungen*, 450–70. Munich: Heyne, 1986.
———. "Unser Recht auf Bewohner anderer Welten." *Frankfurter Zeitung*, October 16, 1910.
Lehr, Thomas. *42*. Berlin: Aufbau, 2005.
Lessing, Doris. *The Memoirs of a Survivor*. New York: Vintage Books, 1988. First published 1974.
Lieckfeld, Claus-Peter, and Frank Wittchow. *427. Im Land der grünen Inseln*. Ulm: Schönberger Verlag, 1986.
Liu, Cixin. *The Three-Body Problem*. New York: Tor Books, 2014.
Moini, Bijan. *Der Würfel*. Zurich: Atrium Verlag, 2018.
Otremba, Hendrik. *Kachelbads Erbe*. Hamburg: Hoffmann & Campe, 2019.
Pätzold, Oliver. *Die Letzten: Zerfall*. Scotts Valley, CA: CreateSpace Independent Publishing Platform, 2016.
Pausewang, Gudrun. *Die Wolke*. Ravensburg: Otto Maier, 1987.
P.M. *Weltgeist Superstar*. Munich: dtv, 1983.
Pohl, Frederik, and C. M. Kornbluth. *The Space Merchants*. London: Gollancz, 2003. First published 1953.
Porter, Chana. *The Seep*. New York: Soho Books, 2020.
Powers, Richard. *Galatea 2.2*. London: Atlantic Books, 2010. First published 1995.

Rabisch, Birgit. *Duplik Jonas 7.* Munich: dtv, 1997.
Randt, Leif. *Planet Magnon.* Cologne: Kiepenheuer & Witsch, 2017.
Ransmayr, Christoph. *Morbus Kitahara.* Frankfurt: Fischer, 1995.
Rieks, Josefine. *Serverland.* Munich: Hanser, 2018.
Rottensteiner, Franz, ed. *The Black Mirror & Other Stories: An Anthology of Science Fiction from Germany and Austria.* Middletown, CT: Wesleyan University Press, 2008.
Sansdal, Boualem. *2084: The End of the World.* New York: Europa Editions, 2017.
Saramago, Jose. *Die Stadt der Sehenden.* Reinbek: Rowohlt, 2006.
Schätzing, Frank. *Limit.* Cologne: Kiepenheuer & Witsch, 2009.
———. *Der Schwarm.* Cologne: Kiepenheuer & Witsch, 2004.
———. *Die Tyrannei der Schmetterlinge.* Cologne: Kiepenheuer & Witsch, 2018.
Scheerbart, Paul. *Die große Revolution: Ein Mondroman.* Leipzig: Insel Verlag, 1902.
———. *Lesabéndio: An Asteroid Novel.* Cambridge, MA: Wakefield Press, 2012. First published 1913.
Schmidt, Arno. *Die Gelehrtenrepublik.* Frankfurt: Suhrkamp, 2006. First published 1957.
Schnabel, Johann Gottfried. *Insel Felsenburg: Wunderliche Fata einiger Seefahrer (1731–1743).* Edited by Günter Dammann and Marcus Czerwionka. Frankfurt: Zweitausendeins, 1997.
Shippey, Tom, ed. *The Oxford Book of Science Fiction Stories.* Oxford: Oxford University Press, 1992.
Shriver, Lionel. *The Mandibles: A Family, 2029–2047.* London: The Borough Press, 2016.
Sorokin, Vladimir. *Telluria.* Cologne: Kiepenheuer & Witsch, 2015.
———. *Der Zuckerkreml.* Cologne: Kiepenheuer & Witsch, 2010.
Starhawk. *The Fifth Sacred Thing.* New York: Bantam, 1993.
Stein, Benjamin. *Replay.* Munich: C. H. Beck, 2012.
Steinhäuser, Gerhard R. *Unternehmen Stunde Null 1986: Leben nach dem jüngsten Tag.* Frankfurt: Fischer, 1975.
Steinmüller, Angela, and Karlheinz Steinmüller. *Andymon: Eine Weltraum-Utopie.* Munich: Golkonda, 2018.
Stoppard, Tom. *The Coast of Utopia.* London: Faber & Faber, 2008.
Suarez, Daniel. *Bios.* Berlin: Rowohlt, 2017.
Timm, Uwe. *Ikarien.* Cologne: Kiepenheuer & Witsch, 2017.
Trojanow, Iliya. *EisTau.* Munich: Carl Hanser, 2011.
Uhrmann, Erwin. *Ich bin die Zukunft.* Innsbruck: Limbus, 2014.
VanderMeer, Jeff. *Southern Reach Trilogy (Annihilation, Authority, Acceptance).* London: 4th Estate, 2014.
Voltz, William, ed. *Perry Rhodan. Die Dritte Macht.* Rastatt: Pabel-Moewig, 1978.
von Harbou, Thea. *Frau im Mond.* Munich: Heyne, 1989. First published 1928.

———. *Die Insel der Unsterblichen.* Berlin: Scherl, 1926.
———. *Metropolis.* Frankfurt: Ullstein, 1984. First published 1926.
von Steinaecker, Thomas. *Die Verteidigung des Paradieses.* Frankfurt: Fischer, 2016.
Weiner, Richard M. *Das Miniatom-Projekt: Ein Wissenschafts- und Kriminalroman.* Marburg: LiteraturWissenschaft, 2006.
———. *Aufstand der Denkcomputer.* Marburg: LiteraturWissenschaft, 2014.
Wells, H. G. *A Modern Utopia.* London: Penguin, 2005. First published 1905.
———. *The Shape of Things to Come.* London: Gollancz, 2011. First published 1933.
Werfel, Franz. *Stern der Ungeborenen: Ein Reiseroman.* Frankfurt: Fischer, 1998. First published 1946.
Whey, Florian Felix. *Toggle.* Berlin: Galiani, 2012.
Wolf, Christa. *Kein Ort. Nirgends.* Frankfurt: Suhrkamp, 2007. First published 1979.
Zeh, Juli. *Corpus Delicti: Ein Prozess.* Munich: btb, 2010.
———. *Leere Herzen.* Munich: Luchterhand, 2017.
Zelter, Joachim. *Schule der Arbeitslosen.* Tübingen: Klöpfer & Meier, 2006.
Ziegler, Thomas. *Alles ist Gut.* Meitingen: Corian, 1983.
———. *Stimmen der Nacht.* Berlin: Golkonda, 2014. First published 1993.

Films and Television Series

Baichwal, Jennifer, Nicholas de Pencier, and Edward Burtynsky, dirs., *Anthropocene: The Human Epoch.* 2018; Toronto, Canada: Mercury Films, 2019.
Bernhardt, Kurt, dir. *Der Tunnel.* 1933; Munich: Bavaria Film, 1933.
Braun, Michael, dir. *Raumpatrouille Orion.* 1966; Munich: Bavaria Film, 1966.
Emmerich, Roland, dir. *Das Arche Noah Prinzip.* 1984; Berlin: Centropolis Film, 1985.
Erler, Rainer, dir. *Operation Ganymed.* 1977; Dietramszell: Pentagramma Filmproduktion, 1980.
Fassbinder, Rainer Werner, dir. *Welt am Draht.* 1973; Cologne: Westdeutscher Rundfunk 1973.
Fehlbaum, Tim, dir. *Hell.* 2011; Munich: Caligari Film, 2011.
Fleischmann, Peter, dir. *Es ist nicht leicht, ein Gott zu sein.* 1990; Munich: B.A. Produktion, 1991.
Herwig, Michael Bully, dir. *Traumschiff Surprise. Periode 1.* 2004; Munich: herbX Film 2004.
Herzog, Werner, dir. *Lo and Behold, Reveries of the Connected World.* 2016; Los Angeles: Saville Productions, 2016.
———, dir. *The Wild Blue Yonder.* 2005; Munich: Werner Herzog Filmproduktion, 2007.

Hilger, Sebastian, dir. *Wir sind die Flut.* 2016; Berlin: Anna Wendt Filmproduktion, 2016.
Hilpert, Heinz, dir. *Der Herr vom andern Stern.* 1948; Berlin: Comedia-Film, 1948.
Kraume, Lars, dir. *Die kommenden Tage.* 2011; Berlin: Badlands Film, 2011.
Kutter, Anton, dir. *Weltraumschiff I startet.* 1937; Munich: Bavaria Film, 1937.
Lang, Fritz, dir. *Frau im Mond.* 1929; Berlin: Universum Film, 1929.
———, dir. *Metropolis.* 1927; Berlin: Universum Film, 1927.
Lucacevic, Damir, dir. *Transfer: Der Traum vom ewigen Leben.* 2010; Berlin: Schiwago Film, 2010.
Nolan, Christopher, dir. *Interstellar.* 2014; Los Angeles: Paramount Pictures, 2014.
Pölsler, Julian, dir. *Die Wand.* 2012; Vienna: Coop 99 Filmproduktion, 2012.
Ruzowitzky, Stefan, dir. *Acht Tage.* 2019; Munich: Neuesuper, 2019.
Schübel, Rolf, dir. *Blueprint.* 2003; Hamburg: Relevant Film, 2003.
Spotnitz, Frank, dir. *The Man in the High Castle.* 2015; Santa Monica, CA: Amazon Studios, 2015.
Tyldum, Morten, dir. *Passengers.* 2016; Los Angeles: Columbia Pictures, 2016.
Villeneuve, Denis, dir. *Blade Runner 2049.* 2017; Los Angeles: Alcon Entertainment, 2017.
von Trier, Lars, dir. *Melancholia.* 2011; Copenhagen: Zentropa Entertainments, 2011.
Vuorensula, Timo, dir. *Iron Sky.* 2012; Helsinki: Blind Spot Pictures, 2012.
Zschoche, Hermann, dir. *Eolomea.* 1972; Berlin: VEB DEFA Studio, 1972.

Secondary Literature

Adams, Max. *The Firebringers. Art, Science and the Struggle for Liberty in 19th Century Britain.* London: Quercus, 2009.
Adams, Robert M. "Devil's Brew." *New York Review of Books*, March 5, 1981.
Adelson, Leslie A. "The Future of Futurity: Alexander Kluge and Yoko Tawada." *Germanic Review: Literature, Culture, Theory* 83, no. 3 (2011): 153–84.
Adorno, Theodor, and Max Horkheimer. *Dialectics of Enlightenment.* London: Verso, 1979. First published 1944.
Affeldt-Schmidt, Birgit. *Fortschrittsutopien: Vom Wandel der utopischen Literatur im 19. Jahrhundert.* Stuttgart: Metzler, 1991.
Alberro, Heather. "Utopia Isn't Just Idealistic Fantasy—It Inspires People to Change the World." The Conversation, June 21, 2019. https://theconversation.com/utopia-isnt-just-idealistic-fantasy-it-inspires-people-to-change-the-world-118962.
Albrecht, Thorben. "A Human-Centred Agenda for the Future of Work." *Social Europe*, January 22, 2019.

Alderman, Naomi. "Dystopian Dreams: How Feminist Science Fiction Predicted the Future." *Guardian*, March 25, 2017.
Aldiss, Brian, ed. *The Penguin Science Fiction Omnibus*. Harmondsworth: Penguin, 1973.
Aldiss, Brian, and David Wingrove, eds. *Trillion Year Spree: The History of Science Fiction*. London: Gollancz, 1986.
Alexander, Jennifer Karns. *The Mantra of Efficiency*. Baltimore: Johns Hopkins University Press, 2008.
Al-Fodhan, Nayef, ed. *There's a Future: Visions for a Better World*. Madrid: Banco Bilbao Vizcaya Argentaria, 2013.
Alpers, Hans-Joachim, Werner Fuchs, Ronald M. Hahn, and Wolfgang Jeschke, eds. *Lexikon der Science Fiction Literatur*. Munich: Heyne, 1988.
Amend-Söchting, Anne. "Doppelte Inversion der Schöpfung, Killerinsekten, Action im Übermaß: 'Die Tyrannei des Schmetterlings' von Frank Schätzing." literaturkritik.de. June 13, 2018. https://literaturkritik.de/schaetzing-tyrannei-schmetterlings-doppelte-inversion-schoepfung-killerinsekten-action-uebermass,24593.html.
Anderson, Jenny. *The Future of the World. Futurology, Futurists, and the Struggle for the Post-Cold War Imagination*. Oxford: Oxford University Press, 2018.
Anthony, Andrew. "The Idea of Free Information is Extremely Dangerous." Interview with Yuval Noah Harari. *Observer*, August 5, 2018.
Antosik, Stanley. "Utopian Machines: Leibniz's 'Computer' and Hesse's Glass Bead Game." *The Germanic Review* 67, no. 1 (1992): 35–45.
Arendt, Hannah. *The Human Condition*. Chicago: University of Chicago Press, 1958.
Ashley, Mike. *Out of This World. Science Fiction, but Not as You Know It*. London: The British Library, 2011.
Assheuer, Thomas. "NS Vergangenheit: Hauptsache, starke Bilder." *Die Zeit*, January 23, 2019.
Assmann, Aleida. *Einführung in die Kulturwissenschaft: Grundbegriffe, Themen*, Fragestellungen. Berlin: Erich Schmidt Verlag, 2006.
———. *Ist die Zeit aus den Fugen? Aufstieg und Fall des Zeitregimes der Moderne*. Munich: Hanser, 2013.
Atwood, Margaret. "Dire Cartographies," In *In Other Worlds: Science Fiction and the Human Imagination*, 66–96. London: Virago, 2012.
———. "When Privacy Is Theft." *New York Review of Books*, November 21, 2013.
Baccolini, Raffaella, and Tom Moylan, eds. *Dark Horizons: Science Fiction and the Dystopian Imagination*. New York: Routledge, 2003.
Bamforth, Iain. "The Method." *British Journal of General Practice* 62, no. 602 (September 2012): 489.
Banerjee, Anindita, and Sonja Fritzsche, eds. *Science Fiction Circuits of the South and East*. Oxford: Peter Lang, 2018.

Barmeyer, Eike, ed. *Science Fiction. Theorie und Geschichte.* Munich: Fink, 1972.
Bartels, Gerrit. "Und raus bist du. 'Die Tyrannei des Schmetterlings' von Frank Schätzing." *Der Tagesspiegel*, April 25, 2018.
Bartels, Gunda. "Männer sind Knalltüten." *Der Tagesspiegel*, February 17, 2016.
Bastani, Aaron. *Fully Automated Luxury Communism.* London: Verso, 2019.
Battegay, Caspar. "Gleichzeitigkeit. Utopie und Exil in Franz Werfels Stern der Ungeborenen." In *Utopie im Exil. Literarische Figurationen des Imaginären*, edited by Marisa Siguan and Linda Maeding, 173–94. Bielefeld: Transcript, 2017.
Bauman, Zygmunt. *Liquid Modernity.* Cambridge: Polity Books, 2012. First published 2000.
———. *Retrotopia.* Berlin: Suhrkamp, 2017.
Beaumont, Matthew. *The Spectre of Utopia. Utopian and Science Fictions at the Fin de Ciècle.* Oxford: Peter Lang, 2012.
Bebel, August. *Die Frau und der Sozialismus.* Bonn: Dietz Verlag, 1994. First published 1879.
Beck, Ulrich. *Risikogesellschaft: Auf dem Weg in eine andere Moderne.* Frankfurt: Suhrkamp, 1986.
———. *Weltrisikogesellschaft. Auf dem Weg in eine andere Moderne.* Frankfurt: Suhrkamp, 2007.
Beckett, Andy, "Fully Automated Luxury Communism by Aaron Bastani—a Manifesto for the Future." *Guardian*, May 29, 2019.
Beiser, Frederic C. *Weltschmerz: Pessimism in German Philosophy, 1860–1900.* Oxford: Oxford University Press, 2016.
Benjamin, Walter. "Zentralpark." In *Gesammelte Schriften*, edited by Hermann Schweppenhäuser and Rolf Tiedemann, 1.2: 651–90. Frankfurt: Suhrkamp, 1991.
Berardi, Franco Bifo. *Futurability: The Age of Impotence and the Horizon of Possibility.* London: Verso, 2017.
Bernard, Elena. "Überlegene Maschinen." *Spektrum der Wissenschaft*, November 23, 2017.
Bernhard, Marcus, Wolfgang Blösel, Stefan Brakensiek, and Benjamin Scheller, eds. *Möglichkeitshorizonte. Zur Pluralität von Zukunftserwartungen und Handlungsoptionen in der Geschichte.* Frankfurt: Campus Verlag, 2018.
Biess Frank. *Republik der Angst. Eine andere Geschichte der Bundesrepublik Deutschland.* Reinbek: Rowohlt, 2019.
Biesterfeld, Wolfgang. *Die literarische Utopie.* Stuttgart: Metzler, 1982.
Blackford, Russell. *Science Fiction and the Moral Imagination: Visions, Minds, Ethics.* Cham: Springer International Publishing, 2017.
Blage, Judith. "Wie Science-Fiction die Wissenschaft inspiriert." *Süddeutsche Zeitung*, June 16, 2019.
Bloch, Ernst. *Geist der Utopie.* Frankfurt: Suhrkamp, 1977. First published 1918.

———. *Das Prinzip Hoffnung*. Frankfurt: Suhrkamp, 1985. First published 1954.

———. *The Utopian Function of Art and Literature*. Cambridge, MA: MIT Press, 1988.

Bloch, Jan Robert. *Utopie: Ortsbestimmung im Nirgendwo. Begriff und Funktion von Gesellschaftsentwürfen*. Opladen: Leske+Budrich, 1997.

Bölsche, Wilhelm. *Vom Bazillus zum Affenmenschen: Naturwissenschaftliche Plaudereien*. Leipzig: Diederichs, 1900.

Böhmer, Daniel-Dylan, and Martin Scholz. "Auch Deutsche dürfen unterhalten." *Die Welt*. March 4, 2014.

Bohmeyer, Michael, and Claudia Cornelsen. *'Was würdest du tun?' Wie uns das bedingungslose Grundeinkommen verändert. Antworten aus der Praxis*. Berlin: Ullstein, 2019.

Boldt, Ralf, ed. *Fiktion in Serie: 50 Jahre Perry Rhodan*. Duisburg: Science Fiction Club Deutschland, 2011.

Böll, Heinrich. "Galopp mit der Raum-Zeit-Maschine." *Die Zeit*, October 4, 1974.

Bollhöfener, Klaus, Klaus Farin, and Dierk Spreen, eds. *Spurensuche im All: Perry Rhodan Studies—Wissen, Theorien, Perspektiven*. Berlin: Speed Comics, 2003.

Booker, M. Keith. *The Dystopian Impulse in Modern Literature: Fiction as Social Criticism*. Westport CT: Greenwood Press, 1994.

———. *Dystopian Literature: A Theory and Research Guide*. Westport, CT: Greenwood Press, 1994.

Borgards, Roland. "Posthumanismus und Anthropozän." In *Faust-Handbuch*, edited by C. Rohde, T. Valk, and M. Mayer, 568–74. Stuttgart: J. B. Metzler, 2018.

Born, Eric. "Some Omissions in the Universal Library: Kurd Laßwitz and the Emergence of Science Fiction." *Monatshefte* 110, no. 4 (2018): 529–51.

Bostrom, Nick. *Superintelligenz: Szenarien einer kommenden Revolution*. Berlin: Suhrkamp, 2014.

Both, Wolfgang, Hans-Peter Neumann, and Klaus Scheffler, eds. *Berichte aus der Parallelwelt: Die Geschichte des Science Fiction-Fandoms in der DDR*. Passau: Erster Deutscher Fantasy Club e.V., 1998.

Böttiger, Helmut. "Wenn plötzlich die Zeit stillsteht." *Die Zeit*, October 13, 2005.

Bowler, Peter J. *A History of the Future: Prophets of Progress from H. G. Wells to Isaac Asimov*. Cambridge: Cambridge University Press, 2017.

Braidotti, Rosi. "Jenseits des Menschen: Posthumanismus." *Aus Politik und Zeitgeschichte* 37/38 (2016): 33–38.

———. *The Posthuman*. Cambridge: Polity Books, 2013.

Brake, Mark. *The Science of Science Fiction: The Influence of Film and Fiction on the Science and Culture of Our Times*. New York: Skyhorse, 2018.

Brandt, Dina. *Der deutsche Zukunftsroman 1918–1945: Gattungstypologie und sozialgeschichtliche Verortung*. Tübingen: Niemeyer, 2007.

Bregman, Rutger. *Utopia for Realists*. London: Bloomsbury, 2017.

Brehmer, Arthur, ed. *Die Welt in 100 Jahren.* Hildesheim: Olms, 2012. First published 1910.
Brians, Paul. *Nuclear Holocausts: Atomic War in Fiction, 1895–1984.* Kent, OH: Kent State University Press, 1987.
Bridges, Elizabeth. "Nasty Nazis and Extreme Americans: Cloning, Eugenics, and the Exchange of National Signifiers in Contemporary Science Fiction," *Studies in 20th and 21st Century Literature* 38, no. 1 (2014): Article 7.
Bridle, James. *The New Dark Age: Technology and the End of the Future.* London: Verso, 2018.
Briegleb, Klaus, and Sigrid Weigel, eds. *Gegenwartsliteratur seit 1968.* Munich: dtv, 1992.
Brittnacher, Hans Richard. "Auf der Rückseite von Ordnung und Vernunft. Überlegungen zur Phantastik." literaturkritik.de. March 8, 2018. https://literaturkritik.de/auf-der-rueckseite-von-ordnung-und-vernunft-ueberlegungen-zur-phantastik,24270.html.
Brittnacher, Hans Richard, and Markus May, eds. *Phantastik. Ein interdisziplinäres Handbuch.* Stuttgart: Metzler, 2013.
Brockmann, Stephen. *A Critical History of German Film.* Rochester, NY: Camden House, 2010.
———. "Review." *Monatshefte* 101, no. 4 (2009): 612–14.
Broderick, Damian, "Reading SF as a Mega-Text." *New York Review of Science Fiction* 47, no. 1 (July 1992): 8–11.
Brühl, Jannis. "Merkel warnt vor 'Vernichtung der Individualität.'" *Süddeutsche Zeitung*, December 4, 2018.
Brundage, Miles, and Shahar Avin. *The Malicious Use of Artificial Intelligence: Forecasting, Prevention, and Mitigation.* Oxford: Futures of Humanity Institute, 2018.
Bruns, Karin. *Kinomythen 1920–1945: Die Filmentwürfe der Thea von Harbou.* Stuttgart: Metzler, 1995.
Buber, Martin. *Pfade in Utopia: Über Gemeinschaft und deren Verwirklichung.* Heidelberg: Lambert, 1950.
Bude, Heinz. *Solidarität: Die Zukunft einer großen Idee.* Munich: Carl Hanser, 2018.
Bühler, Walter. "Positive ökologische Utopie und politische Science Fiction." *Quarber Merkur* 57 (July 1982): 38–57.
Burkeman, Oliver. "Is the World Really Better Than Ever?" *Guardian*, July 28, 2017.
Burow, Olaf-Axel, ed. *Schule Digital—wie geht das? Wie die Digitale Revolution uns und die Schule verändert.* Weinheim: Beltz, 2019.
Buß, Christian. "Stunde Null Roman von Uwe Timm: Sex in den Trümmern des Übermenschen." *Der Spiegel*, September 4, 2017.
Campbell, Bruce, Alison Guenther-Pal, and Vibeke Rützou Petersen, eds. *Detectives, Dystopias and Poplit: Studies in Modern German Genre Fiction.* Rochester, NY: Camden House, 2014.

Carey, Frances, ed. *The Apocalypse and The Shape of Things to Come*. London: British Museum Press, 1999.
Carey, John, ed. *The Faber Book of Utopias*. London: Faber & Faber, 1999.
———. *The Intellectuals and the Masses: Pride and Prejudice among the Literary Intelligentsia, 1880–1939*. London: Faber & Faber, 1992.
Checcin, Louise. "Wir müssen ein neues Verhältnis zur Utopie gewinnen." *Süddeutsche Zeitung*, September 5, 2019.
Chilese, Viviana, and Heinz-Peter Preusser, eds. *Technik in Dystopien*. Heidelberg: Winter, 2013.
Chlada, Marvin. *Der Wille zur Utopie*. Aschaffenburg: Alibri Verlag, 2004.
Chodorkoff, Dan. "The Utopian Impulse: Reflections on a Tradition." *Harbinger: The Journal of Social Ecology* 1, no. 1 (Winter 1983). Available at http://social-ecology.org/wp/1983/12/the-utopian-impulse-reflections-on-a-tradition/.
Chronister, Necia. "Narrating the Fault Lines: German Literature since the Fall of the Wall." *World Literature Today* 88, no. 6 (November 2014).
Cirkel-Bartelt, Vanessa. "Beautiful Destruction. The Aesthetic of Apocalypse in Hans Dominik's Early Science Fiction." *Approaching Religion* 7, no. 2 (December 2017): 37–49.
Claeys, Gregory, ed. *The Cambridge Companion to Utopian Literature*. Cambridge: Cambridge University Press, 2010.
———. *Dystopia: A Natural History*. Oxford: Oxford University Press, 2017.
———. *Searching for Utopia: The History of an Idea*. New York: Thames & Hudson, 2011.
Claeys, Gregory, and Lyman Tower Sargent, eds. *The Utopia Reader*. New York: New York University Press, 1999.
Clareson, Thomas D., ed. *The Other Side of Realism: Essays on Modern Fantasy and Science Fiction*. Bowling Green, OH: Bowling Green University Press, 1971.
Clarke, Arthur C. *Profiles of the Future: An Enquiry into the Limits of the Possible*. New York: Harper & Row, 1973. First published 1962.
Clute John. *Canary Fever: Reviews*. Harold Wood: Beccon Publications, 2009.
Conter, Claude D., and Johannes Birgfeld, eds. *Christian Kracht: Zu Leben und Werk*. Cologne: Kiepenheuer & Witsch 2009.
Cooper, Davina. *Everyday Utopias: The Conceptual Life of Promising Spaces*. Durham, NC: Duke University Press, 2013.
Coordes, Gesa. "Ein Physik-Roman zwischen Realität und Fiktion." *Frankfurter Rundschau*, February 14, 2007.
Corkhill, Alan. *Spaces for Happiness in the Twentieth-Century German Novel*. Bern: Peter Lang, 2012.
Cornick, Lisa. "Identity in Women's Writings: The Proclivity of Solitude and Self—Marlen Haushofer's Austrian Utopia and Anna LaBastille's American Wilderness." *Mount Olive Review: Images of Women in Literature*. no.6 (Spring 1992): 25–36.

Cornils, Ingo. "Alles Kaputt? Visions of the End in West German and Austrian Science Fiction." *Foundation* 30, no. 82 (Summer 2001): 57–74.
———. "Between Bauhaus and Bügeleisen: The Iconic Style of Raumpatrouille," In *Alternative Worlds: Blue-Sky Thinking since* 1900, edited by Ricarda Vidal and Ingo Cornils, 283–302. Oxford: Peter Lang, 2015.
———. "Ein Glasperlenspiel im Internet: Hesse lesen im globalen Zeitalter." In *Hermann Hesse und die literarische Moderne*, edited by Andreas Solbach, 399–413. Frankfurt: Suhrkamp, 2004.
———. "The Martians Are Coming! War, Peace, Love and Scientific Progress in H. G. Wells's *The War of the Worlds* and Kurd Laßwitz's *Auf zwei Planeten*." *Comparative Literature* 55, no. 1 (Winter 2003): 24–41.
———. "The Matrix Preloaded: Rainer Werner Fassbinders Welt am Draht." In *Abendländische Apokalyptik: Kompendium zur Genealogie der Endzeit*, edited by Veronika Wiesner, Christian Zolles, Catherine Feik, Martin Zolles, and Leopold Schlöndorff, 285–98. Berlin: Akademie Verlag, 2013.
———. "Problems of Visualisation: The Image of the Unknown in German SF." In *Text into Image: Image into Text*, edited by Jeff Morrison and Florian Krobb, 287–95. Amsterdam: Rodopi, 1997.
———. "Reisen in Zeit und Raum: Die Renaissance der deutschen Science Fiction." *Literatur für leser* 4 (2006): 275–90.
———. "Utopian, Dystopian and Subversive Strategies in Recent German Alternate History Fictions." In *Collision of Realities. Establishing Research on the Fantastic in* Europe, edited by Lars Schmeink and Astrid Böger, 325–38. Berlin: de Gruyter, 2012.
———. *Writing the Revolution: The Construction of "1968" in Germany*. Rochester, NY: Camden House, 2016.
Crim, Brian E. *Our Germans: Project Paperclip and the National Security State*. Baltimore: Johns Hopkins University Press, 2019.
Crowley, John. *Totalitopia*. Oakland, CA: PM Press, 2017.
Csicsery-Ronay, Istvan Jr. *The Seven Beauties of Science Fiction*. Middleton, CT: Wesleyan University Press, 2008.
Cunningham, Vinson. "The Bad Place: How the Idea of Hell has Shaped the Way We Think." *New Yorker*, January 21, 2019.
Dath, Dietmar. "Ein schöner Albtraum ist sich selbst genug." *Frankfurter Allgemeine Zeitung*, October 15, 2008.
Dath, Dietmar, and Barbara Kirchner. *Der Implex: Sozialer Fortschritt; Geschichte und Idee*. Berlin: Suhrkamp, 2012.
de Berg, Henk. "Mia gegen den Rest der Welt: Zu Juli Zeh's Corpus Delicti." In *Mediale Repräsentationen des Ethischen. Festschrift für Prof. Dr. Joanna Jablowska*, edited by Kalina Kupczynska and Artur Pelka, 25–48. Würzburg: Königshausen & Neumann, 2013.
———. "Warum wir keine Utopien brauchen." *Berliner Debatte Initial* 23, no. 4 (2012): 5–17.

de Berg, Henk, and Duncan Large, eds. *Modern German Thought from Kant to Habermas: An Annotated German-Language Reader.* Rochester, NY: Camden House, 2012.

Delabar, Walter. "Wann kommt der Prinz? '42': Thomas Lehrs Gegenstück zu Dan Browns Sensationsgeschichten." literaturkritik.de, January 2006. https://literaturkritik.de/id/8905.

Demerjian, Louisa MacKay, ed. *The Age of Utopia: One Genre, Our Fears and our Future.* Newcastle: Cambridge Scholars Publishing, 2016.

Detje Robin. "Die Rache des Killerschleims." *Süddeutsche Zeitung*, March 4, 2004.

Deutscher Bundestag. *The Committee on the Digital Agenda.* Berlin: German Bundestag Public Relations Division, 2019.

Dickel, Sascha. "Der neue Mensch—Ein (Technik)Utopisches Upgrade." *Aus Politik und Zeitgeschichte* 37–38 (2016): 16–21.

Dickens, Peter. "Alternative Worlds in the Cosmos." In *Alternative Worlds: Blue-Sky Thinking since* 1900, edited by Ricarda Vidal and Ingo Cornils, 255–81. Oxford: Peter Lang, 2015.

Dluzen, Doug. "How and Why CRISPR Will Change the World." Clarkesworld. September 2018. http://clarkesworldmagazine.com/dluzen_09_18/.

Docx, Edward. "*The Circle* by Dave Eggers." *Guardian*, October 9, 2013.

Donner, Wolf. "EDV-Elegie." *Die Zeit*, October 19, 1973.

Dörr, Julian. "Frauen im Netz: Ferne Welten." *Süddeutsche Zeitung*, March 25, 2019.

Dörr, Julian, and Olaf Kowalski. "Vom Tal auf die Insel? Vom kalifornischen Liberalismus zur Sozialutopie Seasteading." *Aus Politik und Zeitgeschichte* 32–33 (2018): 16–21.

Dörting, Torsten. "Besser paranoid als tot." *Der Spiegel*, February 11, 2010.

Dorson, James. "Cormac McCarthy and the Genre Turn in Contemporary Literary Fiction." *European Journal of American Studies.* 12, no. 3 (2017).

Draut, David. *Zwiespältige Zukunftsvisionen. Das Autorenpaar Steinmüller und die ostdeutsche utopische Science Fiction.* Marburg: Tectum Verlag, 2014.

Druckfrisch: Neue Bücher mit Denis Scheck. Erstes Deutsches Fernsehen (ARD), January 13, 2009.

Duncan, Andy. "Alternate History." In *The Cambridge Companion to Science Fiction*, edited by Edward James and Farah Mendlesohn, 209–18. Cambridge: Cambridge University Press, 2003.

Dürbeck, Gabriele, Urte Stobbe, Hubert Zapf, and Evi Zemanek, eds. *Ecological Thought in German Literature and Culture.* Lanham, MD: Lexington Books, 2017.

Eberl, Ulrich. *Zukunft 2050: Wie wir schon heute die Zukunft erfinden.* Weinheim: Beltz, 2011.

Eberspächer, Achim. *Das Projekt Futurologie: Über Zukunft und Forschung in der Bundesrepublik 1952–1982.* Paderborn: Schöningh, 2019.

Eco, Umberto. *The Book of Legendary Lands*. London: MacLehose, 2013.
Edwards, Caroline. *Utopia and the Contemporary British Novel*. Cambridge: Cambridge University Press, 2019.
Eisfeld, Rainer. "Frau im Mond: Technische Vision und psychologisches Zeitbild." In *Thea von Harbou. Frau im Mond*, edited by Rainer Eisfeld, 207–37. Munich: Heyne, 1989.
———. *Die Zukunft in der Tasche: Science Fiction und SF-Fandom in der Bundesrepublik. Die Pionierjahre 1955–1960*. Lüneburg: Dieter von Reeken, 2007.
Ellis, Erle C. *Anthropocene: A Very Short Introduction*. Oxford: Oxford University Press, 2018.
Elsaesser, Thomas. *Metropolis*. London: Palgrave Macmillan, 2000.
Encke, Julia. "Hauptsache, gebrüllt." *Frankfurter Allgemeine Zeitung*, February 18, 2016.
———. "Wo geht's zum Abgrund?" *Frankfurter Allgemeine Zeitung*, November 16, 2017.
Enzensberger, Hans-Magnus, ed., *Kritik der Zukunft*. Kursbuch 14. Frankfurt: Suhrkamp, 1968.
Ernst, Hans. *Utopie und Wirklichkeit mit Blick auf den Utopiebegriff bei Paul Tillich*. Würzburg: Königshausen & Neumann, 1982.
Eschbach, Andreas. *Das Buch von der Zukunft: Ein Reiseführer*. Berlin: Rowohlt, 2004.
———. "Werdet erwachsen!" *Technology Review*, September 2018.
Esselborn, Hans, ed. *Die Erfindung der Zukunft in der Literatur. Vom technisch-utopischen Zukunftsroman zur deutschen Science Fiction*. Würzburg: Königshausen & Neumann, 2019.
———. "H. W. Frankes Roman Im Zentrum der Milchstraße als Beispiel für Intertextualität in der Science Fiction." *Literatur für Leser* 4 (2006): 237–54.
———. "Möglichkeiten der (westdeutschen) Science Fiction, gespiegelt im Kurd Laßwitz-Preis." *Zeitschrift für Fantastikforschung* 1 (2013): 70–87.
———. "Symbiose oder Ignoranz? Beziehungen zwischen Science Fiction, Wissenschaft und Technik am Beispiel der Erkundung des Weltraums." In *Neue Utopien. Zum Wandel eines Genres*, edited by Rolf Steltemeier, Sascha Dickel, Sandro Gaycken, and Tobias Knobloch, 36–54. Heidelberg: Manutius, 2009.
———. *Utopie, Antiutopie und Science Fiction im deutschsprachigen Roman des 20. Jahrhunderts*. Würzburg: Königshausen & Neumann, 2003.
———. "Der Wandel der deutschen Science Fiction. Vom technischen Zukunftsroman zur Darstellung alternativer Welten." In *Fremde Welten. Wege und Räume der Fantastik im 21. Jahrhundert*, edited by Lars Schmeink and Hans-Harald Müller, 443–56. Berlin: de Gruyter, 2012.
European Commission. *The European AI Landscape. Workshop Report*, April 18, 2018.
Everett, Wendy, and Axel Goodbody, eds. *Revisiting Space: Space and Place in European Cinema*. Oxford: Peter Lang, 2005.

Fassbinder, Rainer Werner. "Einige allgemeine Überlegungen." In Fritz Müller-Scherz and Rainer Werner Fassbinder, *Welt am Draht: Drehbuch*, 179–84. Berlin: Matthes & Seitz, 2010.
Featherstone, Mark. "The Kinetic Utopia." *New York Journal of Sociology* 3, no. 1 (2010): 1–20.
———. *Planet Utopia: Utopia, Dystopia, and Globalisation*. London: Routledge, 2017.
Fechner, Gustav Theodor. *Nanna, oder Über das Seelenleben der Pflanzen*. Hamburg: Leopold Voß, 1903. First published 1848.
Fennell, Jack, ed. *Sci-Fi: A Companion*. Oxford: Peter Lang, 2019.
Fest, Joachim. *Der zerstörte Traum: Vom Ende des utopischen Zeitalters*. Berlin: Siedler, 1991.
Feyerabend, Paul. '*The Tyranny of Science*. Cambridge: Polity Books, 2011.
Finlay, Frank "'Surface is an Illusion but so is depth.' The Novels of Christian Kracht." *German Life and Letters* 64, no. 2 (April 2013): 211–31.
Fischer, William B. *The Empire Strikes out: Kurd Laßwitz, Hans Dominik, and the Development of German SF*. Bowling Green OH: Bowling Green University Popular Press, 1984.
———. "German Theories of Science Fiction: Jean Paul, Kurd Laßwitz, and After." *Science Fiction Studies* 10, no. 3 (November 1976): 254–65.
Fitting, Peter. "A Short History of Utopian Studies." *Science Fiction Studies* 36, no. 1 (March 2009): 121–31.
———. "Utopia, Dystopia and Science Fiction." In *The Cambridge Companion to Utopian Literature*, edited by Gregory Claeys, 135–54. Cambridge: Cambridge University Press, 2010.
Flechtheim, Ossip. *Futurologie: Der Kampf um die Zukunft*. Cologne: Verlag Wissenschaft und Politik, 1970.
———. *Futurologie: Möglichkeiten und Grenzen*. Frankfurt: Edition Voltaire, 1968.
———. *Ist die Zukunft noch zu retten?* Hamburg: Hoffmann & Campe, 1987.
Foucault, Michel. "Of Other Spaces: Utopias and Heterotopias." *Architecture / Movement / Continunité*, October 1994. Also available at http://web.mit.edu/allanmc/www/foucault1.pdf.
Frank, Benedict. "Serie '8 Tage'—Apokalypse light." *Süddeutsche Zeitung*, March 1, 2019.
Frase, Peter. *Four Futures: Visions of the World after Capitalism*. London: Verso, 2016.
Freedman, Carl. "Science Fiction and Utopia: A Historico-Philosophical Overview." In *Learning from other Worlds: Estrangement, Cognition and the Politics of Science Fiction and Utopia*, edited by Patrick Parrinder, 72–97. Durham, NC: Duke University Press, 2001.
Freitag, Jan. "'Transfer' im ZDF: Der Traum vom ewigen Leben." *Berliner Zeitung*, August 18, 2013.

Friedrich, Hans-Edwin. "'Das deutsche Volk schlief schlecht seit dem größten Sieg seiner Geschichte.' Drittes Reich und Nationalsozialismus im alternativhistorischen Roman." *Literatur für Leser* 4 (2006): 255–74.

———. *Science Fiction in der deutschsprachigen Literatur: Ein Referat zur Forschung bis 1993.* Tübingen: Niemeyer, 1995.

Friend, Tad. "Silicon Valley's Quest to Live Forever." *New Yorker*, April 3, 2017.

Fritzsche, Sonja. "East Germany's 'Werkstatt Zukunft': Futurology and the Science Fiction Films of 'defa-futurum.'" *German Studies Review* 29, no. 2 (March 2006): 367–86.

———. "German SF." In *A Virtual Introduction to Science Fiction*, edited by Lars Schmeink. 2012. Available at http://virtual-sf.com/?page_id=62.

———, ed. *The Liverpool Companion to World Science Fiction Film.* Liverpool: Liverpool University Press, 2014.

———. *Science Fiction Literature in East Germany.* Bern: Peter Lang, 2006.

Frost, Sabine. "Looking Behind Walls: Literary and Filmic Imaginations of Nature, Humanity, and the Anthropocene in Die Wand." In *Readings in the Anthropocene: The Environmental Humanities, German Studies, and Beyond*, edited by Sabine Wilke and Japhet Johnstone, 62–88. New York: Bloomsbury, 2017.

Fuchs, Christian. "Fortschritt und Utopie." *Vorschein* 24/25 (2003): 41–63.

Fulk, Kirkland. "Through the Wormhole with Karl Marx: Science Fiction, Utopia, and the Future of Marxism in P. M.'s Weltgeist Superstar." *German Quarterly* 90, no. 1 (Winter 2017): 55–70.

Gallagher, James. "Human Embryos Edited to Stop Disease." BBC News. August 2, 2017. https://www.bbc.com/news/health-40802147.

Galle, Heinz J. *Wie die Science Fiction Deutschland eroberte: Erinnerungen an die miterlebte Vergangenheit der Zukunft.* Lüneburg: Dieter von Reeken, 2017.

Garforth, Lisa. *Green Utopias: Environmental Hope Before and After Nature.* Cambridge: Polity Books, 2017.

Gelderloos, Carl. "Breaking Open Utopia: Science Fiction as Critique in the GDR." *Monatshefte* 107, no. 3 (2015): 468–82.

———. "'Jetzt kommt das Leben': The Technological Body in Alfred Döblin's Berge Meere und Giganten." *German Quarterly* 88, no. 3 (2015): 291–316.

Gellai, Szilvia. "Welten am Draht bei Daniel F. Galouye und Rainer Werner Fassbinder." *Zeitschrift für Fantastikforschung* 1 (2016): 50–72.

Gerstenberger, Katharina. "Nach der Postapokalypse: Thomas von Steinaeckers dystopischer Roman 'Die Verteidigung des Paradieses.'" *Zeitschrift für Germanistik* 29, no. 3 (2019): 587–601.

Gerstenberger, Katharina, and Patricia Herminghouse, eds. *German Literature in a New Century: Trends, Transitions, Transformations.* New York: Berghahn Books, 2008.

Geser, Guntram. *Fritz Lang. Metropolis und Die Frau im Mond: Zukunftsfilm und Zukunftstechnik in der Stabilisierungszeit der Weimarer Republik.* Meitingen: Corian, 1996.
Geuter, Jürgen. "Nein, Ethik kann man nicht programmieren." *Die Zeit*, November 27, 2018.
Giddens, Anthony, and Christopher Pierson. *Making Sense of Modernity: Conversations with Anthony Giddens.* Stanford, CA: Stanford University Press, 1998.
Gidley, Jennifer M. *The Future: A Very Short Introduction.* Oxford: Oxford University Press, 2017.
Giesler, Markus. "Die Furcht vor KI wird immer größer." brandeins. September 28, 2019. https://www.brandeins.de/magazine/brand-eins-wirtschaftsmagazin/2019/wahrnehmung/markus-giesler-die-furcht-vor-ki-wird-immer-groesser.
Gnüg, Hiltrud. *Literarische Utopie-Entwürfe.* Frankfurt: Suhrkamp, 1982.
———. *Utopie und utopischer Roman.* Stuttgart: Reclam, 1999.
Goodbody, Axel. "Catastrophism in Post-War German Literature." In *Green Thought in German Culture*, edited by Colin Riordan, 159–80. Cardiff: University of Wales Press, 1997.
———, ed. *The Culture of German Environmentalism: Anxieties, Visions, Realities.* New York: Berghahn Books, 2002.
———. "Ecocritical Theory: Romantic Roots and Impulses from Twentieth-Century European Thinkers." In *The Cambridge Companion to Literature and the Environment*, edited by Louise Westling, 61–74. Cambridge: Cambridge University Press, 2014.
———. "Melting Ice and the Paradoxes of Zeno: Didactic Impulses and Aesthetic Distanciation in German Climate Change Fiction." *Ecozona: European Journal of Literature, Culture and Environment* 4, no. 1 (2013): 92–102.
———. *Nature, Technology and Cultural Change in Twentieth-Century German Literature.* Basingstoke: Palgrave Macmillan, 2007.
Goodbody, Axel, and Adeline Johns-Putra, eds. *Cli-Fi: A Companion.* Oxford: Peter Lang, 2018.
Gottlieb, Eva. *Dystopian Fiction East and West: Universe of Terror and Trial.* Montreal: McGill-Queen's University Press, 2001.
Gottwald, Ulrike. *Science Fiction (SF) als Literatur in der Bundesrepublik der siebziger und achtziger Jahre.* Frankfurt: Peter Lang, 1990.
Grandits, Ernst A., ed. *2112: Die Welt in 100 Jahren.* Hildesheim: Olms, 2012.
Grass, Günter. "Im Wettlauf mit den Utopien." In Günter Grass, *Essays—Reden—Briefe—Kommentare*, edited by Daniela Hermes, 715–36. Vol. 9 of *Werkausgabe in zehn Bänden*, edited by Volker Neuhaus,. Darmstadt: Luchterhand, 1987. First published June 16, 1978 in *Die Zeit*.
Griffin, Michael J., and Tom Moylan, eds. *Exploring the Utopian Impulse: Essays on Utopian Thought and Practice.* Oxford: Peter Lang, 2007.

Grimm, Reinhold, and Jost Hermand, eds. *Deutsches utopisches Denken im 20. Jahrhundert*. Stuttgart: Kohlhammer, 1974.
Gross, Dominik. "Deus ex Machina or E-Slave? Public Perception of Healthcare Robotics in the German Print Media." *International Journal of Technology Assessment in Health Care* 28, no. 3 (2012): 265–70.
Guérot, Ulrike. *Warum Europa eine Republik werden muss! Eine politische Utopie*. Bonn: Dietz, 2016.
Gunn, James. "Science Fiction around the World." *World Literature Today* 84, no. 3 (May/June 2010): 27–29.
Günther, Gotthard. *Science Fiction als neue Metaphysik?* Lüneburg: Dieter von Reeken, 2015.
———, ed. *Überwindung von Zeit und Raum: Phantastische Geschichten aus der Welt von morgen*. Düsseldorf: Karl Rauch, 1952.
Guthke, Karl S. *Der Mythos der Neuzeit. Das Thema der Mehrheit der Welten in der Literatur- und Geistesgeschichte von der kopernikanischen Wende bis zur Science Fiction*. Berne: Francke, 1983.
———. "Nightmare and Utopia: Extraterrestrial Worlds from Galileo to Goethe." *Early Science and Medicine* 8, no. 3 (2003): 173–95.
Haase, Christine. *When Heimat meets Hollywood: German Filmmakers and America, 1985–2005*. Rochester, NY: Camden House, 2007.
Habermas, Jürgen. "The Concept of Human Dignity and the Realistic Utopia of Human Rights." *Metaphilosophy* 41, no. 4 (July 2010): 464–80.
———. *The Future of Human Nature*. Malden, MA: Blackwell, 2003.
———. *Der philosophische Diskurs der Moderne: Zwölf Vorlesungen*. Frankfurt: Suhrkamp, 1985.
Haeming, Anne. "Politik und Science Fiction sind nicht fern voneinander." *Der Spiegel*, December 21, 2018.
Hahn, Hans-Joachim. *Narrative des neuen Menschen: Vom Versprechen einer besseren Welt*. Berlin: Neofelis, 2018.
Hahn, Susanne. "Das Vernichtungslager für Arbeitslose in Joachim Zelters 'Schule der Arbeitslosen': SPHERICON als Konzentrationslager des 21. Jahrhunderts." Seminararbeit, University of Erfurt, 2008. https://www.grin.com/document/161713.
Hake, Sabine. *German National Cinema*. London: Routledge, 2002.
Hall, Alex, "'A Way of Revealing': Technology and Utopianism in Contemporary Culture." *Journal of Technology Studies* 35, no. 1 (Fall 2009): 58–66.
Hall, Alexander Charles Oliver. *Dyscontent: The Critical Dystopia in 21st Century American Culture*. Fayetteville, AR: University of Arkansas Press, 2009.
———. "'I am trying to believe': Dystopia as Utopia in the Year Zero Alternate Reality Game." *Eludamos: Journal for Computer Game Culture* 3, no. 1 (2009): 69–82.
Hallenberger, Gerd. *Macht und Herrschaft in den Welten der Science Fiction: Die politische Seite der SF: eine inhaltsanalytische Bestandsaufnahme*. Meitingen: Corian, 1986.

Hamilton, Clive. *Defiant Earth: The Fate of Humans in the Anthropocene.* Cambridge: Polity Books, 2017.
Harari, Yuval Noah. *Homo Deus: A Brief History of Tomorrow.* London: Vintage, 2017.
———. "Homo Sapiens as We Know Them Will Disappear in a Century or so." *Guardian*, March 19, 2017.
———. "Ist künstliche Intelligenz autoritär?" *Die Tageszeitung*, December 11, 2018.
———. "Life 3.0 by Max Tegmark—We Are Ignoring the AI Apocalypse." *Guardian*, September 22, 2017.
———. *Sapiens: A Brief History of Humankind.* London: Vintage, 2014.
———. *21 Lessons for the 21st Century.* London: Jonathan Cape, 2018.
———. "We Need A Post-Liberal Future Now." *Economist*, September 26, 2018.
Haraway, Donna J. *Staying with the Trouble: Making Kin in the Chthulucene.* Durham, NC: Duke University Press, 2016.
Harris, Stefanie. "Calling the Nation: Karl Hartl's *F.P.1 antwortet nicht.*" *South Central Review* 29, no. 1–2 (Spring/Summer 2012): 21–40.
Hartmann, Joerg. "'An Absolutely Fascinating Period Piece. . .': Weltraumschiff I Startet." *Zeitschrift für Fantastikforschung* 1 (2016): 1–23.
Haupts, Tobias. "The Empty Sky: A Brief History of German Science Fiction Film." In *Future Imperfect: Science Fiction Film*, edited by Rainer Rother and Annika Schäfer, 65–81. Berlin: Bertz & Fischer, 2017.
Hawking, Stephen. *Brief Answers to the Big Questions.* London: John Murray, 2018.
Hayles, N. Katherine. *How We Became Posthuman: Virtual Bodies in Cybernetics, Literature and Informatics.* Chicago: University of Chicago Press, 1999.
Hayles, N. Katherine, and Nicholas Gessler. "The Slipstream of Mixed Reality. Unstable Ontologies and Semiotic Markers in 'The Thirteenth Floor,' 'Dark City,' and 'Mulholland Drive.'" *Publications of the Modern Language Association* 119, no. 3 (2004): 482–99.
Hayter, Irena. "Robotics, Science Fiction and the Search for the Perfect Artificial Woman." The Conversation, October 24, 2017. https://theconversation.com/robotics-science-fiction-and-the-search-for-the-perfect-artificial-woman-86092.
Hedges, Inez. "Faust and Utopia: Socialist Visions." *Socialism and Democracy* 13, no. 1 (1999): 47–72.
Heermann, Christian. *Eisbomber aus Bitterfeld: Hans Dominik und Hugo Junkers.* Dessau: Anhalt Edition, 2014.
Heffernan, Valerie, and Gillian Pye, eds. *Transitions: Emerging Women Writers in German-Language Literature.* Amsterdam: Rodopi, 2013.
Hegemann, Lisa. "Wenn Politik auf künstliche Intelligenz trifft." *Die Zeit*, November 16, 2018.
Heidegger, Martin. *The Question Concerning Technology, and Other Essays.* New York: Garland, 1977. First published 1953.

Heidtmann, Horst. *Utopisch-phantastische Literatur in der DDR: Untersuchungen zur Entwicklung eines unterhaltungsliterarischen Genres von 1945–1979*. Munich: Wilhelm Fink, 1982.
Heise, Ursula K. "Science Fiction and the Time Scales of the Anthropocene." *English Literary History* 86, no. 2 (Summer 2019): 275–304.
Heller, Agnes. *Von der Utopie zur Dystopie: Was können wir uns wünschen?* Vienna: Edition Konturen, 2016.
Hellmann, Christian. *Der Science Fiction Film*. Munich: Heyne, 1983.
Herbrechter, Stefan. *Posthumanism: A Critical Analysis*. London: Bloomsbury, 2013.
Hermand, Jost. *Der alte Traum vom neuen Reich: Völkische Utopien und Nationalsozialismus*. Frankfurt: Athenäum, 1988.
———. *Grüne Utopien in Deutschland: Zur Geschichte des ökologischen Bewußtseins*. Frankfurt: Fischer, 1991.
———. *Old Dreams of a New Reich: Volkish Utopias and National Socialism*. Translated by Paul Levesque and Stefan Soldovieri. Bloomington: Indiana University Press, 1992.
———."Von der Notwendigkeit utopischen Denkens." In *Deutsches utopisches Denken im 20. Jahrhundert*, edited by Reinhold Grimm and Jost Hermand, 10–29. Stuttgart: Kohlhammer, 1974.
Hester, Vanessa. "'Die Schranken zwischen Tier und Mensch fallen sehr leicht': Die Wandlung der weiblichen Protoagonistin in Marlen Haushofers 'Die Wand.'" *Literatur für Leser* 3 (2016): 197–209.
Heyer, Andreas. *Der Stand der aktuellen deutschen Utopieforschung*. 3 vols. Hamburg: Kovac, 2010.
———. *Studien zur politischen Utopie: Theoretische Reflexionen und ideengeschichtliche Annäherungen*. Hamburg: Kovac, 2005.
Higgins, David M. "Toward a Cosmopolitan Science Fiction." *American Literature* 83, no. 2 (June 2011): 331–54.
Higgs, John. *The Future starts Here. Adventures in the 21st Century*. London: Weidenfeld & Nicholsen, 2019.
Hilger, Josef. *Raumpatrouille: Die phantastischen Abenteuer des Raumschiffes Orion*. Berlin: Schwarzkopf & Schwarzkopf, 2000.
Hillenbrand, Tom. "Eine verführerische Logik." *Die Zeit*, April 14, 2016.
Hinrichs, Boy. *Utopische Prosa als längeres Gedankenspiel: Untersuchungen zu Arno Schmidts Theorie der Modernen Literatur und ihrer Konkretisierung in "Schwarze Spiegel," "Die Gelehrtenrepublik" und "Kaff auch Mare Crisium."* Tübingen: Niemeyer, 1986.
Hintermeier, Hannes. "Krimi im Überwachungsstaat: Drohnenland riecht angebrannt." *Frankfurter Allgemeine Zeitung*, June 28, 2014.
Hollinger, Veronica. "Genre vs. Mode." In *The Oxford Handbook of Science Fiction*, edited by Rob Latham, 139–54. Oxford: Oxford University Press, 2014.
Holmes, Richard. *The Age of Wonder: How the Romantic Generation Discovered the Beauty and Terror of Science*. London: Harper Collins, 2008.
Hölscher, Lucian. *Die Entdeckung der Zukunft*. Göttingen: Wallstein, 2016.

---, ed. *Die Zukunft des 20. Jahrhunderts: Dimensionen einer historischen Zukunftsforschung*. Frankfurt: Campus, 2017.
Hölscher, Lucian, Elke Seefried, and Stefan Berger, eds. *Politische Zukünfte im 20. Jahrhundert: Parteien, Bewegungen, Umbrüche*. Frankfurt: Campus Verlag, 2019.
Honey, Christian. "Niemals unsterblich, aber ewig jung." *Die Zeit*, April 4, 2018.
Hood, Bryan. "Ursula Le Guin: 'I Wish We Could All Live in a Big House with Unlocked Doors.'" *Guardian*, October 18, 2016.
Horn, Eva. *The Future as Catastrophe: Imagining Disaster in the Modern Age*. New York: Columbia University Press, 2018.
---. "Der Untergang als Experimentalraum: Zukunftsfiktionen vom Ende des Menschen." *Aus Politik und Zeitgeschichte*. 62, no. 51/52 (December 2012): 32–38.
---. *Zukunft als Katastrophe*. Frankfurt: Fischer, 2014.
Horx, Matthias. *Zukunft wagen: Über den Umgang mit dem Unvorhersehbaren*. Munich: DVA, 2013.
Hühnerfeld, Paul. "Heliopolis oder die Stadt ohne Liebe." *Die Zeit*, February 2, 1950.
Hupertz, Heike. "Ihr neuer Körper sitzt wie ein Maßanzug." *Frankfurter Allgemeine Zeitung*. August 19, 2013.
Hutton, Will. "Machines Are Not Our Masters—But the Sinister Side of AI Demands a Smart Response." *Observer*, February 17, 2019.
Hüttmann, Oliver. "Der traurige Klon." *Der Spiegel*, January 1, 2004.
Huyssen, Andreas. "The Vamp and the Machine: Technology and Sexuality in Fritz Lang's Metropolis." *New German Critique* 24/25 (1981/82): 221–37.
Ings, Simon. "The Method by Juli Zeh." *Guardian*, April 6, 2012.
Innerhofer, Roland. *Deutsche Science Fiction 1870–1914: Rekonstruktion und Analyse der Anfänge einer Gattung*. Vienna: Böhlau, 1996.
---. "Science Fiction als Social Fantasy? Tendenzen der deutschen SF im ausgehenden 20. Jahrhundert." *Literatur für Leser* 4 (2007): 263–75.
Jabkowska, Joanna. *Literatur ohne Hoffnung: Die Krise der Utopie in der deutschen Gegenwartsliteratur*. Wiesbaden: Deutscher Universitätsverlag, 1993.
Jacobsen, Michael Hviid, and Keith Tester, eds. *Utopia: Social Theory and the Future*. Farnham: Ashgate, 2012.
Jacoby, Russell. *Picture Imperfect: Utopian Thought for an Anti-Utopian Age*. New York: Columbia University Press, 2005.
Jaeger, Mona. "Ein Visionär aus Offenbach: Portrait Ludwig Dexheimer." *Frankfurter Allgemeine Zeitung*, February 16, 2014.
Jäger, Stefan. "Mit dem Grüntee-to-go zum Waterboarding." literaturkritik.de. November 20, 2017. https://literaturkritik.de/zeh-leere-herzen-mit-dem-gruentee-to-go-zum-waterboarding,23929.html.
James, Edward. *Science Fiction in the 20th Century*. Oxford: Oxford University Press, 1994.

James, Edward, and Farah Mendlesohn, eds. *The Cambridge Companion to Science Fiction*. Cambridge: Cambridge University Press, 2003.
Jameson, Fredric. *Archaeologies of the Future: The Desire called Utopia and other Science Fictions*. London: Verso, 2005.
Jauernig, Henning, and Isabella Reichert. "Wie wir 2037 leben werden." *Der Spiegel*, January 3, 2018.
Jeschke, Wolfgang. "Gibt es eine eigenständige deutsche Science Fiction? Nachtrag zu einer Diskussion." *Science Fiction Times* 12 (1983): 4–7.
———. *Das Science Fiction Jahr 1999*. Munich: Heyne, 1999.
Jucker, Rolf, ed. *Zeitgenössische Utopieentwürfe in Literatur und Gesellschaft: Zur Kontroverse seit den achtziger Jahren*. Amsterdam: Rodopi, 1997.
Jung, Irene. "Wie der 'Schwarm' weiterzog." *Hamburger Abendblatt*, November 5, 2005.
Jungen, Oliver. "Ich bin die Lüge in euren Ängsten." *Frankfurter Allgemeine Zeitung*, April 26, 2013.
———. "Und hätte die Liebe nicht." *Frankfurter Allgemeine Zeitung*, March 14, 2016.
Jungk, Robert. *Heller als tausend Sonnen: Das Schicksal der Atomforscher*. Munich: Heyne, 1990. First published 1956.
Kaku, Michio. *The Future of Humanity: Terraforming Mars, Interstellar Travel, Immortality, and Our Destiny Beyond Earth*. New York: Doubleday, 2018.
———. *Physics of the Future: How Science Will Shape Human Destiny and Our Daily Lives by the Year 2100*. New York: Doubleday, 2011.
Kant, Immanuel. "Idee zu einer allgemeinen Geschichte in weltbürgerlicher Absicht." *Berlinische Monatsschrift*, November 1784, 385–411.
———. *Zum ewigen Frieden, Ein philosophischer Entwurf*. Stuttgart: Reclam, 2008. First published 1795.
Kaiser, Gerhard R., ed. *Poesie der Apokalypse*. Würzburg: Königshausen & Neumann, 1991.
Kaplan, E. Ann. *Climate Trauma: Foreseeing the Future in Dystopian Film and Fiction*. New Brunswick: Rutgers University Press, 2016.
Kedves, Alexandra, and Edgar Schuler, "Christian Kracht: Ich meine es todernst." *Badische Zeitung*. May 5, 2010.
Kelly, Kevin. *The Inevitable: Understanding the 12 Technological Forces that will Shape our Future*. London: Penguin, 2016.
———. *Out of Control: The New Biology of Machines, Social Systems, and the Economic World*. New York: Perseus, 1994.
Kincaid, Paul. "This is Science Fiction?" *Los Angeles Review of Books*, December 3, 2016.
Kirchknopf, Géza. "Vom elastischen Familienverband zur Kommune." *Kursbuch* 14 (August 1968): 110–15.
Kirsch, Adam. *The Global Novel: Writing the World in the 21st Century*. New York: Columbia Global Reports, 2017.
———. "The Strange Paradise of Paul Scheerbart." *New York Review of Books*. December 16, 2015.

Kleeberg, Michael. "70 Jahre Glasperlenspiel: Warum nicht alles auserzählen?" *Frankfurter Allgemeine Zeitung*, June 21, 2013.
Klein, Naomi. *This Changes Everything: Capitalism vs The Climate*. New York: Simon & Schuster, 2014.
Kluge, Manfred, and Rudolf Radler, eds. *Hauptwerke der deutschen Literatur: Einzeldarstellungen und Interpretationen*. Munich: Kindler, 1974.
Kniebe, Tobias. "'Blade Runner 2049'ist grandioser als das Original." *Süddeutsche Zeitung*, October 4, 2017.
Kniesche, Thomas W. "Germans to the Final Frontier: Science Fiction, Popular Culture, and the Military in the 1960s Germany: The Case of Raumpatrouille." *New German Critique* 101 (Summer 2007): 157–85.
Koellner, Sarah. "Data, Love, and Bodies: The Value of Privacy in Juli Zeh's Corpus Delicti." *Seminar* 52, no. 4 (Nov 2016): 407–25.
Koepnick, Lutz. *The Dark Mirror: German Cinema between Hitler and Hollywood*. Berkeley, CA: University of California Press, 2002.
———. "Screening Fascism's Underground: Kurd Bernhardt's *The Tunnel*." *New German Critique* 74 (1998): 151–78.
Koller, Catharina. "Das Implantat." *Die Zeit*, February 21, 2013.
Körte, Peter. "Das Gespenst in der Maschine: Frank Schätzings neuer Roman." *Frankfurter Allgemeine Zeitung*, April 22, 2018.
Krah, Hans. "Die Apokalypse als literarische Technik. Ernst Jüngers Heliopolis im Schnittpunkt denk- und diskursgeschichtlicher Paradigmen," in *Ernst Jünger: Politik—Mythos—Kunst*, edited by Lutz Hagestedt, 225–52. Berlin: de Gruyter, 2004.
Kretzmann, Edwin M. J. "German Technological Utopias of the Pre-war Period." *Annals of Science* 3, no. 4 (1938): 417–30.
Kreye, Andrian. "Wie aus Hippie-Utopien Monopolkapitalismus wurde." *Süddeutsche Zeitung*, January 22, 2018.
Krysmanski, Hans-Jürgen. *Die utopische Methode: Eine literatur- und wissenssoziologische Untersuchung deutscher utopischer Romane des 20. Jahrhunderts*. Cologne: Westdeutscher Verlag, 1963.
Kümmel, Anja. "Postpragmatischer Genuss." *Fixpoetry*, June 8, 2015.
———. "Im Todesrausch." *Die Zeit*, June 9, 2015.
Kurzweil, Ray. *The Age of Intelligent Machines*. Cambridge, MA: MIT Press, 1990.
Kutzmutz, Oliver, ed. *"Danke, Jesus!' Andreas Eschbachs fantastische Welten."* Bundesakademie für kulturelle Bildung: Wolfenbüttel, 2018.
Lanchester, John. "Climate Change is the Deadliest Legacy We Will Leave the Young." *Guardian*, February 6, 2019.
Land, Karl-Heinz. *Erde 5.0: Die Zukunft provozieren*. Cologne: Future Vision Press, 2018.
Lange, Britte. *Die Entdeckung Deutschlands: Science Fiction als Propaganda*. Berlin: Verbecher Verlag, 2014.
Langheiter, Christa. *Mut zur Auszeit: Mit Sabbatical, Langzeiturlaub und Ausstieg auf Zeit zu mehr Lebensqualität und neuen Perspektiven*. Munich: Redline, 2012.

Langner, Beatrix. "Der Mensch schafft sich ab." *Deutschlandfunk Kultur,* August 7, 2013. https://www.deutschlandfunk.de/der-mensch-schafft-sich-ab.700.de.html?dram:article_id=256896,

Lanier, Jaron. *Dawn of the New Everything: A Journey through Virtual Reality.* London: Bodley Head, 2017.

Laßwitz, Kurd. *Geschichte der Atomistik vom Mittelalter bis Newton.* Leipzig: Leopold Voss, 1926. First published 1890.

Latham, Rob. "American Slipstream: Science Fiction and Literary Respectability." In *The Cambridge Companion to American Science Fiction*, edited by Eric Carl Link and Gerry Canavan, 99–110. Cambridge: Cambridge University Press, 2015.

———. *The Oxford Handbook of Science Fiction.* Oxford: Oxford University Press, 2014.

Layne, Priscilla. "The Darkening of Europe: Afrofuturist Ambitions and Afropessimist Fears in Damir Lukacevic's Dystopian Film 'Transfer' (2010)." *Seminar: A Journal of Germanic Studies* 55, no. 1 (February 2019): 54–75.

Lee, Dave. "Amazon's Next Big Thing May Redefine Big." BBC News. June 14, 2019. https://www.bbc.com/news/technology-48634676.

Lehmann-Wacker, Sigrid. "Die völlige Irrationalität der Bundesagentur darstellen." *Junge Welt,* December 1, 2007.

Lehnert, Gertrud. "Endzeitvisionen in der Science Fiction." In *Poesie der Apokalypse,* edited by Gerhard R. Kaiser, 297–313. Würzburg: Königshausen & Neumann, 1991.

Leiner, Friedrich. "Carl Amery: Der Untergang der Stadt Passau. Science-Fiction-Roman." In *Deutsche Romane von Grimmelshausen bis Walser. Interpretationen.* Vol.2, edited by Jacob Lehmann, 525–43. Königstein/Taunus: Scriptor, 1982.

Lent, Jeremy. *The Patterning Instinct: A Cultural History of Humanity's Search for Meaning.* New York: Prometheus Books, 2017.

Lenzen, Manuela. *Künstliche Intelligenz: Was sie kann & was uns erwartet.* Munich: C. H. Beck, 2018.

Leonhardt, David. "The Problem with Putting a Price on the End of the World. *New York Times,* April 9, 2019.

Lepore, Jill. "A Golden Age for Dystopian Fiction." *New Yorker,* June 5, 2017.

Lesch, Harald, and Klaus Kamphausen. *Die Menschheit schafft sich ab: Die Erde im Griff des Anthropozän.* Munich: Droemer Knaur, 2018.

Leucht, Robert. *Dynamiken politischer Imagination: Die deutschsprachige Utopie von Stifter bis Döblin in ihren internationalen Kontexten, 1848–1930.* Berlin: De Gruyter, 2016.

Levitas, Ruth. *Utopia as Method: The Imaginary Reconstruction of Society.* Basingstoke: Palgrave Macmillan, 2013.

Levy, Michael M., and Farah Mendlesohn, eds. *Aliens in Popular Culture.* Santa Barbara, CA: ABC-CLIO, 2019.

Lewis, Michael J. "Paradise Possible." *First Things,* August 2017.

Lobe, Adrian. "Wie Google und Amazon die Wikipedia gefährden." *Süddeutsche Zeitung*, February 18, 2019.
Löchel, Rolf. *Utopias Geschlechter: Gender in deutschsprachiger Science Fiction von Frauen*. Sulzbach im Taunus: Ulrike Helmer Verlag, 2012.
Löffler, Siegrid. "Grobschlächtige Weltsicht in Romanform." *Deutschlandradio Kultur*, March 11, 2016.
Lorenz, Christoph F., ed. *Lexikon der deutschsprachigen Science Fiction-Literatur seit 1900: Mit einem Blick auf Osteuropa*. Frankfurt: Peter Lang, 2016.
Lubich, Frederick. "Günter Grass' Kopfgeburten: Deutsche Zukunftsbewältigung oder ‚Wie wird sich Sisyphos in Orwells Jahrzehnt verhalten?'" *German Quarterly* 58, no. 3 (1985): 394–408.
Lueckel, Wolfgang. "From Zero Hour to Eleventh Hour? German Fiction in the Nuclear Age between 1945 and 1963." *Monatshefte* 107, no. 1 (Spring 2015): 84–107.
Luppa, Iris. "Madonna in Moon Rocket with Breeches: Weimar SF Film Criticism during the Stabilisation Period." In *Red Planets: Marxism and Science Fiction*, edited by Mark Bould and China Miéville, 159–77. Middletown: Wesleyan University Press, 2009.
Madera, Judith. "Interview mit Theresa Hannig." *Phantast* 18 (July 2017): 13–17.
Maibohm, Ludwig. *Fritz Lang: Seine Filme—sein Leben*. Munich: Heyne, 1981.
Malkmus, Bernhard. "Maikäfer, flieg! Das Sterben der Arten und das Schweigen der Literaten." *Merkur* 72, no. 826 (March 2018): 34–43.
Malmgren, Carl D. *Worlds Apart: Narratology of Science Fiction*. Bloomington, IN: Indiana University Press, 1991.
Mamczak, Sascha. *Die Zukunft: Eine Einführung*. Munich: Heyne, 2014.
Mann-Borgese, Elisabeth. *Ascent of Women*. New York: George Braziller, 1963.
Mannheim, Karl. *Ideologie und Utopie*. Bonn: F. Cohen, 1929.
Manuel, Frank E., ed. *Utopias and Utopian Thought*. London: Souvenir Press, 1973.
Manuel, Frank E., and Fritzie P. Manuel. *Utopian Thought in the Western World*. Cambridge, MA: Harvard University Press, 1979.
Marantz, Andrew. "The Dark Side of Techno-Utopianism." *New Yorker*, September 23, 2019.
Marcuse, Herbert. *The Aesthetic Dimension*. London: Macmillan, 1979.
———. *Der eindimensionale Mensch*. Neuwied: Luchterhand, 1967.
———. *Das Ende der Utopie*. Berlin: Verlag Peter von Maikowski, 1967.
———. *Triebstruktur und Gesellschaft*. Frankfurt: Suhrkamp, 1965.
———. *Versuch über die Befreiung*. Frankfurt: Suhrkamp, 2008. First published 1969.
Maresch, Rudolf, and Florian Rötzer, eds. *Renaissance der Utopie: Zukunftsfiguren des 21. Jahrhunderts*. Frankfurt: Suhrkamp, 2004.

Markovits, Andrei S., and Philip S. Gorski. *The German Left: Red, Green, and Beyond*. Cambridge: Polity Books, 1993.
Marks, Peter. *Imagining Surveillance: Eutopian and Dystopian Literature and Film*. Edinburgh: Edinburgh University Press, 2015.
Markwardt, Nils. "Im All liegt das Paradies." *Die Zeit*, March 13, 2015.
Martin-Jung, Helmut. "Warum Deutschland bei künstlicher Intelligenz abgehängt werden könnte." *Süddeutsche Zeitung*, April 29, 2019.
Marven, Lyn, and Stuart Taberner, eds. *Emerging German-Language Novelists of the Twenty-First Century*. Rochester, NY: Camden House, 2011.
März, Ursula. "Ein Buch wie ein Sprengsatz." *Die Zeit*, April 16, 2019.
Mason, Paul. *PostCapitalism: A Guide to our Future*. London: Allen Lane, 2015.
Mattenklott, Gert. "Faust." In *Deutsche Erinnerungsorte*. Vol. 3. Edited by Etienne Francois and Hagen Schulze, 603–19. Munich: C. H. Beck, 2001.
Matthews, Malcolm. "Ex Machina and the Fate of Posthuman Masculinity: The Technical Death of Man." *Journal of Posthuman Studies* 2, no. 1 (2018): 86–105.
Matzig, Gerhard. "Tief im Westen schmilzt der Streifen Abendrot." *Süddeutsche Zeitung*, April 27, 2018.
Mayr, Sabine. *Juli Zeh: Corpus Delicti. Ein Prozess*. Paderborn: Schöningh, 2013.
McCalmont, Virginia. "Juli Zeh's Corpus Delicti (2009): Health Care, Terrorists, and the Return of the Political Message." *Monatshefte* 104, no. 3 (Fall 2012): 375–92.
McIsaac, Peter, Gabriele Mueller, and Diana Spokiene, eds. *Visions of Tomorrow: Science and Utopia in German Culture*. Seminar 48, no. 1 (February 2012).
McMillan, Graeme. "Dave Eggers' *The Circle*: What the Internet Looks Like if You Don't Understand It." *Wired*, November 10, 2013.
Mehnert, Antonia. "Climate Change Futures and the Imagination of the Global in Maeva! by Dirk C. Fleck." *Ecozona: European Journal of Literature, Culture and Environment* 3, no. 2 (2012): 27–41.
Menasse, Eva. "Das Kollektiv der gebrochenen Herzen." *Der Standard*, November 20, 2016.
Metz, Markus, and Georg Seeßlen. *Schnittstelle Körper*. Berlin: Matthes & Seitz, 2018.
Metzl, Jamie. *Hacking Darwin: Genetic Engineering and the Future of Humanity*. Naperville, IL, Sourcebooks, 2019.
Meyer, Stephan. *Die anti-utopische Tradition: Eine ideen- und problemgeschichtliche Darstellung*. Frankfurt: Lang, 2001.
Milburn, Colin. *Nanovision: Engineering the Future*. Durham, NC: Duke University Press, 2008.
Miller, Claire Cain. "The Plus in Google Plus? It's mostly for Google." *New York Times*, February 14, 2014.

Milner, Andrew. "Archaeologies of the Future: Jameson's Utopia or Orwell's Dystopia?" *Historical Materialism* 17 (2009): 101–19.
Milner, Andrew, and J. R. Burgmann. "Ice, Fire and Flood: Science Fiction and the Anthropocene." *Thesis Eleven* 131, no. 1 (2015): 12–27.
Milner, Andrew, and Sean Redmond. "Introduction to the Special Edition on Science Fiction." *Thesis Eleven* 131, no. 1 (2015): 3–11.
Minden, Michael, and Holger Bachmann. *Fritz Lang's Metropolis*. Rochester, NY: Camden House, 2000.
———. *Modern German Literature*. Cambridge: Polity Books, 2011.
Monbiot, George. *Out of the Wreckage: A New Politics for an Age of Crisis*. London: Verso, 2017.
Morais, Betsy. "Sharing is Caring is Sharing." *New Yorker*, October 30, 2013.
Morgan, Ben. "Technology and Ordinary Life in Thea von Harbou's and Fritz Lang's Frau im Mond." *Literatur für Leser* 4 (2007): 195–211.
Morgan, Jamie. "The Fourth Industrial Revolution Could Lead to a Dark Future." The Conversation, January 9, 2020. https://theconversation.com/the-fourth-industrial-revolution-could-lead-to-a-dark-future-125897.
Morrison, Michael. "The Abolition of Species by Dietmar Dath." *World Literature Today*, May 2018.
Morrow, James, and Kathryn Morrow. *SFWA European Hall of Fame: Sixteen Masterpieces of Contemporary Science Fiction from the Continent*. New York: Tor Books, 2007.
Moylan, Tom. *Demand the Impossible: Science Fiction and the Utopian Imagination*. New York: Methuen, 1986.
———. "The Locus of Hope: Utopia versus Ideology." *Science Fiction Studies* 27, no. 9 (July 1982): 159–66.
———. *Scraps of the Untainted Sky: Science Fiction, Utopia, Dystopia*. Boulder: Westview Press, 2000.
Moynihan, Thomas. "The End of the World: A History of How a Silent Cosmos Led Humans to Fear the Worst." The Conversation, August 7, 2019. https://theconversation.com/the-end-of-the-world-a-history-of-how-a-silent-cosmos-led-humans-to-fear-the-worst-120193.
Mueller, Gabriele. "'Rattenfänger' von Europa: Generationsnarrative und Zukunftsbilder im gegenwärtigen deutschsprachigen Science-Fiction-Film." *Zeitschrift für interkulturelle Germanistik* 9, no. 1 (2018): 137–54.
Müller, Burkhard. "Eine Mauer um die ganze Insel." *Die Zeit*, January 30, 2019.
Müller, Götz. *Gegenwelten: Die Utopie in der deutschen Literatur*. Stuttgart: Metzler, 1989.
Müller, Henrik. "Stell dir vor, alles wird gut." *Der Spiegel*, August 26, 2018.
Mumford, Lewis. *The Story of Utopias: Ideal Commonwealths and Social Myths*. New York: Boni and Liveright, 1922.
Münch, Detlef. *Carl Grunert: Der Pionier der deutschen Science-Fiction-Kurzgeschichte 1903–1914*. Dortmund: Synergen Verlag, 2005.

Münkler, Heribert. *Die Deutschen und ihre Mythen.* Berlin: Rowohlt, 2009.
Muschg, Adolf. "Hesses Glasperlenspiel." In *"Der Dichter sucht Verständnis und Erkanntwerden." Neue Arbeiten zu Hermann Hesse und seinem Roman Das Glasperlenspiel,* edited by Eva Zimmermann, 125–38. Frankfurt: Peter Lang, 2002.
Nagl, Manfred. "National Peculiarities in German SF: Science Fiction as a National and Topical Literature." *Science Fiction Studies* 8, no. 1 (March 1981): 29–34.
———. *Science Fiction in Deutschland: Untersuchungen zur Genese, Soziographie und Ideologie der phantastischen Massenliteratur.* Tübingen: Vereinigung für Volkskunde, 1972.
Neumann, Hans-Peter. *Die große illustrierte Bibliographie der Science Fiction in der DDR.* Berlin: Shayol, 2002.
Neusüss, Arnhelm, ed. *Utopie: Begriff und Phänomen des Utopischen.* Neuwied: Luchterhand, 1968.
Nicholls, Peter. *The Encyclopedia of Science Fiction.* London: Granada, 1981.
Nida-Rümelin, Julian, and Klaus Kufeld eds. *Die Gegenwart der Utopie: Zeitkritik und Denkwende.* Freiburg: Verlag Karl Alber, 2011.
Nida-Rümelin, Julian, and Nathalie Weidenfeld, eds. *Digitaler Humanismus: Eine Ethik für das Zeitalter der Künstlichen Intelligenz.* Munich: Piper, 2018.
Nocun, Katharina. *Die Daten, die ich rief: Wie wir unsere Freiheit an Grosskonzerne verkaufen.* Cologne: Bastei, 2018.
———. "Populisten im schlüsselfertigen Überwachungsstaat." *Süddeutsche Zeitung,* October 19, 2018.
Norberg, Johan. *Progress: Ten Reasons to Look Forward to the Future.* London: Oneworld Publications, 2016.
O'Connell, Mark. *To Be a Machine: Adventures Among Cyborgs, Utopians, Hackers, and the Futurists Solving the Modest Problem of Death.* New York: Doubleday, 2017.
Oliveira, Susana. "Paul Scheerbart's Kaleidoscopic Fantasies." *Brumal: Research Journal on the Fantastic* 5, no. 2 (Autumn 2017): 11–26.
Oliver, Kelly. *Earth and World: Philosophy after the Apollo Missions.* New York: Columbia University Press, 2015.
Olsberg, Karl, Claudia Ruby, and Uwe Marquardt. *2057: Unser Leben in der Zukunft.* Berlin: Aufbau Taschenbuch Verlag, 2007.
Oppenheimer, Maja. "Designed Surfaces and the Utopics of Rejuvination." In *Alternative Worlds: Blue-Sky Thinking since 1900,* edited by Ricarda Vidal and Ingo Cornils, 167–96. Oxford: Peter Lang 2015.
Päch, Susanne. *Utopien: Erfinder, Träumer, Scharlatane.* Braunschweig: Westermann, 1983.
"Paradox of Progress." Office of the Director of National Intelligence. Accessed February 28, 2020. https://www.dni.gov/index.php/global-trends-home.
Paris, Jeffrey. "The End of Utopia." *Peace Review* 14, no. 2 (2002): 175–81.

Parrinder, Patrick. *Learning from Other Worlds: Estrangement, Cognition, and the Politics of Science Fiction and Utopia*. Durham: Duke University Press, 2001.

———. *Science Fiction: Its Criticism and Teaching*. London: Methuen, 1980.

Partsch, Cornelius. "Paul Scheerbart and the Art of Science Fiction." *Science Fiction Studies* 29, no. 2 (July 2002): 202–20.

Paskins, Matthew. "History of Science and its Utopian Reconstructions." *Studies in History and Philosophy of Science*, Part A, August 20, 2019). https://doi.org/10.1016/j.shpsa.2019.08.001.

Pehlke, Michael, and Norbert Lingfeld. *Roboter und Gartenlaube: Ideologie und Unterhaltung in der Science-Fiction-Literatur*. Munich: Carl Hanser, 1970.

Peperhove, Roman, Karlheiz Steinmüller, and Hans Liudger Dienel, eds. *Envisioning Uncertain Futures: Scenarios as a Tool in Security, Privacy and Mobility Research*. Berlin: Wiesbaden, 2018.

Petersen, Vibeke Rützou. "Freud in the Future: Work in German SF." *Extrapolation* 47, no. 1 (2006): 77–94.

———. "German SF: Its Formative Works and Its Postwar Uses of the Holocaust." In *Detectives, Dystopias and Poplit: Studies in Modern German Genre Fiction*, edited by Bruce Campbell, Alison Guenther-Pal, and Vibeke Rützou Petersen, 31–48. Rochester, NY: Camden House, 2014.

———. "What Is the Holocaust Doing in German SF?" *Extrapolation* 55, no. 2 (2014): 221–43.

Pinker, Steven. *The Better Angels of our Nature: Why Violence Has Declined*. London: Penguin, 2012.

Platt, Charles. *Dream Makers: The Uncommon People Who Write Science Fiction*. New York: Berkley Books, 1980.

Ponzi, Mauro. "'Red Rosa': Rosa Luxemburg's Utopia of Revolution., *links: Zeitschrift für deutsche Literatur- und Kulturwissenschaft* 18 (2018): 15–20.

Popper, Karl. "Utopie und Gewalt." In *Utopie: Begriff und Phänomen des Utopischen*, edited by Anselm Neusüss, 313–26. Neuwied: Luchterhand, 1968.

Poschardt, Ulf. "'In Lenins Schriften ist viel Nützliches.' Dietmar Dath im Interview." *Die Welt*, August 28, 2008.

Poulain, Béatrice. "Das Glasperlenspiel: Mythos oder Utopie?" In *Utopie, Antiutopie und Science Fiction im deutschsprachigen Roman des 20. Jahrhunderts*, edited by Hans Esselborn, 67–82. Würzburg: Königshausen & Neumann, 2003.

Precht, Richard David. *Jäger, Hirten, Kritiker: Eine Utopie für die digitale Gesellschaft*. Munich: Goldmann, 2018.

Preußer, Heinz-Peter. "Dystopia and Escapism: On Juli Zeh and Daniel Kehlmann." *Literatur für Leser* 33, no. 2 (2010): 95–104.

Pye, Gillian, and Sabine Strümper-Krobb, eds. *Imagining Alternatives: Utopias—Dystopias—Heterotopias*. Vol. 9 of *Germanistik in Ireland*. Constance: Hartung-Gorre, 2014.

Qual, Hannelore. *Natur und Utopie: Weltanschaung und Gesellschaftsbild in Alfred Döbins Roman Berge, Meere und Giganten.* Munich: Iudicum, 1992.
Quinn, Erica. "At War: Thea von Harbou, Women, and the Nation." *Women in German Yearbook* 33 (2017): 52–76.
Radick, Gregory. "Genes and Genocide. The Questionable Use of Scientific Endeavour." *Times Literary Supplement*, May 8, 2019.
Radisch, Iris. "Dieses Buch ist quälend, arrogant, verlabert, technikbesoffen. Es ist eine Erleuchtung." *Die Zeit*, October 21, 2008.
Radkau, Joachim. *Geschichte der Zukunft: Prognosen, Visionen, Irrungen in Deutschland von 1945 bis heute.* Munich: Hanser, 2017.
Ramge, Thomas. *Mensch und Maschine: Wie künstliche Intelligenz und Roboter unser Leben verändern.* Stuttgart: Reclam, 2018.
Rapp, Tobias. "Die 'German Angst' war eine Erfindung." *Der Spiegel*, February 16, 2019.
Raworth, Kate. *Doughnut Economics: Seven Ways to Think Like a 21st-Century Economist.* White River Junction, VT: Chelsea Green Publishing, 2017.
Reginald, Robert. *Xenograffiti: Essays on Fantastic Literature.* Rockville, MD: Wildside Press, 2005.
Reichardt, Sven. *Authentizität und Gemeinschaft: Linksalternatives Leben in den siebziger und frühen achtziger Jahren.* Berlin: Suhrkamp, 2014.
Renn, Jürgen, and Bernd Scherer, eds. *Das Anthropozän: Zum Stand der Dinge.* Berlin: Matthes & Seitz, 2015.
Ricinski, Francisca. "Zeit und Zeitbegriff: Thomas Lehr im Gespräch." poetenladen.de, January 2, 2009. http://www.poetenladen.de/francisca-ricinski-thomas-lehr.htm.
Rickels, Laurence A. *Germany: A Science Fiction.* Fort Wayne, IN: Anti-Oedipus, 2014.
Ridley, Matt. *The Rational Optimist.* New York: Harper & Collins, 2010.
Riedel, Sonja. *Utopie als alternative Ordnung: Hermann Hesses "Glasperlenspiel" und Arno Schmidts "Gelehrtenrepublik" vor dem Hintergrund der Gattung "Utopie."* Munich: Grin Verlag, 2008.
Rieder, John. "On Defining SF, or Not. Genre Theory, SF, and History." *Science Fiction Studies* 37, no. 2 (July 2010): 191–209.
Riffel, Hannes, ed. *Jenseits von Raum und Zeit: Phantastische Literatur im 21. Jahrhundert. Neue Rundschau* 130, no. 1. Frankfurt: Fischer, 2019.
Roidner, Jan. "Vom Verschwinden der Utopie in Johann Gottfried Schnabels Insel Felsenburg." *Literatur für Leser* 4 (2007): 177–93.
Romm, Joseph. *Climate Change: What Everyone Needs to Know.* Oxford: Oxford University Press, 2018.
Roob, Helmut, ed. *Kurd Laßwitz: Handschriftlicher Nachlass und Bibliographie.* Gotha: Forschungsbibliothek Gotha, 1981.
Rose, Mark. *Alien Encounters: Anatomy of Science Fiction.* Cambridge: Harvard University Press, 1981.
———. *Science Fiction: A Collection of Critical Essays.* Englewood Cliffs, NJ: Prentice-Hall, 1976.

Rosenfeld, Gavriel D. *The World Hitler Never Made: Alternative History and the Memory of Nazism.* Cambridge: Cambridge University Press, 2005.
Rosling, Hans. *Factfulness: Ten Reasons We're Wrong About the World—And Why Things Are Better Than You Think.* London: Sceptre, 2018.
Rosner, Peter. "Theodor Hertzka and the Utopia of 'Freiland.'" *History of Economic Ideas* 14, no. 3 (2006): 113–37.
Rother, Rainer, and Annika Schaefer, eds. *Future Imperfect: Science, Fiction, Film.* Berlin: Bertz+Fischer, 2017.
Rothstein, Edward. "A Crunchy-Granola Path from Macramé and LSD to Wikipedia and Google." *New York Times,* September 25, 2006.
Rottensteiner, Franz, ed. *The Black Mirror and other Stories: An Anthology of Science Fiction from Germany and Austria.* Middletown, CT: Wesleyan University Press, 2008.
———. "Der Vater der Weltraumstation." *Wiener Zeitung,* October 15, 2010.
———. "Was ist Science Fiction, was ist Fantasy? Ein Überblick über die phantastischen Genres." Tor Online, August 12, 2016. https://www.tor-online.de/feature/und-der-ganze-rest/2016/08/was-ist-science-fiction-was-ist-fantasy-ein-ueberblick-ueber-die-phantastischen-genres-teil-1/was-ist-science-fiction-was-ist-fantasy-ein-ueberblick-ueber-die-phantastischen-genres-teil-2/.
Ruppert, Wolfgang, ed. *Um 1968—Die Repräsentation der Dinge.* Marburg: Jonas Verlag, 1998.
Rüsen, Jörn, Michael Fehr, and Thomas W. Rieger, eds. *Thinking Utopia: Steps into Other Worlds.* New York: Berghahn, 2005.
Saage, Richard. *Innenansichten Utopias: Wirkungen, Entwürfe und Chancen des utopischen Denkens.* Berlin: Duncker & Humblot, 1999.
———. *Politische Utopien der Neuzeit.* Bochum: Winkler, 2000.
Safranski, Rüdiger. *Romantik: Eine deutsche Affäre.* Munich: Carl Hanser, 2007.
———. *Schiller, oder Die Erfindung des Deutschen Idealismus.* Munich: Carl Hanser, 2004.
Sample, Ian. "Group of Biologists Tries to Bury the Idea that Plants are Conscious." *Guardian,* July 3, 2019.
Sansom, Ian. "A Place for Tougher People." *Guardian,* October 23, 1999.
Sargent, Lyman Tower. "The Three Faces of Utopianism Revisited." *Utopian Studies* 5, no. 1 (1994): 1–37.
———. *Utopianism: A Very Short Introduction.* Oxford: Oxford University Press, 2010.
Sarrazin, Thilo. *Wunschdenken: Europa, Währung, Bildung, Einwanderung—warum Politik so häufig scheitert.* Munich: DVA, 2016.
Schenk, Ralf. "Bin ich? Oder bin ich nicht? In neuem Glanz: Rainer Werner Fassbinders Welt am Draht." *film-dienst* 6 (2010).
Scherpe, Klaus R. "Krieg, Gewalt und Science Fiction: Alfred Döbins Berge Meere und Giganten." In *Internationales Alfred-Döblin-Kolloquium,*

edited by Hartmut Eggert and Gabiele Prauß, 141–56. Berlin: Peter Lang, 2001.

Scheunpflug, Annette. "Zukunftsbewältigung: Über die spontane Vernunft hinausdenken." In *Phänomen Mensch: Brockhaus Mensch—Natur—Technik*, edited by Brockhaus-Redaktion, 589–90. Brockhaus: Leipzig, 1999.

Schleider, Tim. "Voller Kraft, Verzweiflung, Gewalt und Anarchie." *Stuttgarter Zeitung*, June 9, 2007.

Schmeink, Lars. *Biopunk Dystopias: Genetic Engineering, Society and Science Fiction*. Liverpool: Liverpool University Press, 2016.

Schmeink, Lars, and Astrid Böger, eds. *Collision of Realities: Establishing Research on the Fantastic in Europe*. Berlin: de Gruyter, 2012.

Schmeink, Lars, and Hans-Harald Müller, eds. *Fremde Welten: Wege und Räume der Fantastik im 21. Jahrhundert*. Berlin: de Gruyter, 2012.

Schmidt, Burghart. "Utopie ist keine Literaturgattung." In *Literatur ist Utopie*, edited by Gert Ueding, 17-44. Frankfurt: Suhrkamp, 1978.

Schmiechen, Frank. "Die Zukunft der Menschheit wird fantastisch." *Die Welt*, January 7, 2013.

Schmitter, Elke. "Utopien—was von den Träumen übrig blieb." *Der Spiegel*, December 30, 2016.

Schmitz, Michaela. "Die Geburt der Rassenhygiene aus dem Geist der Utopie." Deutschlandfunk, October 29, 2017. https://www.deutschlandfunk.de/uwe-timm-ikarien-die-geburt-der-rassenhygiene-aus-dem-geist.700.de.html?dram:article_id=399391.

Schneider, Daniel. "Evolution und Beziehungen bei Monika Maron und Dietmar Dath." *Literatur für Leser* 2 (2012): 109–19.

Schneider, Johannes. "Die Apokalypse ist leider auserzählt." *Die Zeit*, July 31, 2019.

Schnell, Ralf. *Geschichte der deutschsprachigen Litearatur seit 1945*. Stuttgart: Metzler, 1993.

Schölderle, Thomas. *Geschichte der Utopie*. Cologne: Böhlau, 2017.

Schönfellner, Sabine. "Erzählerische Distanzierung und scheinbare Zukünftigkeit: Die Auseinandersetzung mit biomedizinischer Normierung in Juli Zehs Romanen 'Corpus Delicti' und 'Leere Herzen.'" *Zeitschrift für Germanistik* 28, no. 3 (2018): 540–54.

Schossböck, Judith. "Letzte Menschen: Die Heldinnen und Helden des Weltuntergangs." *Aus Politik und Zeitgeschichte* 62, no. 51/52 (December 2012): 38–44.

Schröder, Christoph. "Deutschland ist zerstört." *Die Zeit*, March 16, 2016.

———. "Männer sind der Welten Untergang." *Die Zeit*, February 23, 2016.

Schröder, Torben. *Science-fiction als social fiction: das gesellschaftliche Potential eines Unterhaltungsgenres*. Münster: LIT Verlag, 1998.

Schultz, Stefan. "Was nach der Leistungsgesellschaft kommt." *Der Spiegel*, February 9, 2019.

Schulz, Hans-Joachim. *Science Fiction*. Stuttgart: Metzler, 1996.

Schulz, Matthias, "Himmelfahrt auf Usedom." *Der Spiegel*, May 28, 2001.

Schumacher, Hanna Elisabeth. *Zur Verhandlung der Conditio Posthumana in der zeitgenössischen deutschsprachigen Gegenwartsliteratur—Gesellschaftskonstitution, Subjektivitätsentwicklung und Kunst*. PhD diss., University of Warwick, 2018.

Schweikert, Rudi. "Von Martiern und Menschen, oder: Die Welt, durch Vernunft dividiert, geht nicht auf." In *Auf zwei Planeten* by Kurd Laßwitz, 913–1045. Munich: Heyne, 1998.

Schwendter, Rolf. *Utopie: Überlegungen zu einem zeitlosen Begriff*. Berlin: Edition ID-Archiv, 1994.

Schwickert, Martin. "Gefangen in sich selbst." *Die Zeit*, October 11, 2012.

Schwonke, Martin. *Vom Staatsroman zur Science Fiction: Eine Untersuchung über Geschichte und Funktion der naturwissenschaftlich-technischen Utopie*. Stuttgart: Ferdinand Enke Verlag, 1957.

Scott, Anthony. "Fassbinder's Vibrating Sci-Fi Questions About Reality." *New York Times*, April 14, 2010.

Seefried, Elke. "Steering the Future. The Emergence of 'Western' Futures Research and Its Production of Expertise, 1950s to Early 1970s." *European Journal for Futures Research* 2, no. 29 (2014). https://doi.org/10.1007/s40309-013-0029-y.

———. *Zukünfte: Aufstieg und Krise der Zukunftsforschung, 1945–1980*. Berlin: de Gruyter, 2015.

Seeger, Sean, and Daniel Davison-Vecchione. "Dystopian literature and the sociological imagination." *Thesis Eleven* 155, no. 1 (2019): 45–63.

Seel, Martin. "Drei Regeln für Utopisten." *Merkur* 5 (2001): 747–55.

Seibring, Anne, ed. "Weltuntergang." *Aus Politik und Zeitgeschichte* (2012): 51–52.

Seibt, Gustav, "Selbstsicher: Jede Gesellschaft braucht eine Dosis Amok." *Süddeutsche Zeitung*, November 14, 2017.

Senzel, Dennis. "Die Physik kann uns erlösen." *Die Zeit*, March 21, 2013.

Seredkina, Elena. "Drei Modelle der Planetarkultur im Kontext des Romans von Hermann Hesse Das Glasperlenspiel." Hermann Hesse Page. 2002. Also available at http://www.gss.ucsb.edu/projects/hesse/papers/modelle.pdf.

Shaffer, Elinor, ed. *The Third Culture: Literature and Science*. Berlin: de Gruyter, 1998.

Shanahan, Murray. *The Technological Singularity*. Cambridge, MA: MIT Press, 2015.

Shermer, Michael. *The Moral Arc: How Science and Reason Lead Humanity toward Truth, Justice, and Freedom*. New York: Henry Holt and Company, 2015.

Shippey, Tom. *Hard Reading: Learning from Science Fiction*. Liverpool: Liverpool University Press, 2016.

———. "Introduction." In *Magill's Guide to Science Fiction and Fantasy Literature*, edited by Tom Shippey, 1–16. Englewood Cliffs, NJ: Salem Press, 1996.

Shriver, Lionel. "Lionel Shriver's Guide to Dystopia: from Orwell's 1984 to Atwood's The Handmaid's Tale." *Telegraph*. May 5, 2016.
Simmons, James R. "Utopian Cycles: Trends in American Visions of the Alternative Society." *Extrapolation*. 39, no. 3 (1998): 199–218.
Simon, Christian. "Keine Panik, es ist nur künstliche Intelligenz." *Süddeutsche Zeitung*, October 12, 2018.
Simon, Eric. "Die Science Fiction Literatur der DDR: Ein Überblick." Tor Online. August 10, 2019. https://www.tor-online.de/feature/buch/2019/07/die-science-fiction-literatur-in-der-ddr-ein-ueberblick/.
Simon, Sunka. "Women as Biocontrol: Rereading Donna Haraway through German SF." *Women in German Yearbook* 24 (2008): 119–41.
Sloterdijk, Peter. *Regeln für den Menschenpark: Ein Antwortschreiben zu Heideggers Brief über den Humanismus*. Frankfurt: Suhrkamp, 1999.
———. Rules for the Human Zoo: A Response to the Letter on Humanism. *Environment and Planning D: Society and Space* 27 (2009): 12–28.
Smith, John Maynard. "Eugenics and Utopia." In *Utopias and Utopian Thought*, edited by Frank E. Manuel, 150–68. London: Souvenir Press, 1973.
Smith-Prei, Carrie. "Relevant Utopian Realism: The Critical Corporeality of Juli Zeh's Corpus Delicti." *Seminar: A Journal of Germanic Studies* 48, no. 1 (February 2012): 107–23.
Sommer, Bernd, and Harald Welzer. *Transformationsdesign: Wege in eine zukunftsfähige Moderne*. Munich: oekom, 2017.
Sontag, Susan. "The Imagination of Disaster." In *Science Fiction: A Collection of Critical Essays*, edited by Mark Rose, 116–31. Englewood Cliffs, NJ: Prentice-Hall, 1976.
Sorg, Reto, and Stefan Bodo Würffel, eds. *Utopie und Apokalypse in der Moderne*. Munich: Wilhelm Fink, 2010.
"Sozialkredit-Ranking in China. Reiseverbot für Millionen Menschen." Tagesschau. March 3, 2019. https://www.tagesschau.de/ausland/sozialkredit-ranking-china-101.html.
Spiegel, Simon. *Die Konstitution des Wunderbaren: Zu einer Poetic des Science Fiction Films*. Marburg: Schüren Verlag, 2007.
———. "Things Made Strange: On the Concept of 'Estrangement' in Science Fiction Theory." *Science Fiction Studies* 35 (2008): 369–85.
Spies, Bernhard, ed. *Ideologie und Utopie in der deutschen Literatur der Neuzeit*. Würzburg: Königshausen & Neumann, 1995.
Stapleford, Brian. "Ecology and Dystopia." In *The Cambridge Companion to Utopian Literature*, edited by Gregory Claeys, 259–81. Cambridge: Cambridge University Press, 2010.
Stapleton, Amy. *Utopias for a Dying World: Contemporary German SF's Plea for a New Ecological Awareness*. New York: Peter Lang, 1993.

Steinmüller, Karlheinz. "Das Ende der Utopischen Literatur: Ein themengeschichtlicher Nachruf auf die DDR-Science-fiction." *Germanic Review* 67, no. 4 (Fall 1992): 166–73.

———. "Laudatio auf Carl Amery anläßlich der Verleihung des Deutschen Fantasy Preises 1996." In *Traditionslinien der deutschen Phantastik*, edited by R. Gustav Gaisbauer, 13–16. Passau: EDFC, 1996.

Steinmüller, Angela, and Karlheinz Steinmüller. *Visionen 1900, 2000, 2100: Eine Chronik der Zukunft*. Hamburg: Rogner & Bernhard, 1999.

Steltemeier, Rolf, Sascha Dickel, Sandro Gaycken, and Tobias Knobloch, eds. *Neue Utopien: Zum Wandel eines Genres*. Heidelberg: Manutius, 2009.

Stern, J. P. "A Game of Utopia." *German Life and Letters* 34, no. 1 (October 1980): 94–107.

Stern, Lukas. "Ebbedrama 'Wir sind die Flut': Grenzenloses Grau." *Der Spiegel*, November 10, 2016.

Stöcker, Christian. "Der Untergang taugt nicht als Utopie." *Der Spiegel*, July 16, 2017.

———. "Wir sind zu dumm für künstliche Intelligenz." *Der Spiegel*, July 30, 2017.

Stöhr, Sonja. "Das Ein-Körper-Problem." *Die Zukunft: Die Welt von Morgen in Science und Fiction*, March 30, 2018.

Stone, Ronald H. "On the Boundary of Utopia and Politics." In *The Cambridge Companion to Paul Tillich*, edited by Russell Re Manning, 208–20. Cambridge: Cambridge University Press, 2009.

Straubhaar, Thomas. *Die Stunde der Optimisten: So funktioniert die Wirtschaft der Zukunft*. Hamburg: Edition Körber, 2019.

Ströbele, Carolin. "'Acht Tage': In Zweierreihen zur Apokalypse." *Die Zeit*, February 13, 2019.

Stürzer, Michael. "Als Hitlers Raketen ins Weltall flogen." *Der Spiegel*, September 29, 2017.

Suchsland, Rüdiger. "Lars Kraumes düstere Vision von Deutschland." *Die Welt*, November 4, 2010.

Suerbaum, Ulrich, Ulrich Broich, and Raimund Borgmeier, eds. *Science Fiction: Theorie und Geschichte, Themen und Typen, Form und Weltbild*. Stuttgart: Reclam, 1981.

Sukrow, Oliver. *Arbeit. Wohnen. Computer: Zur Utopie in der bildenden Kunst und Architektur in der DDR in den 1960er Jahren*. Heidelberg: Heidelberg University Publishing, 2018.

Suslov, Mikhail, and Per-Arne Bodin, eds. *The Post-Soviet Politics of Utopia: Language, Fiction and Fantasy in Modern Russia*. London: Bloomsbury, 2019.

Suvin, Darko. *Poetik der Science Fiction: Zur Theorie und Geschichte einer literarischen Gattung*. Frankfurt: Suhrkamp, 1979.

Taberner, Stuart. *Aging and Old-Age Style in Günter Grass, Ruth Klüger, Christa Wolf, and Martin Walser*. Rochester, NY: Camden House, 2013.

———, ed. *Contemporary German Fiction: Writing in the German Republic*. Cambridge: Cambridge University Press, 2007.
———, ed. *The Novel in German since 1900*. Cambridge: Cambridge University Press, 2011.
———. *Transnationalism and German-Language Literature in the Twenty-First Century*. Basingstoke: Palgrave Macmillan, 2017.
Taberner, Stuart, and Paul Cooke, eds. *German Culture, Politics and Literature into the Twenty-First Century: Beyond Normalization*. Rochester, NY: Camden House, 2006.
Tally, Robert Jr. *Fredric Jameson: The Project of Dialectical Criticism*. London: Pluto Press, 2014.
———. "In the File Drawer Labelled 'Science Fiction': Genre after the Age of the Novel." *English Language and Literature* 63, no. 2 (2017): 201–17.
———. *Utopia in the Age of Globalization: Space, Representations, and the World System*. New York: Palgrave Macmillan, 2013.
Tate, Andrew. *Apocalyptic Fiction*. London: Bloomsbury, 2017.
Taylor, Gordon Rattray. *How to Avoid the Future*. London: Secker & Warburg, 1975.
Tegmark, Max. *Life 3.0: Being Human in the Age of Artificial Intelligence*. London: Allen Lane, 2017.
Theisohn, Philipp. "Literarische Droge." *Neue Zürcher Zeitung*, November 11, 2015.
———. "Die Zukunft verhören: Dietmar Daths Science-Fiction-Roman." *Neue Zürcher Zeitung*, June 29, 2013.
Thompson, Peter, and Slavoj Zizek, eds. *The Privatisation of Hope: Ernst Bloch and the Future of Utopia*. Durham and London: Duke University Press, 2013.
Thöne, Eva. "Im Schatten des Kängurus." *Der Spiegel*, September 22, 2017.
Thör, Jacqueline. "Gibt es noch Hoffnung in Dunkeldeutschland?" *Die Zeit*, November 14, 2017.
Thornhill, John. "Preparing for the D-Day of Technological Change Will be Vital." *Financial Times*, January 28, 2019.
Thorpe, Vanessa. "What Lies Beneath the Brave New World of Feminist Dystopian Sci-Fi?" *Guardian*, June 24, 2017.
Thurnau, Julia. "German Science-Fiction: Iron and Pencil Sharpener." *Goethe Institut Norway* (blog), February 2017. https://www.goethe.de/en/kul/flm/20918315.html.
Tillich, Paul. *Politische Bedeutung der Utopie im Leben der Völker*. Berlin: Weiss, 1951.
Topp, Dominic. "Retrospective 2017: Future Imperfect. Science—Fiction—Film. 67th Berlin International Film Festival." *Alphaville: Journal of Film and Screen Media* 13 (Summer 2017): 189–94.
Torner, Evan. "Casting for a Socialist Earth: Multicultural Whiteness in the East German/Polish Science Fiction Film 'Silent Star.'" In *The*

Liverpool Companion to World Science Fiction Film, edited by Sonja Fritzsche, 118–37. Liverpool: Liverpool University Press, 2014.

———. "A Future-History Out of Time: The Historical Context of Döblin's Expressionist Dystopian Experiment, Berge Meere und Giganten." In *Detectives, Dystopias and Poplit: Studies in Modern German Genre Fiction*, edited by Bruce Campbell, Alison Guenther-Pal, and Vibeke Ruetzou Petersen, 49–66. Rochester, NY: Camden House, 2014.

Tostevin, Bob. *The Promethean Illusion: The Western Belief in Human Mastery of Nature*. Jefferson, NC: McFarland, 2010.

Traverso, Enzo. *Left-Wing Melancholia: Marxism, History, and Memory*. New York: Columbia University Press, 2017.

Trojanow, Ilija, and Juli Zeh. *Angriff auf die Freiheit: Sicherheitswahn, Überwachungsstaat und der Abbau bürgerlicher Rechte*. Munich: dtv, 2010.

———. "Nie gut, aber besser." *Die Tageszeitung*, April 18, 2019.

Turner, Fred. *From Counterculture to Cyberculture: Steward Brand, the Whole Earth Network and the Rise of Digital Utopianism*. Chicago: University of Chicago Press, 2006.

Turney, Jon. *The Rough Guide to the Future*. London: Penguin, 2010.

Ueding, Gert, ed. *Literatur ist Utopie*. Frankfurt: Suhrkamp, 1978.

Uerz, Gereon, ed. *ÜberMorgen: Zukunftsvorstellungen als Elemente der gesellschaftlichen Konstruktion von Wirklichkeit*. Munich: Fink, 2006.

Unfried, Peter. "Wir sind das Tätervolk." *Die Tageszeitung*, July 13, 2011.

"Utopia Now: The Problem with the Green New Deal." *Economist*, February 11, 2019.

Vandermeer, Ann and Jeff, eds. *The Big Book of Science Fiction*. New York: Vintage Books, 2016.

van Munster, Rees, and Casper Sylvest. "Appetite for Destruction: Günter Anders and the Metabolism of Nuclear Techno-Politics. *Journal of International Political Theory*, September 7, 2018. https://doi.org/10.1177/1755088218796536.

Viacheslav, Yakobchuk. "Can Robots Ever Have a True Sense of Self? Scientists are making Progress." The Conversation, February 27, 2019. https://theconversation.com/can-robots-ever-have-a-true-sense-of-self-scientists-are-making-progress-112315.

Vidal, Ricarda, and Ingo Cornils, eds. *Alternative Worlds: Blue-Sky Thinking since 1900*. Oxford: Peter Lang, 2015.

Vieira, Fatima. "The Concept of Utopia." In *The Cambridge Companion to Utopian Literature*, edited by Gregory Claeys, 3–27. Cambridge: Cambridge University Press, 2010.

Vint, Sherryl. *Science Fiction: A Guide for the Perplexed*. London: Bloomsbury, 2014.

———, ed. *Science Fiction and Cultural Theory: A Reader*. Abingdon: Routledge, 2015.

Voigts, Eckart, and Alessandra Boller, eds. *Dystopia, Science Fiction, Post-Apocalypse: Classics—New Tendencies—Model Interpretations.* Trier: WVT, 2015.
von Braun, Wernher. "Crossing the Last Frontier." *Collier's Weekly*, March 22, 1952, 25–29, 72–74.
von Cranach, Xaver. "Und plötzlich ist die Welt am Ende." *Die Zeit*, April 26, 2016.
von Kittlitz, Alard. "Besser als ein zähes Entrecote. 'Die Tyrannei des Schmetterlings.'" *Die Zeit*, May 2, 2018.
von Reeken, Dieter, ed. *Über Kurd Laßwitz: Tagebuch 1876–1883, Bilder, Aufsätze.* Lüneburg: Dieter von Reeken, 2014.
von Suttner, Bertha. "Die Numenheit." In *Kurd Laßwitz: Lehrer, Philosoph, Zukunftsträumer: Die ethische Kraft des Technischen*, edited by Dietmar Wenzel, 109–16. Meitungen: Corian 1987.
von Weizsäcker, Carl Friedrich. *Bewußtseinswandel.* Munich: Hanser, 1988.
Vondung, Klaus. "Die Faszination der Apokalypse." In *Apokalypse: Zur Soziologie und Geschichte religiöser Krisenrhetorik*, edited by Alexander Nagel, Bernd Schipper, and Ansgar Weymann, 177–96. Frankfurt: Campus, 2008.
Vosskamp, Wilhelm. *Emblematik der Zukunft: Poetik und Geschichte literarischer Utopien von Thomas Morus bis Robert Musil.* Berlin: de Gruyter, 2016.
———. *Utopieforschung: Interdisziplinäre Studien zur neuzeitlichen Utopie.* 3 vols. Stuttgart: Metzler, 1982.
Vosskamp, Wilhelm, Günter Blamberger, and Martin Roussel, eds. *Möglichkeitsdenken: Utopie und Dystopie in der Gegenwart.* Munich: Fink, 2013.
Wallace-Wells, David. *The Uninhabitable Earth: A Story of the Future.* London: Allen Lane, 2019.
Walsh, Toby. *Android Dreams: The Past, Present and Future of Artificial Intelligence.* London: Hurst, 2017.
Watkins, Susan. "Future Shock: Rewriting the Apocalypse in Contemporary Women's Fiction." *Lit: Literature, Interpretation, Theory* 23, no. 2 (2012): 119–37.
Weber, Nadja. "Science Fiction, Mystery, Drama: 'Wir sind die Flut' von Sebastian Hilger steht zwischen den Genres." literaturkritik.de, November 10, 2016. https://literaturkritik.de/science-fiction-mystery-drama-wir-sind-die-flut-von-sebastian-hilger-steht-zwischen-den-genres,22655.html.
Weidermann, Volker. *Lichtjahre: Eine kurze Geschichte der deutschen Literatur von 1945 bis heute.* Cologne: Kiepenheuer & Witsch, 2006.
Weizenbaum, Josef. *Computer Power and Human Reason: From Judgment to Calculation.* New York: Freeman & Company, 1976.
———. *Computermacht und Gesellschaft.* Frankfurt: Suhrkamp, 2001.

———. *Die Macht der Computer und die Ohnmacht der Vernunft*. Frankfurt: Suhrkamp, 1978.
Welzer, Harald. *Alles könnte anders sein: Eine Gesellschaftsutopie für freie Menschen*. Frankfurt: Fischer, 2019.
———, and Claus Leggewie. *Das Ende der Welt, wie wir sie kannten: Klima, Zukunft und die Chancen der Demokratie*. Frankfurt: Fischer, 2009.
———. "Erinnerungskultur und Zukunftsgedächtnis." *Aus Politik und Zeitgeschichte* 25–26 (2010): 16–23.
Weninger, Robert K. *Sublime Conclusions: Last Man Narratives from Apocalypse to Death of God*. London: Routledge, 2017.
Wennerscheid, Sophie. *Sex Machina: Zur Zukunft des Begehrens*. Berlin: Matthes & Seitz, 2019.
Wenzel, Dietmar, ed. *Kurd Laßwitz: Lehrer, Philosoph, Zukunftsträumer: Die ethische Kraft des Technischen*. Meitungen: Corian, 1987.
Werlitz, Julian. "Was wir gewesen sein werden. Historizität der Gegenwart im Science-Fiction-Roman: Georg Kleins Die Zukunft des Mars und Reinhard Jirgls Nichts von Euch auf Erden." *Germanica. La prose alllemande contempriane* 55 (2014): 229–47.
Wessels, Dieter. *Welt im Chaos: Struktur und Funktion des Weltkatastrophenmotives in der neueren Science Fiction*. Frankfurt: Akademische Verlagsgesellschaft, 1974.
"When Science Fiction Inspires Real Technology." *MIT Technology Review*, April 5, 2018.
Wiener, Norbert. *Cybernetics: Or Control and Communication in the Animal and the Machine*. Cambridge, MA: MIT Press 1948.
Wiening, Jens. "Eckpunktepapier der Bundesregierung: Künstliche Intelligenz made in Germany." Tagesschau, July 18, 2017. https://www.tagesschau.de/inland/deutschland-standort-ki-101.html.
Wieser, Veronika, Christian Zolles, Catherine Feik, Martin Zolles, and Leopold Schlöndorff, eds. *Abendländische Apokalyptik: Kompendium zur Genealogie der Endzeit*. Berlin: Akademie Verlag, 2013.
Willer, Stefan. "Dietmar Daths enzyklopädische Science Fiction." *Arcadia: International Journal of Literary Culture* 48, no. 2 (November 2013): 391–410.
Willer, Stefan. "Die Zukunft der Literatur nach dem Ende der Menschheit in der Mitte des 20. Jahrhunderts: Arno Schmidt und Marlen Haushofer." In *Die Zukunft des 20. Jahrhunderts. Dimensionen einer historischen Zukunftsforschung*, edited by Lucian Hölscher, 121–41. Frankfurt: Campus, 2017.
Willis, Rebecca. "The Green New Deal is Already Changing the Terms of the Climate Action Debate." The Conversation, February 28, 2019. https://theconversation.com/the-green-new-deal-is-already-changing-the-terms-of-the-climate-action-debate-112144.
Winkels, Hubert. "Außerirdisch ambitioniert." *Die Zeit*, July 4, 2013.

Winter, Jay. *Dreams of Peace and Freedom: Utopian Moments in the 20th Century*. New Haven, CT: Yale University Press, 2006.
Wolchover, Natalie. "A Different Kind of Theory of Everything." *New Yorker*, February 19, 2019.
Wolfangel, Eva. "Künstliche emotionale Intelligenz: Das richtige Gefühl." *Spektrum* 21 (2018).
Wolfe, Gary. *The Known and the Unknown: The Iconography of Science Fiction*. Kent, OH: Kent State University Press, 1979.
Wörtche, Thomas. "Ein futuristischer Hightech-Politthriller." Deutschlandfunk Kultur, April 9, 2015. https://www.deutschlandfunkkultur.de/score-von-martin-burckhardt-ein-futuristischer-hightech.950.de.html?dram:article_id=316470.
Wuketits, Franz M. "Apokalyptische Rhetorik als politisches Druckmittel." *Aus Politik und Zeitgeschichte* 62, no. 51/52 (December 2012): 11–16.
———. *Die Boten der Nemesis: Katastrophen und die Lust auf Weltuntergänge*. Gütersloh: Gütersloher Verlagshaus, 2012.
Wright, Eric Olin. *Envisioning Real Utopias*. London: Verso, 2010.
Yaszek, Lisa, and Patrick B. Sharp, eds. *Sisters of Tomorrow: The First Women of Science Fiction*. Middletown, CT: Wesleyan University Press, 2016.
Zeißler, Elena. *Dunkle Welten: Die Dystopie auf dem Weg ins 21. Jahrhundert*. Marburg: Tectum, 2008.
Zemsauer, Christian. "Wortschöpfungen für Zukünftiges in Franz Werfels Stern der Ungeborenen." PhD diss., University of Vienna, 2013. http://othes.univie.ac.at/26603/1/2013-02-14_9217490.pdf.
Zinkant, Kathrin. "Forscher reparieren erstmals Gendefekt an menschlichen Embryonen." *Süddeutsche Zeitung*, August 2, 2017.
———. "Pflanzenforscher wollen neues Gentechnikgesetz." *Süddeutsche Zeitung*, November 27, 2018.
———. "So leicht ist das Editieren von Genen." *Süddeutsche Zeitung*, November 29, 2018.
Zuboff, Shoshana. *The Age of Surveillance Capitalism: The Fight for a Human Future at the Frontier of Power*. London: Profile Books, 2018.
———. "Wie wir Googles Sklaven wurden." *Frankfurter Allgemeine Zeitung*, March 5, 2016.
———. "Facebook, Google and the Dark Age of Surveillance Capitalism." *Financial Times*, January 25, 2019.

Index

Affeld-Schmidt, Birgit, 51
Agenda 2010, 194
Alderman, Naomi, 2, 201
Allensbach Institut, 8, 33
Amazon, 11
American Eugenics Society, 121
Amery, Carl, 7, 140, 143, 157, 161
Amery, Carl, works by: *Der Untergang der Stadt Passau*, 82, 135, 138–40, 229
Anders, Günter, 38
Anholt, Mark, 21
anthropocene, 207, 208, 247n21
apocalypse, 55, 56
Arab Spring, 9
Arendt, Hannah, 9
artificial intelligence, 43, 44
Ashley, Mike, 64
Asimov, Isaac, 67, 218
Assmann, Aleida, 56, 78
Atwood, Margaret, 207
augmented reality, 37
Auschwitz, 167

Babbage, Charles, 165
Ballhaus, Michael, 151, 152
Bamforth, Iain, 172
Bastani, Aaron, 21
Bauhaus, 125, 129
Bauman, Zygmunt, 21
Bay, Michael, 188
Bebel, August, 22
Beck, Ulrich, 39
Benjamin, Walter, 57
Berlin Wall, 33, 211, 216
Berners-Lee, Tim, 30
Beuys, Josef, 40
Bewußtseinswandel, 24, 56, 133
Biess, Frank, 39, 181

Biesterfeld, Wolfgang, 51, 123
Bildungsroman, 115
Blackford, Russell, 66
Blake, William, 230
Bloch, Ernst, 1, 2, 9, 31, 47, 116, 119, 227
Bloch, Ernst, works by: *Geist der Utopie*, 22–23; *Das Prinzip Hoffnung*, 23
Bloch, Jan Robert, 51, 52
Bohmeyer, Michael, 30
Böll, Heinrich, 4
Booker, Keith M., 47
Borgards, Roland, 82
Borges, Jorge Luis, 218
Bostrum, Nick, 9
Bothe, Walter, 168
Böttiger, Helmut, 225
Boyle, Danny, 144
Braidotti, Rosi, 4
Bramkamp, Robert, works by: *Prüfstand 7*, 73
Brandhorst, Andreas, 180
Brandhorst, Andreas, works by: *Das Erwachen*, 180–83; *Ewiges Leben*, 190–92
Brecht, Bertolt, 151
Bregman, Rutger, 19, 35
Brehmer, Arthur, 39, 40
Brenner, Robert, 232
Brexit, 50, 213, 246n66
Bridges, Elizabeth, 189
Brockmann, Stephen, 80, 173
Brown, Dan, 181
Buber, Martin, 23
Bülow, Ralf, 114
Bundesnachrichtendienst, 177
Burckhardt, Martin, works by: *Score*, 195–98, 201, 229
Bush, George W., 100

Cabet, Etienne, 120
Callenbach, Ernest, 59, 135
Campbell, John W. Jr., 67
Card, Orson Scott, 217
Carey, John, 46
CERN, 223, 225
Chaucer, Geoffrey, 8
Chiang, Ted, 99
Chlada, Marvin, 52
Chodorkoff, Dan, 17
Churchill, Winston, 163
Claeys, Gregory, 5, 18, 19, 49, 50, 63
Clarke, Arthur, 99, 107, 118
Clarkesword, 66, 232
cli-fi (climate fiction), 55, 102
climate change, 148
Clinton, Hillary, 213
Club of Rome, 34, 140
Clute, John, 218, 219
Cold War, 4, 38, 125, 137, 138, 216
Confucius, 199
Conrad, Josef, 158, 161
Cornick, Lisa, 216
Coppola, Francis, 158, 161
Cousteau, Jaques, 261n14
Cranach, Lucas, 188
Crichton, Michael, 101, 181
CRISPR, 191
Csicsery-Ronay, Istvan, 64
Cuaran, Alfonso, 144
Cybernetics, 130

Dammann, Günter, 110, 111
DARPA, 186
Darwin, Charles, 207
Dath, Dietmar, 1, 159, 160, 207, 214
Dath, Dietmar, works by: *Die Abschaffung der Arten*, 207–9, 230, 234
Davison-Vecchione, 49
de Berg, Henk, 172
de Gaulle, Charles, 163
Defoe, Daniel, 111
DeLillo, Don, 2
Der Spiegel, 44, 168
Detje, Robin, 102
Deutsche Kinemathek, 81
Deutscher Buchpreis, 145

Dexheimer, Ludwig, 113
Dexheimer, Ludwig, works by: *Das Automatenzeitalter*, 113–14
Dick, Philip K., 149, 157, 263n1
Digitalisierung (digitalization), 10, 43
Döblin, Alfred, 105, 106, 258n5
Dominik, Hans, 69, 77, 105, 112
Draut, David, 118
Dür, Dora, 39
Duwe, Karen, 1
Duwe, Karen, works by: *Macht*, 198–201

Eberl, Ulrich, 42
Edwards, Caroline, 231
Eggers, Dave, 40, 153
Ehrhardt, Ludwig, 130
Eisenach, Alexander, 234
Eisner, Lotte, 108
Elsaesser, Thomas, 80
Emmerich, Roland, 56, 81, 144, 232
Emmerich, Roland, works by: *Das Arche Noah Prinzip*, 56, 82; *The Day after Tomorrow*, 56; *2012*, 56
Engels, Friedrich, 244n27
Enke, Julia, 205
Enquete Kommission Künstliche Intelligenz (Enquete commission on artificial intelligence), 4
Erde, Karl Heinz, 42
Erlenberger, Maria, 59
Erler, Rainer, 81
Ernsting, Walter, 122
Eschbach, Andreas, 6, 73, 230
Eschbach, Andreas, works by: *Die Haarteppichknüpfer*, 217–19, 220, 221, 222, 228, 229; *Nationales Sicherheitsamt*, 5, 165–69, 173, 231; *Perry Rhodan. Das größte Abenteuer*, 123–25; *Quest*, 217, 219–23
Esselborn, Hans, 70, 71, 72, 77, 123
Europäische Datenschutz-Grundverordnung, 170
European Union, 17, 38, 162
Everett, Hugh, 164

Fassbinder, Rainer Werner, 7

Fassbinder, Rainer Werner, works by: *Welt am Draht*, 73, 81, 149–52, 229
Featherstone, Mark, 19
Fechner, Gustav, 94
Fechner, Gustav, works by: *Nanna, oder Über das Seelenleben der Pflanzen*, 94
Fehlbaum, Tim, 1
Fehlbaum, Tim, works by: *Hell*, 82, 144
Fest, Joachim, 25
Finney, Jack, 161
Fischer, Joschka, 100
Fischer, William, 69, 78, 105, 133
Fitting, Peter, 64
Flechtheim, Ossip K., 34, 232
Fontane, Theodor, 91
Fortschrittsoptimismus, 39
Foucault, Michel, 246n64
Frank, Anne, 166
Franke, Herbert, 68, 143
Franke, Herbert, works by: *Zone Null*, 135, 136–38
Freedman, Carl, 63
Freie Deutsche Jugend, 213
Fridays for Future, 232
Friedrich, Hans-Edwin, 69
Fritsch, Valerie, 145
Fritzsche, Sonja, 78, 229
Fukushima, 43
Fukuyama, Francis, 223
Futurama, 202
FutureWork, 38
Futurium Berlin, 4, 44
Futurologie, 39

Galouye, Daniel, 7, 149
Garland, Alex, 107, 178, 216
Gdeck, Martina, 216
GDR (German Democratic Republic), 67, 79, 118, 154, 177, 194, 210, 211, 267n21
Gelehrtenrepublik (republic of scholars), 51
German Book Prize, 3, 210, 225
Germanistentag, 5

Gesellschaft für Fantastikforschung, 3, 5, 70
Gestapo, 166, 170
Gibson, William, 143
Gidley, Jennifer, 33
Gilliam, Terry, 144
Gnüg, Hiltrut, 51
Goethe, Johann Wolfgang, 21, 175, 230, 257n21
Goethe, Johann Wolfgang, works by: *Faust I*, 82, 154, 225, 231, 266n26; *Faust II*, 225, 273n5
Golding, William, 224
Goodbody, Axel, 133
Google, 26, 40, 174, 177, 198
Gore, Al, 34
Gottschalk, Günter, 116
Grass, Günter, 4, 234
Green New Deal, 232
Green Party, 39
Grundgesetz, 170, 194
Gruppe 47, 4
Guérot, Ulrike, 30
Gunn, James, 61
Günther, Gotthard, 67
Guthke, Karl, 68

Haase, Christine, 56
Habermas, Jürgen, 25, 26
Hahn, Otto, 168
Hallenberger, Gerd, 69
Hannig, Theresa, 174, 177
Hannig, Theresa, works by: *Die Optimierer*, 174–76, 193
Harari, Yuval Noah, 10
Harari, Yuval Noah, works by: *Homo Deus*, 10, 37, 214
Haraway, Donna, 9, 94, 98
Hartl, Karl, 108
Hartz IV, 194
Haupts, Tobias, 81
Haushofer, Marlen, works by: *Die Wand*, 58, 215–17, 228, 229, 234
Hawking, Stephen, 35, 164, 180, 181
Heidtmann, Horst, 79
Heimat, 82, 140
Heine, Heinrich, 21
Heinlein, Robert, 188

Heisenberg, Werner, 168
Herbrechter, Stefan, 207
Hermand, Jost, 24, 69
Herminghouse, Patricia, 173
Hertzka, Theodor, 50
Herzog, Werner, 232
Hesse, Hermann, 114
Hesse, Hermann, works by: *Das Glasperlenspiel*, 114–16, 198
Higgs, John, 148
Hilger, Sebastian, works by: *Wir sind die Flut*, 82, 226–28
Hillcoat, John, 144
Hillenbrand, Tom, works by: *Drohnenland*, 154–55; *Hologrammatica*, 155–56
Himmler, Heinrich, 166, 167
Hiroshima, 122
Hitler, Adolf, 46, 121, 163
Hitlerjugend, 213
Hollinger, Veronica, 64
Holocaust, 4, 38, 67, 72, 78, 222
Honold, Rolf, 126
Horn, Eva, 56, 57
Houellebecq, Michel, 2, 205
Hoyle, Fred, 99, 179
Hughes, Albert and Allen, 144
Huxley, Aldous, 110, 112, 188, 230

Illing, Werner, 111
Illing, Werner, works by: *Der Herr vom anderen Stern*, 112–13; *Utopolis*, 112, 117
Industry 4.0, 35
Ings, Simon, 172
Innerhofer, Roland, 69
International Space Station, 84
Iraq War, 33
Iron Curtain, 80, 136, 137
Ishiguro, Kazuo, 188
Itskov, Dmitri, 188
Ive, Jonathan, 129

Jacoby, Russell, 48
Jäger, Stefan, 205
James, Edward, 61, 63
Jameson, Fredric, 5, 9, 18
Jeschke, Wolfgang, 168
Jeschke, Wolfgang, works by: *Das Cusanus-Spiel*, 161–65
Jirgl, Reinhard, 214
Jirgl, Reinhard, works by: *Nichts von euch auf Erden*, 209–12, 234
Jonze, Spike, 178
Jungen, Oliver, 146, 210
Jünger, Ernst, 117
Jungk, Robert, 233

Kant, Immanuel, 21, 32, 90
Kellermann, Bernhard, 104
Kerner, Charlotte, 189
Kerner, Charlotte, works by: *Blueprint*, 189
Kersken, Uwe, 41
Kincaid, Paul, 65
Kirchner, Barbara, 189
Kleeberg, Michael, 116
Kling, Marc-Uwe, works by: *Qualityland*, 201–2, 229
Klopstock, Friedrich Gottlieb, 21
Klopstock, Friedrich Gottlieb, works by: *Die Deutsche Gelehrtenrepublik*, 117
Kluge, Alexander, 4, 211
Korda, Alexander, 128
Korean War, 33
Kosinski, Josef, 144
Kracht, Christian, 1, 157, 168
Kracht, Christian, works by: *Ich werde hier sein im Sonnenschein und im Schatten*, 157–61, 190, 233
Krakauer, Siegfried, 108, 109
Kraume, Lars, 1
Kraume, Lars, works by: *Die kommenden Tage*, 82, 144–45, 190, 217, 230
Krummenacher, Michael, 147
Kubrick, Stanley, 130, 178
Kulturindustrie, 74
Künstliche Intelligenz, 178
Kurd Laßwitz Preis, 70, 140, 173, 207
Kutter, Anton, 108
Kyr, Oliver, 145

Lanchester, John, 50
Lang, Fritz, 5, 82

Lang, Fritz, works by: *Frau im Mond*, 72, 73, 81, 105, 107–8; *Metropolis*, 1, 5, 73, 77, 80, 105, 106–7, 108, 126, 151, 229
Langner, Beatrix, 211, 225
Laßwitz, Kurd, 1, 61, 69, 77, 84, 105, 161, 179
Laßwitz, Kurd, works by: *Auf zwei Planeten*, 7, 82, 84–94, 102, 111, 113, 173, 230, 232; *Sternentau*, 94–98, 102, 230; *Über Zukunftsträume*, 93, 165, 227; *Unser Recht auf Bewohner anderer Welten*, 93
Lawrence, Francis, 144
Layne, Priscilla, 190
Leary, Timothy, 116
LeGuin, Ursuala, 252n2
Lehnert, Gertrud, 133
Lehr, Thomas, 1, 73, 223
Lehr, Thomas, works by: *42*, 223–25, 226, 228
Leibniz, Gottfried Wilhelm, 110, 163
Leitkultur, 270n32
Lem, Stanislaw, 99, 122
Lenz, Siegfried, 4
Lessing, Doris, 135
Levitas, Ruth, 19
Lewis, C. S., 262n16
Ley, Wilhelm, 108
Liu, Cixin, 2, 66, 164
Lovelace, Ada, 166
Lukacevic, Damir, 189
Lukacevic, Damir, works by: *Transfer*, 189–90

Maas, Heiko, 44
Maetzig, Kurt, 122
Mann Heinrich, 86
Mannheim, Karl, 25, 31
Manuel, Frank and Fritzie, 17
Marcuse, Herbert, 1, 9, 23, 31, 32, 47, 129, 138, 232, 246n74
Maresch, Rudolf, 52, 53
Marks, Peter, 49
Markwardt, Nils, 213
Marx, Karl, 9, 21
Mason, Paul, 20, 35

McCarthy, Cormac, 146
McIsaac, Peter, 54
Meadows, Danella and Dennis, 133
Menasse, Eva, 213
Merkel, Angela, 43, 204, 205, 265n25
Milburn, Colin, 6
Miller, Walter, 7
Minnesang, 195
Mitchell, David, 164, 273n7
Möglichkeitssinn, 11
Moholy-Nagy, Laslo, 129
Moini, Bijan, works by: *Der Würfel*, 175–76
Monbiot, George, 20
More, Thomas, 8
More, Thomas, works by: *Utopia*, 46, 114
Moylan, Tom, 5, 47, 48, 50, 53, 61
Mueller, Gabriele, 227
Müller, Elfried, 211
Müller, Götz, 51
Mumford, Lewis, 18
Muschg, Adolf, 116

Nagl, Manfred, 68, 123
National Intelligence Council, 34
National Socialism, 17, 25, 49, 67, 113, 115, 120, 151, 166
Neue Rundschau, 231
Nibelungenlied, 82, 147
Nickel, Christian, 216, 234
Nietzsche, Friedrich, 185, 202, 207
Nischwitz, Theo, 127
Nocun, Katharina, 168
Nolan, Christopher, 144, 151, 226
Norberg, Johan, 59
Novalis, 6, 97, 227

Oberth, Hermann, 108
Occupy Movement, 9
Orwell, George, 110
Ostwald, Wilhelm, 114

Pannwitz, Rudolf, 115
Peters, Carl, 3
Petersen, Vibeke Rützou, 78, 79, 167, 221, 222
Petersen, Wolfgang, 56

Petras, Armin, 233
Pew Research Center, 33
Piel, Harry, 108
Ploetz, Alfred, 120
Pölsler, Julian, 216
Popper, Karl, 25, 31
Porter, Chana, 59
Poulain, Béatrice, 116
Precht, Richard David, 10, 35, 175, 195
Precht, Richard David, works by: *Jäger, Hirten, Kritiker*, 26–27
Prometheus, 230

Rabisch, Birgit, 189
Rams, Dieter, 129
Randt, Leif, works by: *Planet Magnon*, 212–14, 229, 234
Raumpatrouille, 73, 125–32, 230
Red Army Faction, 145, 152
Reich-Ranicki, Marcel, 3
Reynolds, Kevin, 144
Rhodan, Perry, 5, 98, 122–24, 188, 230
Rice, Condoleezza, 100
Rickels, Laurence A., 72
Riefenstahl, Leni, 109
Riffel, Hannes, 231
Rittberger, Kevin, 234
Roberts, Keith, 157
Robinson, Kim Stanley, 59, 157
Roddenberry, Gene, 127
Rothenhäusler, Felix, 234
Rottensteiner, Franz, 6, 78, 254n45
Rose, Mark, 62
Rötzer, Florian, 52, 53
Rühmann, Heinz, 112
Rumsfeld, Donald, 100
Ruppert, Wolfgang, 129
Ruzowitzki, Stefan, 147

Sagan, Carl, 73
Samson, Ian, 46
Sansal, Boualem, 2
Sargent, Lyman Tower, 18
Schätzing, Franz, 6, 73, 230

Schätzing, Franz, works by: *Der Schwarm*, 8, 99–102; *Die Tyrannei des Schmetterlings*, 8, 183–87
Schäuble, Wolfgang, 43
Scheer, Karl-Herbert, 122
Scheerbart, Paul, 104
Schlegel, Friedrich, 6
Schleider, Tim, 151
Schlöndorf, Volker, 4, 144
Schmeink, Lars, 58
Schmidt, Arno, 210
Schmidt, Arno, works by: *Die Gelehrtenrepublik*, 117–18, 229; *Schwarze Spiegel*, 58
Schmidt, Burghard, 51
Schmitter, Elke, 30
Schnabel, Johann Gottfried, 110
Schnabel, Johann Gottfried, works by: *Insel Felsenburg*, 110–11, 112, 117, 118
Schneider, Peter, 4
Schölderle, Thomas, 29, 110
Schröder, Christoph, 146
Schröder, Torben, 69
Schübel, Rolf, 189
Schwendter, Rolf, 51
Schwesinger, Marie, 234
Schwonke, Martin, 68
Scott, Antony, 152
Scott, Ridley, 178
Sebald, W. G., 234
Seeger, Sean, 49
Seel, Martin, 29
Seredkina, Elena, 116
Shaffer, Elinor, 6
Shakespeare, William, 31, 230, 273n5
Shippey, Tom, 62, 65
Shriver, Lionel, 50
Silicon Valley, 9, 186, 213, 229
Simmons, Dan, 178, 207, 262n20
Snow, C. P., 2
Snowden, Edward, 174
Soarez, Daniel, 188
Society for Utopian Studies, 18
Soderbergh, Steven, 99
Sorokin, Vladimir, 2
Soviet Union, 79, 118, 122, 137
Spengler, Oswald, 202

Spielberg, Steven, 144
Stapledon, Olaf, 105, 119, 207
Stapleford, Brian, 55
Stapleton, Amy, 135
Star Trek, 123, 126, 127, 130
Stasi, 170, 265n24
Stein, Benjamin, works by: *Replay*, 152–54
Steinmüller, Angela and Karlheinz, 41
Steinmüller, Angela and Karlheinz, works by: *Andymon*, 80, 118–20
Steinmüller, Karlheinz, 79
Steltemeier, Rolf, 54
Stöhr, Sonja, 156
Straubhaar, Thomas, 43
Strugatzki, Arkadi and Boris, 161
Suchsland, Rüdiger, 145
Suvin, Darko, 63, 133
Swift, Jonathan, 92, 102

Tarkovsky, Andrei, 99
Tegmark, Max, 9, 35, 36
Teilhard de Jardin, 116
Theisohn, Philipp, 213
Third Reich, 67, 114, 120, 121, 157, 168, 177
Thör, Jaqueline, 205
Thurnau, Julia, 81, 82
Tillich, Paul, 17, 23
Timm, Uwe, 2, 173, 234, 260n35
Timm, Uwe, works by: *Ikarien*, 120–21
Torner, Evan, 105
Towfik, Ahmed Khaled, 2
Trimbuch, Sonja, 41
Trojanow, Ilija, 31, 173
Truffaut, Francois, 73
Trump, Donald, 50, 202
Turing test, 179
Tykwer, Tom, 1

Ueding, Gert, 51
United Nations, 17
Universal Basic Income, 26, 30
Unser Leben in der Zukunft, 41
Utopian Studies Society, 18

VanderMeer, Ann and Jeff, 65, 232

Vergangenheitsbewältigung, 3, 28, 74, 78, 222, 234
Verne, Jules, 61
Vieira, Fatima, 47
Villeneuve, Denis, 99, 107, 144, 216
Vint, Sherryl, 5, 6, 65
virtual reality, 37
Vogels, Werner, 11
Voigts, Eckardt, 57
von Armin, Achim, 6
von Braun, Wernher, 72, 84, 108, 124, 232
von Harbou, Thea, 72, 82
von Harbou, Thea, works by: *Frau im Mond*, 72, 73, 81, 105, 107–8; *Metropolis*, 1, 5, 73, 77, 80, 105, 106–7, 108, 126, 151, 229
von Kittlitz, Alard, 184
von Steinaecker, Thomas, 1
von Steinaecker, Thomas, works by: *Die Verteidigung des Paradieses*, 145–47, 229
von Suttner, Bertha, 39, 88, 257n10
von Trier, Lars, 144, 147
von Trotta, Margarete, 4
von Weizsäcker, Carl Friedrich, 24, 168
Vonnegut, Kurt, 149
Vosskamp, Wilhelm, 28–29

Wagner, Richard, 147
Wahlster, Wolfgang, 43
Walsh, Toby, 35, 36
Watkins, Susan, 201
Weber, Nadia, 226
Weimar, 88, 166, 265n22
Weimar Republic, 112, 129
Weiner, Richard M., 178
Weiner, Richard M., works by: *Aufstand der Denkcomputer*, 178–80
Weizenbaum, Josef, 35
Wells, H. G., 57, 61, 164, 207
Wells, H. G., works by: *Anticipations of the Reaction of Mechanical and Scientific Progress upon Human Life and Thought*, 34; *War of the Worlds*, 7, 82, 84, 86

Welzer, Harald, 26, 35, 40, 175, 195
Welzer, Harald, works by: *Alles könnte anders sein*, 27–28, 31
Weninger, Robert, 58
Werfel, Franz, works by: *Stern der Ungeborenen*, 73, 117
Werlitz, Julian, 211
Werner, Oskar, 73
Wessels, Dieter, 143
Weyandt, Hans-Jost, 211
Weyh, Florian, 173
Wilde, Oscar, 243n12
Winkels, Hubert, 211
Wolf, Christa, 4
Wolfe, Gary, 62
World Health Organization, 172
World War I, 84, 105, 166
World War II, 112, 120, 133, 159, 166
Wörtche, Thomas, 198
Wright, Eric Olin, 19

Wyndham, John, 99

Zeh, Juli, 1, 2, 6, 170, 177
Zeh, Juli, works by: *Corpus Delicti*, 170–73, 193, 233; *Leere Herzen*, 203–6
Zeißler, Elena, 53, 54
Zeitschrift für Fantastikforschung, 3, 70
Zelter, Joachim, works by: *Die Schule der Arbeitslosen*, 193–95, 197
Ziegler, Thomas, 143
Ziegler, Thomas, works by: *Alles ist gut*, 135, 141–43; *Stimmen der Nacht*, 73
Zschoche, Hermann, 81
Zuboff, Shoshana, 35, 40
Zuckmayer, Carl, 31
Zukunftsbewältigung, 5, 7, 9, 74, 143, 222, 230, 234
Zukunftsoptimismus, 38
Zukunftsroman, 67, 73, 103, 105